Ius Gentium: Comparative Perspectives on Law and Justice

Volume 94

Ius Gentium is a book series which discusses the central questions of law and justice from a comparative perspective. The books in this series collect the contrasting and overlapping perspectives of lawyers, judges, philosophers and scholars of law from the world's many different jurisdictions for the purposes of comparison, harmonisation, and the progressive development of law and legal institutions. Each volume makes a new comparative study of an important area of law. This book series continues the work of the well-known journal of the same name and provides the basis for a better understanding of all areas of legal science.

The *Ius Gentium* series provides a valuable resource for lawyers, judges, legislators, scholars, and both graduate students and researchers in globalisation, comparative law, legal theory and legal practice. The series has a special focus on the development of international legal standards and transnational legal cooperation.

More information about this series at https://link.springer.com/bookseries/7888

Vera Lúcia Raposo · Roy G. Beran
Editors

Medical Liability in Asia and Australasia

Springer

Editors
Vera Lúcia Raposo
University of Coimbra
Coimbra, Portugal

University of Macau
Macau, China

Roy G. Beran
South Western Clinical School
Liverpool Hospital
University of New South Wales
Sydney, NSW, Australia

School of Medicine
Griffith University
Southport, QLD, Australia

Medical Law
Sechenov Moscow First State University
Moscow, Russia

ISSN 1534-6781 ISSN 2214-9902 (electronic)
Ius Gentium: Comparative Perspectives on Law and Justice
ISBN 978-981-16-4854-0 ISBN 978-981-16-4855-7 (eBook)
https://doi.org/10.1007/978-981-16-4855-7

This Springer imprint is published by the registered company Springer Nature Singapore Pte Ltd.
The registered company address is: 152 Beach Road, #21-01/04 Gateway East, Singapore 189721, Singapore

Foreword I

High rates of litigation in the area of medical liability are currently an inexorable reality in the context of clinical activity in most countries. In some of them, this situation has reached crisis promotions, seriously affecting professional practice in some specialties, particularly those that bring with them the expectation of a positive result, which, when not verified, leads to an immediate action by the judiciary.

The reports published by the US Institute of Medicine at the beginning of the twenty-first century (To Err is Human: Building a Safer Health System, 2000 and Crossing the Quality Chasm: A New Health System for the 21st Century, 2001) are a clear example of the multiple studies that alerted to the worrying reality of medical error and the importance of reflecting intensely on this subject. They showed the disturbing dimension of multiple situations, namely, the alarming number of adverse events that could have been prevented but that occurred, implying the admission of patients to hospitals; the concerning number of patients injured due to errors during hospitalizations; the significant number of temporary and permanent damage resulting from such errors; or the impressive number of deaths that could be prevented annually.

It is now obvious that a professional qualification to practice medicine does not constitute a passport to impunity. It is obvious that when health professionals commit an intentional or gross negligence, resulting in damage to a patient entrusted to their care, they should be held responsible for the damages they inflict like any other professional. The existing law, in many jurisdictions, sometimes seems to be inconsistent with what the current reality of health care, leading, in some cases, to unacceptable deviations from what would be fair and to an excessive number of lawsuits involving cases where such responsibility does not really exist. The medical error should not be considered synonymous with negligence. The former is largely depended on the existing circumstances, and only the latter expresses effective malpractice.

The health professional is required to exhibit reasonable care, skill, and diligence, that is, to act with the same degree of care and competence that can reasonably be expected from a moderately competent, prudent, and responsible colleague, intervening in the same general line of health practice, with the same academic and professional qualifications, and acting in the same or similar circumstances. Nowadays, a professional practices in an environment with complex interactions between multiple variables, such as the disease process itself, health personnel and equipment, the infrastructure in which it operates, policies, and organizational procedures. Unlike most professional areas, the health sector does not involve a clearly defined process.

What is the exact dimension of these medical errors? We do not know. Epidemiological data are extremely inaccurate, as most of the published studies are not truly comparable, and the actual numbers are difficult to know. Even the official numbers of cases involving situations of alleged medical malpractice fail to give us a correct picture of the reality. Many victims of malpractice do not trigger health liability lawsuits. This is also the case because, in some contexts, these situations and disputes seem to function more as a lottery than as a mechanism for quality control or fair compensation. As Meadow, Bell, and Lantos wrote in 1997, "[p]atients and their families are likely to win at random, but those who win can win big. The costs of this lottery are enormous—doctors are increasingly demoralized, patients are increasingly suspicious, and the lottery payouts are, inevitably, passed on to consumers or taxpayer".

It is very important to reflect on what must be done in the twenty-first century regarding health systems and legal systems of medical responsibility to try to control such a concerning situation and of such dire consequences. We must look for legal rules more in line with contemporary scientific medicine and the existing realities. As Carroll and Buddenbaum also wrote in 2007, "[m]any feel that our current liability system is broken, pointing issues such as rising medical malpractice premiums, untimely and inequitable compensation for truly injured patients, and the questionable impact that litigation has on health care quality cost, and access to care". Even if this is not exactly the case, the fact is that a growing number of researchers have considered arbitration as a resource to be explored more intensely, concluding (fairly) that abolishing health responsibility, as some countries have done, without adopting a system of alternative sanctioning measures for negligent health care actions may in some cases lead to an uncontrolled increase in the number and costs. Others have argued that more important than changing legal systems is to improve patient safety, and that an essential way to do this is to improve the detection and reporting of errors and adverse events, as many errors go underreported, including the ones particularly harmful. Transparency in the disclosure of errors seems far from being a rule of action in health.

In order for a path to be opened for the future and for it to be pursued with confidence, serenity, and true justice, it is essential to know the legal solutions we have today for dealing with this matter. The book by Profs. Vera Lúcia Raposo and Roy G. Beran represents a very valuable contribution in this area.

This book lets us know the reality in Asia and Australasia in what regards medical responsibility. These two important geographic areas represent almost half of the world population, have been registering solid economic growth and assuming an increasingly important role in the international panorama. Two geographical areas that are a mosaic of multiple social, cultural, economic, political, and legal realities ... Two geographical areas that involve multiple truths in terms of health responsibility, and which, in this domain, are very unknown to most international scholars from other continents. This book represents a very relevant contribution for deepening the knowledge about international realities, an essential element for the joint reflection that will allow us to decide the future once and for all. The fact that it is edited by two names of reference in the international panorama of medical responsibility, and the quality of the authors who contributed to it, ensure a final result whose reading is strongly recommended and which is essential for all those, directly or indirectly, to participate are interested in such a relevant topic.

Coimbra, Portugal Duarte Nuno Vieira

Duarte Nuno Vieira Full Professor at the University of Coimbra. Chairman of the Scientific Advisory Board of the International Criminal Court. Past President of the International Academy of Legal Medicine, of the International Association of Forensic Sciences, of the European.

Foreword II

First of all, I would like to congratulate the editors and contributors of this book, Medical Liability in Asia and Australia. Their great efforts have paid off.

Legal discourse, to a certain extent, follows the law of fashion (and eventually the law of imitation) in sociology. Intriguing is how a legal topic suddenly or gradually turned fashionable.

The emergence of medical liability as a favorite topic (thus a fashion) in legal discourse owes many reasons; some of them legally intrinsic (such as its openness comparing to the traditional division of branches of law), while others legally extrinsic (such as the drastic changes both in the supply and demand of medical services and the implications they brought to ethics).

After several decades, the data generated from legal practice and theoretical debates could flood a traditional library, while the social consciousness about medical liability, in each and many communities, eventually consolidated themselves into regulations and case law, reflecting different conceptions in this particular field of our social life.

Publications in medical law or medical liability are abundant, yet this book distinguishes itself from other existing works in many aspects, namely, the solid information it provides to the readers, its method of exposition, and its comprehensiveness and succinctness.

Focusing on the topic of medical liability, the book covers 17 jurisdictions across the Asia-Pacific Region, each addressed by renowned experts of the field, assuring readers with accurate and fundamental information (concise theoretical exposition on the topic and most relevant regulations and case law cited).

The book deliberately avoids the kind of rigidity or standardization adopted by conventional legal publications. It is a succinct and comprehensive textbook, allowing an easy access to the core theme of the topic.

Finally, it is our pleasure to see a Macau academic participating and coordinating such a big project of international cooperation. The cooperation between Professor Vera Lucia Raposo and Professor Roy G. Beran, both active researchers and leading scholars in the area, sets a good example for young colleagues.

Tong Io Cheng
Dean of the Faculty of Law
of the University of Macau
Macau, China

Preface

Medical liability is a recurrent topic in medical law and legal medicine and has given rise to publications all around the world. Factors, such as the growth of litigation and the consequent increased attention from law firms, the strengthening of patient's rights, and the acquired relevance of medical law, made medical liability a trendy theme about which to produce this textbook.

This book covers medical liability, in the law and in the practice of legal medicine, in jurisdictions across Asia and Australasia, collecting contributions from some of the most reputed scholars working in those jurisdictions. Various reasons led to the selection of this particular region of the world.

There is an astonishing level of growth that is apparent in the Asia-Pacific Region which accounts for ~50% of the world's population. In the last 25 years, this region has been the world's economically fastest growing area. According to reports, "[i]ts share of global GDP (at purchasing power parity exchange rates) has risen from around 20% in the early 1980s to 41.2% in 2019".[1] An overview of what is happening in Asia and Australasia is crucial for companies (private health providers and law firms) to guide their business strategy in this geographical domain.

There is an enormous diversity between these different jurisdictions, across this region. They are substantially different with regard to culture (including religions), economic factors (with very different levels of development), politics, social structure, and with disparate legal systems. Some of them are based on common law, others in civil law, and others represent a combination and hybrid legal framework that encompasses both these two main systems. A good way to understand the existing laws and practices, in the Asia and Australasia, is to know the background scenario(s).

In many cases, there remain "legal hidden pearls". While some of these jurisdictions have filled hundreds of publications with their solutions on medical liability (Australia, for instance), others remain obscure and require further delineation. In some of them, medical liability is not a widely researched domain. In other cases, there is a substantial volume of publications but, because of the language in which they are written, those studies remain hidden from the outside world. The aim of this

[1] The Economist Intelligence Unit, Asia and Australasia Regional overview, September 2020, http://ftp01.economist.com.hk/CN_HTML_Singapore/Research&Analysis/ACB, p. 2.

book is to bring, to the spotlight, the rules and practice on medical liability in some of those less well-known jurisdictions.

Those contributing to this book come from differing jurisdictions and differing backgrounds with differing writing styles. The editors were more concerned with content, than format, and hence have accepted the styles of the various authors, including either footnotes or endnotes, referencing. This augmented free expression by the contributing authors, without depreciating their input to the overall theme of comparing and contrasting that which prevails within each jurisdiction.

This book does not intend to provide an exhaustive description of all existing regulations and case law, involving medical liability in these regions and countries. More modestly, the aim is to highlight the particularities (eventually the inconsistencies) that distinguish these jurisdictions from others within the region. The editors sincerely hope to have achieved this goal and anticipate that this text will become compulsory reading for anyone with an interest in legal lability in legal medicine and medical law, especially those who reside in Asia and Australasia.

Macau, China Vera Lúcia Raposo
Sydney, Australia Roy G. Beran

Contents

Medical Negligence Law in Australia 1
John Devereux and Roy G. Beran

Medical Malpractice Liability in China (Mainland) 13
Hongjie Man

Medical Negligence Law in Fiji 27
Ian Freckelton AO QC

Clinical Liability in Hong Kong: Revisiting Duty and Standard of Care 41
Albert Lee

Law of Medical Liability in India 61
V. Nandimath Omprakash

Medical Liability in Indonesia: Overview and Regulatory Trends 83
Farah Purwaningrum

Public Health Care Law and Ethics in Israel 97
Jonathan Davies

Medical Injury Litigation and Compensation Systems in Japan 117
Robert B. Leflar

Medical Liability in Macao 147
Vera Lúcia Raposo

'Medical Negligence in Malaysia: Selected Issues of Liabilities and Damages'? 163
Sharon Kaur, Charlaine A. Chin, and Mohammad Firdaus bin Abdul Aziz

Medical Liability in New Zealand 177
Fiona McDonald

Medical Negligence Law in Papua New Guinea 195
Ian Freckelton AO QC

Medical Liability in Qatar 207
Barry Solaiman

Negligence in Russia: Expert Legal Analysis of Adverse Outcomes of Medical Care 225
Svetlana I. Pospelova, Natalia A. Kamenskaya, Yulia V. Pavlova, and Sergey V. Erofeev

The Patient-Centric Turn in Medical Liability in Singapore 245
Calvin Wai-Loon Ho

Medical Liability in South Korea 267
Hyuna Bae

Medical Malpractice in Taiwan 283
Kevin Chien-Chang Wu and Ching-Ting Liu

Contributors

Mohammad Firdaus bin Abdul Aziz Faculty of Law, University of Malaya, Kuala Lumpur, Malaysia

Hyuna Bae School of Law, Ewha Womans University, Seoul, Republic of Korea

Roy G. Beran South Western Clinical School, Liverpool Hospital, University of New South Wales, Sydney, NSW, Australia;
School of Medicine, Griffith University, Southport, QLD, Australia;
Medical Law, Sechenov Moscow First State University, Moscow, Russia

Charlaine A. Chin Advocate & Solicitor of the High Court of Malaya, Kuala Lumpur, Malaysia

Jonathan Davies LLM, WAML, Tel Aviv, Israel

John Devereux University of Queensland, St Lucia, QLD, Australia

Sergey V. Erofeev Department of Forensic Medicine and Medical Law, Ivanovo Medical Academy, Chief of the Bureau of Forensic Medicine, Honored Health Worker of the Russian Federation, Ivanovo, Russia

Ian Freckelton AO QC Castan Chambers, Melbourne, VIC, Australia;
Supreme Court of Nauru, Yaren, Nauru;
University of Melbourne, Parkville, VIC, Australia;
Krieger School of Arts and Sciences, Washington, DC, USA;
Johns Hopkins University, Baltimore, MD, USA

Calvin Wai-Loon Ho Faculty of Law, The University of Hong Kong, Hong Kong, People's Republic of China

Natalia A. Kamenskaya Medical Law Department, Sechenov First Moscow State Medical University (Sechenov University), Moscow, Russia

Sharon Kaur Faculty of Law, University of Malaya, Kuala Lumpur, Malaysia

Albert Lee The Chinese University of Hong Kong, Hong Kong, China;
Honorary Fellow of Faculty of Public Health, London, UK

Robert B. Leflar National Taiwan University College of Law, National YangMing ChiaoTung School of Law, University of Arkansas School of Law (retired 2020), Fayetteville, AR, USA

Ching-Ting Liu College of Law, Fu Jen Catholic University, Taipei City, Taiwan

Hongjie Man Shandong University Law School, Qingdao, Shandong, China

Fiona McDonald Australian Centre for Health Law Research, Queensland University of Technology, Brisbane, Australia;
Department of Bioethics, Dalhousie University, Halifax, Canada;
New Zealand Centre for Public Law, Victoria University of Wellington, Wellington, New Zealand

V. Nandimath Omprakash Professor of Law, Think Tank on Health, National Law School of India University, Bengaluru, Karnataka, India

Yulia V. Pavlova Medical Law Department, Sechenov First Moscow State Medical University (Sechenov University), Moscow, Russia

Svetlana I. Pospelova Medical Law Department, Sechenov First Moscow State Medical University (Sechenov University), Moscow, Russia

Farah Purwaningrum School of Social Sciences, Universiti Sains Malaysia, Penang, Malaysia;
Sydney Asia Pacific Migration Centre, The University of Sydney, Sydney, Australia

Vera Lúcia Raposo Faculty of Law of Coimbra University, Coimbra, Portugal;
Faculty of Law of the University of Macau, Macau, China

Barry Solaiman College of Law, HBKU, Doha, Qatar

Kevin Chien-Chang Wu Department/Graduate Institute of Medical Education and Bioethics, National Taiwan University College of Medicine, Taipei City, Taiwan;
Department of Psychiatry, National Taiwan University Hospital, Taipei City, Taiwan

Medical Negligence Law in Australia

John Devereux and Roy G. Beran

Abstract Liability for medical negligence in Australia follows the common law pattern, viz a plaintiff needs to prove duty, breach, and causation of damage which is not too remote. Australian law distinguishes sharply between two aspects of a doctor's duty. On the one hand, diagnosis and treatment is governed largely by a standard of what is widely accepted by peer professional opinion by a significant number of respected practitioners in the field, as competent professional practice. On the other hand, doctors have a duty to advise of material risks. A risk is material if a reasonable person, in the patient's position, if warned of the risk, would be likely to attach significance to it or if the medical practitioner is, or should be, reasonably aware that the particular patient, would do so.

1 Introduction

The Commonwealth of Australia is a nation of approximately 25 million people (Australian Bureau of Statistics). A boy born in 2015–2017 can expect to live to the age of 80.5 years and a girl would be expected to live to 84.6 years (Australian Institute of Health and Welfare). Aboriginal and Torres Strait Islander people, in Australia, born between 2010 and 2012 will live an estimated 10 years less than non-Indigenous people (Hospitals Contribution Fund). The Closing the Gap Prime Minister's Report 2018 found nearly 3 in 4 Indigenous deaths were from chronic

J. Devereux
University of Queensland, St Lucia, QLD, Australia

R. G. Beran (✉)
South Western Clinical School, Liverpool Hospital, University of New South Wales, Sydney, NSW, Australia
e-mail: roy@royberan.com

School of Medicine, Griffith University, Southport, QLD, Australia

Medical Law, Sechenov Moscow First State University, Moscow, Russia

V. L. Raposo and R. G. Beran (eds.), *Medical Liability in Asia and Australasia*,
Ius Gentium: Comparative Perspectives on Law and Justice 94,
https://doi.org/10.1007/978-981-16-4855-7_1

diseases, including heart disease and cancer, which accounted for 79% of the gap in mortality between Indigenous and non-Indigenous Australians (Closing the Gap).

Australia is a federation, containing a National government (referred to variously as the Federal government or the Commonwealth government) plus six states and two territories. The governing document regulating the division of legislative competence, between the Federal government and State governments, is the Constitution of the Commonwealth of Australia 1900 (Imp), an Act of the Parliament at Westminster. That document does not contain a plenary grant of health powers to the Federal government. The constitution does assign the Federal parliament powers over quarantine, some pensions, pharmaceutical benefits and insurance.

Australia has a vertical fiscal imbalance, which is to say that while the Federal government has the majority of money (raised through exclusive levying of income tax and a Goods and Services tax)—the States have the majority of legislative powers. The Commonwealth parliament has made good use of the power in the Constitution to make grants to the states "on such terms as it sees fit" to fund the provision of health services by the States.

Australians enjoy a scheme of universal healthcare (Medicare) which provides subsidised (or some cases free) medical treatment. Alongside state run hospitals, there is a thriving private general practitioner, specialist and private hospital medical system. Private medical providers are eligible to provide Medicare rebated treatment, acknowledging that, unless the health care provider accepts the Medicare rebated amount, as full payment for the services rendered, there usually remains a significant gap, between the fee set by the health care provider and that offered by the rebate, for which the patient is responsible to pay, in addition to the rebate that is covered by Medicare.

The Australian legal system is based on the common law model. Each state and territory has its own courts. The Federal system tier also has a series of courts.

2 Negligence

Australia follows the common law pattern of defining negligence as consisting of:

- Duty
- Breach
- Causing Damage
- Which is not too Remote.

3 Duty of Care

The High Court of Australia has established a doctor owes a single duty of care to a patient which encompasses diagnosis, treatment and advising of material risks (Rogers v Whitaker). The law now needs to be read in light of the Civil Liability Act, or its equivalent in each state, which purports to restrict liability in personal injuries matters. This chapter uses, as its example, the Civil Liability Act 2003 (Qld).

4 To Whom is the Duty Owed?

It is indesputable that a duty of care is owed by a doctor to his/her patients (Rogers v Whitaker).

There is some controversy as to whether a duty of care can, in exceptional circumstances, be owed to a person, not previously a patient of the doctor. There is case law to support liability if the doctor foresees or ought to foresee that if he/she does not attend, harm might come to the patient (Lowns v Woods). This, is subject to, in all the circumstances, it being reasonable for the doctor to assist. In Dekker, where a motor vehicle collision occurred at night, where the doctor did not have a mobile phone, nor medical equipment with her, her decision not to stop and render aid, but rather rush to a nearby police station to raise the alarm, was held to be a reasonable response (Dekker v WASAC).

5 Duties to Third Parties

It has been held that if the doctor is retained by a employer to conduct tests, as to the suitability of a potential employee, the doctor's duty to properly conduct the tests and to advise of any follow-up tests that may be required, extends beyond owing a duty to the employer, and the duty extends also to the patient (Thomsen v Davison).

Duties of care can be owed to a third party, who is not the patient of the doctor, if that third party would be injured in the event that the doctor provided negligent treatment to a patient. In BT v Oei, a doctor was held liable to the sexual partner of one of his patients, where the doctor's failure to correctly counsel the patient resulted in transmission of a serious sexually transmitted infection (STI) to the partner (BT v Oei).

Where two people are both patients of the same doctor (such as, husband and wife)—a doctor needs to carefully ensure that the duty owed to one patient, does not conflict with a duty owed to the other. In Harvey v PD, a doctor was consulted by two people who indicated they were shortly to commence sexual relations, but wanted to first have STI checks, the Court held the doctor should have clarified with both parties that it would be acceptable for him (the doctor) to divulge each other's results, to each other (Harvey v PD).

6 By Whom is a Duty Owed?

It is not just doctors who owe duties of care. Nurses and ancillary health care workers owe duties of care to their patients. A nurse who was administering heparin, via a needle, and inserted the needle at an angle which allowed the needle to penetrate deeper tissues and cause nerve damage in the plaintiff's left thigh, was held to be negligent as he had acted "*below the standard of care to be expected of a nurse in his position.*" (Kempster v Healthscope Operations Pty Ltd) [2019] ACTSC 248.

Ambulance officers and other ancillary health workers are not judged by the standard expected of a reasonable doctor. They are to be judged by the standard of a reasonable ambulance officer, or ancillary health practitioner, respectively (Masson v State of Queensland).

Both a doctor's receptionist and a doctor owe a duty of care to properly triage patients to ensure that delay in seeing a patient does not cause damage (Alexander v Heise).

Medical staff can be liable for failing to counsel a patient to not leave a medical facility, if the patient is, or might be, suffering from a serious medical condition which could get worse. In Wang v Central Sydney Area Health Service, a patient who had suffered a blow to the head was not counselled to not leave after he decided to depart, following an extensive wait in a hospital emergency room. The patient went from the emergency room to a private clinic where he was counselled on the need to return to the hospital for a scan. The doctor, in the clinic, said it was acceptable for the patient to return home, provided that if his condition got markedly worse (as indicated by some specific symptoms which were outlined to the patient)—he must immediately return to the hospital. Overnight his condition deteriorated. There were some problems raising an ambulance (due to some communication difficulties). By the time he returned to the hospital, the plaintiff had suffered serious brain damage. The hospital (but not the doctor in the private clinic) were found liable in negligence (Wang v Central Sydney Area Health Service).

Wang should be compared with the recent English decision of *Darnley v Croydon Health Services NHS Trust*. In that case a patient was assaulted by an unknown person in South London. He called a friend who collected him and took him to a hospital run by the defendant. He complained of feeling very ill. The Court found that he was incorrectly told that his wait to be seen would be some 4–5 h. The plaintiff said that he felt very ill and was worried he might collapse. The staff member he saw said that, if he did collapse, he would then be treated as an emergency. After 19 min, the plaintiff asked his friend to take him back to his sister's place so he could take some painkillers and lie down. In the middle of the night, he took ill. An ambulance was called. It was then diverted, and a second ambulance was despatched. The plaintiff was rushed to surgery for a haematoma. He suffered hemiplegia.

It transpired that the actual wait time projected to be seen in the hospital was 30 min. Had he known of the correct wait time, the Court accepted the plaintiff would have remained in the hospital and, upon collapse, would have been promptly treated, avoiding the damage he suffered. The court found the hospital liable.

7 Duty to Diagnose and Treat

The relevant standard is a duty to exercise reasonable care and skill in the provision of professional services (Boehm v Deluil).

Breach of duty of care is now determined by reference to the 3 stage test in Sect. 9 of the Civil Liability Act (Qld) 2003.

Step 1 Is the potential for harm something that a reasonable person should have foreseen?

Step 2 Is the risk of harm not insubstantial?

Step 3 Is the risk of harm something against which a reasonable person would take the burden of precautions?

In deciding the question in step 3 a court is required to take into account, amongst other matters:

- The probability of the harm
- The magnitude of the harm
- The cost of avoiding the harm
- The social utility of the harmful activity
- Sect. 9 (2) Civil Liability Act 2003 (Qld).

For an example of how courts apply the three stage test of breach, in a medical negligence setting, see Naidoo v Brisbane Waters Administration Pty Ltd trading as Brisbane Waters Private Hospital.

The standard of care is not a standard that requires perfection, irrespective of circumstance. The duty is to act reasonably. Courts can take into account, in determining whether the standard has been breached, that the situation facing the doctor was an emergency (Sheppard v Swann). In that case a patient went into labour, the labour was difficult and the child weighted 11 pounds. Given the circumstances, it was held that the obstetrician was not negligent in not stopping and offering the patient a caesarean section, rather than proceeding to a vaginal delivery.

8 Duty to Diagnose is an On-Going One

The duty to diagnose is an on-going duty. In Elysee v Hassam, a doctor who failed, over a number of years, to monitor the patient's renal function, or refer the patient to a specialist, was liable for failing to diagnose the problem, causing the patient's kidneys to deteriorate. faster than might otherwise have been the case (Elysee v Hassam).

In McKay v McPherson, a patient admitted to a rural health facility with cardiac symptoms was successful in his claim that the duty of the hospital failed to monitor him and, if his situation deteriorated, transfer him to a city hospital which had better medical facilities (McKay v McPherson).

The allegation made by the plaintiff, in Coffey v Murrumbidgee Local Health District, formerly known as the Greater Murray Area Health Service, that a hospital should have referred her to a city facility in respect of the birth of her son, failed on the particular facts before the court.

9 Diagnosis and Treatment Includes Follow-Up

A doctor may be liable for failing to "follow up" a patient where the doctor has detected something serious but, despite being asked to return, the patient does not do so. In Kite v Malycha, a doctor who, on conducting a fine needle aspiration of some tissue from a woman's breast, was sent a note, by pathological services, advising that the tissue was malignant. The doctor did not follow-up the patient who failed to return to a scheduled appointment. There was, admittedly, a mix up in receiving the advice from the pathology services (Kite v Malycha).

Contrast Kite with the decision in Grinham v Tabro Meats Pty Ltd & Anor; Victorian WorkCover Authority v Murray. In that case a doctor was held not liable for ensuring proper follow-up in circumstances where it was not clear whether or not a patient (who had recently commenced work in an abattoir) had sero-converted a Q fever vaccination. The patient was provided with a pathology test request, asked to undergo another blood test and then return to see the doctor in a month, He neither had the blood test done, nor did he return to see the doctor. The doctor did not "follow up" and the plaintiff subsequently developed Q fever, and suffered Post Q fever syndrome. The Court accepted that it was the plaintiff's decision, not the doctor's, which resulted in the damage to the plaintiff. The court also found that the plaintiff understood that, absent further testing, he could still acquire Q fever and that the doctor had warned him of the consequences of a failure of returning.

Following BT v Oei, liability for failure, a failure follow-up can extend not only to the patient, but a third party who suffers damage. In Idameneo (No 123) Pty Ltd v Gross, a patient received indeterminate test results for HIV. She moved address but failed to advise the clinic of the change and the clinic, in a departure from its usual practice, failed, at the time of her attendance at the practice, to confirm her current contact details. A doctor failed to inform the patient of the need to undergo confirmatory blood tests. By the time she was contacted by the clinic, some two and a half months later, the patient had transmitted HIV to her partner.

The Court found that the medical practice had failed to maintain adequate records, failed in its duty to follow up with the patient to advise of the need for further testing and failed to take steps open to it to make contact. The Court suggested the practice could have searched the phone directory, contacted family members or searched the electoral roll.

10 Defence in the Case of Diagnosis and Treatment

Pursuant to the Civil Liability Act, a doctor is not negligent if he or she acts in accordance with what was widely accepted by peer professional opinion by a significant number of respected practitioners in the field, as competent professional practice.

The practice, widely accepted by peer professional opinion, as being appropriate, is considered to be so, except when that opinion is irrational or contrary to law—section 21 Civil Liability Act 2003 (Qld) (Dobler v Halverson).

It is important that there be an established practice relied upon. If there is no practice, there can be no defence (McKenna v New England and Hunter Local Health District).

A dispute exists as to whether the defence is limited as to the existence of a particular practice (see, most recently for this view, Child & Adolescent Health Service v Mabior), or is broad enough to encompass, not just a specific method of performing an activity but also the response of a professional to a situation which calls for their expertise (see Boxell & Ors v Peninsula Health).

In terms of the irrationality, exception to the peer professional defence, the Court in Boxell stated:

> … a plaintiff must establish that the peer professional opinion which determines a standard of competent professional practice cannot withstand logical analysis. It will be a rare case in which it is demonstrated that an opinion held by a significant number of respected practitioners in the field is unreasonable, in the sense that those practitioners have not directed their minds to the comparative risks and benefits of a particular response to the circumstances under consideration, or because the opinion has no logical basis.

One of the few cases in which an Australian court has established a medical practitioner's opinion was irrational, is Naidoo v Brisbane Waters Administration Pty Ltd trading as Brisbane Waters Private Hospital. In that case, a patient was discharged from a hospital while "*suffering from tiredness, drowsiness and/or sedation*". She was on a combination of psychoactive drugs and suffered from known insomnia and fatigue. While driving home, she either fell asleep or blacked out, and had a car crash. The Court decided that an opinion offered by one psychiatrist, that suggested that the role of a psychiatrist did not include that practitioner deciding to "*allow or prohibit driving by their patients on the basis of the medications they have prescribed or [sic] their mental state*" and that the practitioner "*…does not consider the circumstances where, by reason of the medication or lethargy/tiredness, the patient is not "mentally competent"—did not have any rational basis and amounted to an abrogation of a psychiatrist's duty of care to a patient…*" (Naidoo v Brisbane Waters Administration Pty Ltd trading as Brisbane Waters Private Hospital).

11 Duty to Advise of Material Risks

A doctor has a duty to advise a patient of material risks. A risk is material if a reasonable person in the patient's position, if warned of the risk, would be likely to attach significance to it or if the medical practitioner is or should be reasonably aware that the particular patient would do so (Rogers v Whitaker). See also section 22 Civil Liability Act Qld (2003).

12 Factual Causation

The primary test for causation, applied in Australia, is referred to as "the but for test". 'But for' the actions of the defendant, would the harm have occurred to the plaintiff? Section 11(1) (a) Civil Liability Act 2003 (Qld). In Sochorova v Durairaj & Anor, a court was not satisfied that the administration of thrombolysis, in circumstances where it may have been contraindicated, led to a plaintiff having a stroke (Sochorova v Durairaj & Anor).

By contrast, in Lazarevski v North Metropolitan Health Service, where the plaintiff attended hospital, complaining of pain radiating down her arm, the hospital failed to conduct blood tests, in order to check her Troponin levels, a test for cardiac dysfunction. The Court accepted that, had she been tested, these tests would have indicated raised troponin levels. The plaintiff would have remained in hospital for appropriate management which would have prevented her later heart attack (Lazarevski v North Metropolitan Health Service).

In Chester v WA Country Health Service, the court accepted that the hospital negligently recorded the incorrect injury suffered by the plaintiff. The court also accepted that a doctor, at the hospital, omitted to write in the discharge summary reference to the need for the plaintiff to seek immediate orthopaedic review to facilitate choice between conservative or surgical treatment for his acromioclavicular joint dislocation. The Court held that it had not been proved that the plaintiff's ongoing left shoulder pain had been caused by a failure to proceed with early reduction surgery (Chester v WA Country Health Service).

The situation is the same, whether the allegation is a failure in diagnosis and treatment—or a failure to advise of material risks. In Cowie v Quinn, a plaintiff alleged that he had experienced an adverse advent, following the administration of cryotherapy to treat skin cancer. He alleged that, had he been warned about the risk of the procedure, he would have not undergone the procedure. The Court found that the plaintiff had failed to establish that the procedure had caused his side effect, the latter having developed some 17 days after the cryotherapy was performed (Cowie v Quinn).

In *East Metropolitan Health Service v Jane Elizabeth Popovic as executrix of the Will of Emil Popovic*, the Court of Appeal had to consider whether or not, following complications after surgery to remove a brain tumour, the surgeon should have advised, in a telephone call he received from the plaintiff, that there was a risk the plaintiff might be suffering from bacterial meningitis and that the plaintiff needed to urgently attend a hospital. On the facts, the Court was not satisfied that the surgeon had breached his duty (East Metropolitan Health Service v Jane Elizabeth Popovic as executrix of the Will of Emil Popovic).

In failure to advise of material risk cases, the plaintiff is generally required to prove causation by proving that, had he or she be informed of the risk, he or she would not have proceeded with the medical procedure. In Bustos v Peter Wearne Transplants, where the court described the plaintiff as "*keen to the point of desperation*" to have a hair transplant, the court did not accept the plaintiff's evidence that had he been told of the potential side effects of the hair transplant procedure, he would not have had the procedure (Bustos v Peter Wearne Transplants).

The plaintiff's task in proving causation is now made harder by the Civil Liability Act which makes inadmissible (except where the statement is one against interest), for a plaintiff to give evidence of what he or she might have done—section 11(3) Civil Liability Act 2003 (Qld).

The Civil Liability Act permits, in exceptional cases, "*established rules at common law*" to apply instead of the "*but for*" test—section 11(1) (b) Civil Liability Act 2003 (Qld).

These exceptions have allowed a court to imply "robust inferences of causation" as a matter of common sense, to find that causation has been proved. In Chappel v Hart, a woman was not warned of the risk of mediastinitis as a possible side effect of surgery. Mediastinitis can occur by random chance. Despite not giving evidence, that, had she known of the risk, she would not have undergone the surgery, the High Court held that, since the very risk that materialised was the risk of which she complained, causation could be inferred, in the absence of evidence to the contrary (Chappel v Hart).

Attempts to by-pass the strictness of the *sine qua non* rule, by arguing that a patient was deprived of the chance of a better medical outcome, have failed on the basis that a chance of something is not the same of proving a matter, on the balance of probabilities (Tabet v Gett, Phelan v Melbourne Health).

13 Scope of Liability

In order to recover for damage, the plaintiff must prove that the damage is not too remote i.e. that the damage is within the scope of liability.

The primary test focusses on whether the type or kind of harm suffered was reasonably foreseeable (The Wagon Mound). The precise sequence of events need not be foreseen (Chapman v Hearse).

A court is required to determine, even if the doctor's negligence has caused the harm to the plaintiff, that the type or kind of harm is a matter which, in all the circumstances, is one where liability should be imposed. The court must consider whether or not and why responsibility for the harm should be imposed on the negligent party.

In Wallace v Kam, the plaintiff had an operation on his back. There were two potential side effects- the first was bilateral femoral neuropraxia (a temporary condition). The second was paralysis. The surgeon, Mr Kam, did not warn of either risk, The Court accepted that, had he been warned of the second risk, the patient would not have had the operation. The plaintiff had the operation, and the first side effect developed.

The court decided that the damage suffered was not within the scope of liability. This was because it would be wrong to impose liability for a risk which the patient was willing to accept.

14 Contributory Negligence

A patient's contributory negligence can reduce the damages awarded to him/her (Makaroff v Nepean Blue Mountains Local Health District).

15 Damages

As is customary in the common law world, damages for negligence are compensatory in nature. They are designed to put the plaintiff in the position he or she would have been in, had the tort not been committed (Livingstone v Rawyards Coal Co).

One controversial area for Australian law has been the situation where a person claims damages for the birth of a child.

Australian law refers to an action brought by the parents in such circumstances, as wrongful birth.

16 Wrongful Birth

Wrongful birth actions are open as a matter of law (Cattanach v Melchior). This includes actions brought by the parents of a child, arising out of a negligent failure to correctly diagnose a pregnancy (CES v Superclinics), as well as a negligent failure to warn of the magnitude of a risk that a sterilisation operation might prove unsuccessful (Cattanach v Melchior).

The plaintiff in such a matter is still required to prove causation (Nouri v Australian Capital Territory).

Queensland has limited the award of damages in such claims—Section 49 A Civil Liability Act 2003 (Qld).

17 Wrongful Life

Wrongful Life actions—where a person born disabled claims they would rather not have been born, are not actionable in Australian law (Harriton v Stephens).

18 Vicarious Liability

The employer of a health care practitioner may be liable to a patient for the negligence of the health care practitioner, under a principle referred to as vicarious liability (Alexander v Heise).

19 Non-delegable Duty of Care

A hospital owes a non delegable duty of care to patients. This duty is independent of, and additional to any duty of care owed by a health practitioner to a patient. This means that a hospital may be liable in negligence to a patient even where the health practitioner carrying out the procedure is not an employee of the hospital (e.g. he or she is a VMO) (Stefanyszyn v Brown).

References

Alexander v Heise [2001] NSWSC 69
Australian Bureau of Statistics. Website https://www.abs.gov.au/AUSSTATS/abs@.nsf/Web+Pages/Population+Clock?opendocument&ref=HPKI. Accessed 28 June 2020
Australian Institute of Health and Welfare. Website https://www.aihw.gov.au/reports/life-expectancy-death/deaths-in-australia/contents/life-expectancy. Accessed 28 June 2020
Boehm v Deleuil & Anor [2005] WADC 55
Boxell & Ors v Peninsula Health [2019] VSC 830
BT v Oei [1999] NSWSC 1082
Bustos v Hair Transplant Pty Ltd and Peter Wearne, Unreported, District Court of NSW, 20 December 1994
Cattanach v Melchior [2003] HCA 38
CES v Superclinics (1995) 38 NSWLR 47
Chapman v Hearse (1961) 106 CLR 112
Chappel v Hart [1998] HCA 1
Chester v WA Country Health Service [2019] WADC 152
Child & Adolescent Health Service v Mabior [2019] WASCA 151
Closing the Gap 2018 Report https://www.pmc.gov.au/sites/default/files/reports/closing-the-gap-2018/sites/default/files/ctg-report-20183872.pdf?a=1
Coffey v Murrumbidgee Local Health District formerly known as Greater Murray Area Health Service [2019] NSWSC 1265

Cowie v Quinn [2019] SADC 71
Darnley v Croydon Health Services NHS Trust [2018] UKSC 5
Dekker v Medical Board of Australia [2014] WASCA 216
Dobler v Halverson [2007] NSWCA 335
East Metropolitan Health Service v Jane Elizabeth Popovic as executrix of the Will of Emil Popovic [2019] WASCA 18
Elysee v Hassam [2018] NSWDC 137
Grinham v Tabro Meats Pty Ltd & Anor; Victorian WorkCover Authority v Murray [2012] VSC 491
Harriton v Stephens [2006] HCA 15
Harvey v PD [2004] NSWCA 97
Hospital Contributions Fund of Australia. Website https://www.hcf.com.au/health-agenda/health-care/research-and-insights/life-expectancy-in-australia. Accessed 28 June 2020
Idameneo (No 123) Pty Ltd v Gross [2012] NSWCA 423
Kempster v Healthscope Operations Pty Ltd [2019] ACTSC 248
Kite v Malycha (1998) 71 SASR 3
Lazarevski v North Metropolitan Health Service [2019] WADC 84
Livingstone v Rawyards Coal Co (1880) 5 App Cas 25
Lowns v Woods [1996] Aust Torts Reports 81
Makaroff v Nepean Blue Mountains Local Health District [2019] NSWSC 715
Masson v Queensland [2019] QCA 80
McKay v McPherson [2010] VCC 585
McKenna v New England and Hunter Local Health District [2013] NSWCA 476
Naidoo v Brisbane Waters Administration Pty Ltd trading as Brisbane Waters Private Hospital [2017] NSWDC 372
Nouri v Australian Capital Territory [2020] ACTCA 1
Phelan v Melbourne Health [2019] VSCA 205
Rogers v Whitaker (1992) 175 CLR 479
Sheppard v Swann [2004] WASCA 215
Sochorova v Durairaj & Anor [2019] QSC 251
Stefanyszyn v Brown; brown v Newcastle Private Hospital Limited T/As Newcastle Private Hospital [2016] NSWC 826
Tabet v Gett [2010] HCA 12
The Wagon Mound [1961] AC 388
Thomsen v Davison [1975] Qd R 93
Wallace v Kam [2013] HCA 19

Medical Malpractice Liability in China (Mainland)

Hongjie Man

Abstract The Tort Law of China, in 2009, reaffirmed that medical malpractice liability is a sort of fault-based tort liability. This law adopted an objective standard of fault, with provisions of presumption of fault under certain circumstances. The new law also overthrew the regulation of the Supreme People's Court which required the defendant to prove the lack of causation. In malpractice of medical products and blood transfusion, the physician will assume non-fault liability.

In mainland China jurisdiction, the history of medical malpractice liability can only be traced back to the 1990s. To deal with the increased number of medical malpractice cases, the courts applied the fault-based tort liability, stipulated by the Art. 106 of the General Principles of Civil Law of 1986. In 2009, the Chinses legislator stipulated the Tort Liability Law, of which the Chap. 7 (Art. 54 to Art. 64) is Medical Malpractice Liability. After more than ten years of practice, the Tort Liability Law was codified as the Book VII of the Chinese Civil Code, passed by the 3rd session of the 13th National People's Congress on May 28th, 2020, with minor modifications. This chapter aims to outline the medical liability in the context of the new Civil Code.

1 An Overview

Chapter 6 (hereinafter "the Chapter") of the Book VII (Tort Liability) is the main resource of the legal regulation for medical liability in the Civil Code. Following the model of Chap. 7, of the Tort Liability Law, the chapter consists of 11 articles, namely Art. 1218 to 1228. With the 11 articles, the medical liability regulation demonstrates several characteristics, including the enterprise liability of medical institutions

H. Man (✉)
Shandong University Law School, Qingdao, Shandong, China
e-mail: hman@sdu.edu.cn

Shanghai, China

V. L. Raposo and R. G. Beran (eds.), *Medical Liability in Asia and Australasia*,
Ius Gentium: Comparative Perspectives on Law and Justice 94,
https://doi.org/10.1007/978-981-16-4855-7_2

(hospitals and other health facilities); a fault-based tort liability for malpractice; the liability for infringing on the right to informed consent; and a non-fault liability for medical product and blood transfusion.

Besides the chapter, some of the relevant regulations, concerning medical law, are the "*Regulations on the Prevention and Handling of Medical Disputes*" (hereinafter "the Regulations") stipulated by the State Council, in July 2018, and the "*Interpretation of the Supreme People's Court on Several Issues Concerning the Application of Laws in the Trial of Disputes over Medical Liability*" (hereinafter "*the Interpretation*") of December 2017. The former is mainly an administrative regulation to safeguard patient safety and resolve disputes between patients and physicians, caused by a medical practice by an administrative method. It includes some provision, useful in the tort liability context, such as the duty of the medical institution to document and preserve medical records. The latter is a detailed interpretation for the provisions of Chap. 7 of the Tort Law, providing substantive and procedural and instructions to the judges. Interpretations of statutes, issued by the SPR (The Supreme People's Court), are binding to the SPR and all lower courts.

2 Enterprise Liability of the Medical Intuitions

2.1 The Subject to Assume the Liability

Unlike most of the other jurisdictions, the Chinese law takes the medical institution, instead of the physician or other health practitioners, liable for the damage suffered by the patient. Art. 1218 of Civil Code (formerly Art. 54 of the Tort Liability Law) says: "*Where a patient sustains any harm during diagnosis and treatment if the medical institution or any of its medical staff is at fault, the medical institution shall assume the compensatory liability.*" Prof. Chen Tsung-Fu pointed out that this legislation assumed enterprise liability for medical institutions, rather than the individual liability of health practitioners.[1]

According to Chinese laws, there are two types of healthcare providers, namely medical institutions and individual physicians. Article 2 of the "*Regulations for the Administration of Medical Institutions*" states: "*These regulations apply to medical institutions such as hospitals, health centers, nursing homes, outpatient departments, clinics, health centers and emergency stations engaged in disease diagnosis and treatment activities.*" These institutions need to apply for the "*license for medical institutions*" before delivering healthcare services.

Medical personnel are generally not the subject of liability for medical compensation. Art. 14 of the Law on Practicing Physicians stipulates: "*After registration, physicians can practice in the medical, preventive, and health care institutions according to the registered location, type of practice, and scope of practice, and engage in*

[1] Chen (2015).

corresponding medical, preventive, and health care practice." Physicians are mainly engaged in practising activities in medical (including prevention and health care) institutions and considered as employees of medical institutions. The medical practices are organized and carried out by the medical institution, through its affiliated medical personnel, in which case the medical institution bears the responsibility.

There are also individual doctors in the healthcare system. Art. 19 of the Law on Practicing Physicians states: "Practicing physicians applying for individual medical practice must register for five years in medical, preventive, and health care institutions, and go through the examination and approval procedures in accordance with relevant state regulations." Qualified practitioners who meet certain criteria can apply for individual healthcare practice by application and approval. An individual practicing physician is an independent healthcare provider and s/he shall bear the responsibility for the practice for her/his supporting staff (such as nurses).

2.2 *Nature of the Institution's Liability*

There are different opinions, concerning the nature of the institution's liability. Some scholars explained the liability as vicarious liability which is the medical institution's liability as an employer for the activities of its physicians and other practitioners as employees. It tries the connect the fault of the physician and the liability of institution with the employment theory. Many other scholars have correctly pointed out that vicarious liability does not meet the need to improve patient safety in a health care system. Health care service, in the modern age, is manifested more as a systemic activity of the healthcare system, rather than the diagnosis and treatment provided by a single physician. It is the "*organizational healthcare*", that is, "*an organizational service jointly provided by a group of medical personnel, sharing their own professional involvement of the chain of health care*".[2] In this organizational system, any factor or combination of factors may contain medical risks and be actualized as damage to the patient. Medical risks are mostly manifested as organizational risks. The patient damage is rather the result of the failure of the system than the personal negligence of the physician. The diagnosis and treatment performed by the medical practitioners should be viewed as part of the organizational healthcare delivery, in which case the medical institute is held liable for the damages of the patient, not because it is the employer, but for its fault in organizing the health providing system.

The organizational liability theory explains the nature of healthcare service better while giving a positive impact on patient safety and the protection of patient's right. It can encourage medical institutions to examine their medical systems with maximum caution and fulfil their organizational duties to minimize systematic risks. It can reduce the burden of proof for the patient, namely in a medical liability case, the patient has to prove neither that the fault of diagnosis and treatment was performed by a certain physician, nor other medical staff, nor what specific part of the medical

[2] Huang (2013).

system has made an error, but (s)he only needs to prove that the health care delivered, by the medical institutions, committed a fault, according to Art. 1219, 1221 and 1222 of the Civil Code. The burden of proof, on the patient's side, is eased. It can establish a uniform medical liability in the light of the institution's organizational liability, including, not only liability caused by the practitioner's individual faulty but also the failure of the designing and implementation of the healthcare system.

According to the Civil code, a medical institute may assume liability for the damage to the patient under 3 circumstances, namely: medical negligence; violation of the informed consent principle; the defective medical product; and blood transfusion.

3 Liability for Medical Negligence

A medical institution shall take liability for any damage to the patient due to its negligence in diagnosis and treatment. Art. 1165 of the Civil Code (Art. 6 of the Tort Liability Law) states, "*One who is at fault for infringement upon a civil right or interest of another person shall be subject to the tort liability.*" In the area of medical malpractice, Art. 1221 of the Civil Code (Art. 57 of the Tort Liability law) demonstrates more precisely by saying: "*Where any medical staff member fails to fulfill the obligations of diagnosis and treatment up to the standard at the time of the diagnosis and treatment and causes any harm to a patient, the medical institution shall assume the compensatory liability.*" According to these regulations, there are four elements to establish liability.

3.1 Malpractice

Malpractice is the misconduct in healthcare delivery. Art. 88 of the "Implementation Rules of the Administrative Regulations of Medical Institutions" stipulates that "diagnostic and therapeutic activities" refers to "the use of various examinations, the use of medicine, equipment and surgery to diagnosis and treat the disease, relieve the condition, alleviate pain, improve functions, prolong life, helping the patients to reclaim health." The legal basis of healthcare delivery usually is medical service contracts but there are other possibilities, such as compulsory medical treatment, voluntary medical service and medical emergent danger prevention. The purpose of healthcare delivery is to treat diseases, maintain health, alleviate pain, improve function and prolong life but also includes medical conduct implemented for other subjective purposes, such as medical cosmetology. Art. 88 of the "Implementation Rules for the Regulations of Medical Institutions" defines medical cosmetology as "cosmetic treatment using drugs and surgical, physical and other invasive or invasive methods." Art. 1 of the Interpretation states the interpretation applies to cases on the grounds of personal or property damage in medical and cosmetic activities carried out by cosmetic medical institutions or other medical institutions. Malpractice in medical cosmetic conduct, causing injuries or even death to the patient, may commit a negligent medical liability.

3.2 Negligence

3.2.1 Reasonable Physician Standard

Negligence is theoretically regarded as the subjective element of tort liability, namely the carelessness or over-confidence of the tortfeasor. In Chinese tort law, both legal theory and practice use the objective approach of "*a reasonable person*" to decide whether the negligence can be proved. In medical negligence liability, a professional standard is used. Art. 1221 of the Civil Code applies "*healthcare in compliant with the professional level at the time of the diagnosis and treatment*" standard in examining medical negligence. This standard is similar to the "*a reasonable physician standard*", which makes a comparison between the healthcare provided by the defendant, with that which could have been provided by a reasonable, hypothetical healthcare practitioner, under the same circumstances. In practice, the following factors are taken into consideration:

The development of healthcare level, accepting that medical science and healthcare are always developing. Art. 1221 emphasizes the level of healthcare should be examined with the level of the healthcare at the time of the incident, rather than the level of the latest development, or that in the time of the litigation.

Locality deference, acknowledging that the geological distribution of medical resources varies vastly all over the country, which translates to there being huge gaps in the level of healthcare in different places. In this case, the "*locality rule*", in the examination of the negligence, shall apply.

The function of the medical institution for which the Chinese government is pushing to establish a hierarchical medical system. Primary, secondary and tertiary institutions play different roles in the system in which various levels of practice shall be admitted.

The courts should keep in mind, in the examination of the negligence, all the circumstances of the specific case. In some cases, the court mistakenly used a "*routine treatment*" standard, examining the negligence with the routine treatment of the certain category of disease, while ignoring other factors, such as the urgency of treatment or the personal idiosyncrasy of the patient.[3]

[3] See Dou Haiyang: Analysis of the Court's Judgment Basis for Medical Staff's Negligence-Taking the Related Judgment Since the Implementation of the "Torture Liability Law" as the main object of investigation, Modern Law, 2015(2).

3.2.2 Presumption of Negligence

Article 1222 of the Civil Code states: "When the patient is damaged in the diagnosis and treatment activities, if one of the following circumstances occurs, the medical institution is presumed to be at fault: (1) Violating laws, administrative regulations, rules and other relevant diagnostic and treatment regulations; (2) Conceal or refuse to provide medical records related to the dispute; (3) Loss, falsification, tampering or illegal destruction of medical records." The defendant medical institution's fault is presumed.

Whether this presumption of negligence is allowed to be overruled by further evidence, provided by the defendant, is under considerable debate, in academia and legal practice, since the similar provision of Art. 58 came into force in 2010.[4] Some scholars think this "*presumption*" here means "*regarded as*", in which case it cannot be overruled.[5] The alternative opinion is that the presumption, stipulated by this prevision, should be allowed to be overruled with evidence; otherwise, it will deprive the defendant's procedure rights.

The first sentence of this provision is about the presumption of negligence due to the violation of medical regulations, including laws and administrative regulations. This rule stems from the practitioner's obligation to comply with the laws and regulations for healthcare. Art. 22, paragraph 1 of the "*Practicing Physicians Law*" stipulates that physicians should abide by laws, regulations and technical operation specifications, aiming to guarantee the standardization and institutionalization of healthcare, through the implementation of regulatory norms, and to prevent arbitrary diagnosis and treatment.

In the case of violation of the regulations, the healthcare practitioner is more likely to have negligence than not, which justifies the presumption of the negligence. Medicine is a constantly evolving science, while all the medical regulations are the achievement of past experience. There are possibilities of the necessary breakout of the regulations, in the healthcare provided, for the best of the patient when there is a rational scientific, medical basis, in which case, the defendant should have the opportunity to overrule the presumption by providing sufficient evidence.

Sentence 2 and 3, of the Art. 1222, are about the presumption of negligence due to obstruction of proof. When the medical institution refuses to provide the medical record, without reason (Sentence 2) or unjustified reasons (Sentence 3), the negligence in the healthcare will be presumed, due to the impossibility to prove the negligence by the patient. When there is a disagreement, on the existence of specific diagnosis or treatment provided, due to the lack of medical record, the patient's claim shall prevail, according to Art. 112 of the Civil Procedure Law.

---

[4] Wang et al. (2010).

[5] Wang Xiongfei, Study on the Fact Inference and the Presumption of Law, Hebei Law Science, 2008(6).

3.3 Causation

Similar to other civil law countries, causation is the legal and logical connection between the infringer's wrongful behaviour and the injury suffered by the infringed. In the medical malpractice case, causation is always difficult to prove. It is not easy to tell if the damage of the patient is the result of the physician's malpractice or it is merely the natural consequence of a patient's disease or injury. It is even more difficult for the patient who is usually a layman, without any knowledge or training of medical science, to do so. In 2001, the People's Supreme Court promulgated the Relations Concerning Evidence in Civil Procedure. Art. 4 para 8 of the regulation reads, "*In the tort liability suit caused by medical malpractice, it is the duty of the medical institution to prove that there was no causation between the malpractice and the damage of the patients, as well as there is no fault in the health care provided.*" This paragraph has arisen numerous debates thereafter. The medical professionals argued that this regulation was far too severe to them, for the causation was unclear in many cases, even from the professional point of view. The physician shall not take all the risks of uncertainties in health care; otherwise, this career will be unreasonably risky. It turned out that this regulation, of the burden of proof, was overruled by the Tort Liability Law in 2009. By reconfirming that medical malpractice liability is a fault-based liability, Art. 54 returned the traditional orbit of distribution of the burden of proof. It is the patient's duty to prove the causation, according to tort law. Theoretically, a "*conditio sine qua non*" test is used in examining the causational link to establish the liability. In practice, the courts lose the tendency to shift the burden of proof for causation to the physician. Many of them use a proportional approach which allows the patient to establish partial causation and get partial compensation, by proving there is a certain percentage of probability of the causation, between the malpractice and patient's damage. This approach gives the patient more possibility to overcome the difficulties in proving their case, while placing more burden on the healthcare provider. In 14302 medical negligent liability cases, all over the country, decided from 2014 to 2018, 83.29% of all the decisions were in favour of the patients and allowed them to get at least a partial compensation.[6] The application of "*proportional liability*" is not in compliant with the requirement of the standard of proof, stipulated by the Civil Procedural Law, and put too much burden on the medical providers which will cause suffering to all the patients byways of defending medicine and a rise of the medical expenses.

3.4 Damage

The patient should have suffered personal and/or mental damage consequent to the malpractice in healthcare. In recent years, some courts adopted the loss of

---

[6] See Man Hongjie, The Absence of Causation Requirement in Medical Damage Liability and its Solution, Law Science, 2018(7).

chance theory in medical negligence cases, namely the patient's chance to avoid adverse consequences, such as a chance to survive or to be cured, is compensable damage, independent from the ultimate personal damage. These courts further used a "*proportional compensation*" approach to calculate the patient's damages. If the court finds the malpractice caused the patient's loss of 40% chance to survive, resulting in his/her death, 40% of the damage, caused by the death, should be compensated. Loss of chance damage is always connected with the ultimate damage. The so-called loss of change results from the cognitive ignorance of the causation between the malpractice and the ultimate damage. The proportional compensation approach, of loss of chance, is a tool to evade the causational requirement to establish the liability, in the disguise of independent damage.[7]

4 Strict Liability of Medical Product and Blood Transfusion

In the Chinese Civil Code, there is also space for strict liability in medical liability, in the area of medical products and blood transfusion.[8] Art. 1223 of the Civil Code says, "*Where any harm to a patient is caused by the defect of any medicine, medical disinfectant or medical instrument, or by the transfusion of substandard blood, the patient may require compensation from the marketing authorization holder of the medicine or the manufacturer, or institution providing blood, or require compensation from the medical institution. If the patient requires compensation from the medical institution, the medical institution that has paid the compensation shall be entitled to be reimbursed by the liable marketing authorization holder of the medicine, the manufacturer, or the institution providing blood.*" In case of medical injury, caused by medical product defects or blood transfusion, the medical institution will assume strict liability to the patient, even if it successfully proved there is no fault of the physician during the health care service.

4.1 Liability for Defective Medical Product

In the case of a patient's damage, caused by the defective medical product, the patient has the right to claim compensation either from the medical institute or from the marketing authorization holder of the medicine (hereinafter "MAH") or the producer.

---

[7] See Man Hongjie, Research on the Compensation for Loss of Chance in Medical Malpractice, The Jurist, 2019(4).

[8] Wang Zhu, Liability Rules of Medical Products and Their Applicability: Focusing on Article 59 of the Tort Law of the People's Republic of China, Studies in Law and Business, 2013(3).

Regarding defect of the product, Art. 46 of the "Product Quality Law" stipulates: "Defect refers to products that have unreasonable dangers that endanger the safety of personal and property of others; defect can be found if the product does not meet the quality standard whereas there is the national or industrial standard for the protection of human health and the safety of personal and property." The defects of medical products mainly refer to the unreasonable safety of medical products that endanger patients. Because medical products are closely related to human health, there are many legal regulations and standards on the safety and effectiveness of medical products. When the product is incompliant with the regulations or standards concerned, the product is regarded as defective.

In August 2019, there was a major amendment to the "*Pharmaceutical Administration Law*", in order to introduce the MAH, as the main stakeholder of pharmaceutical production and sale. According to Art. 6 of the Pharmaceutical Administration Law, a MAH is responsible for the safety, effectiveness and quality controllability of medicine in the entire process of development, production, operation and usage.

In a medical product liability case, the patient is entitled to make a claim for compensation against either the MAH, producer or the medical institution. If the product is found to be a defective product, the causational requirement is satisfied, the defendant shall bear the liability, no matter whose activity is the course of the defect. After assuming the compensation, the medical institution may reclaim its loss from the MAH or producer. Only when the defect was caused by the medical institution, the MAH or producer may recover its loss from the medical institution.

According to Art. 23 of the interpretation, if the producers and sellers of medical products produce or sell the medical product, with obvious knowledge that there are defects in medical products, causing death or other serious damage to patient's health, the injured patient is entitled to claim punitive damages less than twice the actual loss suffered by the patient. It is based on Art. 55 of the Consumer Protection Law

4.2 Blood Transfusion Liability

Article 1223 also gives provision for blood transfusion. Following the Art. 59 of Tort Liability Law, it stipulates that the patient may claim his damage caused by transfusion of "*substandard*" blood, from the blood supply institution, or the medical institution.

There are three different opinions about whether blood is regarded as a product.[9] Some argue that blood is a product, while the blood supply institution is the producer and the medical institution is the seller of the product.[10] Others hold that blood should not be considered as blood, because the source of blood is a donation, and it doesn't

[9] Dong (2015).

[10] Dong (2015).

meet the definition of a product provided by the Product Quality Law.[11] The third option is that blood is a quasi-product hence the regulations, for no-fault product liability, shall be applied.

Art. 1223 uses the wording of "*substandard blood*" rather than "*defective product*".[12] Some believe it is no more than a legal wording, without any specific meanings. Another view is that "*substandard*" is different from "*defective*", because there are many statutory regulations concerning the collecting, testing, storage, transportation, packaging and transfusion, such as the "*Basic Standards for Blood Stations*" issued by the Ministry of Health, "*Basic Standards for Single Blood Collection Station*" and other administrative regulations. If the medical institution, or blood supply institution, follows the above regulations, the blood is "*meeting the standard*", in which case they are not liable for the patient's damage. Only when the blood doesn't meet the standard, the blood supply institution and the medical institution are responsible.

The nature of this debate lies in whether medical institutions and blood providers should bear the development risks. The first scenario is that a certain virus or bacteria is known but limited by the current technical conditions which cannot be checked out, even with no-fault, according to the statutory regulations. The second scenario is the existence of a certain virus or bacteria is unknown at the time the blood transfusion is conducted.

The risk of development should not be attributed totally to blood supply institutions nor medical institutions, in the blood transfusion responsibility, which does not meet the risk characteristics of blood transfusion, resulting in the excessive responsibilities of blood supply institutions and medical institution. Art. 1223 juxtaposes defective products with substandard blood. The legislator's intention is to treat the two different things in the same way. Blood transfusion liability should be considered as non-fault based. In order to justify the distribution of development risks, the provisions of Art. 41, paragraph 2 of the Product Quality Law shall be applied, that when the defect of the product "*cannot be found by science and technology at the time of putting the product into circulation.*" The defence of development risks can be used by the defendant and the blood supply institution and the medical institution should prove that all of their all procedure were compliant with the statutory regulations concerning the safety of blood transfusion.

[11] Dong (2015).

[12] Dong (2015).

5 The Liability for the Violation of Informed Consent

Informed consent is the dominant doctrine, in the physician-patient relationship.[13] Introducing Chinese law in the 1990s, the patient's right to informed consent is a protection by Art. 55 of the Tort Liability law, as well as the Art. 1219 of the Civil Code.

The latter provision states that: "Medical personnel should explain the condition and medical measures to patients during the diagnosis and treatment activities. If operations, special examinations, and special treatments are required, medical staff should promptly explain to the patient medical risks, alternative medical plans, etc., and obtain their explicit consent. If it is unable or unsuitable to explain to the patient, the medical staff should explain to the patient's close relatives, and get their explicit consent. If the medical staff fails to fulfil the obligations of the preceding paragraph and causes damage to the patient, the medical institution shall bear the liability for compensation."

The first sentence of the first paragraph stipulates the medical staff's general duty of providing information to the patient, regarding diagnosis and treatment, while the second sentence stipulates the medical staff's special obligation to secure informed consent. Paragraph 2 is about the liability of medical institutions for violations of patients' right to informed consent.

5.1 General Duty of Informing

A healthcare practitioner bears a general duty to explain the condition, diagnosis and treatment measures to the patient which means, in the entire process of diagnosis and treatment, the patient should be informed of the condition, possible diagnosis/es and treatment measures, in a timely, accurate and comprehensive manner, including the description of the nature and degree of development of the disease, as well as the detailed explanation of the use of medicine.

5.2 Informed Consent in "Special" Medical Measures

When surgery or special diagnosis and treatment activities are necessary, the practitioner shall inform the patient of the nature, functioning, effectiveness, risks and side effects of the measures, possible alternatives and costs, and obtain the patient's consent, before any of the measures can be taken. Article 88 of the "*Implementation Rules for the Administration Regulations of Medical Institutions*" provides: "*Special*

[13] See Man Hongjie, Emergency Treatment with Exception to the Principle of Informed Consent: Reflections on the Incident of Pregnant Mother's Death After the Public Opinion Is Cooling Down, 2008(5).

examination and special treatment refer to the diagnosis and treatment activities in one of the following situations: (1) Examination and treatment with certain risks and possible adverse consequences; (2) Due to the special physical condition of the patient or the critical condition, the examination and treatment that may have adverse consequences and dangers to the patient; (3) Clinical trial examination and treatment; (4) The examination and treatment that may cause a large financial burden to the patient Treatment." Special examinations and treatments mainly include invasive examinations and treatments which may cause visible (such as surgery) or invisible (such as high-dose radiation) damage to the patient's body, as well as those cause high cost on the patient.

The informing shall be made in a way that patients can understand. Article 17 of the "Regulations on the Prevention and Handling of Medical Disputes" states, "Medical institutions shall establish and improve the communication mechanism between doctors and patients, and shall patiently explain and explain the consultations, opinions and suggestions made by patients during the diagnosis and treatment process, and handle them in accordance with the regulations; any questions raised by the patient regarding the diagnosis and treatment should be promptly verified and self-examined, and the relevant personnel should be appointed to communicate with the patient or his close relatives and truthfully explain the situation."

5.3 Physician Privilege

The patient is the recipient to be informed and the decision-maker thereafter. Under special circumstances, the healthcare practitioner may enjoy medical privileges; that is, when the relevant information will obviously cause serious damage to the patient, they can be exempted from informing the patient. This "*physician privilege*" is recognized by the article. Unlike other jurisdictions, the Chinese Civil Code requires the practitioner to inform the patient's close relatives, rather than being exempt from informing. When this is "*unsuitable*", it is the patient's close relatives that shall give the informed consent.

5.4 Incapable Patient

By using the word "*unsuitable*", Art. 55 of the Tort Liability Law does not take into account the situation where patients have no ability to exercise their right to informed consent. Some patients lack legal capacity, such as minors or adults under custodianship. Some patients lose their consciousness temporarily or even permanently, due to injury or illness. Art. 1219 of the Civil Code stipulates when it is impossible to inform the patient, to deal with the above situation, the practitioner shall inform the close relatives and get informed consent from them. The opinions and willingness of the minors and adults under custodianship, with certain cognitive abilities, should also be properly considered, in accordance with their cognitive abilities.

5.5 Compensation Liability

Paragraph 2 of Art. 1219 stipulates that if medical personnel fail to fulfill the obligations of Paragraph 1 of this article, causing damage to the patient, the medical institution shall bear liability for compensation. Regarding the nature of the "*damage*", there has been a lot of debate since the same provision was stipulated by "*Tort Liability Law*".[14] Some believe only when a patient suffers from a physical injury, due to the health care provided without informed consent, can (s)he claim compensation from the medical institution.[15] Others argue that the right to informed consent is a manifestation of a patient's autonomous interest, namely a compensable interest itself.

The right to informed consent is the key to patient's rights. From a dogmatic point of view, it is necessary to define the "*damage*" in compliant with the context. Art. 1218 is a general description of fault-based medical liability, including the liability stipulated in Art. 1219 and Art. 1220 (liability for medical negligence). The "*damage*" used in the above 3 article (Art. 1218, Art. 1219 and Art. 1220) should hold the same definition, namely from Art. 1218, it is the physical damage suffered by the patient.

Article 17 of the Interpretation states: "When medical personnel violated the obligations under Article 55, paragraph 1, of the Tort Liability Law, but did not cause physical injury to patients, the patient's claim for compensation should not be allowed." If the failure of obtaining informed consent does not cause physical damage to the patient, the patient is unable to claim compensation, applying Art. 1219. Art. 1165 of the Civil Code allows compensation for all civil rights and interests, thus it is possible for the patient to claim compensation for non-pecuniary damages, through Art. 1165.

5.6 Emergency Treatment

Although it is a general principle that no surgery or other special diagnosis or treatment may be performed, without informed consent from the patient or his/her close relative, under certain circumstances, the Civil Code allows treatment without informed consent in case of emergency. Art. 1220 states that in case of an emergency situation, such as rescuing a patient in life-threatening conditions, the necessary

[14] Zhang Gu, Study on Medical Obligation to Inform, Zhejiang Social Sciences, 2010(2).

[15] Gou (2013).

medical treatment may be implemented immediately upon approval by the head of the medical institution or authorized person when the informed consent of the patient or its close relatives is unable to obtain.

6 Compensation

In accordance with Art. 1179 of the civil code, the tortfeasor shall compensate the victim for the reasonable costs and expenses for treatment and rehabilitation, such as medical treatment expenses, nursing fees and travel expenses, as well as the lost wages. If the victim suffers any disability, the tortfeasor shall also pay the costs of disability assistance equipment required by the victim plus disability indemnity. If it causes the death of the victim, the tortfeasor shall also pay the funeral service costs and death compensation. The scope of compensation of medical malpractice concludes: (1) Costs for health care, including treatment and nursing cost; (2) Loss of income, including wages loss, and loss of potential working ability in case of disability; and (3) Death compensation when the victim is dead.

The Civil Code also allows non-pecuniary compensation. Art. 1183 says "Where any harm caused by a tort to a personal right or interest of another person inflicts serious mental distress on the victim of the tort, the victim of the tort may require compensation for the infliction of mental distress." In case that the mental distress, caused by medical malpractice, is serious, the patient is entitled to the right to claim further compensation as well.

References

Dong C (2015) Positive study on imputation principle of blood transfusion liability. J Huazhong Univ Sci Technol (Social Science Edition) (5)

Huang D (2013) New theory of medical law. Law Press, p 450

Wang L, Zhou Y, Gao S (2010) China tort liability law course. People's Court Press, p 603

Gou M (2013) The protection of the patient's right of privacy, science of law. J Northwest Univ Polit Sci Law (3)

Chen T (2015) Organization and responsibility of legal persons in medical institutions. In: Xuede C (eds) Legal system and practice of medical dispute handling. Taipei Angle Publishing Company, pp 230–232

Medical Negligence Law in Fiji

Ian Freckelton AO QC

Abstract The law as to the legal liability for medical negligence is evolving in its own individual way in Fiji, drawing upon English and Australian authorities. As yet claims have not been made in the courts by reference to the important constitutional "right of every person to health, and to the conditions and facilities necessary to good health, and to health care services, including reproductive health care." However, it is apparent that significant sums of damages are available to persons who are proved to have suffered loss by virtue of a breach of duty of care on the part of medical practitioners. Awards of damages are rising in order to provide plaintiffs with adequate compensation for harm that they have suffered from medical negligence. While vicarious liability will generally lie for a hospital where negligence takes place, it will be rare for contributory negligence to lead to a reduction in damages.

1 Introduction

Fiji is a Pacific nation of approximately 900,000 people, its indigenous inhabitants being a mixture of Polynesian and Melanesian. It also has a substantial population of citizens of Indian descent. Fiji consists of approximately 330 islands, only about a third of which are permanently inhabited. In 2016 the life expectancy at birth for males was 67 years and for females 73 years (World Health Organization 2017) and 4.49% of the gross national product was spent on health. In 2020 Fiji celebrated its 50 year anniversary of independence from Britain, granted by the *Fiji Independence Act 1970* (UK) (Lal 2008). Fiji is a unicameral democracy and has a legal system

I. Freckelton AO QC (✉)
Castan Chambers, Melbourne, Australia
e-mail: i.freckelton@vicbar.com.au

Supreme Court of Nauru, Yaren, Nauru

Law and Psychiatry, University of Melbourne, Melbourne, Australia

Krieger School of Arts and Sciences, Johns Hopkins University, Baltimore, USA

V. L. Raposo and R. G. Beran (eds.), *Medical Liability in Asia and Australasia*, Ius Gentium: Comparative Perspectives on Law and Justice 94,
https://doi.org/10.1007/978-981-16-4855-7_3

that is based on the English model. Its constitution was revised for the fourth time in 2013 (https://www.wipo.int/edocs/lexdocs/laws/en/fj/fj013en.pdf).

Fiji has a well established judicial system (see Lee and Pittard 2018; Corrin and Paterson 2008), with a High Court, a Court of Appeal and a Supreme Court. There have been controversies about its governmental systems and about political interference in courts' decision-making since a coup in 2000 (Hassall and Saunders 2002; Farran 2009; Jowitt and Cain 2010; International Bar Association 2009), reducing somewhat since the democratic election of 2014 (Ratuva and Lawson 2016; Ratuva, Compel and Aguilar 2019; Freedom House 2019). Fiji has sought to develop its law in a context of preservation of its rich cultural heritage (see Techera 2011).

Article 38 of the Fiji Constitution provides that:

(1) The State must take reasonable measures within its available resources to achieve the progressive realisation of the right of every person to health, and to the conditions and facilities necessary to good health, and to health care services, including reproductive health care.
(2) A person must not be denied emergency medical treatment.
(3) In applying any right under this section, if the State claims that it does not have the resources to implement the right, it is the responsibility of the State to show that the resources are not available.

However, the right to health has not yet been the subject of a significant trial or appellate judgment in Fiji (see though *Phillip v Permanent Secretary for Health* 2016), by contrast with South Africa, Kenya and Uganda (see Freckelton 2020).

The United Nations Special Rapporteur on the Right to Health, Dainius Pūras, presenting a preliminary statement at the end of his eight-day mission, in December 2019 welcomed "*Fiji's strong political will to ensure that people can realise their right to health, and I am pleased that it has very good opportunities to do so. Of course it is important to continue investing in a sustainable health care system with a focus on primary care, but it is equally essential to seriously address the major determinants of health, such as violence, discrimination and inequalities that threaten the effective realisation of people's right to health. The key to success is critical analysis, recognising the current gaps and identifying the measures needed to close those gaps.*" However, the Special Rapporteur said more attention needed be paid to violence against women and children, including implementing existing laws (UNOCHCR, 5 December 2019).

2 Duty of Care in Negligence

Fiji's tort law continues to be closely aligned with that of England, although it is developing distinctive features (see Offei 2006) and little by little is evolving. Medical negligence law commands a level of controversy in Fiji. In 2016 the Consumer Council of Fiji recorded that seeking justice for both medical negligence and unprofessional conduct by medical practitioners has long been a struggle for many aggrieved patients (Kalouniviti 2016).

As of 2018 Fiji continued to apply earlier English law as set out by Phillips in his 1997 book, *Medical Negligence Law* (at pp. 16–17), namely that:

> …The test for medical negligence is essentially objective, and does not therefore take formal account of a doctor's experience, level of qualifications, the resources available within that doctor's practice or hospital, or even how many hours may have been worked prior to the incident. It therefore concentrates upon the relationship between the doctor and patient and generally excludes other considerations. Unsurprisingly, the test is retrospective, but although deterrence of negligent conduct is one aim claimed for the law, there is no formal mechanism for improving the standard of care as a result of any lessons learned in litigation. Nor does it consider a doctor's record or the standards to which she or he may have practised in the past: where negligence is alleged, it is only the incident(s) in question which is (are) examined. Indeed, the most blatant cases of negligence, being indefensible, are likely to be settled out of court (*Chand v Permanent Secretary for Health* 2018, at [26]; see too *Ali v Ministry of Health* 2017).

In *Manu v McCaig* (2011, at [1]) Inoke J captured the dichotomy between advantageous and disastrous surgical practice colourfully: "*The surgeon's scalpel cuts away bad and good flesh. When it cuts away bad flesh it is a miracle. When it cuts good flesh, it becomes a curse. And when the curse is for life, the patient prays for a miracle. Unfortunately, all that this Court can do is to do its best to compensate the patient justly according to law.*" He commented that the law needed to change so that the negligent practices of doctors employed by the government should not be indemnified by the public purse: "*I do not think it is right that a doctor should be allowed to practice with such impunity over many years and then move into private practice and take advantage of the seniority and experience that he gained under indemnity by the public purse.*" He also observed that: "*the amount and extent of the compensation which the Court should award to a patient who has suffered at the hands of the negligent doctor*" needed to increase". (*Manu v McCaig* 2011, at [1]).

It has been held that it is the duty of a doctor to act in the patient's best interests (*Kumar v Permanent Secretary for Health* 2006) but it has been noted by the Fiji Court of Appeal, as it was put by Denning LJ in *Hatcher v Black* (1954) in dealing with the duty to exercise reasonable skill and care, that "*You must not, therefore, find him negligent simply because something happens to go wrong; … You should only find him guilty of negligence when he falls short of the standard of a reasonably skilful medical man…*" . (*Permanent Secretary for Health v Voliti* 2016, at [21]).

The test for medical negligence has been viewed as objective, not taking formally into account the doctor's experience, level of qualifications, the resources available at the doctor's practice or hospital or how many hours the doctor may have worked before the incident (*Moli v Bingwor* 2003). In *Moli v Bingwor* (2003), though, a South Australian authority (*Giurelli v Girgis* 1980) taking account of whether a doctor was a specialist was factored into formulation of the content of the doctor's duty of care.

In a case involving a failure to diagnose appendicitis, Pathik J found a doctor "*completely negligent*"—she "*failed dismally*" in her duty: "*The doctor did not find what caused abdominal pain and vomiting which it was her bounden duty to do.*" (*Moli v Bingwor* 2003).

In a case where an infant was delivered without monitoring of oxygen, it was held (*Kumar v Permanent Secretary for Health* 2006) that adverse consequences including loss of sight should have been foreseeable to the clinicians (*Kumar v Permanent Secretary for Health* 2006) and that damages should be awarded for the negligent failure to do so.

In *Kumari v Taoi* (2005), too, Finnigan J stated:

> I am bound to hold that every person who enters into the medical profession undertakes to bring to the exercise of it a reasonable degree of care and skill, that is a fair reasonable and competent degree of skill. I take reasonable skill to be skill that reasonable according to the standards of what the profession does in a given situation. The course I believe I must adopt, so long as there is evidence, is to consider what the profession does in a given situation and then determine for myself what the reasonable doctor would have done.

Similarly Gates J (as he then was) in *Shah v Narayan* (2003) cited Lord Scarman in *Maynard v West Midland Regional Health Authority* (1984, at 639) for the proposition that:

> … in the realm of diagnosis and treatment negligence is not established by preferring one body of professional opinion to another. Failure to exercise the ordinary skill of a doctor (in the appropriate speciality, if he be a specialist) is necessary (emphasis added).

He concluded that: "*Ultimately it will be for the court to decide if the doctor had reached a defensible conclusion.*"

In *Bilitaki v Medical Superintendent Colonial War Memorial Hospital* (2011) at [54] Judge Hettiarachchi summarised the law straightforwardly in the context of determining whether a doctor had breached his duty of care to refer a patient overseas:

> It was the doctors' duty to act in the best interest of his patient's health and well being and not to expose him to the risk of unnecessary pain and suffering. Further, it was also their duty to examine the plaintiff's eye and give consideration to the history while prescribing treatments and make every possible effort to cure, if not, at least to control the plaintiff's eye condition. … it is the prerogative of the attending clinician to make the decision whether the patient can be improved by overseas medical treatment.

He concluded that:

> the hospital authorities have shown a very lethargic attitude in treating the plaintiff despite the fact that the plaintiff had series of uveitis attacks and other complications secondary to uveitis. They treated the plaintiff as if he was suffering from some trivial illness which could be dealt with some basic treatments.
>
> When a person presented himself with a serious eye condition and the treatments given to him do not show a positive response, it is the duty and responsibility of the doctors to decide whether he should be referred to overseas treatment or should continue with the same treatments (*Bilitaki v Medical Superintendent Colonial War Memorial Hospital* (2011) at [55, 56]).

There is ongoing controversy about the content of the duty of care in tort on the part of medical practitioners in Fiji. Practical and cultural issues are highly relevant to the formulation of a duty of care for doctors and also their obligations in terms of obtaining informed consent from their patients. Fijians have bestowed the title of "*vuniwai vakaviti*" ("healer") onto doctors which bespeaks expectations (Leckie 2019). It is a title of respect, derivative of traditional healing customs (see Singh 1986; Shah 2012; Jain 2015), and it is indicative of a belief that treatment provided by doctors will be efficacious and commanding of a level of spiritual authority.

This, along with other practical considerations, impacts upon requirements and expectations of levels of communication by doctors with patients. As Prasad (2009) has argued:

> The literacy factor also raises issues about the ability of patients to communicate and understand the information imparted to them by their doctors. The economic situation and the costly medical bills in the private health care tend to sway most of these people to access the public health care facilities. The public hospitals are under resourced with limited beds, medical equipments and treatment facilities. They are understaffed with most of the doctors overworked. The surgical patients tend to be on the waiting list for months before undergoing treatment. In situations like this, it is a relief to the patient to receive any sort of treatment instead of waiting in pain and agony.

The duty of care has been held to come into existence whenever there is a doctor-patient relationship (*Kumar v Permanent Secretary for Health* 2006) and it has been found to be breached if a court finds that a reasonable person, in the position of the defendant, would have foreseen that his or her conduct involved a risk of injury to the plaintiff or to a class of people of which the plaintiff was a member and proceeded regardless (*Kumar v Permanent Secretary for Health* 2006). The Fiji High Court has held there to be close agreement between the English and American cases on the standard of care required to be discharged by hospitals, medical practitioners, doctors and surgeons:

> One can safely deduce from the cases that a doctor could be 'liable for negligence' in respect of diagnosis and treatment despite a body of professional opinion sanctioning his/her conduct where it has not been demonstrated to the Court's satisfaction that the body of opinion relied on was reasonable or responsible. It boils down to saying that it is the Court not for medical opinion to decide what the standard of care required is of a professional in the circumstances of each particular case (*Kumar v Permanent Secretary for Health* 2006).

For the present, the law of Fiji, for the most part, applies the test set out in *Bolam v Friern Hospital Management Committee* (1957: 586–587) (see Montrose 1958), namely that the content of the test for a doctor's duty of care is the

> standard of the ordinary skilled man exercising and professing to have that special skill. A man need not possess the highest expert skill; it is well-established law that it is sufficient if he exercises the ordinary skill of an ordinary competent man exercising that particular art. A doctor is not guilty of negligence if he has acted in accordance with a practice accepted as proper by a responsible body of medical men skilled in that particular art … Putting it the other way round, a doctor is not negligent, if he is acting in accordance with such a practice, merely because there is a body of opinion that takes a contrary view.

In *Singh v Attorney General of Fiji* (2008) at [82–91] and *Saulaki v Ministry of Health* (2008) at [36–41]) Hickie J catalogued multiple decisions by the High Court of Fiji which had applied the *Bolam* test and proceeded to do so (see too *Voliti v The Attorney General of Fiji* 2014). In 2002 Baledrokadroka identified that Fiji is far from alone in this regard (referring particularly to *Ismail v Medical Superintendent* 2000); many South Pacific courts continue to apply the *Bolam* test.

An example of where *Bolam* has been applied in Fiji is the decision of *Votimaisiru v General Manager Labasa Hospital* (2013) where the deceased, a man who had been a military officer, was admitted to the Labasa Hospital where he was diagnosed with cellulitis and an ulcer on his left foot and on two occasions was discharged and suffered osteomyelitis and septicaemia. Wati J applied *Bolam* and concluded that there was no contrary medical evidence to say what the doctors decided in the circumstances of the case was not the proper medical practice, accepted as proper by a responsible body of medical men skilled in the particular art (*Votimaisiru v General Manager Labasa Hospital* (2013) at [41]). He found no negligence in the provision of treatment to the patient.

In more recent times, the High Court of Fiji has also applied the test set out by the Australian High Court decision of *Rogers v Whitaker* (1992), which held that "*a doctor has a duty to warn a patient of a material risk inherent in the proposed treatment; a risk is material if, in the circumstances of the particular case, a reasonable person in the patient's position, if warned of the risk, would be likely to attach significance to it or if the medical practitioner is or should reasonably be aware that the particular patient, if warned of the risk, would be likely to attach significance to it*" (at [16]).

The distinct nature of the two tests was acknowledged by Judge Inoke in *Dre v Ministry of Health* (2009) who (at [33]) described Fijian law as to the appropriate test as "*not yet settled*". He stated agreement (at [37]) with Judge Byrne in *Narayan v Ministry of Health* (2008) at [51]) that the *Rogers v Whitaker* line of authority was to be preferred, namely that the *Bolam* line of authority should no longer be applied and that the question is not whether the conduct accords with the practice of the medical profession, or some part of it, but whether it conforms to the standard of reasonable care demanded by the law.

The test in *Rogers v Whitaker* was also referred to by the Court of Appeal in *Din v Khan* (2017, at [15]) but it was found not to be necessary to determine whether it should be followed. In *Attorney-General v Narayan* (2011, at [29]) the Court of Appeal again found it not to be necessary to determine which test should be the law of Fiji.

In light of the adoption by the United Kingdom Supreme Court in *Montgomery v Lanarkshire Health Board* (2015) of the *Rogers* test (see Hobson, 2016; Freckelton 2016), it is likely in due course that Fiji will adopt this approach.

Part of the medical landscape in Fiji is that basic requisites can be in scarce supply. A judgment in which such a deficit of resources figured was *Waqabaca v Vuniniabola* (1998) where damages were awarded in relation to a child who suffered a convulsion prior to being operated on. He needed oxygen because of the convulsion but none was available on the ward and it took three minutes to find an oxygen cylinder with the result that he died. Negligence was found against the hospital but not the child's doctor. The extent to which unavailability or inaccessibility of resources constitutes a defence has not been finally resolved and whether it is enough for a hospital or the government to claim that it has a discretion in how to allocate its resources (see *R v Cambridge Health Authority; ex parte B* (1995) remains to be determined authoritatively for Fiji (see Balededrokadroka 2014).

3 Proof of Negligence

Negligence has been held to be able to be proved inferentially. An instance of where this was achieved by a plaintiff was in *Manu v McCaig* (2011) where Mr Manu on the recommendation of the orthopedic surgeon, Mr McCaig, admitted himself to the CWM Hospital in Suva to be operated on his bad back by the surgeon. He was discharged some seven months later with permanent loss of bladder, bowel and sexual function. He successfully sued the surgeon for damages for negligence and his employer, the Government of Fiji, was found liable to compensate Mr Manu. During the operation the dura covering the spinal cord was torn 1–1.5 cm, resulting in a leak of fluid into the spinal cord and bleeding around the cord.

Inoke J found that there had been damage to the pelvic or sacral nerve(s) during what should have been a straightforward the operation. There was no direct evidence that the surgeon cut or damaged the sacral nerve, and he denied doing so. Inoke J concluded that "*there is no other possibility on the evidence other than want of care on the part of the respondent. On the probabilities it is likely that there was 'a cut too far' by the respondent which damaged the nerve causing the appellant's condition. There is no evidence that the nerve was damaged by some rare or unavoidable misadventure. Indeed, the respondent gave no explanation of what might constitute a rare or unavoidable misadventure*" (*Manu v McCaig* (2011) at [31]).

The doctrine of *res ipsa loquitur* ("the situation speaks for itself") has been held to apply to allegations of medical negligence (*Kumar v Permanent Secretary for Health* 2006), although it was unnecessary for the plaintiff to rely on it in *Manu v McCaig* (2011) at [32]). Where the situation is shown to be under the management of the defendant or the defendant's servants and the outcome is such as in the ordinary course of things does not happen if those who have responsibility for management of the patient use proper care, in the absence of explanation, it may be inferred that the outcome arose from want of care (*Kumar v Permanent Secretary for Health* 2006; *Seru v Lautoka City Council* 2018).

4 Causation

The test for causation applied in Fiji is the "*sine qua non test*" and an inquiry is made as whether the cause in question was the real and effective cause of the outcome (*Moli v Bingwor* 2003). In *Bilitaki v Medical Superintendent Colonial War Memorial Hospital* (2011) Judge Hettiarachchi identified that the issue of causation was a major point of contest. The plaintiff proved that the defendant was in breach of his duty to him by failing to refer him to overseas treatment when he suffered complications or in failing to revise his diagnosis. The more difficult question was whether there would have been any difference to outcome for the plaintiff had he been referred for overseas treatment. Judge Hettiarachchi summarised the alternatives pithily: "*If it is proved that the overseas referral and treatment would have cured the eye then the causal connection is established. If not the plaintiff fails.*" (*Bilitaki v Medical Superintendent Colonial War Memorial Hospital* (2011) at [78]). He observed that: "*Mere speculative evidence is not sufficient to arrive at a conclusion that the delay in referring the plaintiff to overseas treatment would have contributed to his blindness.*" (*Bilitaki v Medical Superintendent Colonial War Memorial Hospital* (2011) at [82]). Because the evidence adduced for the plaintiff did not reach this point, his action did not succeed.

5 Contributory Negligence

The defence of contributory negligence has been held to exist in principle in medical negligence cases. The test is whether the defendant proves that the plaintiff failed to take "*ordinary care*" for himself or herself, or, put another way, such care as an ordinary person would take for his or her own safety and that the failure to take care was contributory of the cause of the harm (*Nisha v Basant* 1997; *Moli v Bingwor* 2003). In the English decision of *Grayson v Ellerman Lines Ltd* (1920, at 477), Lord Parmour held that "*the question of contributory negligence depends upon any breach of duty as between the plaintiff and a negligent defendant; it depends entirely on the question whether the plaintiff could reasonably have avoided the consequences of the defendant's negligence.*" This test has been applied by the Fiji Court of Appeal (*Permanent Secretary for Health v Voliti* (2016, at [20]).

In *Moli v Bingwor* (2003), an argument of contributory negligence was advanced in a case involving a failure to diagnose appendicitis in a child, asserting that parents who were local villagers were unduly slow to bring their child back to hospital. Judge Pathik rejected the argument as "*preposterous*".

6 Expert Evidence

Expert opinion evidence, as to the content of the duty of care, matters of causation and the effects of negligence and the needs of a plaintiff, are vital in medical negligence cases (see Freckelton 2019). In *Narayan v Ali* (2018 at [17]), Judge Tuilevuku observed that a "*medical negligence case is won or lost on the battle of the respective expert medical opinions for each party's case. In terms of the law of evidence, clinical records kept in a patient's medical folder is the best and is the primary evidence of patient information and the care rendered. An expert opinion on whether or not that care rendered falls below the standard of care needed is secondary evidence.*

In essence, the opinion is an interpretation of the clinical records in the medical folder."

7 Contribution Between Tortfeasors

Medical negligence recovery in Fiji is governed, amongst other things by section 6 of the *Law Reform (Contributor Negligence and Tortfeasors) Act* which provides that:

> (1) Where damage is suffered by any person as a result of a tort (whether a crime or not):
>
> (a) Judgment recovered against any tortfeasor liable in respect of that damage shall not be a bar to an action against any other person who would, if sued, have been liable as a joint tortfeasor in respect of the same damage;
>
> (b) if more than one action is brought in respect of that damage by or on behalf of the person by whom it was suffered, or for the benefit of the estate, or of the wife, husband, parent or child of that person, against tortfeasor's liable in respect of the damage (whether as joint tortfeasors or otherwise) the sums recoverable under the judgments given in those actions by way of damages shall not in the aggregate exceed the amount of the damages awarded by the judgment first given; and in any of those actions, other than that in which judgment is first given, the plaintiff shall not be entitled to costs unless thc court is of opinion that there was reasonable ground for bringing the action;
>
> (c) any tortfeasor liable in respect of that damage may recover contribution from any other tortfeasor who is, or would if sued have been, liable in respect of the same damage, whether as a joint tortfeasor or otherwise, so, however, that no person shall be entitled to recover contribution under this section from any person entitled to be indemnified by him in respect of the liability in respect of which the contribution is sought.
>
> (2) In any proceedings for contribution under this section the amount of the contribution recoverable from any person shall be such as may be found by the court to be just and equitable having regard to the extent of that person's responsibility for the damage; and the court shall have power to exempt any person from liability to make contribution, or to direct that the contribution to be recovered from any person shall amount to a complete indemnity.

8 Vicarious Liability

In *Shankar v Fortech Construction Ltd* (2005) the Fijian law on vicarious liability was accepted as being that:

> A master is not responsible for a wrongful act done by his servant unless it is done in the course of his employment. It is deemed to be so done if it is either (i) a wrongful act authorised by the master; or (ii) a wrongful and unauthorised mode of doing some act authorised by the master... On the other hand, if the unauthorised and wrongful act of the servant is not so connected with the authorised act as to be a mode of doing it, but is an independent act, the master is not responsible: for in such a case the servant is not acting in the course of his employment, but has gone outside of it.

It is necessary to have regard to the closeness of the connection between the duties which, in broad terms, the employee was engaged to perform and his or her wrongdoing (*Wati v Buliruarua* 2005).

In *Bilitaki v Medical Superintendent Colonial War Memorial Hospital* (2011) at [89] Judge Hettiarachchi confirmed that in a medical negligence action a hospital can be liable in two ways: if the liability asserted can be directly attributed to the hospital, and vicariously through the actions of one of its doctors or staff. The basis of asserted liability must be identified explicitly by a plaintiff.

An illustrative case in which vicarious liability was straightforwardly established is *Muakalou v Ministry of Health* (2011) which concerned a circumcision which was negligently undertaken by an unqualified dresser (the third defendant) with no significant medical supervision and resulted in gangrenous necrosis of the glans and a fistulous opening of the urethra onto the shaft of the penis, resulting in the likelihood that the plaintiff would have difficulty in achieving normal penile erections and sexual intercourse. Judge Wati found that the employee who undertook the circumcision was employed by the Ministry of Health, was unqualified and did not possess any academic or professional training to carry out the circumcision on the plaintiff: "*His self professed experience and training is flabbergasting when it comes to dealing with an important matter like circumcision which involves a procedure to one of the most important organs of a person's body.*" (*Muakalou v Ministry of Health* (2011) at [46]). He concluded that the previous acts of circumcision undertaken by a dresser and the fact that he was permitted by the doctors to conduct the procedure on the plaintiff were "*meaningless*" and did not mean that it was within his job description to conduct such a procedure. Relevantly, the dresser did not obtain consent from the plaintiff's parents or keep any operative or post-operative notes. To make things worse, when the child was admitted to hospital after the complications, no-one looked at his treatment folder to ascertain the method of circumcision that had been employed or ask the doctor named on the file as the person who had undertaken the procedure how he had carried it out: "*This in itself shows ill management of a patient's condition by the doctors.*" (*Muakalou v Ministry of Health* (2011) at [64]). On the balance of probability and having regard to the evidence as a whole, he found that there was negligence during the circumcision process and/or after the circumcision process and/or the wound management process by virtue of which the third defendant was liable in negligence to the plaintiff. He also found against the Ministry of Health, concluding that such liability was vicarious.

9 Damages

The Fijian courts apply the English approach in relation to the award of damages for medical negligence—to attempt to place the plaintiff in the position he or she would have been in had the negligence not occurred (*Waqabaca v Vuniniabola* 1998). This generally involves an estimation of a plaintiff's past and prospective pain and suffering, special damages in the form of loss of earnings, costs of future care and medical treatment. In *Mahotra v Dr Rege* (2010), for instance, Judge Calanchini awarded damages arising from a negligent hysterectomy for pain and suffering to a plaintiff who had experienced pain, infection and inflammation as a result of corrective surgical procedures that needed to be undertaken and for loss of amenities in that the plaintiff was no longer able to enjoy sexual intercourse with her husband without experiencing pain, resulting in her having lost all interest in sexual activity.

In *Rokobutabutaki v Rokodovu* (2000), the Fiji Court of Appeal noted that each case must depend on its own circumstances but pain and suffering and loss of amenities of life are not susceptible of measurement in terms of money and a conventional figure derived from experience and awards in comparable cases must be assessed. In the case at hand there were no helpful precedents as there were no Fijian reports of damages being awarded for paraplegia, with the consequence that the court "*should aim at a level which bears a reasonable proportion to awards made in other cases, in the light of the relative severity of the injuries and of the pain, suffering and loss of amenities: the assessment should also be made in the light of local experience.*" (*Rokobutabutaki v Rokodovu* (2000)). The Court of Appeal noted that the level of damages for personal injuries in Fiji had traditionally been markedly below that of its more prosperous common law associates, reflecting the differences in their socio-economic conditions. It emphasised that the figure awarded "*must be one appropriate for Fiji and the conditions which apply here*":

> the Judge's task is to fix general damages for personal injury at a proper figure in current Fiji dollars, referring to other awards as no more than broad guidelines to ensure that he or she is on the right track. The use of such guidelines is encouraged as tending to secure fairness and consistency between awards. However, as there are no reports of damages awarded in Fiji for paraplegia, the Court should aim at a level which bears a reasonable proportion to awards made in other cases, in the light of the relative severity of the injuries and of the pain, suffering and loss of amenities. The assessment should also be made in the light of local experience: *Marika Lawanisavi v Pesamino Kapieni* (CA 49/98;13 August 1999), adopting the warning by the Judicial Committee against paying regard to awards in other jurisdictions unless similar social and economic conditions exist (*Li Ping Sun v Chan Nai Tong* [1985] 1 Loyd's Rep. 87). Inflation should be taken into account when considering the present worth of past awards used for comparison.

In *Muakalou v Ministry of Health* (2011) at [72] Judge Wati reiterated that the socio-economic conditions of Fiji needed to be taken into account in determining the quantum of compensation to be awarded to the plaintiff whose penis had been irreparably damaged by a circumcision operation conducted by an unqualified dresser. He declined to order aggravated damages, such damages having been determined to be inappropriate in negligence cases by English authority (*Kralj v McGrath* 1986; *AB v Southern Water Services* 1993; see though *Shah v Narayan* 2003).

It was held that an award of exemplary/punitive damages can be made in an "*appropriate case*". It can only be done when the person wronged is the victim of "*punishable behaviour*" (*Moli v Bingwor* 2003). A claim for exemplary damages needs to be pleaded specifically. Fiji has followed the English authority of *Rookes v Barnard* (1964) in awarding exemplary damages where there has been "*oppressive, arbitrary or unconstitutional action by servants of government*" and Australian authority (*XL Petroleum (NSW) Pty Ltd. v Caltex Oil (Australia) Pty Ltd.* 1985) that the conduct must be worthy of punishment as showing a conscious and contumelious disregard for the plaintiff's rights and to deter the defendant from engaging in such conduct again (*Rokotuiviwa v Seveci* 2008). This is extremely rare in medical negligence cases in Fiji.

Nonetheless significant sums in damages have been awarded in some situations. For instance in *Manu v McCaig* (2011, at [62]) where as a result of a negligently conducted operation Mr Manu had impaired bladder sensation and a series of other impairments: "*the Plaintiff continued to leak urine and self administer his catheter, and remove his faeces by hand. In both of these processes his wife has remained intimately involved. Even though she finds them distasteful, they are tasks to which she has dedicated herself. It quickly dawned on them both that his sexual function had ceased entirely as well.*" Ultimately Mr Manu was awarded $PNG410,000: made up of:

Damages for pain and suffering and loss of amenities	$300,000
Interest thereon	$48,000
Extra cleaning expenses	$10,400
Nursing care	*$52,000*
Total	*$410,400*

An appeal was dismissed as "without merit" (*McCaig v Manu* 2012, at [40]). The assessment of damages is indicative of Papua New Guinea courts' preparedness to order significant damages where it is necessary to do so in order to recognise and compensate for the impact of tortious conduct.

10 Conclusion

The law as to the legal liability for medical negligence is evolving in its own individual way in Fiji, drawing upon English and Australian authorities. As yet claims have not been made in the courts by reference to the important constitutional "*right of every person to health, and to the conditions and facilities necessary to good health, and to health care services, including reproductive health care.*" However, it is apparent that significant sums of damages are available to persons who can be proved to have suffered loss by virtue of a breach of duty of care on the part of medical practitioners. While vicarious liability will generally lie for a hospital where negligence takes place, it will be rare for contributory negligence to lead to a reduction in damages.

References

AB v Southern Water Services [1993] QB 507

Ali v Ministry of Health [2017] FJHC 907

Attorney-General v Narayan [2011] FJCA 27

Baledrokadroka J (2002) The interface of law and medicine in the South Pacific. J S Pac Law 6:14. http://www.paclii.org/journals/fJSPL/vol06/9.shtml

Bilitaki v Medical Superintendent Colonial War Memorial Hospital [2011] FJHC 774

Bolam v Friern Hospital Management Committee [1957] 1 WLR 583

Chand v Permanent Secretary for Health [2018] FJHC 434

Corrin J, Paterson D (2008) Introduction to South Pacific law. Routledge

Din v Khan [2017] FJCA 148

Dre v Ministry of Health [2009] FJHC 129

Farran S (2009) Human rights in the South Pacific: challenges and changes. Routledge

Freckelton I (2016) Bolam buried belatedly. J Law Med 24(3):525–537

Freckelton I (2019) Expert evidence: law, practice, procedure & advocacy, 6th edn. Thomson Reuters

Freckelton I (2020). The rights to life and to the highest attainable standard of health: internationally influential jurisprudence from Kenya and Uganda. J Law Med 28(1):9

Freedom House (2020) Fiji, 2019. https://freedomhouse.org/country/fiji/freedom-world/2019. Accessed 12 April 2020

Giurelli v Girgis (1980) 24 SASR 264

Grayson v Ellerman Lines Ltd [1920] AC 466

Hassall G, Saunders C (2002) Asia-Pacific constitutional systems. Cambridge University Press

Hatcher v Black (2 July 1954) The Times

Hobson C (2016) No (,) More Bolam Please: *Montgomery v Lanarkshire Health Board*. Modern Law Rev 79(3):488–503

International Bar Association (2009) Dire straits: a report on the law of law in Fiji, an international bar association human rights institute report

Ismail v Medical Superintendent [2000] FJHC 87

Jain M (2015) A comparative analysis of medical pluralism in Fiji and the United States. Honors Theses, Union College, Schenectady, New York, p 336. https://digitalworks.union.edu/cgi/viewcontent.cgi?article=1335&context=theses

Jowitt A, Cain TN (2010) Passage of change: law, society and governance in the Pacific. ANU E-Press

Kalouniviti M (20 August 2016). Justice for medical negligence. The Fiji Times. https://www.fijitimes.com/justice-for-medical-negligence/. Accessed 12 October 2021

Kralj v McGrath [1986] 1 All ER 54

Kumar v Permanent Secretary for Health [2006] FJHC 130

Kumari v Taoi [2005] FJHC 347

Lal BV (2008) A time bomb lies buried: Fiji's road to independence, 1960–1970. ANU E-Press

Leckie J (2019) Colonizing madness: asylum and community in Fiji. University of Hawaii Press

Lee HP, Pittard M (ed) (2018) Asia-Pacific judiciaries: independence impartiality and integrity. Cambridge University Press

Mahotra v Dr. Rege [2010] FJHC 278

Manu v McCaig [2011] FJHC 49

Maynard v West Midland Regional Health Authority [1984] 1 WLR 634

McCaig v Manu [2012] FJCA 20

Moli v Bingwor [2003] FJHC 279; HBC0355.1998

Montrose JL (1958) Is negligence a ethical or sociological concept? 21:259–264. https://doi.org/10.1111/j.1468-2230.1958.tb00473.x

Muakalou v Ministry of Health [2011] FJKC 220

Narayan v Ali [2018] FJHC 435

Montgomery v Lanarkshire Health Board [2015] 1 AC 1430

Nisha v Basant [1997] FJHC 288
Offei S (2006) Law of torts in the South Pacific. Vandeplas Publishing
Permanent Secretary for Health v Voliti [2016] FJCA 131
Phillip v Permanent Secretary for Health [2016] FJHC 526
Phillips AF (1997) Medical negligence law: seeking a balance. Taylor & Francis
Prasad NN (2009) The law of medical negligence: consent to medical treatment and failure to warn: drafting a model bill. Thesis submitted in satisfaction of the requirements of the degree of Masters of law, University of the South Pacific. http://digilib.library.usp.ac.fj/gsdl/collect/usplibr1/index/assoc/HASHbe93.dir/doc.pdf. Accessed 20 April 2020
R v Cambridge Health Authority; ex part B [1995] 1 WLR 898
Ratuva S, Lawson S (ed) (2016) The people have spoken: the 2014 elections in Fiji. ANU Press
Ratuva S, Compel R, Aguilar S (2019) Guns and roses: comparative civil-military relations in the changing security environment. Palgrave
Rogers v Whitaker (1992) 175 CLR 479
Rokobutabutaki v Rokodovu [2000] FJCA 9
Rokotuiviwa v Seveci [2008] FJHC 221
Rookes v Barnard [1964] AC 1129
Saulaki v Ministry of Health [2008] FJHC 186
Seru v Lautoka City Council [2018] FJHC 160
Shah S (2012) Liability of traditional healers. J S Pac Law. http://www.paclii.org/journals/JSPL/2012/6.pdf, https://www.usp.ac.fj/fileadmin/random_images/home_middle_banners/emalus/JSPL/2012/Shah.pdf
Shah v Narayan [2003] FJHC 340
Shankar v Fortech Construction Ltd [2005] FJHC 238
Singh Y (1986) Traditional medicine in Fiji: some herbal folk cures used by Fiji Indians. J Ethnopharmacol 15(1):57–58. https://doi.org/10.1016/0378-8741(86)90104-2
Singh v Attorney General of Fiji [2008] FJHC 393
Techera EJ (2011) Safeguarding cultural heritage: law and policy in Fiji. J Cult Herit 12(3):329–334. https://doi.org/10.1016/j.culher.2011.02.002
United Nations Office of the High Commissioner on Human Rights (5 December 2019) Preliminary observations on country visit, 28 November to 5 December 2019. https://www.ohchr.org/EN/NewsEvents/Pages/DisplayNews.aspx?NewsID=25390&LangID=E
Voliti v The Permanent Secretary for Health, unreported, High Court of Fiji, 25 April 2014
Votimaisiru v General Manager Labasa Hospital [2013] FJHC 475; HBC 29.2004
Waqabaca v Vuniniabola [1998] FJLawRp 19; [1998] 44 FLR 10
Wati v Buliruarua [2005] FJHC 128
World Health Organization (2017), "Fiji". https://www.who.int/countries/fji/en/. Accessed 20 April 2020
XL Petroleum (NSW) Pty Ltd v Caltex Oil (Australia) Pty Ltd (1985) 155 CLR 448

Clinical Liability in Hong Kong: Revisiting Duty and Standard of Care

Albert Lee

Abstract Clinical liability arises when medical practitioner fails to fulfil the duty of care owed to the patient with clinical performance not meeting the reasonable standard. This chapter will start with an introduction to discuss how duty of care arise to be considered as reasonable and foreseeable with authorities from Australia, England, Hong Kong, New Zealand, and how definition of standard of medical care has evolved from *Bolam* to *Montgomery*. Under what circumstances will medical practitioner owed duty of care to third party? The discussion will take reference from a case of infectious disease and a case of psychiatric injuries drawing authorities from common law jurisdictions. What standard should we impose on general practitioner in conducting special medical assessment? The standard should also take into account for disclosing clinical information to address the material risk of that particular patient as reflected by a case of assessment of commercial diver.

1 Introduction

1.1 Duty of Care: Reasonable and Foreseeable

Clinical liability arises when there is a clinical negligent act resulting medical mishap. It would be due to medical practitioner not fulfilling his/her duty of care, owed to the patient, and the clinical performance not meeting the standard to be considered

---

A. Lee (✉)
The Chinese University of Hong Kong, Hong Kong, China
e-mail: alee@cuhk.edu.hk

Honorary Fellow of Faculty of Public Health, London, UK

V. L. Raposo and R. G. Beran (eds.), *Medical Liability in Asia and Australasia*,
Ius Gentium: Comparative Perspectives on Law and Justice 94,
https://doi.org/10.1007/978-981-16-4855-7_4

Table 1 Essential elements to establish negligence and what constitute special relationship

Essential elements to establish negligence: • the existence of a duty of care situation • breach of that duty • causal connection between the defendant's careless conduct and the damage • that the damage was not so unforeseeable as to be too remote
Requirements for special relationship: • A reliance by the plaintiff on the defendant's special skill and judgment • Knowledge, or reasonable expectation of knowledge on the part of the defendant, that the plaintiff was relying on the statement; • It was reasonable in the circumstances for the plaintiff to rely on the defendant

as reasonable medical practice. The essential elements to establish negligence are summarised in Table 1.[1] Duty of care arises where there is a special relationship between the giver and recipient,[2] and it is summarised in Table 1.

In *Yuen Kun Yeu v Attorney General of Hong Kong*,[3] the Privy Council upheld the judgment of the Hong Kong Court of Appeal that the Commissioner of Deposit-taking companies had no special relationship with the claimant who was one of the unascertained members of a huge class of people depositing money with Hong Kong financial institutions, notwithstanding protection of depositors being a function of Commissioner. The economic loss of the claimant was directly caused by a wrongful act of third party and there is no general duty to confer protection against the loss. The Commissioner did not have the legal power nor the resources to control day to day operation of the many companies, so it would not be fair to pose such duty on him.

The Australian case, *Sydney Water Corp v Turano*,[4] and the New Zealand case, *North Shore City Council v Attorney-General* ("*The Grange*"),[5] also adopted the requirement of reasonable foreseeability of harm. In *Turano*, the High Court held that it was not foreseeable that installation of a water main system, by the defendant, would lead to damage to the roots of a tree and cause the tree to fall after twenty years and thus no duty was owed to a road user who was hit by the tree. *The Grange* case defined the reasonableness for duty of care, namely that the duty is owed of '*a reasonable person in the defendant's position could have avoided damage by exercising reasonable care and was in such a relationship to the plaintiff that he or she ought to have acted to do so*'.[6]

[1] Michael Jones, et al., Clerk & Lindsell on Torts (22nd ed. 2017).

[2] *Hedley Byrne & Co Ltd. v Hellers & Partners Ltd.* [1964] AC465.

[3] [1988] A.C. 175.

[4] [2009] HCA 42, (2009) 239 CLR (High Court), Australia.

[5] [2012] NZSC 49, [2012] 3 NZLR 341 (Supreme Court), New Zealand.

[6] Ibid [28].

The defendant Council sought to establish a higher level of responsibility of the Building Industry Authority (BIA) in its regulation of the Council's operations. A building development leaked and the Council was sued, in respect of its alleged negligence, for failing to take reasonable steps to ensure that the construction, of the development, complied with the building code. The Council sought to join the Attorney-General, as a third party (the liabilities of the BIA fall on the Crown), on the basis that the BIA had breached a duty of care owed to the Council by failing to raise concerns about monolithic cladding and weather-tightness and giving the Council "*a clean bill of health*" for the building. Taking reference from *Sacramento*[7] the Court of Appeal held that the BIA owed no duty to building owners to exercise its powers under the Building Act 1991 and the Building Code by taking steps to warn about and to prevent poor building practices leading to the leaky building syndrome.

The defendant, the BIA, being in a position involving supervision and control would not be enough, in itself, to give rise to a duty as there should be a sufficiently close and proximate relation between the parties and, in *The Grange*, the BIA did deal with the Council but the review process could involve any or all councils and a duty could lead to indirect responsibility of the BIA to all homeowners suing councils. The BIA could not, in any event, be responsible for operational negligence.[8]

Caparo Industries Plc v Dickman[9] stated the elements of the three pronged test (tripartite test) determining duty of care:

(i) whether the damage was reasonably foreseeable;
(ii) whether the relationship between the plaintiff and the defendant could be characterised as one of 'proximity' or 'neighbourhood'; and
(iii) whether the situation was one in which the court considers it fair, just and reasonable to impose a duty of the given scope upon the defendant.

In *McFarlane v Tayside Health Board,*[10] the House of Lord determined whether the parents of a healthy child could claim damages for the cost of its upbringing due to negligent act of rendering the father sterile. The judgement was 'NO' and it was held not fair, just and reasonable to impose such liability.

1.2 Standard of Care

The standard is to compare with reasonable practitioner with the relevant skill or qualification. The "Bolam" test from *Bolam vs Friern Health Management Committee*[11]

---

[7] *Attorney-General v Body Corporate* No 200200 [2007] 1 NZLR 95 [*Sacramento*].

[8] Stephen Todd, *Torts in the New Zealand Supreme Court 2004–2013*, Auckland, New Zealand: The New Zealand Supreme Court: The First Ten Years, (13–15 Nov 2014). https://cdn.auckland.ac.nz/assets/facultyconferences/faculty-of-law/Supreme%20Court%20Conference/Todd.pdf Last access 15 July 2020.

[9] [1990] AC 605.

[10] [2000] 2 AC 59.

[11] *Bolam vs Friern Health Management Committee* [1957] 1 WLR 582.

is that a *doctor is not guilty of negligence if he has acted in accordance with a practice accepted as proper by a responsible body of medical men skilled in that particular art*. McNair J, in *Bolam*,[12] made it clear that a doctor would not adopt a practice conctradicting substantial standard. In *Bolitho v City and Hackney Health Authority*[13]:

> …[t]he court is not bound to hold that a defendant doctor escapes liability for negligent treatment or diagnosis just because he leads evidence from a number of medical experts who are genuinely of opinion that the defendant's treatment or diagnosis accorded with sound medical practice……the weighing up of risk against benefits, the judge before accepting a body of opinion as being reasonable, responsible or respectable……, the experts have directed their minds to the questions of comparative risks and benefits and have reached a defensible conclusion on the matter.
>
> …..[i]t will very seldom be right for a judge to reach the conclusion that views genuinely held by a competent medical expert are unreasonable….. ……It is only where a judge can be satisfied that the body of expert opinion cannot be logically supported……………………..

The expert witness must be capable to withstand logical analysis for the decision to be justifiable, fair and reasonable.

The *Montgomery*[14] case has raised the standard of reasonable test as the focus is now on '*reasonable patient*' rather than '*reasonable doctor*'. In *Montgomery* the plaintiff was not told about the risk of shoulder dystocia which would be 9–10%, among babies of diabetic mothers, to deprive the option of elective Caesarian section and the baby was born with cerebral palsy. *Montgomery* has raised the standard of reasonable test as the focus is now on '*reasonable patient*' rather than '*reasonable doctor*'. The law defines material risk as either a risk to which a reasonable person in the patient's position would be likely to attach significance or a risk that a doctor knows or should reasonably know perceived to be significance by this particular patient. Many jurisdictions have moved towards legal standards for risk disclosure, prioritising the preferences of patients.[15] The shift towards '*reasonable or prudent patient test*', focusing on what the patient would want to know, would be construed as '*patient-centred*' care.[16] This is in line with the standard of care expected of medical practitioner.[17]

The judgement of reasonable standard would be based on a balance of probability, according to legal burden to be discharged in civil cases.[18] The standard is dependent upon the subject matter and the seriousness, where the more improbable the event,

---

[12] Ibid.

[13] [1998] A.C. 232 (HL).

[14] *Montgomery v. Lanarkshire Health Board* UKSC 2015 11.

[15] Bismark et al. (2012).

[16] Lee (2017).

[17] General Medical Council General Medical Council. *Consent: Patients and Doctors Making Decisions Together* (2008).

[18] Andrew L.T Choo, "Evidence and Standard of Proof' in Andrew L–T Choo (ed.), *Evidence*. (OUP, 2014); Williams (2003).

the stronger must be the evidence.[19] The Canadian Court has also taken similar approach,[20]

> ...Like the House of Lords, I think that it is time to say, once and for all in Canada, that there is only one civil standard of proof at common law and that is proof on balance of probabilities. Of course, context is all important and a judge should not be unmindful where appropriate, of inherent probabilities or improbabilities or the serious of allegations or consequences. ...[21]

Should liability be imposed on healthcare providers due to faults in the facilities? Third party might lodge a claim on the negligent act of medical practitioner on patient, due to a close relationship of the third party to the patient. Liability would impose, on medical practitioner, when s/he undertakes a routine clinical task notwithstanding some special skills are expected, such as occupational assessment for certain jobs to be performed under special circumstances. Medical doctors are concerned with liability with inadequate disclosure of information. This chapter will use cases to unfold those issues by drawing references to some recent cases in Hong Kong, applying judgement from cases of common law jurisdictions illustrating the principles of proximity, foreseeability and fair, just and reasonable.

2 Outline of Basic Materials Used in the Chapter

2.1 Table of Cases

Australia

Tame v New South Wales (2002) 211 CLR317.

Sydney Water Corp v Turano [2009] HCA 42, (2009) 239 CLR (High Court), Australia.

Canada

FH v McDougall [2008] 3 SCR 41, [40] (Supreme Court), Canada.

Hong Kong

Ho Ying Wai v. Keliston Marine (Far East) Ltd. and Another [2002] HKCU 651.

Luk Mary V Hong Kong Baptist Hosptial [2008] 1 HKC.

Luen Hing Fat Coating & Finishing Factory Ltd. v Waan Chuen Ming [2011] 2 HKC 364, [2011] 2 HKLRD 223, (2011) 14 HKCFAR 14.

Wong Rocky Lok-kun v Wu Kwong Sum [2018] HKDC 70.

---

[19] Heather Keating, *Suspicious, Sitting on the Fence and Standards of Proof*, 21(2) Child and Family Law Quarterly 230 (2009); *Re S-B (Children) (Perpetrator: Non-Accidental Injury)* [2009] UKSC 17, [2010] 1 AC 678 (Supreme Court), UK.

[20] *FH v McDougall* [2008] 3 SCR 41, [40] (Supreme Court), Canada.

[21] Ibid (Rothstein J).

Yuen Kun Yeu v Attorney General of Hong Kong [1988] A.C. 175. (appeal to Privy Council).

New Zealand

Attorney-General v Body Corporate No 200200 [2007] 1 NZLR 95 [*Sacramento*].
North Shore City Council v Attorney-General [2012] NZSC 49, [2012] 3 NZLR 341 (Supreme Court), New Zealand.
South Pacific Manufacturing Co Ltd. v New Zealand Security Consultants & Investigations Ltd. [1992] 2 NZLR.

UK

Bolam vs Friern Health Management Committee [1957] 1 WLR 582.
Bolitho v City and Hackney Health Authority [1998] A.C. 232 (HL).
Caparo Industries Plc v Dickman [1990] AC 605.
Cassidy v Minister of Health [1951] 2 KB 343, [1951] 1 All ER 574 (CA).
Derrick & Ors v Ontario Community Hospital & Ors (1975) 47 Cal Ap 3d 145.
Goodwill v British Pregnancy Advisory Service [1996] 2 All ER 161, [1996] 1. WLR 1397 (CA).
Hedley Byrne & Co Ltd. v Hellers & Partners Ltd. [1964] AC465.
Montgomery v. Lanarkshire Health Board UKSC 2015 11.
Palmer v Tees Health Authority [1999] Lloyd's Rep Med 351 (CA).
Roe v Minister of Health [1954] 2 QB 66, [1954] 2 All ER 131, [1954] 2 WLRD. 915 (CA).
White v Jones [1995] 2 AC 207.
Wisher v Essex [1987] 1 QB 730.

Bibliography

Braithwaite, John, et al., *The Governance of Health Safety and Quality*, Commonwealth of Australia, 2005.
Bismark Maria M, et al., *Legal disputes over duties to disclose treatment risks to patients: A review of negligence claims and complaints in Australia*. 9 (8) PLoS Med e.1001m283 (2012) https://doi.org/10.1371/journal.pmed.1001283.
Choo Andrew L.T., 'Evidence and Standard of Proof' in Andrew L-T Choo (ed.), *Evidence* (OUP, 2014).
General Medical Council, *Consent: Patients and Doctors Making Decisions Together* (2008).
Jackson Emily, *Medical Law: Text, Cases, and Materials* (3rd edn, Oxford University Press 2013).
Keating Helen, *Suspicious, Sitting on the Fence and Standards of Proof*, 21(2) Child and Family Law Quarterly 230 (2009).
Lee Albert, *Bolam' to 'Montgomery' is result of evolutionary change of medical practice towards 'Patient-Centered Care. 93* Postgraduate Medical Journal 46–50 (2017) https://doi.org/10.1136/postgradmedj-2016-134236.

Lee Albert. *Public health action against COVID-19 to protect our rights to health.* 39 (2) Medicine and Law 205–222 (2020).

Sokol Daniel, *Doing the right thing*, 351 BMJ h5288 (2015).

3 Discussion of that Material

Duty of care of hospital warning family members of possibility of being infected by discharging patient.

3.1 The Case

This is a case that the plaintiff ("Ms L") brought an action in negligence against a private hospital ("Hospital") as defendant of providing no advice or warning to family members upon discharge of plaintiff's brother ("Mr L") who had contracted Severe Acute Respiratory Syndrome (SARS) and later died. Ms L also contracted SARS with close contact with Mr. L.[22] The defendant applied to strike out the claim on the ground that no reasonable cause of action was disclosed.

The cause of action is breach of duty of defendant, the Hospital owned to the plaintiff, Ms L. The elements have been described in Table 1 of introduction,[23] and also the requirement of special relationships.[24] The analysis should include:

- whether the damage was reasonably foreseeable;
- whether the relationship between the plaintiff and the defendant could be characterised as one of 'proximity' or 'neighbourhood'; and
- whether the situation was one in which the court considers it fair, just and reasonable to impose a duty of the given scope upon the defendant.
- Consideration of the three requirements (tripartite test[25]) involved value judgments and it was necessary to take a holistic view of foreseeability, proximity and the need to be satisfied that it would be fair, just and reasonable to impose a duty of care

3.2 The Facts and Issues

Table 2 summarise the chronology of the facts.

[22] *Luk Mary V Hong Kong Baptist Hosptial* [2008] 1 HKC.

[23] Michael Jones et al., Supranote 1.

[24] *Hedley Byrne,* Supranote 2.

[25] *Caparo,* Surpanote 9.

Table 2 Chronological summary of the plaintiff case

- 10 March 2003, Mr L was admitted to the Hospital suffering from bilateral epididymitis
- He was admitted under the care of a urologist. During the course of his stay in the hospital, patients in the hospital were infected with SARS
- 16 March 2003, Mr L was discharged home to the care of his wife
- Neither Mr L nor his wife were informed that suspected SARS cases were present in the hospital, in particular that such cases were on the same floor upon which Mr L had been accommodated
- Neither Mr L nor his wife were given any advice or warning of precautions to be takenin relation to SARS
- Ms L, the plaintiff did not live in the same house as Mr L
- SARS is a highly infectious communicable disease and may be transmitted by droplets communicated from one person to another at a distance of less than 1 m
- Between 16 and 22 March 2003, Ms L had daily contact with Mr L
- Neither Mr L, nor members of his family, nor Ms L took precautions against the possible transmission of SARS during this period
- On 22 March 2003, Mr L was admitted to QEH with suspected SARS, which was subsequently confirmed
- On 24 March 2003, Ms L began to have a fever, and isolated herself on 25 March 2003. On 26 March 2003, she attended the Accident & Emergency Department at QEH and she was admitted, and was subsequently confirmed to be suffering from SARS
- On 26 March 2003, Mr L's wife and one of his sons were admitted QEH and both were subsequently confirmed to be SARS positive
- Mr L died from SARS on 14 April 2003
- On 28 March 2003 Mr L's brother's mother-in-law was admitted to PMH with SARS, where she died of that condition

The issues of this case are:

- The plaintiff alleged that the Hospital owed her, as a member of Mr L's family a duty of care to take all reasonable precautions not to expose Mr L's family to the reasonable foreseeable risk of being infected by SARS
- Failure to alert and/or warn Mr L that he might have been exposed to SARS and advised him, and members of his family, of appropriate precautions required, resulting in them being infection was alleged a breach of duty of care
- Mr L was under care of private urologist, not employed by the Hospital nor agent of the Hospital, that was responsible for discharging Mr L
- Should the duty of care be owed by the Hospital, providing the facility for the patient or the attending doctor, who was responsible for Mr L's care?
- Should the duty of care extend beyond the patient?

3.3 The Arguments for Duty of Care

The defendant relied on two decision by Lord Denning in *Cassidy v Minister Health*[26] and *Roe v Minister of Health.*[27] In *Cassidy*, the claimant was a patient, at a hospital run by the defendant, who required routine treatment to set the bones in his wrist. Due to negligence, on the part of one of the doctors, the operation caused his fingers to become stiff. The claimant sued the defendant, in the tort of negligence, on the basis of vicarious liability. Denning LJ (dissenting) said that:

> …[w]henever they accept a patient for treatment, they must use reasonable care and skill to cure him of his ailment. The hospital authorities cannot, of course, do it by themselves: they have no ears to listen through the stethoscope, and no hands to hold the surgeon's knife. They must do it by the staff which they employ; and if their staff are negligent in giving the treatment, they are just as liable for that negligence as is anyone else who employs others to do his duties for him.' and 'where a person is himself under a duty to use care, he cannot get rid of his responsibility by delegating the performance of it to someone else, no matter whether the delegation be to a servant under a contract of service or to an independent contractor under a contract for services.

The Court of Appeal held that the defendant was vicariously liable, as the person was a servant of the defendant if he was chosen for the job by the defendant, and he was fully integrated into the defendant's organisation.

In *Roe*,[28] two claimants had been given an anaesthetic for minor operations. The anaesthetic had been contaminated with a sterilising fluid. This resulted in both claimants becoming permanently paralysed. The anaesthetic had become contaminated during storage. The anaesthetic was stored in glass ampoules which were emerged in the sterilising fluid. It transpired the ampoules had minute cracks which were not detectable with human eye. It was not known that the anaesthetic could be contaminated in this way and the hospital followed a normal procedure in storing them this way. It was held that there was no breach of duty. The risk was not foreseeable as it was an unknown risk at the time.

In *Luk*,[29] it was not related to treatment provided by the attending doctor as Saunders J said: '*If the surgeon makes an error in the course of surgery, …it will be the surgeon, and not the hospital who will be liable. However, hospital is responsible for overall administration of the facility including the precautions to be taken as result of presence of infectious diseases and cleanliness of the facilities.*'[30] Discharging patient should not be only decision of the attending doctor and Saunders J stated: '*once the formal decision is made to discharge the patient it will usually be the hospital staff who will attend to the formalities involved in discharge. These will include matters such as the settling of accounts, checking dressings if necessary, and*

[26] [1951] 2 KB 343 (CA).

[27] [1954] 2 QB 66 (CA) **2 WLR 915** Court of Appeal.

[28] Ibid.

[29] *Luk*, Supranote 22, [24].

[30] *Luk* Supranote 22, [20 G and I].

arguably ensuring that appropriate advice has been given as to any steps the patient might need to take following discharge.'[31]

In *Roy*[32] and *Cassidy*,[33] there were no involvement on the part of the hospital in the act of event causing injury. The court was satisfied that *Luk* was an arguable case: '*[a] duty of care exists on the Hospital to inform patients, when there is an infectious disease such as SARS present in the hospital, upon discharge of a patient, to inform the patient of precautions to be taken to ensure that that disease does not spread to members of the patient's immediate family.*'[34] The Hospital owed a duty of care to advise patients, on discharge, of precautions to be taken to protect the public. The public has the right to be protected from infectious diseases with prompt public health action and healthcare providers have the duty, in this aspect of health protection.[35]

3.4 The Arguments of Proximity, Foreseeability and Fair, just and Reasonable

The second issue is whether the duty of care would be extended to the plaintiff, Ms L. The determination of proximity or neighbourhood, foreseeability of damage and fair, just and reasonable impinge duty upon the defendant would be the key elements as in *Caparo*.[36] Defendant referred to *Derrick & Ors v Ontairo Community Hospital & Ors*[37] that the plaintiff, a minor, contracted a contagious disease from a girl, while in the hospital, and argued that the hospital had failed to notify the plaintiff or his parents of the hazard, inherent in exposure to the girl. The Court of Appeal rejected the argument that the hospital owed the plaintiff a duty of care as it would impose an intolerable burden upon hospitals to notify all members of the public that one of its patients, being released from the hospital, is suffering from a contagious, communicable disease.

The defendant also referred to English cases., *Palmer v Tes Health Authority*[38] and *Goodwill v British Pregnancy Advisory Service*.[39] In *Palmer*, a child was abducted, sexually assaulted and murdered, by a man living in the same street as the child, who was under the psychiatric care of the Health Authority at risk of committing the offence which had occurred. Summon of striking out was held that no duty of care was owed to the child or her parents. The Court of Appeal upheld the decision that,

---

31 *Luk* Supranote 22, [27].

32 *Roy* Supranote 27.

33 *Cassidy* Supranote 26.

34 *Luk* Supranote 22, [30B].

35 Lee (2020).

36 *Caparao* Supranote 9.

37 (1975) 47 Cal Ap 3d 145, Cal App LEXIS 1996.

38 [1999] Lloyd's Rep Med 351.

39 [1996] 1 WLR 1397.

on the facts, there was insufficient proximity for a duty of care to arise. Living in the same street as Armstrong was not a sufficient degree of proximity. In *Goodwill*,[40] it was held that a doctor did not owe a duty of care in giving contraceptive advice to a person, with whom the patient may be, in future, engaged in sexual relationship.

In determining whether the duty of care should be extended to Ms L, the local circumstances should be taken into account.[41]

> …Mr Ozorio is on strong ground when he argues that the concept of family in Hong Kong, including as it does parents, children, siblings, wives or husbands of children or siblings, their children and even parents-in-law, enables him to contend that the determinant cohort of family as it may be found to be in Hong Kong may well include Ms Luk.
>
> If it does, and I am satisfied that it is so arguable, then the decisions in Derrick, Palmer and Goodwill, where, in each case the plaintiff fell outside the determinant cohort, are distinguishable.[42]

It was held that the statement of claim disclosed a course of action and the Hospital's summon was dismissed.

3.5 Principles to Be Applied

Luen Hing Fat Coating & Finishing Factory Ltd. v Waan Chuen Ming[43] states how the HK court approaches these three requirements (tripartite test). The facts of the case are:

- Factory operator (appellant) engaged independent contractor to repair a machine in factory and provided two pallet jacks and two bearing trolleys to the contractor to transport a heavy unit to be detached and removed for repair.
- The unit fell and crushed the respondent employed by the contractor crushing both his legs.

The trial judge found both contractor and factory operator liable.

- Harm in question was **foreseeable**. The operation was dangerous[44]
- He was using equipment on loan from the Factory Operator. **Proximity** existed between the Worker and the Factory Operator.[45]

The issues determining the question of fairness, justifiable and reasonableness to hold that a duty of care owed by the factory operator to the worker are:

---

[40] Ibid.

[41] *Luk* Supranote 22 [46].

[42] *Luk* Supranote 22 [47].

[43] *Luen Hing Fat Coating & Finishing Factory Ltd v Waan Chuen Ming* [2011] 2 HKC 364, [2011] 2 HKLRD 223, (2011) 14 HKCFAR 14.

[44] Ibid [39].

[45] Ibid [40].

- *The factory operator chose to engage an independent contractor who had to borrow makeshift equipment from it. It could have chosen instead to engage an independent contractor who had the equipment needed to do the work in a safe manner. That would presumably have been more costly. But safety is not a thing on which to cut costs like this.*[46]
- *Personal safety being at stake is always significant. This is an area in which legal policy is involved. The policy considerations in favour of personal safety are naturally very powerful.*[47]

The appeal was unanimously dismissed. *Luen Hing Fat* has highlighted that engaging an independent contractor (similar to the Hospital engaging private doctors) would still fulfil the proximity test by utilising the facilities of the contractor. If the task is known to be dangerous or the damage is harmful, posing risk of personal safety, it would be fair, just and reasonable to impose duty on the contractor on third party. SARS was known to be a serious condition and highly infectious at that time. If the patients contracted the infection during their stay, it would be hard to imagine why the hospital did not owe duty of care to advise patients of the precautions of infection control protecting them and their close contacts. It is not uncommon that close family members will be in close contact, from time to time, in the circumstance of Hong Kong. SARS was known to be infectious with high infectivity and would cause morbidity and also mortality, like COVID-19 in 2020, so healthcare professionals have a duty to protect the public.[48] Infection control is an important issue for safety and quality assurance of hospital services. In Australia, the ten National Safety and Quality Health Services Standards include governance for safety and quality in health service organisation (standard 1) and preventing and controlling healthcare associated infection (standard 3).[49] It is hard for a hospital to deny duty of care for better infection control for the safety of patients, staff and those visiting the facilities.

4 Clinical Liability for Psychiatric Injury

4.1 The Case

The plaintiff, ("Mr W") alleged defendant's ("Dr W") clinical negligence causing his wife ("Mrs W") to suffer from physical pain and psychiatric disorders which had caused her to become estranged from the plaintiff, leading to their divorce in 2015 and consequential psychiatric damage or injury to the plaintiff.[50]

[46] Ibid [41].

[47] Ibid [41].

[48] Albert Lee Supranote 35.

[49] John Braithwaite, et al., *The Governance of Health Safety and Quality*, Commonwealth of Australia, 2005.

[50] *Wong Rocky Lok-kun v Wu Kwong Sum* [2018] HKDC 70.

The plaintiff claimed that the defendant knew or foresaw, or ought reasonably to have known or to have foreseen, such consequential damage or injury to the mental wellbeing of the plaintiff. The defendant applied to strike out the plaintiff's claim, on the ground that the plaintiff's statement of claim disclosed no reasonable cause of action.

4.2 Facts

- In 2010, the plaintiff, Mr W, and his wife Mrs W was expecting a baby and was attended by the defendant, Dr W, an obstetrician, on ten occasions until she gave birth.
- On 12 September 2010, Mrs W gave birth to a baby girl in a private hospital, attended by Dr W who performed episiotomy on Mrs W to facilitate the delivery and repaired the wound with absorbable sutures. Mr W was present throughout.
- Mrs W complained of pain in the episiotomy wound, whilst at the hospital and during the follow-up consultation. On 1 October 2010, an object was found protruding from the Mrs W's vagina and removed.
- The object was confirmed to be a retained surgical gauze. Mrs W commenced the claim of personal injuries against Dr W for medical negligence and the case was settled.
- In early 2014, Mrs W was confirmed to be suffering from:

  (i) major depressive disorder, single episode, in partial remission;
  (ii) persistent depressive disorder (dysthymia);
  (iii) female sexual interest/arousal disorder; and
  (iv) genito-pelvic pain/penetration disorder.

- Mrs W filed for divorce in 2015.
- Mr W felt helpless and had '*intense self-blame and feelings of guilt*'.
- Mr W's concentration and attention became poor and this affected his work performance.
- Mr W consulted Dr H for psychiatric assessment for the first time in May 2015. Dr H's diagnosis was '*Major Depressive Disorder Single Episode, Mild*'. Mr W attended further assessments by Dr H in 2015, 2016 and early 2017. He also received therapeutic treatment by Dr C, a specialist in psychiatry
- In November 2015, Mr W commenced action, alleging negligence on Dr W, which led to a train of events culminating in the plaintiff's suffering from major depressive disorder.
- Dr W's negligence caused Mrs W to suffer from physical pain and psychiatric disorders, which had caused her to become estranged from Mr W, leading to their divorce in 2015 and consequential psychiatric damage or injury to the Mr W.
- Mr W claimed that Dr W knew or foresaw, or ought reasonably to have known or to have foreseen such consequential damage or injury to the mental wellbeing of the plaintiff, Mr W.

4.3 Issues

The court adopted three-pronged test[51]:

(i) whether the damage was reasonably foreseeable;
(ii) whether the relationship between the plaintiff and the defendant could be characterised as one of 'proximity' or 'neighbourhood'; and
(iii) whether the situation was one in which the court considers it fair, just and reasonable that the law should impose a duty of a given scope upon the defendant for the benefit of the plaintiff.

Winnie Tsui J said[52]: "*In Hong Kong, the modern starting point of how the court should approach these three requirements must be the Court of Final Appeal's decision in Luen Hing Fat.*[53]"

> ...It is recognised time and again by courts of the highest authority that the consideration of the three requirements involve value judgments and, in grey area cases, the outcome will have to be determined by judicial judgment. In every case, the value or judicial judgment involved is the assessment by the court of whether in a given relationship there ought' to be liability for negligence. See White v Jones [1995] 2 AC 207 at 221F-G, per Sir Donald Nicholls V-C in the Court of Appeal; South Pacific Manufacturing Co Ltd. v New Zealand Security Consultants & Investigations Ltd. [1992] 2 NZLR 282 at 294. These statements were expressly acknowledged to be the proper Caparo approach in Luen Hing Fat (at para 37)...

4.4 Application of Cases

In *White v Jones*,[54] two daughters of their deceased father sued Mr Jones, a solicitor, for failing to follow their father's instructions when drawing up his will as Mr Jones did not change the will of previous instruction of the father to cut his two daughters out of the will so that £9000 would be given to his daughters. His will still stood the same after his death. It was held that a special relationship and the loss was foreseeable and there was a proximate relationship between the client and his will's beneficiaries, and there were no reasons why liability could not be fair, just and reasonable.

In *South Pacific Manufacturing Co Ltd. v New Zealand Security Consultant & investigations Ltd.*[55] have reformulated questions being asked at each stage of inquiry:

- Internal concentrating on the parties themselves and the proximity or nature and closeness of the particular relationship between them

---

[51] *Caparo* Supranote 9; *Wong* Supra note 49 [57].

[52] *Wong* Supranote 50 [58].

[53] *Luen Hing Fat* Supranote 43 [29–37].

[54] [1995] 2 AC 207.

[55] [1992] 2 NZLR 282 (CA).

- External involving an explicit assessment of extraneous considerations of policy or principle for and against a duty

Cooke P said: "*A broad two-stage approach or any other approach is only a framework...... Ultimately the exercise can only be balancing one and the important object is that all relevant factors be weighted........grey area case has to be determined by judicial judgement. Formula can help to organise thinking but they cannot provide answers.*"[56] The two-stage approach can be a more balancing approach to decide liability.

In the previous section, *Luen Hing Fat* highlighted the principles to decide harm, in the question, whether the harm was foreseeable as it was obvious that the operation was dangerous.[57] Proximity existed between the Worker and the Factory Operator.[58] Holding the Factory Operator owing a duty of care to the Worker was found to be fair, just and reasonable, as the Factory Operator chose to engage an independent contractor borrowing makeshift equipment from it but it could have chosen instead to engage an independent contractor with the equipment to do the work in a safe manner.[59] That would presumably have been more costly but personal safety should always be significant and policy considerations in favour of personal safety are naturally very powerful.[60] The appeal by Factory Operator was unanimously dismissed.

4.5 *Principles of Fair, just and Reasonable*

The expert opinion of Dr H whom Mr W consulted, stated that Mr W's illness is closely related to the events that happened following the birth of the daughter and that Mr W had been directly affected by the incident which happened to the wife.[61] Winne Tsui J said:

> ...[h]ow the doctor could have possibly foreseen that because of his negligently leaving behind a gauze inside the wife and failing to realise his mistake in subsequent consultations, the husband of his patient would suffer from psychiatric injury. The risk of such harm is simply too far-fetched...[62]
>
> ...The resulting harm is several steps or levels 'removed' from the original negligent act – the chronological sequence being Dr Wu's negligence; the wife suffering from psychiatric disorders; the wife becoming completely withdrawn from Mr Wong, both emotionally and sexually; the divorce; and, finally, Mr Wong suffering from psychiatric disorders. So, at

[56] Ibid.

[57] *Luen Hing Fat* supranote 44.

[58] *Luen Hing Fat* supranote 45.

[59] *Luen Hing Fat* supranote 46.

[60] Ibid.

[61] *Luen Hing Fat* Supranote 43 [31].

[62] *Luen Hing Fat* Supranote 43 [72].

> least four steps 'removed'....some of the links in the chain of causation is not altogether straightforward. Nor do they come across as a natural development of events[63]
>
> The following passages from Clerk & Lindsell contain a general but helpful discussion on this point in the context of remoteness. I would say that the observations and the reasoning there would similarly apply in the present context of duty of care. **'....The defendant's wrongdoing may trigger a series of events stretching well beyond one's normal expectations of possible consequences. The law does not, however, impose indefinite liability. A line must be drawn to confine the responsibility of the defendant to those consequences of his wrongdoing which it is proper for him to shoulder......'**.......'....In a system of fault liability, holding a person liable for the unpredictable or freakish consequences of his negligence may seem unfair **because of a sense of disproportion between the fault and the damage.**'[64] (at para 2–137) (emphasis added)...[65]

The injury could not reasonably be predicted, was in any event too far-fetched, took place in an unusual or extraordinary manner, and it would be disproportionate to impose liability on the defendant, even if he had acted carelessly, would such carelessness ultimately lead to the injury? The plaintiff, Mr W did not have a clear-cut case of reasonable foreseeability.

Common law stated by the court in *Tame v New South Wales*[66] held that the central question, in determination defendant owing duty of care to avoid recognizable psychiatric injury, was whether in all the circumstances, the risk of plaintiff sustaining such injury was reasonably foreseeable. The resulting damage would not be many steps away from the original negligent act. The causal relationship needs to be strong and the degree of injury should be appropriate to the insulting event. The fault and the damage ought to be proportionate and the law would not impose indefinite liability.

5 Standard of Care in Conducting Medical Assessment

This is a case of allegation of breach of duty of care of a general medical practitioner for omission to test practical experience and health status of a diver, and breach of duty of care of a medical professional for omission to explain the full effect and consequences of injury following diagnosis.[67] The issues are whether the doctor has fulfilled the standard of care, in conducting health assessment, and also disclosing clinical information to the patient.

---

[63] *Luen Hing Fat* Supranote 43 [74].

[64] *Luen Hing Fat* Supranote 43 [79].

[65] *Clerk & Lindsell on Torts* (21st Ed) paras 2–137.

[66] (2002) 211 CLR317.

[67] *Ho Ying Wai v. Keliston Marine (Far East) Ltd. and Another* [2002] HKCU 651.

5.1 Case Summary

Plaintiff ("Mr H") had been diving commercially since approximately 1990. He was admitted to hospital on 19 October 1990 with diagnosis of pneumothorax. Mr H joined the first defendant ("KH") as commercial driver in January 1992. He was referred to second defendant ("Dr Y") for medical examination.

The Code of practice for Diving has stated:

> …Diving is a hazardous occupation and safety requires that the diver should be trained and fit…The aim of this code is to provide guidance on the principle of safe diving practice for the protection of the health of persons employed to work under water…[68]
>
> {2. The employer (diving contractor) has the ultimate responsibility for ensuring the safety of his employees and should take all necessary steps to achieve safe diving practices.
>
> 8. He should appoint a doctor with special experience in underwater medicine to provide medical cover for diving and carry out the examination required by divers. He should arrange for this doctor to be on call when diving operations involve regular decompression or other activity with high risk of illness or injury.
>
> This is a very wide-ranging responsibility which underlines the need for the doctor's special experience in providing "medical cover" and being "on call". A **doctor** without such special experience would not be in a position to meet these requirements. Accordingly the duty of appointing such a **doctor** is clear enough and requires steps to be taken to ensure that he meets that required level of expertise.
>
> 9. He should maintain a diver's fitness register with details of the dates and results of medical examinations including X-rays.
>
> This is clear and illustrates the high **duty of care** imposed upon an employer in respect of it's employees but is no more than reasonably to be expected in a hazardous industry.}[69]

Mr H was referred to Dr Y for medical examination in September/October 1992 whether he would be fit as diver.

5.2 Case Analysis

- Mr H completed the "Health Declaration" form. It is the type of form used by Dr Y for a medical examination, to complete as a preliminary step.[70]
- No part of its content is specifically referable to the examination of a commercial diver, nor does it provide for the recording of a history of matters so referable.[71]
- No copy of this form was kept by Dr Y.[72]
- Mr H was vague how he completed this form, the first question:

---

[68] *Ho* Supranote 67 [22].

[69] *Ho* Supranote 67 [23].

[70] *Ho* Supranote 67 [50].

[71] *Ho* Supranote 67 [51].

[72] *Ho* Supranote 67 [52].

> Have you ever been admitted to Hospital for treatment or observation?[73]

Mr H should have answered "Yes" or a tick in the 'YES' box and if he had answered positively, Dr Y would have followed up to clarify the circumstances.[74] One question asked if Mr H had ever suffered from a number of specified illnesses or diseases including lung diseases and Dr Y should have clarified this but no written record was retained.[75] Mr H did not reveal his hospitalisation in 1990 and Dr Y considered that he was examining a man with no declared adverse medical history.[76] Is this an acceptable standard for medical doctors undertaking the duty to certify someone to be fit as commercial driver with understanding the requirements under code of practice? Hon Seagroatt J said:

> ...Dr Y had no expertise or previous experience in diving medicine, yet he must have realised that he was being asked to certify as fit for diving men who required a specific medical approach. I am satisfied that he treated them as no different from the general run of employees referred to him for an examination for general fitness and yet he recorded nothing in relation to his medical history...[77]

Hon Seagroatt J also raised the issue, if considering Dr Y's clinical notes and records carefully, a number of factors emerged to cast doubt on his thoroughness in dealing with essential matters for a medical examination of a commercial diver.[78] There was nothing, in the entries for 21 September 1992, to support that Dr Y had obtained any information from Mr H, whether by way of a check on the health declaration form or any X-ray or simply by a doctor's normal inquiries, and no record of history of Mr H as a smoker.[79]

Expert witness, Professor Wong expressed that a general medical practitioner, with no such experience or knowledge, who undertook the medical examination of a professional diver, without equipping himself with available information and the current Code of Practice and guidance, in relation to diving medicine and professional divers medical examinations, was acting below the standard to be expected of the reasonably competent practitioner in that field.[80]

[73] *Ho* Supranote 67 [53].

[74] Ibid.

[75] *Ho* Supranote 67 [54].

[76] Ibid.

[77] *Ho* Supranote 67 [55].

[78] *Ho* Supranote 67 [65].

[79] *Ho* Supranote 67 [66].

[80] *Ho* Supranote 67 [83].

5.3 *Would Being a General Medical Practitioner Affect the Standard of Care?*

The standard of care should not be lower for inexperienced doctors. In *Wisher v Essex*,[81] a junior doctor mistakenly inserted a catheter in a vein, instead of an artery, for oxygen monitoring. It was held:

> …That standard of care required of member of a medical unit was that of the ordinary skilled person exercising and professing to have the special skill, and the standard was to be determined in the context of particular posts in the unit rather than according to general rank.
>
> An inexperienced who was called on to exercise a specialist skill and made a mistake nevertheless satisfied the necessary standard of care if he had sought the advice and help o his senior when necessary….

Once the medical practitioner assumed the duty of care, for the particular clinical task, s/he is expected to possess the skills up to the necessary standard to perform such functions. Otherwise, s/he should refer the case to someone with the relevant skills and experience.

The *Grange* case defined the reasonableness for duty of care as duty owed by '*a reasonable person in the defendant's position who could have avoided damage by exercising reasonable care and was in such a relationship to the plaintiff that he or she ought to have acted to do so*'.·[82] Has Dr Y performed adequate assessment to prevent Mr H from further damage to continue as commercial diver?

Medical examination certifying fitness for particular occupation includes information and advice to patients, The purpose of giving information to patients is to ensure informed decision. Patients should have adequate understanding of the relative advantages and disadvantages of the treatment and in the case of Mr H whether he would be fit and safe to be a commercial diver. Doctors will need to tailor their disclosures according to individual patient's priorities and concerns as people have different needs for information.

Doctors should be aware of the *Montgomery* case.[83] The law now requires a doctor to take "*reasonable care to ensure that the patient is aware of any material risks involved in any recommended treatment, and of any reasonable alternative or variant treatments.*"[84] The standard expected for any doctor, performing this type of medical examination, is to assure that the examinee is fit for the job to be designated. Dr Y fell below this standard if he only regarded it as a general physical examination.

---

[81] [1987] 1 QB 730.

[82] *Grange* Supranote 5.

[83] *Montgomery*, Supranote 14.

[84] Daniel Sokol, *Doing the right thing*, 351 *BMJ* h5288 (2015).

6 Conclusion

Patients are not living in isolation. They are usually closely connected to their family members, and also their own social circles. Adverse clinical outcomes would have impact on those with whom they have intimate relationships. Analysis of the cases *Luk*,[85] and *Wong*,[86] drawing references from cases from different common law jurisdictions and academic literature, should enrich the understanding of the essential elements of medical negligence, constitution of special relationship and the tripartite test in applying to third parties' allegation of claims for clinical negligent acts. With advancement of medical technology, some treatments are taken place in various healthcare facilities. The healthcare providers also owe a duty of care to the patients, apart from the attending doctors. The management of healthcare facilities ought to understand what constitutes proximate relationship, between the users (patients) and the providers, and be more vigilant to foresee the possible clinical risk, in order to have safety measures in place. Is the clinical practice accepted as proper by a responsible body of medical men skilled in that particular art in *Ho*[87]? Medical doctors must not forget the standard required for disclosing clinical information to address the material risk of that particular patient. In the *Ho* case, it is not up to standard if the doctor performing the medical examination fails to disclose his risk to be commercial diver as this represents the main purpose of the consultation.

References

Bismark MM et al (2012) Legal disputes over duties to disclose treatment risks to patients: a review of negligence claims and complaints in Australia. PLoS Med 9(8):e.1001m283. https://doi.org/10.1371/journal.pmed.1001283

Lee A (2017) 'Bolam' to 'Montgomery' is result of evolutionary change of medical practice towards 'Patient-Centered Care. Postgrad Med J 93:46–50. https://doi.org/10.1136/postgradmedj-2016-134236

Lee A (2020) Public health action against COVID-19 to protect our rights to health. Med Law 39(2):205–222

Williams CR (2003) Burdens and standards in civil litigation. Syd Law Rev 25(2):165

---

[85] *Luk* Supranote 22.

[86] *Wong* Supranote 50.

[87] *Ho* Supranote 67.

Law of Medical Liability in India

V. Nandimath Omprakash

Abstract Alike other common law jurisdictions, India registers increasing medical negligence litigation. The milestone judgment of IMA v V P Shanta made it clear that doctors do fall under the ambit of Consumer Protection Act—making it easier for the aggrieved patients to proceed to consumer protection commissions, to seek civil remedy. Indian courts/tribunals have built rich jurisprudence on medical negligence, borrowing from other western jurisdictions, with suitable modifications and improvisation to suit local needs. Especially Jacob Mathews case provides much needed procedural safeguard towards meaningless (criminal) prosecution against the doctors. This paper accounts for the development of medical negligence law both in civil and criminal spheres in India.

1 Introduction

In India, alike other common law jurisdictions, medical liability[1] arises primarily from common law. The doctor owes a duty of care towards his/her patient, which is primarily fixed by law. Any shortfall in discharging that duty holds the medical professional liable in law. Greater degree of negligence holds the doctor liable in criminal law in India, for negligence.[2] There are many statutes which govern dedicated aspects of medical treatment and contemplate liability on the treating doctor,

[1] The expression indicates the liability of the medical professional or doctor for his negligence while treating the patient. Words like 'medical liability', 'doctor's liability' and 'liability of medical professional' are used in this paper interchangeably.

[2] See generally Jacob Mathew v State of Punjab & Another,.

[3] Act No. 42 of 1994. This statute provides for regulation of removal, storage and transplantation of human organs and tissues for therapeutic purposes and for the prevention of commercial dealings in human organs and tissues.

V. Nandimath Omprakash (✉)
Professor of Law, Think Tank on Health, National Law School of India University, Bengaluru, Karnataka, India

V. L. Raposo and R. G. Beran (eds.), *Medical Liability in Asia and Australasia*, Ius Gentium: Comparative Perspectives on Law and Justice 94,
https://doi.org/10.1007/978-981-16-4855-7_5

as well as hospital. This also includes, in many cases, criminal liability. The Transplantation of Human Organs & Tissues Act, 1994[3]; The Medical Termination of Pregnancy Act, 1971[4]; The Mental Healthcare Act, 2017[5] are few examples where acts, in contravention of the statutory provision(s), would attract liability under law (including criminal liability).

'Health' is a State subject, as per the constitutional scheme in India.[6] There is much legislation, passed by respective States, which impose liability for their contravention on doctor and/orhospitals, as per the facts of the case.[7] These statutes should be studied deeply and independently, to make sense of their purpose, approach and sanctions. The present paper dwells upon civil liability, arising under common law; and criminal liability, under Indian Penal Code, of medical professional(s) and/or hospital(s).

2 The Disgruntled Patient and Forums

A disgruntled or aggrieved patient has multiple forums, in India, from which to choose, depending upon his/her desire to avail required legal remedy. The following three classifications help, in better understand these multiple forums which often overlap.

2.1 Civil Remedy

If the intent of the aggrieved patient is to seek damages, s/he can choose between jurisdictional Civil Court or Consumer Protection Tribunal. All patients may invoke the jurisdiction of Civil Courts, in case they have any grievance against the doctor. This is based on the principle of law that a treating doctor owes a duty of care towards his/her patient, and would be held liable, when such duty is breached. Alternatively, if the medical services are availed for charge (money consideration), the

---

[4] Act No. 34 of 1971. This Act provides for the termination of certain pregnancies by registered Medical Practitioners and for matters connected therewith or incidental thereto.

[5] Act No. 10 of 2017. The Act to provide for mental healthcare and services for persons with mental illness and to protect, promote and fulfil the rights of such persons during delivery of mental healthcare and services and for matters connected therewith or incidental thereto.

[6] India has federal structure of government (but substantially different compared to US federal structure). The legislative powers are divided between Centre and State, to the extent possible under Schedule VII, appended to the Constitution of India. All residuary powers rest with Centre, making Centre stronger than States. Entry 6, List II of State List, explicitly vests 'public health and sanitation; hospitals and dispensaries' to the ambit of State (provincial) Governments.

[7] The Karnataka Private Medical Establishments Act, can be cited as one example. This statute mandates all private medical establishments in the State of Karnataka to have themselves registered under the statute.

aggrieved patient may opt to Consumer Dispute Redressal Commissions, governed under Consumer Protection Act, 2019. If the medical treatment is provided free of cost - the remedy under Consumer Protection law is not available.

It may not be completely out of place to state that, the erstwhile Consumer Protection Act, 1986[8] established the system of *'better consumer protection'* with tribunals to redress consumer grievances/disputes, for the first time. Till 1986, there were no Consumer Protection Tribunals in India.[9] This would have meant that the disgruntled patient had to take his/her claim to the Civil Courts. In 2019, a brand new Consumer Protection Act replaced the erstwhile (1986) consumer law, with greater emphasis upon overall consumer welfare in mind.

A 'consumer' is defined as a person who either buys a good or avails any service for payment of consideration either in full or in part (with a promise to pay the remaining consideration in due course) or with a promise to pay consideration in future.[10] To litigate in Consumer Tribunals there must be paid consideration, paid part of the consideration or, at least, promised payment of consideration in future. If a medical service is availed free of cost, or as charity, the only avenue is to the Civil Courts.

Two school of thought existed till 1996, speculating the jurisdiction of consumer tribunals vis-a-vis 'medical services'. One believed that the services, rendered by the doctors, are of higher order and do not qualify within *'deficiency of services'*, as contemplated by the then Consumer Protection law.[11] Bringing the medical services (or doctors) within the ambit of Consumer Protection Act (CPA), would mean to reduce high-ranking medical professionals, to be mere technicians like plumbers or carpenters.[12] The other school believed, looking into the objective of the CPA, that doctors are covered by it.[13] In 1996, this speculation ended as the Supreme Court

---

[8] Act 68 of 1986. The Preamble of this statute bring out the basic objective as to 'provide for better protection of the interests of consumers and for that purpose to make provision for the establishment of consumer councils and other authorities for the settlement of consumers' disputes and for matters connected therewith.

[9] It is a three-tier system, comprising of District Forum, State Commission and National Commission, providing quick, economical and effective remedy to the consumers for either defective goods bought or deficiency of services received. These tribunals are popularly known as 'consumer courts' by laymen.

[10] Section 2(7) of the Consumer Protection Act, 2019.

[11] The erstwhile Consumer Protection Act defined services in Section 2(o) as 'any service of any description which is made available to potential users and includes, but not limited to, the provision of facilities in connection with banking, financing, insurance, transport, processing, supply of electrical or other energy, board or lodging or both, housing construction, entertainment, amusement or the purveying of news or other information, but does not include the rendering of any service free of charge or under a contract of personal service'.

[12] For instance, the Division Bench of Madras High Court, while deciding Dr. C. S. Subramanian v Kumarasamy & Another [(1994) 1 MLJ 438] took a view that both medicinal and surgical services, would not come within the ambit of CPA under Section 2(1)(o).

[13] The Division Bench of Andhra Pradesh High Court has held that services rendered for consideration by private medical practitioners, private hospitals and nursing homes do provide service within in the meaning of CPA and therefore, the law is applicable to them.

declared that the CPA is applicable to doctors.[14] With this, the patient became a '*consumer*' in India, provided s/he has availed medical services for money consideration. This decision opened the doors of consumer tribunals for the patient to claim damages or other remedies.

There are obvious advantages in recourse to the Consumer Dispute Commission. Concession from payment of court-fees (which can go up to 10% of total claim value in case of Civil Courts), freedom from technicalities and timely disposal of cases are main among the many advantages. These tribunals are consumer friendly forums—where the consumer is, by culture, treated as '*favoured litigant*'. The patient has the upper hand over doctor in litigating, making this forum probably a favourite, most often if not always! The procedure of the forum is *sans* formalities, making the forum not feasible to examine cases of medical liability, with nuances or cases needing evaluation of complicated scientific evidence.[15] In such cases, probably the ideal forum would be the Civil Court.

A conscious choice has to be made by the patient, between Civil Court or consumer dispute redressal commissions, if eligible to sue in the later forum. The only option that could be exercised is to move the Civil Court. Both these forums have the right to enforce their respective orders; and have wide powers to provide equitable relief to the patient.

2.2 Criminal Remedy

If the aggrieved patient intends to seek criminal remedy, the only concurrent forum available is the jurisdictional Criminal Court. If the patient desires, the proceedings in criminal court may continue concurrently with Civil Court or Consumer commission. If for some reason, the patient is desirous of pursuing only criminal proceedings, then s/he may do so. The CPA provides two years, from the date cause of action, as limitation period for filing the complaint to seek redress.[16] The Limitation Act, 1963, provides a limitation period of three years to seek remedy from Civil Courts.[17] If the cause of action is continuing, then the limitation period is not applicable. If the patient has his/her limb rendered useless after surgery, s/he might bring an action at any time during his/her lifetime, as it is deemed that the requisite cause of

[14] In Indian Medical Association v V. P. Shantha & Others, AIR 1996 AIR 550.

[15] The procedure of civil code, evidence law is not applicable to the procedure of the tribunal. The tribunal is to operate by applying mere principles of natural justice.

[16] Section 24A. Further s. 24A(2) provides the forum with power to condone the delay, if there are reasonable and justifiable reasons.

[17] Act No. 36 of 1963. This Act consolidates the law for limitation of suits and other proceedings in India before Civil Courts. Section 3 of the Act lays down the cardinal principle as 'subject to the provisions contained in Sects. 4 to 24 (inclusive), every suit instituted, appeal preferred, and application made after the prescribed period shall be dismissed, although limitation has not been set up as a defence'.

action is arising every moment.[18] If, after trying one's luck in Consumer Tribunal, the continuing dissatisfaction (including no success) may prompt the claimant to approach the Civil Court, within the period of limitation. Any relief granted by the Civil Court, would be subject to the relief already granted by the Consumer Tribunal. Limitation period of the criminal cases are prescribed in Criminal Procedure Code (CrPC).[19] The limitation is contemplated according to the volume of punishment. If the offence is punishable with fine only, the period of limitation is six months. If the offence is punishable with imprisonment for a term less than one year, the limitation period is one year. In case the offence is punishable with imprisonment for a term exceeding one year, but not exceeding three years, the limitation period is three years.[20] These prescriptions are only for non-cognizable offences.[21] There is no period of limitation for cognizable offences.[22]

3 Complaining to the Professional Regulatory Body

In addition to moving the Civil or Criminal Courts; the aggrieved patient may complain about the medical professional to the concerned Professional Regulatory Body (PRB) to which s/he belongs. In India, there are multiple PRBs regulating different systems of medical professionals. The National Medical Commission regulates the system of 'evidence-based medicine' or 'modern medicine' or 'allopathy'.[23] Those professing Indian system of medicines are regulated by the National Commission for Indian Systems of Medicine.[24] Ayurveda, Siddha, Unani, Naturopathy and Yoga are considered as Indian Systems of Medicine. There are scholastic writings which consider homoeopathy among the Indian System of Medicine, as according them, it has got itself assimilated completely into the Indian Systems of Medicine.[25] The practice of homeopathy is governed by its own respective professional regulatory

[18] S. 23 of Limitation Act. It reads that "In case of a continuing breach of contract or in the case of a continuing tort, a fresh period of limitation begins to run at every moment for the time during which the breach or the tort, as the case may be, continues'".

[19] The Code of Criminal Procedure, 1973.

[20] Ss. 467, 468, 468, 470, 471, 472 and 473 of the Code of Criminal Procedure, 1973.

[21] s. 2(l) of the Code of Criminal Procedure defines non cognizable offences as those "in which the police officer without any warrant has no authority to arrest". There are offences which do not have serious impact upon the society. For instance, assault, cheating, forgery etc.

[22] S. 2(c) of the Code of Criminal Procedure, 1973 defines cognizable offence as those, "in which a police officer may arrest without warrant, as per the First Schedule of the Criminal Procedure Code, 1973 or under any other law for the time being in force". Cognizable offences are usually those which have serious effect upon the society and are heinous.

[23] Vide National Medical Commission Act, 2019.

[24] Vide National Commission for Indian System of Medicine (NCIM) Act, 2020 (the year indicated is to be verified for accuracy).

[25] See generally, Prasad (2002).

body viz., National Commission for Homeopathy.[26] These professional regulatory bodies are tasked to promote medical ethics and to regulate professional conduct, in accordance with their respective regulations and ethical standards.

Anyone having a grievance against doctors can take their grievances to the concerned (State) Medical Councils. After duly enquiring into the matter, the Councils will provide necessary relief to the complainant. The professional bodies, *inter alia*, can suspend the license of the erring medical professional, either temporarily or permanently.

There are several commissions established in India. Commission for Backward Classes,[27] National Human Rights Commission,[28] State Human Rights Commissions,[29] National Commission for Women,[30] Scheduled Tribes Commission[31] are the most prominent. These Commissions are vested with legal power to investigate matters pertaining to their jurisdictional subject. The Commissions can investigate either on their own or on the basis of the complaint received. Most of these Commissions are equipped, while investigating any of the matters—to summon and enforce the attendance of any person (from any part of India) and examine them under oath. They may order 'discovery' and production of any documents, receive evidence on affidavits, requisition public record(s) or copy(ies) thereof from any source. After necessary enquiry, these Commissions may report and recommend action by the concerned State agencies as might be appropriate.

There are instances, especially involving government doctors/hospitals, where complaints are lodged against the doctors in case of medical negligence. Complaints are made to Commissions, such as the Human Right Commissions or the Backward Commission, against private medical establishments. The trend of complaining to these Commissions is on rise in India. Commissions can be taken as another sort of forum, to seek legal help, by disgruntled patient(s).

India provides for multiple (and ample) forums to seek legal redressal for medical negligence, which is parallel to any other advanced jurisdictions. After allowing medical liability cases in Consumer Tribunals, the complaints against doctors (for seeking compensation for medical negligence cases) have increased multiple fold. There is no credible database in India, maintaining the incidence of medical liability cases. The insurance companies are, to the extent practical, collecting the data for conducting their business. Many forums, available for patients, might also make it difficult to establish a credible database. In 2019, 2638 complaints were filed against doctors in various consumer tribunals (District Commission to National Commission).

---

[26] Vide National Commission for Homeopathy Act, 2019.

[27] A Constitutional body under Art. 338A of the Constitution of India, works under the Ministry of Social Justice & Empowerment.

[28] Established under Protection of Human rights Act (PHRA), 1993 in October 1993.

[29] Established under S. 21 of the Protection of Human Rights Act, 1993.

[30] Set up as in January 1992 under the national Commission for Women Act, 1990; and works to protect and promote the interests of women in India.

[31] Established by Art. 338A of the Constitution of India.

4 Civil Liability

Laxman Balkrishna Joshi v Trimbak Bapu Godbole & Another is probably the first case reaching the Supreme Court, dealing with aspects of medical negligence in 1969.[32] As Consumer Tribunals were not in existence, the case commenced from the lower Civil Court and moved to the Supreme Court. An otherwise healthy 20 years old young adolescent had an accident in a western part of India, resulting into a fracture of his left femur.[33] Till the defendant treats him, the only treatment he received, from a local physician, was to have his leg tied to wooden plank (as a splint). The local physician adviced the boy to be taken to Pune for further treatment. After two days, the boy was taken to the Defendant's hospital at Pune, where it was found that he had an overlapping fracture of the femur requiring pin-traction. The appellant doctor (Specialist) asked his deputy, Dr. Irani, to administer two injections of 1/8th grain of morphia and 1/200th grain of Hyoscine HB, at an hour interval. Dr. Irani gave only one injection. The boy was taken to the operation theatre where the injured leg was put into plaster splints. For that procedure the boy was kept in the operation theatre for about an hour and at about 5:30 PM was shifted to his room (at the hospital). At about 6:30 PM, the boy was struggling to breath and his condition deteriorated. Emergency treatment was commenced, but the boy died due to fat embolism.

The Respondent claimed medical negligence, *inter alia* contending that, while putting the leg in plaster, the appellant doctor used manual traction with excessive force. It was argued that such procedure should have been undertaken only under anaesthesia (rather than morphia alone). The rough manipulation was calculated to cause conditions favourable for embolism or shock and proved fatal to the patient. In his defence, the doctor's claim that, taking into consideration the exhausted condition of the patient, they did not find it desirable to give general anaesthetic; and they accordingly reduced the rotational deformity and held the limb in proper position with slight traction and immobilised it in plaster spica. The patient was alleged to be cooperative. The Supreme Court, referring to English cases, held the doctor liable, as his act of not anaesthetising the patient amounted to negligence.

A person who holds himself out ready to give medical advice and treatment impliedly holds-forth that he is possessed of skill and knowledge for the purpose. Such a person, when consulted by a patient, has certain duties, namely, a duty of care in deciding whether to undertake the case, a duty of care in deciding what treatment to give and duty of care in the administering that treatment. A breach of any of these duties gives a right of action for negligence, as noted in this judgment by the court. This dictum is being applied and followed consistently by the Courts in India, to determine liability of the doctors.

---

[32] AIR 1969 128.

[33] At Palshet villege, Ratnagari District in Maharashtra.

The doctor owes a duty of care towards the patient, once the relationship between them is established.[34] The breach of such duty will attract the liability in law for the doctor. In India the doctor's performance (in treating the patient) will be compared with that of a 'reasonable doctor'. If the standard of care falls short of that necessary to meet the standards exhibited by the reasonable doctor, the accused doctor will be held liable; otherwise, the doctor will be exonerated. The most popular method to explain this aspect of law is by adopting the following framework; is evaluating the duty of the doctor while:

1. Accepting the patient for necessary treatment;
2. Determining the course of treatment; and
3. Actual administration of treatment.

5 Accepting the Patient for Treatment

Like other professionals, a doctor may use his/her discretion in accepting a patient for treatment, provided: (i) it is not a case of emergency; and (ii) s/he has not sacrificed such privilege to his/her employer, under any contract of employment. In both of these situations, the doctor will be 'forced' to treat any patient submitted to him. In case of medical emergency, the doctor is believed to have owed a duty of care towards the emergency victim. Such duty arises out of the Hippocratic oath which is administered to the doctor before he is admitted into the profession.[35] There are many versions of the oath today in India. Breach of this oath, or conditions mentioned therein, are taken as violation of ethical standards but may not attract sanction.

With development of time, this duty of a doctor, to render emergency care, is sliced out of the overall duty of care under oath and has been converted as a legal obligation. The following are the three justifications for the same viz.

1. Indian Medical Council's Professional Conduct, Etiquette and Ethics Regulations, 2002;
2. Judicial pronouncements of Supreme Court of India; and
3. New age statutes imposing the said obligation on hospitals.

---

[34] The relationship between doctor and patient begins (i) under contract, when the patient proposes to seek treatment, and in turn accepted by the doctor for consideration of professional fee; and (ii) under tort law, where the patient is been accepted for treatment for free of cost.

[35] Hippocrates is often referred to as father of medicine in western culture. Hippocratic oath is an oath historically taken by physicians. It is one of the most widely known of Greek medical texts. In its original form it requires a new physician to swear, by a number of healing gods, to uphold specific ethical standards. Scholars widely believe that Hippocrates or one of his students wrote the oath between 5th and 3rd century BC.

Section 2.1 of the Regulations[36] state as follows:

Though a physician is not bound to treat each and every person asking his services, he should not only be ever ready to respond to the calls of the sick and the injured, but should be mindful of the higher character of his mission and the responsibility he discharges in the course of his professional duties. In his treatment he should never forget that the health and the lives of those entrusted to his care depend on his skill and attention. A physician should endeavour to add to the comfort of the sick by making his visits at the hour indicated to the patients. A physician advising a patient to seek service of another physician is acceptable, however in a case of emergency a physician must treat the patient. No physician shall arbitrarily refuse treatment to the patient. however, for good reason, when a patient is suffering from an ailment which is not within the range of experience of the treating physician, the physician may refuse treatment and refer the patient to another physician.

It becomes mandatory for the doctor to render his service to the emergency victim. Every doctor is expected to sign, at the time of his/her professional registration, a document which states that the concerned doctor shall abide by the code of medical ethics, as enumerated in the Indian Medical Council (Professional Conduct, Etiquette and Ethics) Regulations, 2002.

While deciding *Pt. Parmanad Katara v Union of India & Others*, the Supreme Court observed as follows, emphasising upon the duty of the doctor in emergency[37]:

1. There can be no second opinion that preservation of human life is of paramount importance. That is so on account of the fact that once life is lost, the status quo ante cannot be restored as resurrection is beyond the capacity of man;
2. Every doctor, whether at a Government hospital or otherwise, has the professional obligation to extend his services with due expertise for protecting life;
3. No law or State action can intervene to avoid/delay the discharge of the paramount obligation cast upon members of the medical profession. The obligation being total, absolute and paramount, laws of procedure whether in statute or otherwise which would interfere with the discharge of this obligation cannot be sustained and must, therefore, give way;
4. It is clear that there is no legal impediment for a medical professional when he is called upon or requested to attend to an injured person needing his medical assistance immediately. There is also no doubt that the effort to save the person should be the top priority, not only of the medical professional but even of the police or any other citizen who happens to be connected with the matter or who happens to notice such an incident or a situation;
5. The members of the legal profession, our law courts and everyone concerned will also keep in mind that a man in the medical profession should not be unnecessarily harassed for purposes of interrogation or for any other formality and should not be dragged during investigations at the police station and it should be avoided as far as possible;

---

[36] Indian Medical Council's Professional Conduct, Etiquette and Ethics Regulations, 2002.

[37] 1989 AIR 2039. This is a Public Interest Litigation, based on the newspaper report concerning the death of the scooterist being knocked down by the speeding car. The accident victim was denied treatment, when taken to the nearest hospital; and was advised to be taken to another hospital (allegedly authorised to handle medico-legal cases) situated away by 20 Kms., which caused the death due to delay in treatment.

6. Law courts will not summon a medical professional to give evidence unless the evidence is necessary and even if he is summoned, attempt should be made to see that the men in this profession are not made to wait and waste time unnecessarily.

The decision clearly lays down that a doctor shall do all possible to safeguard life during the emergency.

In *Paschim Banga Khet Mazdoorsamaity v State of West Bengal & Another*, the Supreme Court touched upon the issue.[38] The Petitioner fell off the train and suffered serious head injuries and brain haemorrhage. He was immediately rushed to the nearest Primary Health Center; thence taken from one hospital to another, till he was admitted in Calcutta Medical Research Institute, a private hospital where he was treated as an 'indoor patient'. An expenditure of approximately INR 17,000 was incurred. Most of the hospitals, to which he was taken, were either lacking facilities or reluctant to admit him, stating that it was a medico-legal case. Aggrieved by the incident and callous attitude, on the part of the medical authorities at various State run hospitals, in Calcutta, in treating serious injuries, the Petitioner filed a writ-petition to the Supreme Court.

The issue was whether non-availability of facilities for treatment of serious injuries in various government hospitals (in Calcutta) amounted to denial of a fundamental right, guaranteed under Art. 21 of the Constitution of the Petitioner? Was the question framed by the Supreme Court for its consideration. After due assessment, the Court answered the question in affirmative. It also ordered immediate upgrading of all government hospitals, so that such situation did not recur. Although such upgrades would be costly to the State exchequer; it was to be carried out immediately, as it is one among the paramount constitutional obligations of the State to discharge. This judgement imposed a direct duty upon the State to provide for necessary facilities to care for medical emergencies.[39] In discharging this paramount constitutional responsibility, the State strategically roped in private medical practitioners/hospitals as well.

In *Savelife Foundation v Union of India*,[40] the Supreme Court observed, in categorical terms, that lack of response by a doctor, in an emergency situation pertaining to road accidents, shall constitute professional misconduct,under MCI Ethical regulations, and disciplinary action shall be taken against such doctor. Although this case is applicable only to road accidents, it can easily be stretched to other emergencies. The medical professional is reminded of this ethical responsibility by these few Supreme Court verdicts.

---

[38] 1996 SCC (4) 37.

[39] The Court observed that "it is no doubt true that financial resources are needed for providing these facilities. But at the same time it cannot be ignored that it is the constitutional obligation of the State to provide adequate medical services to the people. Whatever is necessary for this purpose has to be done. In the context of the constitutional obligation to provide free legal aid to poor accused this Court has held that the State cannot avoid its constitutional obligation in that regard on account of financial constraints".

[40] Writ Petition (Civil) No. 235 of 2012 (Supreme Court).

The Law Commission of India, in its Report, basing its recommendation on the basis of above cases, states as follows[41]:

> We have provided that no hospital or medical practitioner shall refuse to provide emergency medical care to victims of accidents or those in emergency medical condition on the ground that it is a medico-legal case or that the person is not able to pay immediately or that he has no medical insurance or other reimbursement facilities. If they refuse without justifiable reason, that will be an offence.

There are various State legislations to regulate private medical establishments of their respective jurisdiction.[42] *Inter alia*, these legislations stipulate various standards for private medical establishments and prescribe statutory obligations to be performed by them. This is the contemporary trend in India. The Karnataka legislation (KPME) imposes an obligation in the following words viz., "*administer necessary first aid and take other life saving or stabilising emergency measures in all medico-legal or potentially medico-legal cases such as victims of road accidents, accidental or induced burns or poisoning or criminal assaults and the like which present themselves or are brought before it at the establishments; in the event of such emergencies without insisting on advance payment*".[43] The same approach is being followed with little variance by most of the States in India. Delhi mandates medical care in emergency, without worrying about payment of fees therein. It also states that if any such emergency is attended by the hospitals, fees will be reimbursed by the state government.

6 Determining the Course of Treatment

Indian Courts have adopted the Bolam's principle that, the medical practitioner, as a qualified professional, may exercise his discretion in choosing the course of treatment, if alternative modes of treatments are available.[44] The doctor has a discretion in choosing treatment which he proposes to give to the patient and such discretion is relatively ampler in cases of emergency, said the Supreme Court, adopting the Bolam principle in the case of *Dr. Laxman Balkrishna Joshi v Trimbak Bapu* Godbole's case.[45] In *Haribabu Khodwa v State of Maharashtra*, the Court observed that the skill of medical practitioners differs from doctor to doctor. The nature of the profession is such that there may be more than one course of treatment which may

---

[41] "Emergency Medical Care to Victims of Accidents and the During Emergency Medical Condition and Women under Labour", Law Commission of India, 20 1st Report, p. 4.

[42] For example, in Karnataka the Karnataka Private Medical Establishments Act, 2007.

[43] Section 11(i) of the Karnataka Private Medical Establishments Act, 2007.

[44] The principle laid down in Bolam v Friern Hospital Management Committee, (insert the citation). Lord McNair laying down the principle as "if he (doctor) has acted in accordance with a practice accepted as proper by a responsible body of medical men skilled in that particular art" can't be held liable in law.

[45] 1969 AIR 128 or 1969 SCR (1) 206.

be advisable for treating a patient. Courts would be slow to attribute negligence, on the part of the doctor, if s/he performed his/her duties to the best of his/her ability and with due care and caution. Medical opinion may differ, with regard to the course of action to be taken by a doctor treating a patient, but as long as a doctor acts in a manner which is acceptable to the medical profession and the Court finds that s/he has attended on the patient with due care, skill and diligence and if the patient still does not survive, or suffers a permanent ailment, it would be difficult to hold the doctor guilty of negligence. It was observed that "*in cases where the doctors act carelessly and in a manner which is not expected of a medical practitioner, then in such a case an action in torts would be maintainable*". In *State of Haryana & Others v Smt. Santra* and *Dr. Suresh Gupta v NCT*, Delhi, the Supreme Court applied the Bolam principle.

In the United Kingdom, the Bolam test is criticised, especially in the Bolitho's case.[46] The House of Lords substantially shift from the Bolam approach. Experts, when consulted by the Court, feel that some class of doctors would have adopted the line of treatment, as adopted by the defendant doctor in the case.[47] If the Bolam approach was followed, the defendant doctor would have been held not guilty for negligence, as a class of doctors would have followed the practice akin to that of the defendant. Not following the Bolam principle, Lord Farquaharson LJ, stated that "*it is not enough for the defendant to call a number of doctors to say that what he had done or not done was in accord with the accepted clinical practice. It is necessary for the judge to consider that evidence and decide whether that clinical practice puts the patient unnecessarily at risk*".[48]

In English Law, Bolam has lost much of its sheen.

Indian courts have applied both Bolam and Bolitho in the recent past. It appears that Indian courts have shown more allegiance to the approach of Bolam than Bolitho. This might be by considering the Indian socio-economic conditions. The arguments that Bolam has lost its vigour, after the pronouncement of Bolitho, does not hold water in India. In *Samera Kohli v Dr. Prabha Manchanda & Another*, the Supreme

---

[46] Bolitho v City and Hackney Health Authority, (1993) PLQR 334.

[47] At the age of two young Patrick Bolitho was diagnosed with a patent ductus arterioles, a condition that prolongs the foetal circulation after birth to the detrimental of the normal oxygenation of blood. A surgery to correct the anomaly had been undertaken in 1983; and he made considerable recovery. A year after the surgery he gets admitted into St. Bartholomew's Hospital with croup. During the course of his admission he experienced a precipitous deterioration in his breathing on several occasions, a sequence of events which culminated in a respiratory collapse and cardiac arrest from which Patrick emerges with severe brain damage and subsequently dies. When judicial review begins, the prime question arises for answer is whether or not the hypothetical act of omission would have represented a breach of duty and also whether or not incubation would have prevented the injuries that were sustained by Patrick Bolitho.

[48] Five years later, Lord Brown Wilkinson writes "*the effect of Bolam test is that the defendant must live up to the standard of the ordinary skilled man exercising and professing to have special skill. The existence of the practice is not of itself determinative of the issue of breach of duty. The court has to subject the expert medical evidence to secreting and to decide whether the practice is reasonable. The issue of reasonableness is for the court and not for the medical profession*".

Court got an opportunity to touch upon this aspect almost conclusively. The court observes:

> Having regard to the conditions obtaining in India, as also the settled and recognised practices of medical fraternity in India, we are of the view that to nurture the doctor-patient relationship on the basis of trust, the extent and nature of information required to be given by doctors should continue to be governed by the Bolam test rather than the 'reasonably prudential patient test' evolved in Canterbury. It is for the doctor to decide, with reference to the condition of the patient, nature of illness, and the prevailing established practices, how much information regarding risks and consequences should be given to the patients, and how they should be couched, having the best interest of the patient.

7 Actual Administration of Treatment

The majority of cases arise during the administration of treatment. This is when the doctor actually administers the medicine and provides treatment. The real test is whether the doctor concerned satisfies the expected standard of care (or standards of treatment), in the actual administration of treatment. The standard of care is that which a reasonable competent doctor would adopt in similar circumstances. It is critical to envisage how the reasonable doctor would perform, in a simulated circumstance, by the Court or Tribunal considering the case. While extending the arguments before the court, the doctor shall influence the judge to draw appropriately the 'standard of care' that the reasonable doctor would adopt. There is no universally accepted formula to explain this proposition of law. Few examples might be taken to understand the dynamics the courts have adopted.

8 *RES IPSA Loquitur* Cases

Indian courts have applied *res ipsa loquitur*, where the facts are compelling. In *A H Kodwa v State of Maharashtra* the principle of *res ipsa loquitur* was applied. While performing a sterilisation operation, the surgeon left a swab inside the abdomen of the patient causing serious health problems and finally resulting in her death.[49] When an opportunity was provided (by shifting the burden of proof) to the doctors, they could not provide reasonable and logical defence as to how the mishap occurred, in spite of their diligence. The Supreme Court held the doctors liable by stating '*the facts speak for themselves. Negligence is writ large*'. Not treating the patient properly for what is shown in diagnostic reports was held to be a case of *res ipsa loquitur*. In *Krishna Rao v Nikhil Super Speciality Hospital*, the patient's diagnostic report showed positive smear for malaria parasite, and the Widal test showed negative result for Typhoid. The treatment that was given was for Typhoid and not for malaria. The patient's condition deteriorated, and she was rushed to another hospital. Without yielding any

[49] Achutrao Haribabu Khodwa v State of Maharashtra & ANother, 1996 SCC (2) 634.

positive results the patient died. This was held to be a case of *res ipsa loquitur*. It was also held, by the Supreme Court, that in such cases there is no need to have any expert evidence to determine negligence, on the part of the doctors.

Misreading the prescription by the treating doctor (a deputy to the treating doctor) and delegating responsibility (as a deputy) to the nurse, was held to be a case of *res ipsa loquitur*, as per *Spring Medows Hospital & Another*.[50] A child immediately after the administration of the injection (as part of typhoid treatment) collapsed; and faced several complications. It was found that the nurse who administered the injection had misread the prescription. The treating doctor had prescribed the injection to be administered by another (duty) doctor who delegated his responsibility to the nurse who misread the script. It was held to be a case of *res ipsa loquitur*.

Gangrene developed in the arm of a patient following an intramuscular injection, the doctor failing to diagnose a known complication of surgery on the patient's hand. The spinal anaesthetic was contaminated with disinfectant, as a result of the manner in which it was stored, causing paralysis to the patient. This too was considered an example where Indian courts have applied *res ipsa loquitur*.

9 Not Meeting Standard of Care Parameters

When the skill and knowledge of a treating doctor falls below the established standards, the doctor will be held negligent and liable. It is generally classified as '*deficiency of service scenarios*' in India.

The doctor in *Ram Bihari Lal v Dr. J. N. Srivastava*, is a Civil Assistant Surgeon, Grade I, and was in-charge of the Sohangpur Government Hospital, at Shahdol.[51] The deceased Mrs. Kantidevi developed severe abdominal pain and the defendant was called to Collector's bungalow (she being Collector's wife, lived there) at about 1 AM. Along with abdominal pain she had an elevated temperature. The doctor administerd a Streptopencilin injection and a tablet of Largactyl. After three days, the doctor advised her to undergo surgery for appendicitis. As per his assessment, she was not responding to treatment. Before the operation, consent was obtained for the 'operation of appendicitis'. The civil surgeon made a grid iron incision but found that the appendix was not at all inflamed. He made another Kocher's incision and then removed the gall bladder as he found it to be blackish with stones. During the operation the Plaintiff (the deceased's husband) and others were waiting outside the operation theatre. They were neither informed about this additional surgery, nor was the husband's informed consent sought. After the operation, the defendant disclosed that he had removed the gall bladder and the operation had been successful. After gaining consciousness the patient's condition deteriorated and she succumbed. It got revealed that her death was due to overwhelming toxaemia consequent upon

[50] (1998) 4 SCC 39.

[51] AIR 1985 MP 150.

progressive hepato-renal failure, which developed after the operation was undertaken following prolonged chloroform anaesthesia which led to peripheral circulatory collapse evidenced by progressive fall in blood pressure, rapid threat pulse and high temperature.

When sued, the doctor contended that the advice of surgery was given in good-faith and for the benefit of the patient. He would not have operated if there was any objection raised by the Plaintiff or the deceased. He stated that, on opening the abdomen, the appendix was found not inflamed but on further probing it was found that the gall bladder fundus extended up to right iliac-fossa, which was unusual, as the gall bladder is usually situated higher within the abdomen. The fundus was black and full of stones and it was considered necessary to give a second incision and remove the gall bladder which was successfully performed. The consent of the patient was not taken as she was under chloroform and the consent of the Plaintiff was implied, having already given consent for the appendicectomy. It was held that the doctor was guilty as he had operated without proper consent.

Not counselling the patient post-surgery, and not taking proper precautions was held to be negligence in *State of Haryana v Mrs. Santra.*[52] A woman labourer, working in construction industry, who already had many children and opted for sterilisation, became pregnant and was compelled, by the circumstances, to give birth to a healthy female child. She alleged medical negligence, and filed a suit for recovery of INR 2 lakhs as damages. Partly allowing her claim (to the extent of INR 54,000 with interest at the rate of 12% per annum from the date of institution of the suit till the payment of decretal amount), the court held that the doctor in this case was negligent. The following two factors influenced the judgement. Dr. Sushil Kumar Goyal stated that the operation related only to the right fallopian tube and the left fallopian tube was not touched, which indicated that 'complete sterilisation' was not performed. The patient requested an abortion but was advised not to go in for abortion as this would be dangerous to her life, without proper application of mind.

The doctor was held liable in *Poonam Verma v Dr. Ashwin Patel*, for prescribing a medicine in which he has no expertise.[53] Dr. Ashwin Patel is a homeopath but prescribed allopathic medicine to the deceased Mr. Promod Verma, the patient. Mr. Verma was the sole 'bread earner' of his family, working as Sales Manager in a private company, when he sought treatment from the doctor. Mr. Verma had high fever. Dr. Patel prescribed allopathic drugs for viral fever for first few days and thereafter for typhoid fever. When Mr. Verma's condition deteriorated, he got admitted to Sanjeevani Maternity and General Nursing Home. His condition continued to deteriorate and he was rushed to Hinduja Hospital but could not be saved.

Mrs. Poonam Verma, wife of Promod Verma, sought compensation from the National Commission but the National Commission dismissed her complaint and she appealed to the Supreme Court. It was contended that Dr. Ashwin Patel was not qualified, or even authorised, to practice in allopathic system of medicine and prescribe allopathic drugs and lacked expertise in the allopathic system of medicine

---

[52] AIR 2000 SC 1488.

[53] 1996 SCC (4) 1996.

and was responsible for deficiency in the treatment administered. Dr. Ashwin Patel attempted to defend that he was qualified to practice allopathic medicine but the court held that he was not qualified to prescribe allopathic medicine and was negligent, as he has practised beyond his ordinary skill and competency.

Indian courts appear to treat professional standards as conclusively establishing the standard of care for negligence and do not assume responsibility to lay down standards.

10 Criminal Medical Liability

The process of determining criminal liability of the doctor is no different than determining civil liability. To hold the doctor criminally liable, the degree of negligence has to be necessarily higher than negligence in civil liability. Otherwise, the doctor can be held liable under civil law but not in criminal law.

The entire jurisprudence of criminal liability of the doctor, predominantly revolves round two milestone judgements in India viz., *Dr. Suresh Gupta v NCT of Delhi*[54] and *Jacob Mathew v State of Punjab & Another*.[55] Both these cases deal with same subject viz., the criminal liability of the medical practitioner for the death of the patient under their direct supervision and treatment.

In *Suresh Gupta*, the patient died while he was being operated upon for a nasal deformity, by a team comprising of a plastic surgeon and an anaesthetic. In *Jacob Mathew*, a terminally ill (cancer) patient died during treatment at Ludhiana hospital. It was contended by his son that, his father's death occurred due to carelessness of the doctors and non-availability of oxygen cylinder, in particular at the relevant point in time of treatment. In both of these instances, judicial intervention was sought to hold the medical practitioner criminally liable. The doctors were charged under Section 304A of IPC and, while the situations were different, the facts and principles involved for judicial scrutiny were similar.

In *Suresh Gupta,* the death occurred due to asphyxiation and it was alleged that the doctors failed to insert a cuffed endo-tracheal tube of proper size and in a manner to prevent aspiration of blood blocking respiratory passage which was the ultimate cause of death. The real cause of death could not be ascertained. The investigating authority looking into the matter constituted a special medical board of four eminent doctors which opined that *'the death of a patient was due to sudden cardiac arrest, and the direct cause of the same can't be ascertained'*. The post mortem was conducted very late, when decomposition had occurred and reported *'asphyxia resulting from blockage of respiratory passage by aspirated blood consequent upon surgically incised margin of nasal septum'*, as the cause of death. As the issue was of criminal liability, the Supreme Court framed the question as follows: "*Even considering, not putting a cuffed endow tracheal tube, can the qualifying*

[54] (2004) 6 SCC 422.

[55] (2005) Supp. (2) SCR 307.

degree of negligence sufficient to attract 'criminal liability' under Section 304A of IPC?" (death caused by negligence). The Court, while answering the question in the negative, stated that, unless there is a higher degree of morally blameworthy conduct and gross negligence on the part of the doctor, it is not proper to impose criminal liability upon the doctor. It was also observed that the act, complained against the doctor, must show negligence or rashness of such a higher degree as to indicate a mental state, which can be described as totally apathetic towards the patient. The doctors could not be blamed of criminal negligence. It is not about the judgement of the apex court in *Suresh Gupta*, but reasoning was doubted.

In this context, especially with doubt regarding application of criminal liability to doctors, one must consider *Jacob Mathew*. The case of Jacob Mathew, therefore, provided a golden opportunity to the Supreme Court to re-verify its assessment on the issue.

A terminally ill patient died in hospital. An offence, under Section 304A read with Section 34 of IPC was registered. Judicial Magistrate First Class (JMFC) presided. The Appellant moved to the High Court, under Section 482 of Code of Criminal Procedure, asking for quashing of the FIR and the proceedings which was declined. Therefore, a Special Leave Petition (SLP) was taken to the Supreme Court. During the initial hearing, even the bench expressed its doubt upon the correctness of Dr. Suresh Gupta and referred the matter to a bigger 'constitutional bench'. The bigger bench examined the matter in *Jacob Mathew*.[56] Section 304A reads "*Whoever causes death or any person by doing rash or negligent act not amounting to culpable homicide, shall be punished with imprisonment of either description for a term which may extend two years, or with fine, or with both*". Negligence or recklessness being 'gross' is not the requirement of the provision. If so can it be read into the law? Is it not going beyond the legislative intent?—were the prime issues to be settled. The question also arose regarding the creation of dual standards; one for medical practitioners and another for rest of the community or others?

Not just due to the bench strength, *Jacob Mathew* was a weighty judgement as it had greater consultative value in itself. The medical council of India was asked to assist the Court. 'People for Better Treatment', Kolkatta, Indian Medical Association

[56] The reference to the constitutional bench was on the following counts:

1. Negligence or recklessness being 'gross' is not a requirement of Section 304A of IPC; and if the view taken in Dr. Suresh Gupta's case is to be followed then the word 'gross' shall have to be read into section 304A of IPC for fixing criminal liability on a doctor. Such an approach cannot be countered;
2. Different standards cannot be applied to doctors and others. In all cases it has to be seen whether the impinged act was rash or negligent. By carrying out a separate treatment for doctors by introducing degree of rashness or negligence, violence would be done to the plain and unambiguous language of Section 304A. If by adducing evidence it is proved that there was no rashness or negligence involved, the trail court dealing with the matter shall decide appropriately. But a doctor cannot be placed at a different pedestal for riding out whether rashness or negligence was involved.

and Delhi Medical Association were sought to be heard during the proceedings. The evolution of law, on the point from its inception, was traced to arrive at the decision.

The principle of negligence both in criminal and civil law is the same. It is when the conduct (that is an 'act' or 'omission') of an individual fails to meet the reasonable standards. To fasten liability in criminal law, the degree of negligence has to be higher than civil law. The justification is simple and fundamental. Wrongs that impact society gravely are classified as 'crimes'; and are punished heavily. Wrongs which impact menially are mere civil wrongs and are punished lightly. Simple lack of care is to be distinguished from very high degree of negligence. Simple lack of care results in civil liability; and very high degree of negligence leads to criminal liability. It is up to the victim of the civil wrong to claim remedy under law. It was observed "*the factor of grossness of degree does assume significance while drawing distinction in negligence actionable in tort and negligence punishable as crime. To be latter, the negligence has to be gross or of a very high degree*".[57] The said distinction is the fundamental premise upon which, the Court continued its reasoning.

The principle of negligence relies on a professional possessing a special skill by virtue of his/her education and training. The respective Professional Regulatory Body (PRB) admits him/her into the profession with careful scrutiny. PRB comprises experts in the field, professing the skills over a period of time. The adjudication of law takes place comparing the 'actual alleged act' with that of an 'expected reasonable act' under the circumstances. The benchmark to determine negligence (in law) is the 'reasonable standard'. The reasonable standard is fixed by the law of averages. It's an average between the highest and the lowest standards. It is stated that while dealing with cases of professional negligence, the established jurisprudence is to benchmark by taking the lowest standard of skill and competence a professional is expected to possess.

The *Jacob Mathew* judgement reiterated the principle of benchmarking professional standard, by referring to *Michael Hyde & Associates v J D Williams & Co., Ltd.*, a renowned English Judgement.[58] The celebrated observation of Mc Nair J, in Bolam, is also noted by the court.

While substantiating these points of view, the Supreme Court quoted the words of Lord President (Clyde)[59] as follows:

> In the realm of diagnosis and treatment there is ample scope for genuine difference of opinion and one man clearly is not negligent merely because his conclusion differs from that of other professional men... The true test of establishing negligence in diagnosis or treatment on the part of a doctor is whether he has been proved to be guilty of such failure as no doctor of ordinary skill would be guilty of it acting with ordinary care.

One has to be extremely careful before imposing criminal liability. It may appear that one opinion is more attractive than another; but the judge's preference for one

---

[57] Para 18 of the judgement.

[58] (2001) PNLR 233 CA. Where Sadely LJ. stated that "where a profession embraces a range of views as to what is an acceptable standard of conduct, the competence of the defendant is to be judged by the lowest standard that would be regarded as acceptable".

[59] In Hunter v Hanley, 1955 SLT 213.

body of professional opinion to another shall not be conclusive proof of negligence. Error of judgement, conclusively held by several Supreme Court decisions, on the part of medical practitioner is also not negligence. A mere deviation from normal professional practice is not necessarily evidence of negligence. Reckless disregard for the patient's interest; or grater deviation from the accepted practice is absolutely essential to constitute negligence.

A doctor, unlike in cases involving others, operates with consent of the patient. The requirement of consent differentiates his situation from others. Without linking it to 'consent', the court observed that *'no sensible professional would intentionally commit an act or omission which, would result in loss or injury to the patient as the professional reputation of the person at stake'*.[60] The Court referred to the construction of several provisions of IPC, and pointed out that many illustrations specifically involve instance of doctors.[61] Reading these illustrations further, the premise that a professional and ordinary men of skill is not intended to be treated equally by the framers of IPC. The Court emphasised the commentary in Roscoe's Law of Evidence, a seminal work in the area, such as:

> Where a person, acting as a medical man, whether licensed or unlicensed, is so negligent in his treatment of a patient that death results, it is manslaughter if the negligence was so great as to amount to crime, and whether or not there was such a degree of negligence is a question in each case for the jury. In explaining to juries to test which they should apply to determine whether the negligence in particular case amounted or did not amount to a crime, judges have used many epithets, such as 'culpable', 'criminal, 'gross', 'wicked', 'clear', 'complete'. But whether epithet be used and whether an epithet be used or not, in order to establish criminal liability the facts must be such that, in the opinion of the jury, the negligence of the accused went beyond a mere matter of compensation between subjects and showed such disregard for the life and safety of others as to amount to a crime against the State and conduct deserving punishment.
>
> Whether he be licensed or unlicensed, if he displays gross ignorance, or gross inattention, or gross rashness, in his treatment, he is criminally responsible. Where a person who, though not educated as an accoucheur, had been in the habit of acting as a man-midwife, and had unskilfully treated a woman, who died in childbirth, was indicated for the murder. L. Ellenborough said that there was no evidence of murder, but the jury might convict of manslaughter. To substantiate that charge the prisoner must have been guilty of criminal misconduct, arising either from the grossest ignorance or the most criminal inattention. One or other of these is necessary to make him guilty of that criminal negligence and misconduct which is essential to make out a case of manslaughter.

The Supreme Court held that the word 'gross' is to be suffixed in S. 304A of IPC in case of doctors. It is now settled that, in criminal law, to condemn a medical practitioner, negligence of high degree or gross negligence is absolutely essential. The expression 'rash or negligent act' as occurring in s. 304A has to be read as qualified by the word grossly.

In the overall interest of the society, the Supreme Court continued to state, on record, that before initiating a process of law against medical doctors, due care and

---

[60] Para 29 of the judgement.

[61] Illustrations happened to ss. 88, 93 etc.,.

caution is to be exercised, without which it would prove harmful and counterproductive. Either the investigating officer (in the case of complaint to the police) or the Judicial Magistrate (in the case of private complaint) do not have sufficient knowledge of medical science to determine whether the act of the accused medical doctor amount to rash or negligent act within the domain of criminal law. Hastily initiated action, against the medical doctor, might cause enormous embarrassment and most often harassment. The medical doctor may be exonerated by acquittal or discharge but the loss, which s/he has suffered in his/her reputation, cannot be compensated by any standards.

The court felt that a statutory rule or an executive instruction in this regard be brought out by the Central/State Government. Such executive instructions or rules may be framed by the State, in consultation with the Medical Council of India (which existed during that time). Till such norms are put in place, the Court felt that seeking an expert opinion, to confirm that a prima facie case existed, is mandatory before issuing processes in the case involving medical doctors. The court of investigating officer should, before proceeding against the doctor accused of rash or negligent act or omission, obtain an independent and competent medical opinion preferably from a doctor in government service, qualified in that branch of medical practice, who can normally be expected to give an impartial and unbiased opinion as per the facts. The court also made clear that a doctor accused of rashness or negligence cannot be arrested in a routine manner, due to the fact that, a case is registered against him; unless it becomes inevitable.

Although not elaborated, the unexplained premise of the court is, continuing its attitude of non-intervention into the professional domain, unless it becomes extremely essential. The movement of all professions, hitherto, has been from chaos to organisation; organisation to consolidation and consolidation to autonomy and monopoly. The prime reason for conferring autonomy and monopoly to a profession is the fact that they are body of learned people and the interest of society and individuals is safe in their hands. The hallmark of the profession (like auto regulation, monopoly) is that they assure society highly ethical behaviour and skill sets where financial returns are not the measure of success. It is absolutely imperative that a profession has to constantly endeavour to enhance its learning and uphold high ethical behaviour. The professions are losing the confidence of society, due to over commercialisation. The medical profession is no exception.

11 Conclusion

In India, the litigation for medical liability is constantly on the rise. The inclusion of medical professionals (or services), into the ambit of Consumer Protection Act by Supreme Court, is the first attempt which encouraged many dissatisfied patients to take recourse to legal remedy. Over a period of time the eco-system of medical service provisioning has also changed in India. Unlike earlier (up to late 1980s), nearly two-thirds of medical services are being provided by private medical establishments. The government owned medical establishments, barring few, have diminished in quality. This is another reason for making the cost of medical services dearer. The high cost of medical treatment has also compelled many to take the course of litigation. Doctors are taking professional indemnity coverage (by insurance companies) to mitigate the plausible risk of medical liability.

Reference

Prasad LV (2002) Indian system of medicine and homoeopathy traditional medicine in Asia. In: Chaudhury RR, Fafei UM (ed). WHO-Regional Office for South East Asia: 2002, New Delhi, pp 283–286

Medical Liability in Indonesia: Overview and Regulatory Trends

Farah Purwaningrum

Abstract This book chapter examines how medical liability is regulated in the Indonesian legal civil system and the regulatory trends of medical liability in Indonesia. Medical liability as an issue is gaining prominence in Indonesia as there are more concerns raised on the need to protect patients' rights, and the increasing activism of doctors and other health professionals in Indonesia. There was a Dutch influence in the formation and progression of Indonesian medical law in Indonesia in the beginning. Such colonial influence began to diminish in the 1990s in medical law as evidenced in the usage of code of ethics for medical professionals and increasing regulations on the protection of patients' rights by the Ministry of Health. The patient-doctor relationship is regulated by the code of ethics. Meanwhile, there is still a strong reference to Indonesian civil code and Indonesian criminal code in verdicts and cases of medical liability in Indonesia, both codes of which were legal transplants during the Dutch colonial administration period. Up to now, Dutch legal terms are still frequently used in the Supreme Court and Constitutional Court in Indonesia in medical liability cases. By investigating various court decisions relevant to medical liability issue in Indonesia and looking into trends of medical liability in health and medical regulations in Indonesia in the past ten years, the book chapter presents substantive findings based on desk research.

1 Introduction

There have been numerous cases of medical mistakes conducted by medical professionals in Indonesia. Indeed, one of the most complex issues in health care quality law is regarding which remedies should be available to patients in cases the patients suffer death or injury as a consequence of the alleged negligence of a health care professional or corporation (Rosenbaum 2003).

F. Purwaningrum (✉)
School of Social Sciences, Universiti Sains Malaysia, Penang, Malaysia

Sydney Asia Pacific Migration Centre, The University of Sydney, Sydney, Australia

V. L. Raposo and R. G. Beran (eds.), *Medical Liability in Asia and Australasia*,
Ius Gentium: Comparative Perspectives on Law and Justice 94,
https://doi.org/10.1007/978-981-16-4855-7_6

Medical professionals distribution in Indonesia is largely uneven, with most of them concentrated in Java, Indonesia. An internist physician in Jakarta in March 2020 shared her arduous residency experience in a Health Community Centre (*Puskesmas*) Borneo Kalimantan the due to lack of healthcare facilities and mysticism in Borneo society. The current ratio between physicians and the population in Indonesia is still well below the ideal ratio recommended by the WHO. In 2017, the WHO data showed that Indonesia had 4 doctors per 10,000 people. Ensuring geographical coverage of health services for 17,508 islands from Sabang to Merauke in Indonesia is arduous. That said, patient safety is an issue in Indonesia, particularly in light of medical liability. The Indonesian Doctors Association (*Ikatan Dokter Indonesia* or "IDI") IDI claimed to have received around 20 reports of medical malpractice allegations each month from January to July 2010. This book chapter asks the following research questions: how is medical liability regulated in Indonesian civil legal system? What are the regulatory trends of medical liability in Indonesia?

To probe these research questions, this book chapter employs desk research and documentary study in its research methods. It employs qualitative-normative analysis of regulations in the period of 2015–2020 and it uses a reference to court verdicts in the district court level, high court level, the supreme court as well as the constitutional court in Indonesia which are relevant to medical liability cases. The next section deals with medical liability in Indonesia's medical law. The third section observes medical liability and the protection of patient's rights in health regulations. The fourth section provides the conclusion of the study.

2 Medical Liability in Indonesia's Medical Law

Medical liability is often associated with tort law. The civil law tradition to which the Indonesian legal system hinges upon is doctrinal, based on principles of law as stipulated in statutory provisions, and relies much less on case law. As such legal action taken is initiated by reference to a statute (*undang undang*) or one of a variety of lower-level regulations, such as Government Regulations in Lieu of Law (*Peraturan Pemerintah Pengganti Undang-Undang* or Perppu).[1] Furthermore, there are specific provisions in Indonesia's Criminal Code (*Kitab Undang-undang Hukum Pidana*) and Civil Code (*Kitab Undang-undang Hukum Perdata*) which deal with torts such as arson, theft and minor assault. Liability in medical mistakes is interpreted in line with these codes. There is the influence of the Dutch colonial administration in Indonesia as evident in the application of Indonesian civil code (*Burgerlijk Wetboek*) and Indonesian criminal code (*Wetboek van Strafrecht*). These two codes were legally transplanted during the Dutch colonial administration period in Indonesia. This civil law system and the influence of the Dutch colonial administration are evident in medical law in Indonesia.

[1] Lindsey and Butt (No Year).

There is an emphasis on legal certainty inherent in the civil law system (Otto 2002; Otto and Stoter 2008). This concept consists of five elements as follows[2]; first is that a lawmaker has laid down clear, accessible and realistic rules; second is that the administration follows these rules and induces citizens to do the same; third is that the majority of people accept these rules, in principle, as just; fourth is that serious conflicts are regularly brought before independent and impartial judges who decide cases in accordance with those rules; fifth is that these decisions are actually complied with. Statutory provisions pertaining to torts and medical mistakes are interpreted by judges, prosecutors, attorneys in line with ensuring legal certainty is maintained.

There was a Dutch influence in the formation and development of Indonesian medical law in the beginning. This is evident in the promulgation of laws and cases. The practice of medicine was governed by *Het Reglement de op Dienst der Volksgezondheid–Staatsblad* 1882, which is a regulation of public health service. There were cases such as the Djainun Case 1923, where a patient had an overdose of medicine and Court Decision Raad van Justitie 1938, which ascribes medical liability for wrong prescription of medicine to a medical professional.

There are three important stages of the development of medical law in Indonesia; the first one is criminal liability upon a physician in 1981 which has attracted the public attention toward medical law issues; the second one is medical malpractice crisis taking place in 2003, which stimulated the need to have specific legislation concerning medical malpractice; the third one is the enactment of the Medical Practice Act 2004 on October 6th, 2004 which became the basis of the development of the Indonesian medical law or in particular the medical practice law.

There have been notable deliberations and court decisions (verdicts) within Indonesian health laws prior to the 1980s and 1990s. Prior to that there was the Blume case in 1960. The case of Doctor CL Blume in Jakarta attracted attention in the 1960s. He was charged with practicing abortion for seven years(Hanggoro 2014). Another one was Fong Lan case in 1968 when there were post operation complications. Nonetheless, medical cases which brought more expanded reasoning unfolded in the 1980s and 1990s.

A landmark case for medical liability in Indonesia in the 1980s is the Doctor Setyaningrum Case. In this case, Setyaningrum who was a doctor at the community health center in Pati Central Java District was tried at the Pati District Court because of an injection. Rukmini Kartono who was a patient of Setyaningrum who died due to shock after an injection of streptomycin in the Wedarijaksa Community Health Center in Pati Regency, Central Java. The incident initially started when Rusmini came to see Setyaningrum on 4 January 1979 as she had complaints in her digestive system. Setianingrum then began to treat Rusmini by giving an antibiotic injection in the form of Streptomycin. After that, there were signs that Rusmini was allergic to the antibiotic injection of Streptomycin, as there were signs of vomiting. The second injection given to Rusmini was Cortisone for treatment against allergic reactions from Streptomycin. However, this effort was unsuccessful because Rusmini grew more

[2] Otto and Stoter (2008), p. 55.

critical, and as a last resort Rusmini was given a *Delladryl* injection. Due to her critical condition, Rusmini was transported to Soewondo Pati hospital. Rusmini received help for approximately 15 min, and not long after was declared dead. Setyaningrum was the doctor who was reported to the police on the basis of Article 360 of the Indonesian Criminal Code. On 2 September 1981 the Pati District Court Verdict penalised Setyaningrum with 3 months of probation and 10 months of imprisonment. Pati District Court in its decision dated 2-9-1981 No. 8/1980/Pid.b/PN.Pt. decided the following, among others: first is that it states that that the defendant Setyaningrum was culpable of a crime; "because of her negligence had caused others to die". Second, it sentenced the defendant to 3 months in prison.

Pursuant to the decision of the Pati District Court Verdict, the defendant submitted an appeal to the Semarang High Court. In an examination at the appeal level, the Semarang High Court with its decision dated 19–1-1982 No. 203/1981/Pid/PT.Smg. decided to strengthen the decision of the Pati District Court dated 2–1-1981 No. 8/1980/Pid.b/PN.Pt. There was a cassation request that followed, wherein Setyaningrum submitted a cassation request against the Semarang High Court decision. It is at this cassation level that the Supreme Court, with its decision dated 2–6-1984 Reg. No. 6000 K/Pid/1983, acquitted the defendant, i.e., Setyaningrum of the charge of causing another person to die because of her negligence (Article 359 of the Criminal Code). The consideration of the Supreme Court to acquit Setyaningrum was that the claim that the injection of Streptomycin was too difficult to avoid, and this could claim the patient's life in a very short time.

The case of Setianingrum was the beginning of the development of medical liability in health law in Indonesia. The case indeed established basic principles for medical liability in Indonesian law. These principles which are in author's viewpoint relevant to the case are civil medical liability for malpractice, elements for criminal medical liability for a malpractice, the fact that proof for medical malpractice can be a deviation from the standards, ethical codes medical professionals must adhere to, and a change of patient management pattern from paternalistic to partnership. These principles mark a progress of a more welcome change in the medical law in Indonesia.

In the Muhidin case in 1988, Muhidin argued that the doctor had deliberately taken the patient's eye. This became so because the doctor failed to explain the risks of the operation. Muhidin "lost" an eye after being operated on at Syamsudin General Hospital by a physician named G. Muhammad Husaini. According to Husaini, if Muhidin's right eye were not removed, it would spread to other important organs around the eye such as brain, ear, nose. In this case, parents of Muhidin, Makmun filed a civil lawsuit against Husaini for operating on his son's eye without his knowledge and permission, and demanded that the doctor "replace "the pupil of his son's right eye and it had costs IDR 20 million due to the replacement. In return, Muhammad Husaini did not remain silent, he filed a lawsuit back at Muhidin as he felt his good name was tarnished (Liemena 1990). There was indeed the development of the informed consent of patient as a doctrine thanks to the Muhidin case. What followed thereafter was the issuance of an edict (fatwa) of Indonesian Doctor Association in 1988 reifying the importance of informed consent. It was further reinforced in The

Ministry of Health Regulation of 1989 and then in 2008. It was not only by recourse to Indonesian civil law, liability is pursued. In the Suwarti Case in 2002, Suwarti passed away after giving birth to her first child. The family reported the doctor to the police with allegations of medical malpractice in accordance to Article 359 of the Indonesia Criminal Code. Article 359 of the Indonesian Civil Code prescribes 'Anyone who due to his fault (negligence) causes another person to die, shall be punished by a maximum imprisonment of five years or maximum imprisonment of one year'.

In doctor Bukhari Case, he has been alleged of the offense for not making medical records. The legal basis of this offence is Article 79 (b) of the Indonesian Medical Practice Act. Langsa District Court Decision No. 86/Pid.B/2009/PN/LGS on 26 October 2009 ruled that dr. Bukari is proven guilty of the criminal offence. The penalty is a Rp30.000.000 fine with a 3-month imprisonment. Moreover, in the Aceh High Court Decision No. 191/PID/2009/PT.BNA on 11 February 2010, the judges ruled in favour of the district court of Langsa decision. There was a cassation, however, this cassation was rejected in Cassation Deed No. 05/Akta.Pid/2010/PN.LGS at the Supreme Court. The cassation deed was rejected due to not fulfilling the formal requirements of appeal as stated in Article 45 (a) of Law No. 5 of 2004, hence the penalty and punishment stands.

In 2010, there was a doctor Ayu case. Dewa Ayu Sasiary Prawani, Hendry Simanjutak and Hendy Siagian were all doctors who were alleged for causing a patient's death, Julia Fransiska in a hospital in Manado, North Sulawesi on 10 April 2010. The legal bases are article 359 of ICC joncto article 361 of ICC joncto article 55 (1) of ICC as well as article 76 of Medical Practice Act jo Article 55 (1) of ICC. The Manado District Court Decision No. 90/PID.B/2011/PN.MDO on 22 September 2011, Manado District court imposed punishment to all Dewa Ayu Sasiary Prawani, Hendry Simanjutak and Hendy Siagian who were doctors with 10 months of imprisonment. There was a cassation request, and Supreme Court Decision No. 365 K/PID2012 on September 2012, the Supreme Court reaffirms the previous court decision. However, this was not for long as in a judicial review in a Supreme Court Decision No. 79PK/PID/2013 on 7 February 2014; the Supreme Court conducts judicial review on the case and retracts all previous court decision and declares all 3 doctors to be innocent.

In 2011, there was doctor Bambang case, who was alleged for negligence that led to a patient's death resulting from leaving behind a strand of medical thread in the patient's body during operation on 25 October. The Madiun District Court Decision No. 79/Pid.Sus/2011/PN/Kd/Mn on 6 October 2011, declares that Bambang case as a *onslag can recht vervolging* or that the action does not constitute as a criminal offence. However, upon cassation, the Supreme Court Decision No. 1110 K/Pid.Sus/2012 On 30 October 2013, Supreme Court retracts district court decision and punishes dr. Bambang with 1 year and 5 months of jail time. In 2015, the Supreme Court Judicial Review Decision No. 210PK/Pid.Sus/2014, Supreme Court Judges rule that dr. Bambang is released from all charges. The reason being that articles 75 and 79 of the Indonesian Medical Act, which was the basis for legal medical liability for Bambang are no longer legally binding, pursuant to Constitution

Court Decision No. 4/PUU-V/2007.[3] It is evident from these reasonings in medical liability verdicts and decisions that they make reference to the normative base in Indonesian civil code and Indonesian criminal code; both codes were instilled during the pre-independence period of Indonesia by the Dutch colonial administration.

It is noteworthy that doctors in Indonesia are becoming more active in their constitutional rights, and not only through the Indonesian Doctors Association. In the Constitutional Court Decision No. 14/PUU-XII/2014 applicants (which in this case are doctors) argue for a judicial review because the substance of Article 66 (3) of the Indonesian Medical Practice Act is not aligned with the Article 28D (2) and Article 28G (1) of the Constitution as it causes a contradiction in which doctors who have been deemed innocent by the Indonesian Medical Disciplinary Board (*Majelis Kehormatan Disiplin Kedokteran Indonesia* or "MKDKI") can still be held liable in court proceedings.[4] The next section discusses the protection of patient's rights in health regulations in Indonesia.

3 Medical Liability and the Protection of Patient's Rights in Health Regulations

The Indonesian civil code (ICC) docs regulate medical liability from civil code perspective. To begin with, article 1365 of the ICC regulates negligence in that civil medical malpractice can also constitute as tort (*Perbuatan Melawan Hukum*) with elements of civil medical malpractice as follows: (i) mild negligence or *Culpa Levis*, (ii) financial loss/damage. This article stipulates that a causal relation between medical actions and the loss/damage is needed. At the same time, article 1367 (3) postulates the Respondeat Superior doctrine. 'Respondeat superior' in Latin means 'that the master must answer', it is a legal doctrine according to which an employer is responsible for the actions of its employees.[5] Under the doctrine of respondeat superior, hospitals are vicariously liable for the negligent acts of employees and others whom the hospital has a significant degree of control; wherein the hospital employee is a physician, any change in the practice standard based on customs will be a determining factor of hospital liability under the doctrine of repondeat superior (Knottnerus 1984).

In this sense, akin to the charitable immunity doctrine, wherein the hospital is held liable for the malpractice of its medical staff, namely the doctor in (permanent employee of the hospital). There are three articles which are of relevance in the Indonesian civil code namely article 1320 regarding informed consent, article

[3] For further reference the decision can be read at https://putusan3.mahkamahagung.go.id/direktori/putusan/b5fdb2ab95fdcc7cc88d4d73534b642b.

[4] For further reference the decision can be read at https://mkri.id/public/content/persidangan/putusan/14_PUU-XII_2014.pdf.

[5] Encyclopaedia Brittanica, https://www.britannica.com/topic/respondeat-superior (accessed on 22 September 2020).

1243 which states that civil medical malpractice may also constitute as a breach of contract in relation to informed consent, as well as article 1354 on *zaakwaarneming*. Zaakwaarneming is a legal concept in which that actions carried out as voluntary management for acting in the stead of the person one is representing constitutes as a semi contract as it creates a legal relation (engagement) between the authoriser and the authorised, namely in terms of medical liability, as the doctor of the patient. There are several elements of this semi contract: first, the objective must be for the authorised to act in the interest of the authoriser, second, the authorised must do so willingly and without coercion; third the authorised must also want the same thing as the authoriser; and fourth, there must be a legitimate reason for the authorised to act so.

Liability is ascribed differently in the common law system. According to the common law, there is a "captain of the ship" doctrine, which ascribed the negligence of hospital staff to the attending physician who is perceived as the actual person in charge.[6] Within this doctrine, the surgeon or medical professional is likened to the captain of a ship, and it is his or her duty to control everything that is going on in the operating room (Murphy 1990). Further state legislation establishing anti-corporate practice of medicine prohibitions prolonged this view of hospitals as solely physician workplaces (Rosenbaum 2003). There is another opposing doctrine which assumes liability to the beneficiary of health services, in this case, charity. The charitable immunity doctrine postulates that a beneficiary of the charity, such as a hospital patient, assumes the risk of the charity's negligence and by implication waives any right he may have to recover from the hospital when he accepts benefits (Horty 1964).[7] The charitable immunity doctrine, which exempted charitable corporations from liability in order to preserve their assets for community benefit.[8]

Law No. 29 of 2004 on Indonesian Medical Practice Act provides the basis of the principle of patient autonomy in article 45, which states '*Any Action/treatment in general and dental patients should only be done after the patient signed the consent form and after complete explanation of information*'. This is a reification of the principle of patient autonomy from the Ministry of Health of Indonesia No. 585 of 1989 and Decision of the Indonesian Medical Association No. 319/PB/A.4/1988. The right to information is regulated by Law No 29 of 2009, whereas it is stipulated that doctors shall see to it that their patients understand at the very minimum: diagnosis and medical action; the purpose of the medical action; alternative medical actions and its risks; risks and possible complications; and prognosis of the medical action.

Consent is an important element in doctor-patient relationship. Medical consent is reified in Law No. 29 of 2004 in article 45.4 whereas consent can be given orally or in a written form.

Specifically, in article 45.5, it is stipulated that in high-risk medical procedures which have the risk of causing the patient's death, the approval of medical action from the patient should be given or made in writing.

---

[6] Rosenbaum (2003).

[7] Horty (1964), p. 344.

[8] Rosenbaum, Ibid.

There are amendments indeed, as Indonesia has a Constitutional Court in place which has an authority to examine laws as to whether they are consistent to the 1945 Constitution in Indonesia. In Constitution Court Decision No. 4/PUU-V/2007 on 19 June 2007, it is ruled that first articles 75 which stipulates criminal sanction to Indonesian doctor or Indonesian dentist or foreign doctor or foreign dentist in Indonesia who practice without having a registration letter and article 79 which regulates penal sanction in the form of confinement for doctor or dentist in Law No. 29 of 2004 are both not legally binding. This effectively removes penal sanction in the case of medical malpractice in Law No. 29 of 2004, one has to refer to Indonesian criminal code or administrative law for such criminal sanction.

The Ministry of Health Regulation No. 4 Year 2018 on Obligations of Hospitals and Patients[9] stipulates obligations of the hospital, which include but are not limited to, article 3 regarding the patient's right for information. Further, in article 5 (1), the scope of the patient's right for information include medical service; diagnosis and medical action; purpose of medical action; alternative to medical action; risks and possible complication; rehabilitation, prognosis; and estimate of costs. Article 15 states provisions on the obligation of the hospital to refuse service for patients who seek medical action for matters of illegal abortion; assisted suicide; false information; fraud; and anything that goes against the standard and ethics for the medical profession along with statutory provisions. Article 17 emphasises the patient's right to be treated well which include but are not limited to: obtaining services that are humane, fair, honest and without discrimination; obtain quality health services in accordance to professional standards and standards operational procedures; obtain effective and efficient services so that the patient avoids physical harm and monetary loss. Within the spheres of obligations, article 18 places to the hospital's obligation to establish a code of ethics. Whereas in Article 26 obligations of the patient which include but are not limited to: compliance with regulations enforced at the hospital; usage of Hospital facilities in a responsible manner; respecting the rights of other patients, visitors and rights of health workers and other officers who works in the hospital; providing honest, complete and accurate information with regard to their level of understanding of their medical condition; providing information about financial capabilities and the health insurance that they subscribe to; adhering to the therapy plan recommended by health workers in hospitals that the patient has given their consent to with regard to the regulations that are in force; acknowledging all consequences in the event of rejecting the therapeutic plan recommended by health workers and/or if the patients did not comply with the instructions given by health workers for recovery; and provide compensation for services that are received. Relevant articles to medical liability in the Ministry of Health Regulation No. 4 Year 2018 are first Article 17 (2) q which protects the patients' right includes the right to file for civil and criminal suits. Further in article 30, there are administrative sanctions for non-compliant hospitals which can come from the ministry, Provincial Regional Government, and/or District/city Regional Government in the form of light, moderate

[9] Ministry of Health Regulation No. 4 Year 2018 on Obligations of Hospitals and Patients https://www.persi.or.id/images/regulasi/permenkes/pmk42018.pdf.

and/or severe sanctions. In deliberations for cases which include medical malpractice, article 40 provides provision of what constitutes as evidence for this matter, namely; letters and/or documents; witness statement; expert statement; confession of the reported; and/or physical evidence.

Medical professional association plays a key role in overseeing the adherence of the code of ethics and ensuring there are no violations. Ethical medical malpractice is within the sphere of the Indonesian Code of Ethics. Ethical malpractice is where doctors perform medical acts contrary to Indonesian medical ethics code. Furthermore, medical ethics contain moral obligation contract between doctor with colleagues and patients. The substance is established in accordance to Declaration of Helsinki based on the Geneva Declaration.

As stipulated in the Medical Council Regulation No.4 of 2011 concerning the professional discipline of doctors and dentists, which strictly prohibits doctors from committing violations of the professional discipline of doctors and dentists where there are 28 (twenty-eight) disciplinary violations which are regulated as follows[10]:

- Conducting medical practice incompetently.
- Not referring patients to other doctors or dentists who have the appropriate competence.
- Delegating work to certain health workers who do not have the competence to carry out the work - Doctors and dentists must be sure that the health worker who receives the delegation has the competence to do so.
- Providing a temporary replacement doctor or dentist who does not have the appropriate competence and authority or does not provide notification regarding the replacement.
- Carrying out a medical practice in such a high level of physical or mental health, making it incompetent and can endanger the patient.
- Not taking action or adequate medical care in certain situations that can be dangerous.
- Conducting excessive examination or treatment that does not fit patient's needs.
- Not providing honest, ethical, and adequate explanations (adequate information) to patients or their families in doing medical practice.
- Performing medical action/care without obtaining the consent of the patient or close family, guardian, or guardian.
- Not deliberately creating or keeping medical records.
- Perform actions aimed at terminating pregnancy that are not in accordance with the provisions of the prevailing laws and regulations. In this matter at least two doctors will determine the termination of pregnancy in certain patients who have sacrificed the life of the fetus.
- Doing actions that can end a patient's life at the request of himself or his family. Every doctor is not allowed to do anything that aims to end human life.
- Carrying out medical practice by applying knowledge, skills, or technology that has not been accepted or is outside the proper medical practice procedures. In

[10] Kurniawan (2013), p. 150.

order to maintain patient safety, every doctor and dentist is obliged to use the knowledge, skills and procedures of Medical Practice that have been accepted by the medical or dental profession. laws.

- Conducting research in medical practice using humans as research subjects without obtaining ethical clearance from a recognised government institution.
- Not carrying out emergency aid on humane basis, despite the fact it does not endanger the person/patient, unless the doctor believes someone else is on duty and is able to do it.
- Rejecting or stopping action or treatment against patients without a proper and legal reason in accordance with the provisions of professional ethics or applicable laws and regulations in Indonesia.
- Divulging the patients confidentiality as doctors and dentists are obliged to keep their patients secret.
- Producing medical statements that are not based on the results of examinations that doctor knows to be correct and appropriate.
- Participating in acts that include torture or execution of the death penalty.
- Prescribing or giving drug classified as narcotics, psychotropics and other addictive substances that are not in accordance with the provisions of professional ethics or applicable legislation.
- Committing sexual harassment, acts of intimidation, or acts of violence against patients in the implementation of medical practices.
- Using an academic degree or professional title that is not their right.
- Receiving rewards as a result of referral, requesting examination or providing prescription drugs or medical devices.
- Advertise ability/service or owned either by oral or written means, or another misleading way.
- Addiction (addiction) to narcotics, psychotropics, alcohol, and other addictive substances.
- Practicing by using a registration Certificate, Practice License, and/or Competency Certificate which is not valid or has practice without having a license to practice in accordance with the provisions of the applicable laws and regulations.
- Not honest in determining medical services. Doctors and dentists must be honest in determining medical services in accordance with their actions or medical care for patients.
- Failure to provide information, documents, and other evidence needed by 'MKDKI' at the national level and 'MKDKI P' (at the Provincial Level) to examine complaints of alleged violations of the professional discipline of doctors and dentists.[11]

The Indonesian code of ethics for medical professionals was established through the Decree of the Minister of Health Number 434/Men.Kes/SK/X/1983 regarding code of ethics for medical professionals.[12] A code of ethics is a new code of conduct

---

[11] https://perdatinaceh.files.wordpress.com/2018/01/perkonsil-kki-no-4-tahun-2011-tentang-disiplin-profesional-dokter-dan-dokter-gigi.pdf.

[12] Ibid. P. 150.

that outlines appropriate conduct and behavior guidelines for the medical profession. It fosters human relationships which include the general obligations of a doctor, the relationship between doctors and patients, the obligations of doctors to colleagues and obligations of doctors towards themselves. The relationship between patient-doctor is regulated within this code of ethics.

An analysis of medical malpractice-related regulations shows how this terrain is heavily regulated at the ministerial level by the ministry of health. Indeed, there is increasing regulation in this aspect. Administrative medical malpractice exhibits this legal reality in the past five years. It is within this administrative medical malpractice there is a concentration of regulations. By 'administrative medical malpractice', the author refers to sanction imposed by mainly administrative means by the Ministry of Health.

To begin with, the Ministry of Health Regulation No. 269 of 2008 on Medical Records[13] defines administrative medical malpractice. It occurs when a doctor or other health professionals conduct skilled-practice without a license to practice, perform medical acts not in accordance with the license issued, medical practice with an expired license and practicing without making medical records (Kurniawan 2013). Violations result in administrative sanctions like revocation of license and possibly in criminal penalties as well.

At an organisational level, namely at a hospital, an administrative sanction is elucidated by the Ministry of Health Regulation No. 3 Year 2020 on Classification and Licensing of Hospitals. Article 39 (1) of the Ministry of Health Regulation No. 3 Year 2020 states that a hospital has to obtain an Operational License (*Izin Operational*) and extend it continuously, otherwise risking being sanctioned, unless it shuts down operation until issuance of a new license. Furthermore, article 39 (2) specifies that failure to comply will cause the hospital to be held liable by Indonesian criminal laws. The Ministry of Health Regulation No. 66 Year 2016[14] on Safety of Working at Hospital refers to the standard for safety shall be the Occupational Health and Safety of Hospital (*Keselamatan dan Kesehatan Kerja Rumah Sakit*) as stated in article 1 (3). In article 29 (4), it is specified that hospitals can be given administrative sanctions in the event of non-compliance of provisions in this ministerial regulation. These two ministerial regulations are applicable to the hospital regardless of the private or public nature of hospital in Indonesia.

Similar raison d'etre as the one applicable in the hospital is evident in clinical testing and licence for clearance for health, diagnostic, invitro and household health supply. Sanctions in the event of non-compliance are primarily administrative ones. This type of sanction is demonstrated in the Ministry of Health Regulation No. 63 Year 2017 on Health Tool Clinical Testing[15] and the Ministry of Health Regulation

[13] Ministry of Health Regulation No. 269 of 2008 on Medical Records is available as follows: http://www.apikes.com/files/permenkes-no-269-tahun-2008.pdf.

[14] The Ministry of Health Regulation No. 66 Year 2016 on Safety of Working at Hospital is available as follows: https://www.persi.or.id/images/regulasi/permenkes/pmk662016.pdf.

[15] The Ministry of Health Regulation No. 63 Year 2017 on Health Tool Clinical Testing is available as follows: https://www.persi.or.id/images/regulasi/permenkes/pmk632017.pdf.

No. 62 Year 2017 on License for Clearance for Health, Diagnostic, Invitro and Household Health Supply[16] in Chap. 11. Though for the latter, in article 64 non-compliance can also constitute as a criminal offence in accordance with the Indonesian criminal code.

At the health insurance front, the Ministry of Health Regulation No. 16 Year 2019 on prevention and handling of fraud and implementation of administrative sanction in the execution of health insurance program[17] regulates the implementation of administrative sanctions for fraud of health insurance program. This is exemplified in article 6 (2); whereas article 6 (7) imposes sanction by administrative means which does not eliminate the possibility of being held liable by the Indonesian criminal code.

Revocation of licence is another means of administrative sanction for medical liability. This form of sanction is visible in the Ministry of Health Regulation No. 34 Year 2018 on licensing and management of therapist acupuncture practices[18] in article 3, 5 and 22. Article 3 states that all Acupuncture Therapists must obtain the License to Register as Acupuncture Therapist (*Surat Tanda Registrasi Akupunktur Terapis* or "STRAT"). Article 5 stipulates that all Acupuncture Therapists must obtain the License to Practice Therapeutic Acupuncture (*Surat Izin Praktik Akupunktur Terapis* or "SIPAT"). Article 22 specifies the kind of administrative sanction, namely failure to comply will cause the therapist to be: (i) given an oral warning; (ii) given a written warning; and/or (iii) revocation of SIPAT. It is also apparent as a mechanism of sanction in the event of non-compliance in the Ministry of Health Regulation No. 73 Year 2016 on Pharmaceutical Standard of Service for Pharmacy[19] in article 12. Specifically, article 12 regulates that administrative sanctions are applicable in the event of non-compliance in the forms of: (i) written warning; (ii) temporary probation; and/or (iii) revocation of license. This form of sanction is apparent in oral health in the Ministry of Health Regulation No. 20 Year 2016 on License and Implementation of Mouth and Teeth Medical Practice.[20] Article 3 of this ministerial regulation states that the license for teeth and mouth medical practice include a Registration Letter for Mouth and Teeth Therapist/*Surat Tanda Registrasi Terapis Gigi dan Mulut* ("STRGM"). Article 5, in addition to article 3, states that the license for teeth and mouth medical practice include Permit Letter for Teeth and Moth Therapist to Practice/*Surat Izin Praktik Terapis Gigi dan Mulut* ("SIPTGM"). Article 29 further states that administrative sanctions are applied in the event of non-compliance.

[16] The Ministry of Health Regulation No. 62 Year (2017) on License for Clearance for Health, Diagnostic, Invitro and Household Health Supply is available as follows https://www.perso.or.id/images/regulasi/permenkes/pmk622017.pdf.

[17] The Ministry of Health Regulation No. 16 Year 2019 is available as follows https://www.persi.or.id/images/regulasi/permenkes/pmk162019.pdf.

[18] The Ministry of Health Regulation No. 34 Year 2018 is available as follows http://bppsdmk.kemkes.go.id/web/filesa/peraturan/100.pdf.

[19] The Ministry of Health Regulation No. 73 Year 2016 on Pharmaceutical Standard of Service for Pharmacy is available as follows https://www.perso.or.id/images/regulasi/permenkes/pmk732016.pdf.

[20] The Ministry of Health Regulation No. 11 Year 2017 on the Safety of Patient is available as follows https://www.persi.or.id/images/regulasi/permenkes/pmk202016.pdf.

A notable difference which is more of an exception is the Ministry of Health Regulation No. 11 Year 2017 on the Safety of Patient.[21] In this ministerial regulation, criminal sanction is available for medical malpractice. Article 1 (1) stipulates regarding patient's right for the right to safety. Furthermore, in article 3: the National Committee for Patient Safety (*Komite Nasional Keselamatan Pasien* or "KNKP") is formed for the purpose of conducting an evaluation on allegations of violations against patient safety. In article 30, KNKP can report allegations of violation against patient safety as a criminal offence to the General Directorate.

4 Conclusion

The chapter starts with the following questions: how is medical liability regulated in Indonesian civil legal system? What are the regulatory trends of medical liability in Indonesia? By way of desk research, this research interrogates various court decisions and verdicts that are relevant to medical liability cases in Indonesia. Furthermore, it examines this issue in health regulations in Indonesia. There are two arguments brought forth in this work; first is that when it comes to medical liability verdicts and decisions reference is still made to the normative base in Indonesian civil code and Indonesian criminal code, both codes were transplanted by the Dutch colonial administration. Second is that the relationship between patient-doctor is regulated within this code of ethics for medical professionals, and the analysis of medical malpractice-related regulations shows how this sphere is increasingly regulated at the ministerial level by the ministry of health. However, most if not all sanctions are at the administrative level. At the beginning of the section, it was described how medical liability is often associated with tort law. The civil law system, which is the foundation of the Indonesian legal system is mainly doctrinal. It is based on principles of law as stipulated in statutory provisions, and relies much less on case law. That said, an overview of cases on medical liability shows mostly normative understanding and interpretation of judges in the application of Indonesian civil code and Indonesian criminal code. The relationship between patient and doctor is regulated within the code of ethics of medical professionals, in this case, the Decree of the Minister of Health Number 434/Men.Kes/SK/X/1983 regarding code of ethics for medical professionals in Indonesia. The second section of the book chapter also highlights an increasing trend of regulations in the Ministry of Health, with sanctions for violation mostly in the administrative form.

[21] The Ministry of Health Regulation No. 11 Year 2017 on the Safety of Patient is available as follows https://www.persi.or.id/images/regulasi/permenkes/pmk112017.pdf.

References

Hanggoro HT (2014) Kontroversi Aborsi (Controversion of Abortion). Historia. Jakarta
Horty JF (1964) The status of the doctrine of charitable immunity in hospital cases. Ohio St. Law J 25(343)
Knottnerus W (1984) California negotiated health care: implications for malpractice liability. San Diego Law Rev 21(2):455–476
Kurniawan RA (2013) Medical risk and negligence against medical malpractice in Indonesia. Perspektif XVIII(3):148–156
Liemena F (1990) Note on informed consent (Suatu Catatan tentang Informed Consent). Varia Peradilan No. 60
Lindsey T, Butt S (No Year) Civil liability for criminal acts at Indonesian Law. Accessed from 04 Sept 2020 https://law.unimelb.edu.au/__data/assets/pdf_file/0009/1546299/CivilLiabilityforCriminalActsatIndonesianLaw2.pdf
Ministry of Health Regulation No. 62 Year 2017 on License for Clearance for Health, Diagnostic, Invitro and Household Health Supply is available as follows https://www.persi.or.id/images/regulasi/permenkes/pmk622017.pdf
Murphy EK (1990) Applications of the 'captain of the ship' doctrine. AORN J 52(4):863–866
Otto JM (2002) Toward an analytical framework: real legal certainty and its explanatory factors. In: Chen J Li Y, Otto JM (eds) Implementation of law in the People's Republic of China. The Hague, Kluwer Law International, pp 1–17
Otto JM, Stoter WS (2008) Using legislative theory to improve law and development projects lawmaking for development: explorations into the theory and practice of international legislative projects. In: Rooij BV, Otto JM, Arnscheidt J (eds). Leiden, Leiden University Press, pp 53–74
Rosenbaum S (2003) Medical errors, medical negligence, and professional medical liability reform. Public Health Rep 118(3):272–274
The Ministry of Health Regulation No. 269 of 2008 on Medical Records is available as follows http://www.apikes.com/files/permenkes-no-269-tahun-2008.pdf
The Ministry of Health Regulation No. 66 Year 2016 on Safety of Working at Hospital is available as follows: https://www.persi.or.id/images/regulasi/permenkes/pmk662016.pdf
The Ministry of Health Regulation No. 11 Year 2017 on the Safety of Patient is available as follows https://www.persi.or.id/images/regulasi/permenkes/pmk202016.pdf
The Ministry of Health Regulation No. 11 Year 2017 on the Safety of Patient is available as follows https://www.persi.or.id/images/regulasi/permenkes/pmk112017.pdf
The Ministry of Health Regulation No. 4 Year 2018 on Obligations of Hospitals and Patients is available as follows https://www.persi.or.id/images/regulasi/permenkes/pmk42018.pdf
The Ministry of Health Regulation No. 63 Year 2017 on Health Tool Clinical Testing is available as follows: https://www.persi.or.id/images/regulasi/permenkes/pmk632017.pdf
The Ministry of Health Regulation No. 73 Year 2016 on Pharmaceutical Standard of Service for Pharmacy is available as follows https://www.persi.or.id/images/regulasi/permenkes/pmk732016.pdf
The Ministry of Health Regulation No. 16 Year 2019 is available as follows https://www.persi.or.id/images/regulasi/permenkes/pmk162019.pdf
The Ministry of Health Regulation No. 34 Year 2018 is available as follows http://bppsdmk.kemkes.go.id/web/filesa/peraturan/100.pdf

Public Health Care Law and Ethics in Israel

Jonathan Davies

Abstract The Israeli health care system is considered to be of high quality and economically efficient. The Israeli health system provides equal health care services, under budgetary restrictions, to all its citizens. The Israeli decision-making process, regarding public funding of new medical technologies, is fair, transparent and evidence-based, in a way that fulfills the responsibility of the Israeli government, to provide equal health services to its people. This chapter introduces to the readers a brief overview of the Israeli health care system, covering different health issues, such as public health policy, organization of health services, public health and technology, artificial intelligence (AI), healthcare regulation of medical research and clinical trials. It will review legal aspects, such as the relationships between public health, law, human rights and ethics, protection of patient safety in Israel, Balancing between public health issues and individuals rights. In light of the pandemic that struck the world, it reviews the impact and ramifications of Covid-19 on health system and human rights in Israel.

1 Introduction

Public health law in Israel is a dynamic field that covers many issues with science, medicine and law converge. The main issue in public health law and ethics is to protect public interests, in light of human rights principals that reflect the essence of the state of Israel, being a Jewish democracy. The topics of public health law and ethics, in Israel, range from protecting the rights of the individual to public interests by large. Public health law protects the population, such as patients, minors,

WAML Governor for Israel, President of the Society of Medicine and Law in Israel, Former Editor in Chief of the "Medicine and Law" Journal (2000–2015), Legal Advisor to Ethics committee of HMO, Advocate in personal Injuries and medical malpractice claims.

J. Davies (✉)
LLM, WAML, Tel Aviv, Israel
e-mail: davies@med-law.co.il

V. L. Raposo and R. G. Beran (eds.), *Medical Liability in Asia and Australasia*,
Ius Gentium: Comparative Perspectives on Law and Justice 94,
https://doi.org/10.1007/978-981-16-4855-7_7

handicapped and elderly. Private health law deals with issues, such of pregnancy and childbirth, termination of pregnancy, sperm donation, surrogacy, experiments on humans, biotechnology and law, organ transplants and organ trade, curing diseases, by means of cloning, genes implantation, protection of genetic information and the dying patient. These issues constitute public health policies of the health system, in Israel, and reflect its definition as a welfare state.

Legal medicine in Israel is set by legislation and by court ruling and traverses the boundaries of civil law, criminal law, family law, labor laws, administrative law and evidence law. Public health law and patient's rights derive from legislation and court ruling. The accepted causes of action, in legal medicine, are medical malpractice, wrongful life and informed consent, governed by principles of patient right to autonomy, that is considered as a constitutional right.

The main function of the courts, in interpreting public health law and ethics, is to find an appropriate balance between public and individual interests and applying the appropriate health policy between the many considerations of the various disciplines involved.

Since the outbreak of Covid-19, there has been a sharp transition in the balancing point, on the scale of protecting human rights from an individual to public interests. The world, including Israel, is in a constant battle to recover from the pandemic, trying to return to normal life. Israel experienced a sharp transition, from a normal functioning health system, under a liberal democratic system of government and the civil freedoms, to a national state of emergency. A series of orders and emergency regulations, introduced within months, including lockdown and quarantine, road closures, mobile surveillance by the security services and social distancing have changed the order of life and the economy of Israel.

The chase, to prevent a spread of the pandemic, was drastic, constituting an infringement of basic constitutional rights, enshrined in basic laws, such as freedom of movement, the right to property, freedom of occupation, the right to privacy, freedom of information, freedom of religion and individual human rights.

This chapter provides a brief overview of the Israeli health care system, covering both health and legal aspects: doctor and patient relationship; and patient's rights, through the main causes of action in Israel's legal system.

2 The Health Care System in Israel

The Israeli health care system is considered high quality and economically efficient. Health indicators are comparable with those of developed countries. Life expectancy for males is 81 and for females 84 years and infant mortality is 3.6 per 1000 live births. Inequalities, in health indicators, exist with lower scores for those living in the periphery and for minorities. The Israeli health care system is considered one of the advanced in the OECD countries in the world.[1]

[1] http://www.oecd.org/israel/.

According to The National Health Insurance Law,[2] every Israeli citizen is entitled to an extensive basket of health services, funded by the government, in return for a health tax, constituting 4.8% of the gross salary (up to a certain ceiling). Citizens earning a minimal income taxed only 3.1% and citizens on welfare or retirees are exempt.

Public Health Policy: Since 1995, Israel operates a compulsory National Health Insurance (NHI) scheme, which supplies all Israeli citizens with a wide benefits package. There is co-payment for ambulatory services and drugs. Despite the good quality public system, private health expenditure is increasing. There are indications that some of the poor are forfeiting medical treatment, mostly medicines.

The NHI act, from 1995, provides all citizens, with no discrimination, a basic basket of compulsory medical services. Services provided by four health care providers (HMO) that are state budgeted. These agencies can provide private insurances of all kinds. The health basket is a list of drugs and medical services and technologies to which all citizens are entitled. A national committee that presents public and private views on medical, economical and legal interests meets annually to expand or decrease the health basket.

The committee plays a major bioethical role in deciding which new drugs or medical technologies are to be introduced and which patient is entitled to these free benefits.

In addition to the NHI that provides basic medical services, the HMOs and the insurance companies may offer private insurances and provide services beyond the basic basket. More than half the population holds private insurance.

This situation creates a significant gap and disparity between patients who need the services covered by the NHI and patients who seek the services of private practices. This dichotomy also creates a difference in the quality of the medical services. A substantial number of health providers operate in private practice and dedicate most of their time there, in addition to their work in public healthcare.

Time and resource constraints, especially in the public healthcare system, affect the relationship between the doctor and the patient. Investing time and resources, in private medicine, raises the cost of the treatment and comes at the expense of the quality of the treatment in the public healthcare system, thus lowering the standard of care for those patients or decreasing the number of patients who receive care.

Courts are often requested to rule against health funds, in cases of discrimination, which, in some extreme cases, may mean a death sentence, in cases of patients who cannot afford the lifesaving drugs, which are excluded from the basket. Courts have wide discretion in interpreting the NHI Act based on moral, equality and human rights values. HMO funds will finance necessary procedures abroad that are not executed in Israel, due to lack of experience.

---

[2] The statute enacted on January 1 1995.

Organization of Health Services: The government plays a major role in the health market, as it budgets the system (95%). These include as: regulator; has direct financial and operational responsibility of medical services, such as geriatrics and psychiatry; owner and operator of 40% of hospital beds; and insurer of all medical services, through the insurance scheme for elementary and professional liability of all their activities.

The four health plans funds supply the actual medical services to the public, owned or bought facilities and personnel.

Workforce: There are 3.4 physicians per 1000 people. This ratio is declining, due to an inadequate increase in intake in the medical schools. Corrective measures, to train doctors in peripheral medical centers, will become effective in about 10 years. The system also suffers from a shortage of physicians, in specific specialties, and of nurses in relation to the situation in average of the Organization for Economic Co-operation and Development (OECD) countries.[3] During the second wave of Covid 19 Health, the system suffered a substantial shortage of physicians, especially in intensive care units in peripheral medical centers that were understaffed.

3 Legislation

Israel's legal system is based on the common law. Israel has no constitution. The Israeli parliament (Knesset) has enacted several basic laws, serving as a kind of a constitution based on a common law.

The right to healthcare is recognized as a fundamental right in the Israeli legal system and consists of many rights, scattered among many legislations. Among the rights are included: the right of privacy; right of dignity; right of equality; right to proper medical care; right of information; right for access to medical care; and right to confidentiality.

These rights, regulated by laws, and recognized as having superior status and considered as basic laws that protect human rights. The main basic law that the Knesset has enacted is the **Human Dignity and Liberty Basic law-1992**, which regulates the basic rights for dignity and privacy of an individual in society.

Other legislation protects specific groups in society. **Patient's Rights Law**-1996 regulates the rights of the patient and general physician–patient's relations, **Freedom of Information Law**-1998, allows transparency of information and acknowledges the right of every person to information subject to certain restrictions, **Protection of Privacy Law**-1981 protects the person's right of privacy in the society. **National Health Insurance Law**-1995 regulates the rights of the residents for health insurance and a minimum medical services basket, via the Health Maintenance Organization

[3] Scheffer (2012), the Global Shortage of Health Workers and Pay for Performance. Improving Health and Health care, who is responsiblel? Who is Accountable, Israel National Institute for health policy 2012, pp 87–96.

(HMO) of which (s) he is a member. The Knesset enacted the **Dying Patient Law**-2005, regulating euthanasia and the right of the terminally ill to die with dignity. In 2007, the Ministry of Health established regulations of the dying patient.

National Health Insurance Law is one the most dynamic laws and reflects the tension between the declared protection of the Health Insurance Law of individual rights in general and the right to healthcare, in particular, and administering healthcare economics, within the reality of limited resources.

Since the ratification of the **National Health Insurance Law,** by the Knesset, about 700 changes in legislation, of different and diverse subjects (most of them within the National Healthcare Law and some through the Economic Arrangements Law), were brought before the Knesset for ratification. The majority of the issues, which require frequent legislation changes, are HMO registration policy, HMO administration, coverage of medical services basket, funding of medical services basket, health tax, resource distribution, among the different HMOs and others. Additional laws regulate the rights of underprivileged groups in the society, such as handicapped or minors. The **Equal Rights of Persons with Disabilities Law**-1998 regulates the right of handicapped in the society and the **Legal Capacity and Guardianship Law**-1962 regulates the rights of wards and minors. The **Mentally Ill Law**-1991 regulates the rights of the mentally ill. In 2008, the Knesset enacted the **Organ Transplantation Law** and the law for determining brain-respiratory death. Several committees are continuing to discuss the current health laws and potential new laws (such as the Medical Experimentation Law; Egg Donation Law).

Israeli legislation has explicitly provided a no fault compensation (Absolute liability) in four cases of damages, caused by specific medical treatments: damages to road accident injuries subject to proof of compulsory insurance and driving license; damages caused by vaccination; damages caused by radiation therapy for ringworm of the scalp (Tinea Capitis).and damages caused to patients who suffer polio. These compulsory no fault damages, covered by the State and private insurance (according to the **Road Accident Compensation Act**), notwithstanding causation or negligence. Apart from these, the overall tort regime, in medical law, is subject to proof of negligence and causation.

Financing: Israel spends about US $2,200 per capita per year on health care, 7.8% of its GDP, of which about 57% is public, covering mostly the statutory benefits package, and 43% private. The public resources originate from a dedicated health tax and other general taxes. The pooled public resources distributed between four HMO, via a capitation mechanism adjusted to age.

The committee for the national health basket, restricted by the budgetary limit dictated by the government each year and the budget, usually stands at 0.6 to 0.8% of the total cost of the Health Insurance Law.[4] The estimate of the total cost of technologies, submitted to the TAW for consideration in the 2020 Basket, is approximately 3 billion NIS.[5]

[4] Figures for the 2020 Basket were 500 million NIS ($150 million), with the financing of the Health Insurance Law currently standing at approximately 60 billion NIS($17.5 billion).

[5] $1 = NIS 3.5.

Israel's poverty rate and income inequality measures remain high, relative to most other OECD countries, despite continuing decline in recent years. The multi-ethnic fabric of Israel is culturally enriching in many ways, yet also poses challenges to equal access to care and implementation of culturally appropriate health services and programs.

The government, through services in the community and medical institutions, finances medical services provided by HMOs. The state owns 40% of the hospitals, the HMOs own approximately 40% of the medical institutions and the rest are privately owned hospitals and clinics.

Statutorily permissible supplementary insurance plan have been sold by the health plans to 80% of the population. A citizen is entitled to join with no underwriting and low community premium rates. About 50% of the population purchases supplementary insurance programs.

Due to Covid-19, it is expected that Gross National Product (GNP) of Israel will fall by 6% approximately.

4 Public Health and Technology in Israel

In an era, when new techniques and technologies are constantly evolving, there is growing public demand for prevention and early detection of disease, along with zero tolerance for misdiagnosis. This climate, enhanced by medical malpractice claims, efforts of industry, to promote use of new technologies and a tendency of the media to be overly involved in the formation of public opinion health is important.

Israel is big in health data, is a hub for digital health innovation, implementation and evaluation and is considered amongst the world leaders in the field of medical devices development. According to the recently released Start-Up Nation Central report, the number of digital health companies, operating in Israel, reached 580 in 2019 (more than doubling since 2011), and, in the last year, Israeli digital health start-ups raised $662 million. Such achievements earned Israel the rank of the world's sixth most innovative country by the Bloomberg Innovation Index in 2019.[6]

Israel is into "big data". The National Health Insurance Law provides all Israeli citizens with comprehensive health and medical care, through one of the country's four HMOs. Virtually all the accumulated medical data, on all citizens is digitized and access to the accumulated and digitized data provides a fertile landscape for medical research. Last year, the government approved a 1 billion-NIS ($276 million) investment into digital health, focusing primarily on exploiting the country's digital electronic health records (her) system and medical data repositories. These initiatives offer great promise for advancing medical science and practice, while generating data-security, together with legal and ethical challenges, which are currently the subject of draft guidelines of the Ministry of Health.

---

[6] https://www.bloomberg.com/news/articles/2020-01-18/germany-breaks-korea-s-six-year-streak-as-most-innovative-nation.

Israel has already met targets for maternal, neonatal and under-5 mortality, largely thanks to universal health coverage and free education. Despite these remarkable achievements, maternal and child health disparities persist, particularly between Jews and Arabs, and between center and periphery, and Israel struggles with a very high level of child-poverty.

The Ministry of Health has established a Department of Technology Assessment and appointed a national Basket Committee that would make evidence-based decisions about the inclusion of new technologies in the public basket of services.

Artificial Intelligence (AI), Healthcare and Human Rights

Recent advances in healthcare outcomes are attributed to improvements in the three pillars of healthcare: prevention; diagnosis; and treatment. Artificial intelligence (AI) has applications across all three pillars but its greatest impact has been on improving the accuracy of medical diagnosis, changing the traditional clinical diagnosis.

Clinicians use a wide range of approaches, in order to diagnose disease. The simplest and most widespread is to identify the patient's symptoms and correlate them to conditions or diseases that are characterized by the same pattern of symptoms. The same basic approach applies in interpreting the results of diagnostic tests: a radiologist reviewing magnetic resonance imagining (MRI) or a pathologist analyzing a biopsy sample compare what they are seeing to what they have learned, in order to make a diagnosis.

One of the most advanced AI collaboration, medical research community and high technology, is currently taking place in Israel. This investigator-initiated, prospective, randomized, two-arm, multiple users, interventional, clinical study is aimed to explore the performance and usability of the EVA device (Google LLC). The EVA device is a novel, AI based, automated, real-time lesion detection software, intended to assist adenoma detection in colonoscopy, by highlighting the suspected lesion on the secondary EVA screen. The EVA system is composed of a software, installed on a dedicated personal computer (PC) and monitor, assembled on a portable cart or mounted on the wall. The EVA computer, connected to the colonoscopy, receives the real-time video. The EVA AI algorithm uses a neural network, trained over 7,500 colonoscopies, tested on over 10,000 patients, and is currently in the process of the ethical committee approval.

In the last several years, systems based on machine learning or deep learning began developing to automate the diagnosis of disease, across a range of medical specialties. Few of these technologies are currently in use, though early results suggest that they have great promise in improving the accuracy of medical diagnosis. The promise of AI, to improve our lives, is enormous. AI-based systems are already outperforming medical specialists in diagnosing certain diseases. AI also has downsides. Among these is that AI systems depend on the generation, collection, storage, analysis and use of vast quantities of data with corresponding impacts on the right to privacy. AI techniques are used to discover some of our most intimate secrets by drawing profound correlations out of seemingly innocuous bits of data. AI can easily perpetuate existing patterns of bias and discrimination, since the most common way to deploy these systems is to "train" them to replicate the outcomes achieved by human decision-makers.

5 Regulation of Medical Research and Clinical Trials

The scientific research, based upon principles of the Helsinki Declaration, which mandated the obtaining of informed consent and adherence to a decision-making procedure, upon clinical trials, with a safeguard of basic human rights and the distinction between adults and children participating in trials and medical research.

Wide ranges of medical experiments in Israel are conducted in various fields: pharmaceuticals medical devices; products containing cells and tissues; and epidemiology of diseases. For the last thirty years, primary care in Israel has been computerized. An enormous wealth of data is stored on the mainframe computers of the four HMOs that insure all of Israel's population.

The health ministry closely supervises most research approved by each institution's committee. The local ethical committee must include, amongst others, a head of department of Internal Medicine and a representative of the public. All genetic research needs the additional approval of the Higher Helsinki Committee for Medical Trials in Humans, based in the Ministry of Health.

Ethical committees are required to make their decisions based on transparency, safety and effectiveness of medical care, in accordance with the Declaration of Helsinki, and in accordance with the Genetic Information Act, 2000, Genetic Intervention Prohibition Law (Human cloning and genetic modification in reproductive cells), 1999 and in accordance with the procedure of human experiments.

The higher Helsinki Committee examines and approves proposals for all human studies in Israel concerning the genetic system of humans, research related to fertilization, for studies conducted by Ministry of Health staff and any other research, at the request of the Director General of the Health Ministry.

According to the Pharmacists (Preparations) Regulations, drugs are registered in the State Register of Medicines only after safety, efficacy and quality have been proven. The decisions, to register any drug, is made after information is submitted and thoroughly examined. The registration department establishes the policy on registering drugs containing new substances, authorizing generic drugs and rules for restricting drugs. The Medical Device Division deals with the licensing and supervision process for all types of medical devices and equipment, including rehabilitation and mobility devices.

COVID-19 pandemic illness may be treated with medications, supplied in the absence of prior information, some on an experimental basis. The information and experience, related to this disease, mostly has been scant. The use of certain medications, recommended and in many cases, the treatment procedures have changed "*on the move*". The problem was that insufficient data existed as to the efficiency of the medications and it was necessary for every medical center to formulate its own treatment protocol and to determine what procedure to follow for a patient in a moderate to severe condition. From the very beginning, there were unestablished procedures, based upon unsubstantiated research. It has not been possible to ascertain the effectiveness of the medications. These examples reflect an infringement of ethical principles, by making a shortcut in the name of public interests.

In October 2020, the Ministry of Health allowed, for the first time, researchers in clinical trials to accept informed consent of participants by digital means and distance conferencing, subject to specific restrictions of transparency and protection of privacy.[7]

6 The Relationships Between Public Health, Law, and Ethics

The Public Health Ordinance is an ordinance, enacted in 1940 by the British Mandate authorities, which regulates the activities of the health system in a large scope of areas: public health; births and death registry; water and milk sanitation; burial arrangements; licensing of medical institutions; health; and the environment. By virtue of this ordinance, regulations, such as: medical experiments on humans; in vitro fertilization; and disease control, including infectious diseases, are regulated according to the public health ordinance. Regulations, enacted to fight the Covid 19 pandemic, were enacted under this statute.

The National Health Insurance Act has shaped the relationship between citizens and basic human rights for medical care.

The origins of the relationship, between public health issues and human rights, influenced by the 1964 Helsinki Declaration,[8] was considered as a turning point in the recognition of modern patients' rights. The Helsinki Declaration was adopted and incorporated into the Public Health (Experiments with Humans), Law -1980 and, since then, procedures have been published focusing upon management of general research and particularly in the framework of the Ethics Committees of the Ministry of Health, hospitals, medical institutions and the HMO funds.[9]

There are various models to describe the complex legal relationship between a health provider and the patient.[10] Each of the models has balanced the obligations to inform and the patient's right to receive the substantial information. The balance point has changed over the years: At first, the paternalistic presupposition that the

[7] Ministry of Health in Israel. Guidelines for informed consent in Clinical trials via digital instruments. October 2020.

[8] Recommendations of the medical guidelines for obtaining informed consent in bio-medical research, that involves humans—were adopted at the 18th World Medical Conference in Helsinki, Finland in 1964 and were amended at the 29th World Medical Conference in Tokyo, Japan in 1975.

[9] The Ministry of Health has recently published an informed consent procedure in relation to trials involving humans whose applicability date of 20/5/20 will be deferred. https://documentcloud.adobe.com/link/review?uri=urn%3Aaaid%3Ascds%3AUS%3A05eba217-fad8-4c79-89ff-cc9868c92c51.

[10] Nili Krakow—Eyal, Informed Consent Doctrine, Hapraklit, Volume 49, 181, 171–218.

authority to make decisions, in the matter of a patient given solely to the doctor (*Confidential Model*) was prevalent. Later, the patient's right to agree or refuse the treatment, based on information regarding the nature of the treatment (*Consensual Model*), emerged. An additional development was made when broad interpretation was given to the patient as a right to autonomy. The Supreme Court of Israel decided that a patient has not only the right, to agree or refuse treatment, but also the right to receive additional information regarding the suggested treatment, allowing him/her to make an informed decision. According to this model (*Autonomy Model, Participatory Model*) "*the patient has a material and active role in the decision making process: he must examine the information he was given, weigh the advantages of the suggested treatment and its disadvantages, examine the advantages and disadvantages of alternate treatments and decide, based on information and values, most suitable medical treatment for him*".[11] The health provider has the duty to inform the patient, in addition to the information regarding the nature of the suggested treatment.

In the **Kadosh** case, the Supreme Court in Israel adopted the American approach known as "*The Shared Decision Making Model*". This model, perceives the doctor and the patient as two parties who share making the decisions, which will be best for the patient. The patient him/herself eventually made the final decision, regarding the appropriate treatment. The doctor is obligated to take part in this process and provide all material information needed for the patient decision, as stated in the Matthias ruling[12]:

There are two approaches, in Israel's Supreme Court, regarding the question of which test applied for examining the scope of the duty of disclosure, on the part of the doctor to his/her patient. The opinion of the majority, expressed in the verdict of Justice Rivlin, in the **Kadosh Case**, adopted the reasonable expectation test. According to the approach of Justice Amit in the **Kadosh Case,** the preferred test should be the involved patient in the eyes of the reasonable doctor. It is predicted that Justice Amit school of thought will prevail.

Protection of Patient safety in Israel

A large number of legislative enactments governs human rights. Protecting public and individual interests. Basic Law: Human Dignity and Freedom was enacted in 1992 with a constitutional effect on basic rights, such as the right to privacy, the right to informed consent, property and intellectual property rights, freedom of movement, freedom of speech, the right to access health services and prohibition of discrimination. Prior to these statutes, protection of human rights was recognized in universal conventions, such as the Helsinki Declaration.[13]

Public health law is engaged on private and public levels.

- The right to access medical service in Israel, public health, and national insurance.

---

[11] Judge Rivlin in HCJ 1303/09 **Kadosh v. Bikur Holim Hospital** (2012).

[12] Matthies v. Masromonaco, 160 N.J. 26, 36, 733 A.2d 456, 461 (N.J. Sup. Ct. 1999).

[13] https://www.esahq.org/uploads/media/ESA/Files/Downloads/Resources-PatientSafetySignedHelsinkiDeclaration/Helsinki%20Declaration%20-%20signed.pdf.

- The right to medical information entered in the computerized medical records, remote medicine (telemedicine), medical confidentialityand medical negligence,
- The rights of children, handicapped people and the elderly, pregnancy and birth, sperm donation, surrogacy, termination of pregnancy, dying patients, trials involving humans, biotechnology and law, organ transplantation and trading in organs, fertility treatments, amelioration of terminal illnesses by means of cloning, implantation of genes in the patient's body and protection of genetic information

Health law is governed by legislation and case law, transcending the boundaries of civil law, criminal law, family law, labor law, insurance law, administrative law and the laws of evidence.

Patients' rights in Israel can be charted in the following five correlated circles;

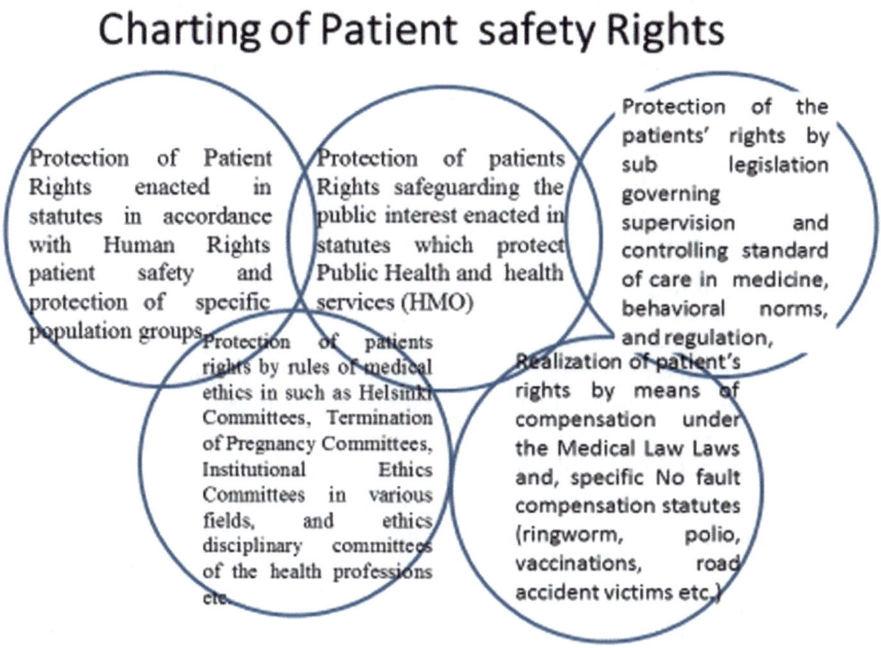

(1) First circle deals with patient rights, designed to protect individual rights of specific groups, such as patients, mental illness (Treatment of Mental Patients Law) the elderly, children, handicapped and other disabled people (Equal Rights for Persons with Disabilities Law), employees (Sick Leave Law) soldiers (Compensation and Rehabilitation of the Disabled Law) and insured persons (Insurance Contract Law).

(2) The second circle comprises various statutory enactments governing protection of the public interest, such as the Public Health Ordinance (1940) and National Health Insurance Law-1994. Numerous orders and regulations were enacted to protect public interests and balance between public interests and protection of rights of the individual.

(3) The third circle reflects legislation and regulations that supervise standards of care, ethical and behavioral norms, regulation that sets the standard of conduct (Director General's Circulars), the institution of the Ombudsman (Public Complaints Commissioner in the Ministry of Health), Disciplinary and Quasi-Judicial Tribunals.
(4) The fourth circle expresses the protection of the rights of patients, by means of a series of rules of medical ethics in various fields, such as Helsinki Committees (governing the rules of ethics in relation to scientific and medical research), termination of pregnancy committees, institutional ethics committees in various fields and ethics disciplinary committees of the health professions.
(5) The fifth circle reflects statutes of no fault compensation acts for disabled individuals that suffer neurological disability, due to ringworm, polio, vaccinations and victims of road accidents. Beyond the right to social benefits that derive from the National Insurance [New Version] Law 5755-1995 and entitles any citizen who suffers substantial disability and compensation to any employee who is injured at work.

The above circles derive their authority from the various legislative enactments and laws on the constitutional hierarchy ladder. In case of a conflict, between public and private matters, the courts balance between such rights with proportionality and in accordance with the purpose of the statute.

Institutional liability in personal Injury and Tort Law

The boundaries of liability in Public Health Law are sensitive to social, cultural, religious, and technological influences and to the tendency courts play an active role in widening tort liability at large and liability in health law in particular. Many of the medical malpractice cases, dealt by Israeli courts, are medical malpractice cases filed against the State and other various health providers, through the principle of vicarious liability. Tort law and medical malpractice claims serve as a tool for reducing a variety of harms to the population's health.

The goals of tort law, although imperfectly achieved, are frequently consistent with public health objectives. The tort system aims to hold individuals and state accountable for their dangerous activities compensate those who are harmed, deter unreasonably hazardous conduct, encourage innovation in product design and labeling and reduce the risk of injury or disease. Civil litigation can provide potent incentives for people and manufacturers to engage in safer, more socially conscious behavior.

Tort law can be an effective method of advancing the public's health but, like any form of regulation, has its limits. The tort system imposes economic costs and personal burdens סח individuals and businesses.

The Supreme Court has considered shifting the pendulum, from protection of human rights of individual to public interests, thus reducing institutional liability of the government.[14] It is to be assumed that case law, post Covid, will follow this trend.

[14] Zandberg (2013).

7 Balancing Between Public Health Issues and Individuals Rights

Public health strives for maximizing benefits for the highest number of people, while protecting human rights. Restrictions on individual rights are justified for two reasons:for the benefit of the individual; or the benefit of the community.

The common example is involuntary admissions and hospitalizations of mentally ill patients, those present medico legal, moral, social and mostly bioethical dilemmas for the western legal systems. Those are mostly due to the necessity to choose between conflicting principles of deprivation of personal freedom and autonomy of the mental patients vis-a-vis the necessity to protect the safety of society.

Autonomy and the freedom to move freely, at one's choice, is a cornerstone in Israeli legal system. A person may suffer a major medical crisis, such as stroke or myocardial infarct, but retains full choice to refuse to be admitted to the hospital, even when the alternative is a serious jeopardy to his/her life. When a psychotic person expresses suicidal thoughts or threatens to harm him/herself or others and refuses to be treated, then (s)he can be involuntarily admitted and hospitalized in a psychiatric secured ward, losing the liberty to leave and move around at his/her free will. This involuntary admittance, is practiced when such patient has assaulted already or has tried to harm him/herself in the past. When involuntarily admitted, such patient(s) can be enforced with medications, against his/her will with no consent to such treatment, contrary to the basic patients' rights statute requiring patient's consent to every medical treatment, is required.

The legal justification for such deprivation of freedom is clear—safeguarding the safety of public interests. The moral or ethical question remains, but these decreased substantially during the Covid 19 crises.

A series of orders and emergency regulations, introduced within months, including lockdown and quarantine, barriers and road closures, mobile surveillance by the security services and social distancing changed the order of life and the delicate balance between protecting public interests and individual interests.

The chase, to prevent a spread of the pandemic, was drastic; constituting an infringement of basic constitutional rights enshrined in basic laws, such as freedom of movement, the right to property, freedom of occupation, the right to privacy, freedom of information, freedom of religion and individual human rights.

Coping with the outcome of the Covid-19 pandemic in Israel

Since the Covid-19 outbreak, the State of Israel has been coping with 3 waves of lockdowns in which over 1,000,000 citizens caught the virus and over 7500 died of Covid 19 or its complications. The government handled the pandemic by closing the boarders, shutting down businesses, forbidding any form of gathering, such as sporting events, weddings, cultural events (theater and cinema), communal parties, restaurants, hotels and a complete shutdown of tourism. Universities and schools moved to distance learning until the pandemic is over. For the first time, since the establishment of the State of Israel, as a democratic state government, declared a state of emergency.

From a medical prospective, little was known about Covid 19 and, very soon after the breakout, health providers realized that serious risk factors included medical background, diabetes, obesity and overweight. The prognosis of Covid is vague but early reports show that post Covid long term damages are wide spread and patients report heart and renal failure, hearing and neurological damages and psychiatric outcomes.

Soon after the outbreak, lockdown was forced upon citizens, by means of emergency regulations and orders, restricting the freedom of the individual and constitutes an infringement of basic human rights, such as the right to privacy, freedom of movement, freedom of religion and the right to protest. Despite the declaration to return to normality, the government has not withdrawn the state of emergency, with the support of the Supreme Court. It has left in place the emergency orders that are an infringement of the right to privacy. The Supreme Court of Justice has approved the denial of sacred human rights if the infringement occurs within the framework of principal legislation.

***Another characteristic of the pandemic, in Israel, was public dispute, between politicians and public health experts, about how to handle the crises. The main fear of the government was that the health system would collapse justifying the extreme enactments that challenged the Ministry of Health's directives to the public. Another issue was the political state that Israel faced, at the time of the outbreak. The coalition formed was an emergency one and large government that was political based rather than evidence based. This dispute added to the uncertainty and distrust of the government. Covid-19 managed, for the first time in modern history, to infringe the absolute trust citizens had in the political regime and health system but, at the same time, health providers were praised as heroes of the time.

Informed consent in the age of Covid

The Patient's Rights Act changed the balance of the doctor-patient relationship and created the doctor's statutory duty of disclosure to the patient, by means of the cause of action for informed consent. In the past, informed consent was handled within the cause of action of negligence tort or battery but since the Patient Right's Law of 1996, the duty to receive informed consent was considered part of the right for autonomy of the patient, protected by law.

The meaning of informed consent is that health providers hold a duty to disclose information to the patient necessitating his/her consent and understanding of the information. In order for the patient to give genuine consent to the suggested treatment, health providers need to supply material information about the diagnosis, alternative treatments and prognosis. Failure to disclose pertinent information, regarding the treatment, undermines the consent given for treatment.

The requirement for "*informed consent*" incorporates two main elements: the one, embodied by the word "informed", relates to the duty of disclosing information to the patient; the second element, embodied by the word "consent", relates to the patient's free will decision regarding the treatment he needs as part of the **right to autonomy**.

Principles of Informed consent, in post Covid age are challenging. Because little is known about the illness, there remains uncertainty regarding the side effects of the Covid-19. Medical publications show that the prognosis of Covid 19 is uncertain and many symptoms can appear even after full recovery.

Doctors are treating the disease with conflicting information, about its ramification and unknown prognosis, which effects, not only adults but also children. Based on this assumption, the rights of the patient to which we have become accustomed, such as the right of informed consent, the right to make free and autonomous decisions, the right to refuse medical treatment, the right of access to medical treatment, freedom of movement and freedom of occupation, no longer constitute cause of action.

Informed consent and the future vaccination for Covid-19

There were calls for special attention, to apply mandatory vaccination, in order to benefit society, including those who refuse to be vaccinate. In some states, vaccination is mandatory with only few exceptions (medical or religious). In others, the law mandates that parents receive educational information re benefits of vaccinations, to the child' family and society, and still other states use pinpointed actions, such as expelling unvaccinated children from school or restricting unvaccinated individuals from visiting public areas.

During 2019, Israel experienced a Measles vaccination crisis, while children, of ultra-religious citizens, were infected with measles, after their parents refused to vaccinate their children. This case demonstrates bioethical questions as to the scope of intervention in imposing on parents to vaccinate their children in order to protect the society.

In extreme situations, such as Covid 19, there may be a need to protect public interests that include the health of an individual that refuses treatment; even by overriding individual/parental autonomy. Many countries have mandatory vaccination. These laws curtail individual autonomy, in order to protect society from infectious diseases, because unvaccinated individuals pose risk to the community—including vaccinated individuals (since vaccines are not 100% efficacious). Scientific evidence can exemplify the need for overriding individual autonomy. A divergence, between individual and community benefits, may also exist when there are ideological beliefs incongruent with vaccination or individuals are unaware of or do not accept available scientific evidence.

When the state curtails individual freedoms, for the benefit of society's interests, it should address several issues, including the magnitude of the individual and community risk, the strength of the individual's conviction, wider and long-term consequences of restricting individual autonomy, effective risk communication, best available scientific evidence and transparency of the decision making process. The global chase for vaccination in the battle against Covid 19 is already razing questions as to what will be the attitude of society to sectors and individuals who refuse to receive vaccination under the right to refuse treatment. The right to refuse treatment is part of the right of autonomy that allows individuals to decide on their body.

What if the individual right to autonomy clashes with public interests like the right to Health?

In the post Covid age, the answer is that public interests will prevail. In pre Covid times, when a constitutional right was infringed, the court examined the proportionality of the infringement, striking a balance between the competing interests (the public interest v. personal interest), and, as far as the infringement is disproportionate, the decision will favor the individual.

The Impact of Covid -19 on Health system and Human Rights

Covid 19 has tremendous impact on all avenues of life. The pandemic followed by economic, social and political crises that its implication are too early to forecast.

The traditional players, participating in health care management, are health providers and medical professionals, such as clinicians and public health practitioners, each of whom has his/her own approach to the subject. Other professionals have played key roles in the determination of standards of care. The decision makers, in public policy, are not only health professionals but also public officials, economists, social scientists, politicians, the media and lawyers. The interests of the public, in health care policy, has increased considerably. The questions that have arisen concern the process by which the different disciplines interact. During the Covid 19 crises, politians took over from the professional's responsibility and made the final decisions.

Infringement of patients' rights, in view of the changing swing of the pendulum, from a liberal approach back to a paternalistic approach, emphasizes the shift of the balance. The decrease of the status, of the individual's right to autonomy, will influence the courts discretion, which will be prepared to sacrifice individual rights, for the benefit of the public interest.

In normal times these methods would be dismissed as patently illegitimate, now they are retrogressive *Vis a Vis* the right to life and physical perfection.[15]

This shift has, in the state attitude, caused uncertainty towards the future. In handling Covid crises, especially when decisions are made by politicians, rather than professionals. Will politicians will be accountable to their decisions?

The rights of the individual are on hold and subordinated to political interest. The rights, to access medical services, which normally is not challenged, has been subordinated to the public interest under emergency orders, which require people to remain in isolation. Owing to this uncertainty, regarding the side effects of the Covid-19, the rights of the patients were infringed.

There are also questions about the rights of people who view themselves aggrieved, because of a decision of the government to introduce a lockdown, thus preventing them from exercising a basic right of freedom of occupation. One cannot challenge the administrative decision, in accordance to principles of administrative law or employment law. This also applies to a person who is suffering from a chronic disease and, because the spread of Covid is unable to obtain proper and adequate treatment. Pursuant to patient safety statutes,[16] (s)he is entitled to remedies. If the

---

[15] Supreme Court of Justice Petition 2435/20 **Yedidia Leventhal, Advocate v. The Prime Minister and others** (published in Nevo 7/4/2020).

[16] Section 5 of the Patents' Rights Law requires health system to provide patients with adequate and reasonable quality health services.

rights of the patient have been subordinated to the general public interest, (s)he probably will not be entitled to compensation. It is too early to evaluate the scope of the pandemic but first data, from the National Insurance released and show a huge grow in compensation payments to Covid 19 casualties, recognizing them as entitled to work compensation from the State.

Post Covid-19 regulations influenced human rights and subordinated to the decision to shut clinics to all elective treatments other than Covid 19. Patients who need elective treatments, such as fertility treatments could not continue due to an age limit, and, in some cases, women could not persist with the treatments and lost the chance for parenthood, which was considered as a basic human right.

The decrease of human rights, of access to public medical services, limited by budgetary considerations post Corona, namely due to the economic crises, the health system resources will decrease and individuals will need to use costly private health services, in additions to other taxes imposed on them.

Under the National Insurance Act, individuals injured during their employment are entitled to compensation. This includes illness correlated to work, if caused during work. With Covid 19, the question arises where the infection with virus take place did. According to the National Insurance publications,[17]. there is an increase of 500% in claims for compensation. Many of the claims raise a question of causation and, if denied, can leave the person without compensation, without a job and with uncertainty of his/her medical situation, due to the uncertain prognosis. A further infringement relates to a pregnant woman to continue to receive a salary, to the end of their pregnancy, unless her absence is due to pregnancy. What is the case of pregnant women who were infected during her pregnancy?

The main crises is economic and it is yet to come. With one million people seeking for work, no budget and growing unemployment, the damages of Covid 19 may be irreversible. It is too early to evaluate the scope of the pandemic but, first data, from the National Insurance, show a huge grow in compensation payments to Covid 19 casualties, recognizing them as entitled to workers' compensation from the State. Other implications will change the face of society in the years to come.

8 Conclusion

The Covid-19 crisis has affords a good opportunity of examining whether this will serve as an historical turning point. The above chapter examined the pre-pandemic status of the health system in Israel, with an attempt to forecast what effect the Covid-19 crisis will have on human rights in general and on patient rights and ethical guidelines in particular.

It is too early to forecast the medical ramification of Covid-19. The prognosis of Covid is vague but early reports show that, post Covid, long term damage will affect children and adults and have a wide spectrum of damage that may include

[17] https://www.btl.gov.il/English%20homepage/Pages/default.aspx

heart and renal failure, hearing and neurological damages and psychiatric outcomes. Damage to muscles may also ensue. The assumption that the illness may result in future immunity from the pandemic is currently under review.

The health system in Israel, in common with those worldwide, did not make adequate preparations to foresee and handle the current pandemic, and its economic outcome. There has been a shift from individual autonomy to a national debate of the public interest and other ethical considerations.

The chase to prevent a spread of the pandemic was drastic, constituting an infringement of basic constitutional rights, enshrined in Israeli basic laws, such as freedom of movement, the right to property, freedom of occupation, the right to privacy, freedom of information, freedom of religion and individual human rights.

The global race, to find a vaccination, calls for special attention to what will happen, once the vaccinations are developed and applied worldwide. In some societies, vaccination is mandatory with only few exceptions (medical or religious). Based on the right to autonomy, Israel did not apply a mandatory vaccination policy, even lately when there was an outburst of measles.

Once a vaccination will be found, it is to be presumed that paternalistic policy will apply, in accordance with the public interests, and vaccination will become mandatory.

The Covid 19 crisis has escalated the use of AI techniques, to track positive Covid carriers (consciously and unconsciously) from spreading the disease, using mobile phones as a tracking machine, and, concurrently, possibly extracting private medical information. This escalation emphasized the dangers surrounding algorithms, making predictions about private information. While existing laws prohibit infringement of privacy, there has been a rapid change in public health interests sacrificing basic human rights principals.[18]

These examples reflect a changing trend, resulting from the Covid-19 pandemic, which has shifted the point of balance from the protection of rights of the patient towards a recognition of the public interest, as possessing greater weight. As the pandemic has not yet completely subsided, it is difficult to make prophesies about the future. This shift of the balance will continue for many years to come until the dangers of the current pandemic are over.

Balancing probabilities, in terms of cost effective damage (direct and indirect), that it has been sustained in the battle against Covid-19, the major question arises as to whether it would have been possible to prepare differently and to prevent the heavy economic damage that will occur to the national economy because of the failures to prepare and anticipate the crises.

The answers, to questions raised in this chapter, concerning pandemic effect on health and ethical issues, will take control of the legal discourse. Public health interests will prevail over the right to autonomy in Israel and worldwide. Once a vaccination becomes available the paternalistic policy will, most likely apply, in accordance with the public interests and the vaccination will become mandatory.

---

[18] Office of the State Comptroller and Ombudsman The 71A Annual Audit Report, Jerusalem | October 2020 . Catalog No. 2020-971A ISSN 0334–9713. https://www.mevaker.gov.il.

Covid has created new opportunities and challenges, and, once a vaccination[19] is found, this will change the world and improve technologies that will adapt humankind to a better place in which to live.

References

Scheffer RM (2012) The shortage of health workers Improving health and health care, who is responsiblel? Who is Accountable, Israel National Institute for health policy, pp 87–96

Zandberg C (2013) Torts claims against the Executive branch—on the Pendulum Movement (in the Advocate's Gazette 2013)

[19] On November 1, 2020 the Biological Institute of Israel started the clinical faze trial on humans and is due to find a vaccination within 9–12 months.

Medical Injury Litigation and Compensation Systems in Japan

Robert B. Leflar

Abstract This chapter explains the essential aspects of formal and informal Japanese systems for assessing, compensating, and prosecuting medical practice-associated harm. Distinctive features of criminal law, civil law, and administrative compensation programs are explored. *Criminal law*: Notorious errors at hospitals of high repute around the turn of the century focused public attention on slipshod practices and dishonesty in the medical world. The criminal justice system, amplified by media reportage, sounded a wake-up call to a medical profession previously lacking in accountability mechanisms. The health ministry and organized medicine implemented measures to improve patient safety; the effectiveness of those measures is unknown. Prosecutors' actions policing medical quality provoked reactions from medical providers eliciting public sympathy, contributing to a string of acquittals of medical defendants and clipping the prosecutors' wings. *Civil law*: Civil Code provisions governing medical injury lawsuits are fault-based and similar to rules applied in North America and Western Europe. The burden of proof of causation is relaxed in informed consent and loss-of-chance cases. Procedural reforms, including creation of health care divisions in some metropolitan district courts, have speeded the pace of judicial proceedings. Damage awards appear not to differ greatly, on average, from awards in the United States, and are applied on a more consistent, standardized basis. The volume of claims filed in court, as well as extrajudicially, is considerably lower than North American levels but has been rising steadily, with some year-to-year variation. Most compensation payments are made outside, not within, the court system. Malpractice insurance premiums, uniform nationwide for physicians in private practice without regard to specialty or geography, are far cheaper than in the U.S. *Administrative compensation programs*: Building on a tradition of no-fault administrative compensation schemes for harm from pollution, defective drugs, vaccines, blood transfusions, and asbestos, Japan instituted in 2009 a no-fault compensation system for infants with severe birth-related brain injuries. Backed by the medical establishment, financed through public funding, administered by a

R. B. Leflar (✉)
National Taiwan University College of Law, National YangMing ChiaoTung School of Law, University of Arkansas School of Law (retired 2020), Fayetteville, AR, USA
e-mail: rbleflar@uark.edu

V. L. Raposo and R. G. Beran (eds.), *Medical Liability in Asia and Australasia*, Ius Gentium: Comparative Perspectives on Law and Justice 94,
https://doi.org/10.1007/978-981-16-4855-7_8

quasi-public entity and offering substantial profit opportunities to private insurers, the obstetrical injury compensation system has achieved universal buy-in by childbirth facilities hoping for protection from future litigation.

1 Introduction

This chapter sets out the essential aspects of Japanese systems, formal and informal, for assessing, compensating and occasionally prosecuting cases of medical practice-associated injuries and deaths. Building on, and updating, the author's earlier overview of these systems,[1] this chapter explains and critiques recent Japanese responses to continuing concerns about patients' safety.

Health insurance coverage, in Japan, is virtually universal. Every legal resident is entitled to receive medical care, through either public or private insurance schemes.[2] Eleven percent of Japan's GDP goes to health care expenditures—a proportion in the middle range of industrialized nations, and far smaller than that of the world's most inefficient health care system, that of the United States (17%).[3] Japan's statistics, regarding lifespan and infant mortality, rank among the best of the world's nations, and Japan's top hospitals offer advanced and sophisticated treatments the equal of any on the globe.

Despite the overall high quality of Japanese health care, public and professional concerns about avoidable medical injury erupted, as a result of a series of highly publicized fatal and near-fatal errors in 1999 and subsequent years. Switched-patient surgery, a fatal toxic injection, a bungled laparoscopic surgery, a series of children's deaths in pediatric heart surgery in Tokyo and Yokohama hospitals of high repute—in all of these cases medical personnel altered patient charts; misled bereaved families or investigating officials; or otherwise acted in untrustworthy ways.[4]

---

[1] Lefla (2012), *reprinted in* Oliphant and Wright (2013) (hereinafter "Leflar, *Medical Misadventure*").

The author benefited from extensive interviews in Tokyo during the summers of 2018 and 2019 with a wide variety of experts on Japanese health law and policy. The interviewees, in alphabetical order within professional categories, included Toshiharu Furukawa (*Sangiin giin*, House of Councillors); Jiro Ezaki, Toru Hama, Jun Izawa, Hiroko Otsubo, Ogusa Shibata, Kenichiro Watanabe (MHLW); Sosuke Kimura, Hiroaki Miyata, Shin Ushiro (MHLW-affiliated research directors); Ryoko Hatanaka, Norio Higuchi, Naoki Ikegami, Futoshi Iwata, Yasuhiro Otaki, Mark Ramseyer (academics); Katsutoshi Hiyama, Yasushi Kodama, Yasuaki Oyama, Junichi Yoshida (private sector experts); and other informants who preferred that their identities remain unrevealed.

[2] A foundational work explaining the structure of the Japanese health care system is Campbell and Ikegami (1998).

[3] OECD.Stat Extracts, http://stats.oecd.org/index.aspx~~,go to~~; input "Health: Health Expenditure and Financing" (last visited September 23, 2020).

[4] For English-language accounts of these events, see, e.g., Leflar and Iwata (2005) (recounting Aoto Hospital story); Leflar (2009a) (hereinafter Leflar, "*Unnatural Deaths*") (recounting Tokyo Women's Medical University Hospital story).

Intense media coverage of these events sparked public questioning of the medical profession's once-pristine reputation for selfless and competent service. This came at a time during which concerns about excessive and irrational drug prescriptions,[5] a scandal over HIV-contaminated blood supply,[6] and a national debate over brain death issues[7] were coalescing to shake public confidence in the medical profession's previously unquestioned beneficence. These developments engendered a growing movement promoting greater transparency in health care, reflecting public pressures for greater openness in other areas of society. Evidencing this trend toward transparency were court decisions based on principles of informed consent,[8] national and local laws enacting freedom of information rules[9] and measures providing patients access to their medical records.[10]

Until the turn of the century, quality control structures in Japanese health care were of doubtful efficacy.[11] Medical licensure and discipline authority, exercised by the *Idō Shingikai* (Medical Ethics Council) under the auspices of the Ministry of Health, Labor & Welfare, seldom inquired into failures of patient safety.[12] Hospitals' internal peer reviews were conducted with a soft touch, if at all; hospitals' claims of thorough, impartial internal reviews of adverse events were met with increasing public skepticism in light of the notorious cases mentioned above. The hierarchical system of medical education and job placement inhibited open questioning of practices taught by revered professors (who controlled career postings), even if such practices were outmoded or scientifically unproven.[13] The hospital accreditation system produced only marginal pressure for proper safety practices. Accreditation is not required for hospitals to qualify for reimbursement for examinations, procedures and medications,

---

[5] See, e.g., Fukushima (1989), Kondo (1988).

[6] See, e.g., Feldman (1999).

[7] See, e.g., Lock (2002), Leflar (1996).

[8] See, e.g., Judgment of Supreme Court February 29, 2000, 54 Minshū 582 (damages awarded Jehovah's Witness for violating her blood transfusion refusal, despite transfusion's life-saving effects), *translated in* Milhaupt et al. (2006).

[9] Gyōsei kikan no hoyū-suru jōhō no kōkai ni kansuru hōritsu (Law on Access to Information Held by Administrative Organs), Law No. 42 of 1999 (hereinafter Information Disclosure Law). This national law was preceded by various local freedom of information ordinances, a process well described in Boling (1998).

[10] Ministry of Health & Welfare (1998), Leflar (2007).

[11] See, e.g., Campbell & Ikegami, *supra* note 2, at 188–189 (criticizing quality assurance and peer review in Japanese hospitals).

[12] See Leflar, "*Unnatural Deaths*," *supra* note 4, at 20 & n. 87 (summarizing research of Dr. Etsuji Okamoto and the author's interview with health ministry staff concerning work of the Ministry's medical discipline committee, the Medical Ethics Council *(Idō Shingikai)*); Ryōko Hatanaka, Iryō jiko no gen'in kyūmei to sekinin tsuikyū o meguru iryō to shihō no tairitsu 16–17 (2018).

[13] See, e.g., Campbell & Ikegami, *supra* note 2; Hashimoto et al. (2011) ("Physicians' practice patterns tend to be idiosyncratically set by the chair and professor of the university clinical department").

and even today, only 26% of Japanese hospitals have received accreditation.[14] Japan's patchwork death inquiry system functioned effectively only in a few metropolitan jurisdictions and, even in those areas, the system seldom focused on patient safety problems and their amelioration.[15] Civil litigation over medical injuries cast a far lighter shadow over medical practice than in the United States.

At the beginning of the twenty-first century, weaknesses in professional self-regulation, health ministry oversight, the death inquest system and civil litigation left Japanese medicine to function within an accountability vacuum.[16] Democratic societies demand professional accountability. *Faute de mieux*, Japan's prosecutors stepped in to attempt to fill the accountability gap.

2 Prosecutions and Their Consequences

A. Prosecutions in Medical Cases

Over the last twenty years, prosecutions of medical personnel have been brought under four statutory grounds. The first, and most frequently employed, is for violation of Article 211 of the Criminal Code, which prohibits "*negligence in the pursuit of social activities*" causing death or injury.[17] The second is for violation of the Criminal Code's Articles 156 and 160, forbidding the creation of, with the purpose to use, false official documents or medical records.[18] The third is the concealment or destruction of evidence, a violation of Article 104.[19]

The fourth statutory basis for prosecution has become the most controversial: Article 21 of the Medical Practitioners' Law. Article 21 requires physicians to notify police, in timely fashion, of "*unnatural deaths*" (*ijōshi)*—a phrase undefined in the law. Physicians once assumed that this requirement applied only to such areas as suicides, violent deaths and infectious diseases threatening public health. In 2000 the CEO of Tokyo's Hirō Hospital submitted a falsified death certificate for a patient, killed by an accidental toxic injection, and delayed reporting the death to police. Prosecutors—fully aware of intense public concern over medical errors—charged

---

[14] Of Japan's 8273 hospitals, 2142 were accredited as of September 2020. Japan Council for Quality Health Care, Byōin kinō hyōka kekka no jōhō teikyō (Information on Results of Hospital Evaluations), *available at* http://www.report.jcqhc.or.jp (last visited September 24, 2020).

[15] See Leflar, "*Unnatural Deaths*," *supra* note 4, at 25–30.

[16] This thesis is more fully developed in Leflar, "*Unnatural Deaths*," ~~supra note 4,~~ and Leflar & Iwata, *supra* note 4.

[17] Keihō (Criminal Code), art. 211.

[18] Keihō (Criminal Code), arts. 156 (Kyogi kō-bunsho sakuseitō) & 160. The CEO of Tokyo's Hirō Hospital was convicted on these grounds.

[19] Keihō (Criminal Code), art. 104 (Shōko inmetsu-tō). See, e.g., Leflar, "*Unnatural Deaths*," *supra* note 4, at 6. Plaintiffs' attorneys charge that tampering with patient charts was a frequent practice, at least in the past. See, e.g., Ishikawa (2006); see also Mark Ramseyer (2010) (hereinafter Ramseyer, *Malpractice Claims*) (citing evidence that chart alteration "commonly happens").

the CEO with violating Article 21. The Supreme Court, affirming his conviction in 2004, confirmed that the "*unnatural death*" notification requirement may encompass deaths causally related to medical mismanagement.[20]

The Hirō Hospital CEO's arrest and conviction threw hospital administrators onto the horns of a dilemma. If a patient dies following less-than-optimal care, should the hospital routinely notify police, inviting a criminal investigation disruptive of hospital routine and patient care? Or should the hospital keep quiet and risk public obloquy for a cover-up and possible criminal prosecution? Article 21's "*unnatural death*" notification requirement, and the concomitant (if variable and sporadic) police oversight of medical practice, generated intense controversy.[21]

The criminal justice system's engagement in monitoring medical mistakes has been strongly attacked. Critics charge that police lack medical expertise, that criminal investigations in the hospital disrupt patient care, that criminal sanctions are disproportionately punitive in light of the mere inadvertence typical of lapses in care, and that criminal law tends to focus on individual blame, rather than addressing more significant problems of system failure.[22] These criticisms have substantial merit.

Criminal law's prominent role in monitoring medical quality in the early years of this century is understandable, for several reasons. The public expects that the criminal justice system's protective reach does not stop at the hospital doors. Police and prosecutors are committed to their professional duty to enforce the criminal codes, applicable by their terms to medical personnel as to everyone else. A democratic society requires public accountability of every institution, including the medical profession, for harms inflicted on the population. This accountability obligation was inadequately fulfilled in Japanese medicine by professional self-regulation, administrative oversight, the death inquest system and civil litigation.

B. Responses by the Health Ministry and the Medical Profession

The Ministry of Health, Labor & Welfare (MHLW) had paid scant attention to patient safety issues throughout the twentieth century. Reacting to highly publicized cases of medical errors as the new century began, the MHLW created a small patient safety office, drafted guidance manuals for hospitals to designate risk management staff,

[20] Judgment of Supreme Court April 13, 2004, 58(4) Keishū 247. One observer affiliated with the Japan Medical Association contended that "violation of Article 21 serves only as a hook for the (criminal) investigation of professional negligence resulting in death." Sawa (2008).

[21] One skirmish in this controversy involved an assertion by antiregulatory critics such as attorney Yasunari Inoue, seeking to limit the reach of the Supreme Court's 2004 Hirō Hospital decision, that the Article 21 requirement to report "unnatural deaths" should be limited to fatalities in which external damage is observed on the corpse, as in suicides, traffic accidents, and situations like the Hirō Hospital case. The health ministry rejected this view, noting that among other reasons, infectious disease deaths lacking external damage to the corpse had always been treated as requiring reports under Article 21. Ministry of Health, Labor & Welfare (MHLW), Ishi ni yoru ijōshitai no todokede no tettei ni tsuite (Thorough Reporting by Physicians of Unnatural Deaths), Medical Policy Notification 0208 No. 3 (February 8, 2019).

[22] See, e.g., Higuchi (2008), Leflar, "*Unnatural Deaths,*" *supra* note 4, at 14 & n. 53 (summarizing criticisms).

set up adverse event tracking systems and review committees,[23] established local "*medical safety support centers*" to handle patients' complaints and questions,[24] required a class of large specialized hospitals to make reports to a quasi-public entity of accidents causing harm,[25] and launched a study of the incidence of adverse events in Japanese hospitals. In this study, reviewers employing criteria based on a previous Canadian study[26] found an adverse event rate of 6.0% and concluded that of those adverse events, about 23% were preventable.[27]

Four leading medical societies, troubled by the prospect of police investigations and possible criminal liability and recognizing social pressures for transparency, proposed to the MHLW a new system, independent of the criminal process, to review patient deaths possibly connected to medical management, inform the parties of facts found and suggest preventive measures. The MHLW, understaffed and eager to demonstrate progress in addressing patient safety issues, agreed to fund a "*Model Project for the Investigation and Analysis of Medical Practice-Associated Deaths.*" The Model Project, aimed at encouraging impartial, high-quality peer reviews of possibly iatrogenic hospital deaths by experts unaffiliated with the hospital in question. Findings were to be reported to both the family and the hospital; case summaries were to be made public, with names of the patient, medical staff, relevant hospital and location redacted; and suggestions for prevention of recurrences were to be offered. The Ministry of Justice and the National Police Agency gave up none of their jurisdiction over medical crime but acquiesced in the Model Project's operation, for the most part holding back from criminal investigations and prosecutions in the regions in which the project operated.[28]

Results from the Model Project were mixed. Case uptake failed to meet expectations. Cooperation from hospitals in participating regions was uneven. Fewer than 100 cases were submitted for review during the project's initial five-year period, and despite the low numbers, delays in issuing case findings were common.[29] The quality

---

[23] Iryō jiko jōhō shūshū-tō jigyō (Medical Accident Information Collection Project), http://www.mhlw.go.jp/topics/bukyoku/isei/i-anzen/jiko/index.html (last visited September 25, 2020); MHLW (2000).

[24] The medical safety support centers (*iryō anzen shien sentā*) received statutory authorization in a 2006 amendment to the Medical Services Law, Iryō Hō art. 6(11).

[25] This entity is the Japan Council for Quality in Health Care (*Nihon iryō kinō hyōka kikō*). For an account of these administrative developments, see Leflar & Iwata, *supra* note 4, at 208–210.

[26] Ross Baker et al. (2004).

[27] Sakai (2006); see also Ikeda (2006) (summarizing study results). Estimates of annual preventable iatrogenic deaths were not given. The study was based on randomly selected patient charts from 18 major hospitals that volunteered to participate. Since hospitals experiencing serious quality difficulties were likely underrepresented in the study, the results cannot be deemed representative of Japanese hospitals as a whole.

[28] For a detailed overview of the Model Project, see Leflar, "*Unnatural Deaths*,"*supra* note 4, at 31–39.

[29] Reasons for the low case uptake included physicians' unfamiliarity with the case review process, rules that the process be invoked by hospitals rather than families, limitation of the Model Project to death cases (excluding nonfatal injuries), and a shortage of pathologists to perform the needed autopsies. See Leflar, "*Unnatural Deaths*,"*supra* note 4, at 36–39; Nakajima et al. (2009).

of case reviews was likely superior to most internal hospital reviews conducted prior to the project's inception, and the project's method, bringing together physicians, nurses, attorneys, academics and health bureaucrats working toward common goals, probably improved interdisciplinary cooperation in a society still hierarchically structured, each field typically in silo-like separation from the others.

Data collection and analysis for the health ministry's other adverse event reporting systems are undertaken by the Japan Council for Quality Health Care (JCQHC), a quasi-public entity that also performs hospital accreditations.[30] The JCQHC's information dissemination efforts have aided the objective of improving health care quality by encouraging medical facilities' experience-based learning. The JCQHC's quality improvement recommendations have provoked adverse feedback from some physicians used to different styles of practice.[31] Another criticism, from the transparency perspective, is that, despite the public's enormous appetite for medical information, neither the health ministry nor the JCQHC has made available much hospital-specific health outcomes information.[32]

C. The Medical Profession Strikes Back

National news broadcasts pictured police leading a handcuffed Dr. Katsuhiko Katō out of Ohno Hospital, in rural Fukushima prefecture, in 2006. Katō, an obstetrician at the hospital, had lost a patient during a particularly difficult childbirth in 2004. Many medical professionals found Dr. Katō's humiliating arrest outrageous. Petitions and remonstrances inundated the National Police Agency from medical organizations nationwide. The furor surrounding Dr. Katō's arrest and prosecution launched a physician-led movement employing the slogan "*iryō hōkai*"—"*the collapsing health care system.*"[33]

The "*iryō hōkai*" movement had a considerable impact on public opinion. The movement offered sympathetic portrayals of the plight of overworked, underappreciated physicians harassed by arrogant police and overreaching prosecutors. The movement's proponents also called attention to the shortage of physicians willing to

---

[30] For example, JCQHC operates the Medical Accident Information Collection Project, *supra* note 23.

[31] Analysis by Prof. Shigeto Yonemura, University of Tokyo Faculty of Law (August 2, 2020) (on file with author).

[32] The health ministry does require hospitals to report the number of operations they conduct annually for various specified procedures. Media outlets obtain this information and compile rankings of hospitals by procedure volume. See, e.g., Shujutsu-sū de wakaru ii byōin (Telling Good Hospitals from the Number of Operations) (Shūkan Asahi ed., 2010). For an analysis based in part on these reports, See Mark Ramseyer (2009) (concluding that price controls diminish the availability of sophisticated care, costing lives).

[33] The slogan was apparently coined by physician Hideki Komatsu. See Komatsu (2006). For an account of the causes of morale problems among Japanese physicians and structural difficulties within Japanese medicine, See Hideo Yasunaga, *The Catastrophic Collapse of Morale among Hospital Physicians in Japan*, 2008 Risk Mgmt. & Health Care Policy 1, *available at* http://www.dovepress.com/getfile.php?fileID=3935 (last visited September 30, 2020).

attend childbirths, especially in rural areas, and to repeated instances of hospital emergency rooms turning away ambulances for fear of liability exposure.[34] The critics attributed these problems, in large part, to abuses of the criminal justice system.[35] Other factors have contributed to Japan's shortages in obstetrical care, such as the adoption of a residency matching system undercutting traditional hierarchical job placement practices, that once ensured a supply of young physicians to smaller hospitals. The Ohno Hospital prosecution became an effective target for critics of the criminal justice system's medical oversight role. One effect of the "*iryō hōkai*" movement, sparked by Dr. Katō's arrest and prosecution, was to arouse sympathy for the medical profession and concomitantly to diminish media and public attention to concerns over medical error.

The "*iryō hōkai*" movement's efforts found success, not only in the court of public opinion, but also in the courts of law. Acquittals in criminal trials are extremely rare in Japan; more than 99% of criminal trials result in convictions.[36] In four successive cases, including Dr. Katō's prosecution, medical personnel were acquitted of all charges and, in the two cases that prosecutors appealed,[37] the acquittals were affirmed.[38] This series of acquittals marked a watershed point in Japanese medical jurisprudence. Police and prosecutors subsequently have been far more cautious in targeting health care personnel.[39]

D. The Politics of Reform: The 2014 Medical Accident Review Law and Its Implementation

Dissatisfaction with police involvement in medical investigations, together with recognition that more transparency and more attentive review of medical injury cases were needed, sparked efforts both by medical societies and by patients' organizations to push reform legislation through the Diet. A first attempt in 2008 failed, due in part to attacks by a well-organized chorus of regulatory critics outside the mainstream medical societies.[40] A second attempt succeeded in 2014, when the Diet enacted a law aimed at setting up a nationwide medical accident review system.

[34] See Komatsu, *supra* note 33.

[35] An analogy might be drawn to the medical "tort reform" movement in the United States.

[36] See Mark Ramseyer and Nakazato (1999) (overall conviction rate in 1994 of 99.9%).

[37] Japanese appellate procedure permits prosecutors to appeal not-guilty judgments on grounds of both fact and law without violating the double jeopardy principle. See id. at 175.

[38] Judgment of Fukushima Dist. Ct. August 20, 2008, 16 Iryō Kaisetsu Hanrei 20 (Ohno Hospital case); Judgment of Tokyo High Ct. March 27, 2009, *aff'g* Judgment of Tokyo Dist. Ct. August 27, 2007, 1282 Hanrei Taimuzu 233 (Tokyo Women's Medical U. Hospital heart surgery case); Judgment of Nagoya Dist. Ct. February 27, 2007, 1296 Hanrei Taimuzu 308 (obstetrics case); Judgment of Tokyo High Ct. November 20, 2008, 1304 Hanrei Taimuzu 304, *aff'g* Judgment of Tokyo Dist. Ct. March 28, 2006 (Kyorin U. *waribashi* (chopstick) case).

[39] The number of medical cases police sent to prosecutors peaked in 2006, the year of the Ohno Hospital arrest and subsequent protests, and has since diminished. Police investigations of medical crimes have not entirely ceased, however.

[40] The failure of the 2008 reform proposal is discussed in Leflar, "*Medical Misadventure*," *supra* note 1.

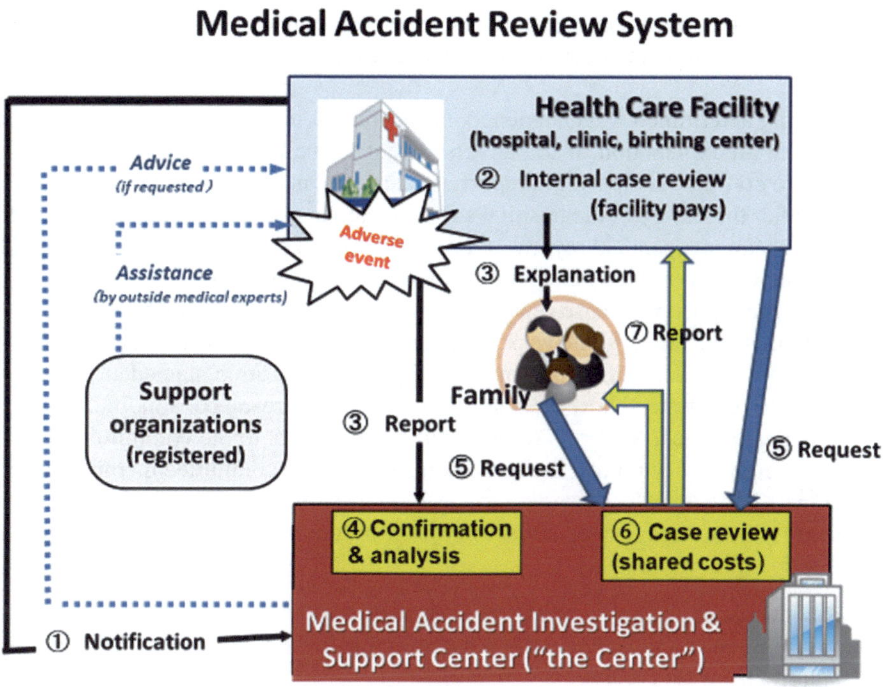

Fig. 1 The medical review system contemplated by the 2014 law

The 2014 law specifically provided:

> When a "*medical accident*" (*iryō jiko*) occurs, the administrators of hospitals, clinics, and birthing centers (hereinafter "*hospital &c*") shall without delay report the time, place and conditions and other items required by ministerial ordinance under article 6(15)(1) to the Medical Accident Investigation & Support Center (*Iryō jiko chōsa shien sentā*).
>
> "*Medical accident*" (*iryō jiko*) means a death or miscarriage caused, or suspected to have been caused, by care provided by employees of the hospital &c, the death or miscarriage being <u>unforeseen</u> (*yoki shinakatta*) by the hospital administration, as defined by (MHLW) regulation.[41]

Serious injuries not resulting in death or miscarriage, even if the result of malpractice, are not considered to be reportable "*medical accidents*" under this law.

The new system's design might best be explained through the accompanying graphic (Fig. 1).

When an "*medical accident*" (as defined) occurs at a health care facility, ① the health care facility is to send a notification to a new entity created by the statute—the Medical Accident Investigation & Support Center (commonly referred to as "the Center"). ② Then the health care facility—suppose it is a hospital—is to conduct an internal case review, at the hospital's own expense. In conducting this review, the

---

[41] Law No. 205 of 2014, amending Iryō Hō (Medical Services Law) Article 6(10) (emphasis added).

hospital may seek assistance of outside experts associated with registered support organizations, such as medical specialty societies, and may also seek advice from the Center.

③ Having determined what happened, the hospital is to send a report to the Center and provide an explanation of the adverse event to the patient and family. ④ The Center is to confirm receipt of the report and perform an analysis of its content.

⑤ If either the family or the hospital submits a request to the Center, ⑥ the Center is to perform an independent review of the case. Costs of that review are to be shared between the Center and the person or entity requesting the review. ⑦ The Center is to provide the report of its case review to both the family and the hospital.

Within this legislative framework of action are many ambiguities requiring interpretation and guidance. The health ministry, in standard fashion, named an advisory committee to recommend how the ambiguities should be resolved, appointing a mix of academics, medical leaders, lawyers, and other experts to the committee, representing a range of viewpoints. Disagreements among the committee members were heated.[42]

Among the most controversial issues raised by the new law's ambiguities were these:

1. Reviewable/reportable events are limited by the law to deaths that are "*unforeseen*" (*yoki shinakatta*). What does that mean? Who makes the determination? By what process?
2. Must the case review be conducted with outside expert assistance or may the review be purely internal?
3. What information about the clinical course should be disclosed to the family of the deceased patient? Should the disclosure be in writing if the family requests?
4. Should the case review focus not only on what caused this patient's death but also on how such accidents could be avoided in the future (*saihatsu bōshi*)?
5. What facts in the hospital's report to the Center should be made public? Names of hospitals? Names of health care personnel? Details of the deceased patient's clinical course?

Opposition to a strong, enforceable accident review system was led by adherents of *Iryō Hōjin Kyōkai* (commonly referred to as *Ihōkyō*), an association of small and medium-sized physician-owned hospitals. *Ihōkyō* adherents advanced arguments such as these:

- Hospital administrators, who are most familiar with the relevant events, should have discretion about what events are reportable.
- It is unfair for local hospitals to be judged by outside specialists from prestigious institutions, who do not understand local circumstances.
- Giving written reports to patients would just provide ammunition for their lawyers, and would preclude cooperation from medical personnel.

---

[42] The author attended several of the advisory committee meetings as an observer.

- Putting accident-recurrence prevention measures into the reports might lead to findings of negligence through hindsight bias, even where providers' conduct met the standard of care.

Bowing to pressure from *Ihōkyō* partisans and their allies in the Diet, the health ministry issued a ministerial ordinance (*shōrei*) creating three safe-harbor exceptions to the statutory duty to report:

A death or miscarriage is *"unforeseen"* (*yoki shinakatta*) if the administrator determines that none of the following apply:

1. The administrator determines that before the provision of care, health care personnel had explained to the patient (or family) that such death or miscarriage was foreseen.
2. The administrator determines that before the provision of care, health care personnel had written in the medical record or other writing that such death or miscarriage was foreseen.
3. The administrator determines from opinions expressed at a hearing or safety committee meeting convened for this purpose that before the provision of care, such death or miscarriage was foreseen by the health care personnel providing the care.[43]

The effect of these three safe-harbor exceptions has been essentially to leave the decision about whether to report an in-hospital death or miscarriage to the Center to the discretion of hospital administrators. According to officials of the health ministry and other key observers, the health ministry decided on this "*soft*" strategy for implementation of the new law in order to persuade skeptical physicians and hospitals to participate in the information reporting system. Improving transparency to the public has not been a major goal of the law's implementation.[44]

How well has the system been working? The health ministry's latest report presented these totals for the first five years of the system's operation, from October 2015 through September 2020:

- Total reported hospital death cases: 1847, or 369 per year. (This works out to 3.1 reported deaths annually per million population.)
- 135 cases were referred to the Center for review during the five-year period. Of these, the Center has issued reports on just 46.[45]

Hospital administrators are employing their discretion to classify the great majority of hospital deaths as "*foreseeable*" and not subject to the law's review and reporting requirements. As a basis for estimating the incidence of medical error in Japanese, health care facilities, the medical accident review system implemented by MHLW under the 2014 law is worth little. As a launching pad for diffusion of

---

[43] MHLW Shōrei (Ministerial Ordinance) No. 100 (May 8, 2015) (emphasis added).

[44] Tokyo interviews, summers 2018–2019, *supra* note 1. Not all interviewees discussed these topics.

[45] MHLW press release, Iryō jiko chōsa seido no genkyō hōkoku (9-gatsu) (Medical Accident Investigation System Report (September 2020)), https://www.medsafe.or.jp/uploads/uploads/files/houdoushiryo20201006.pdf (October 6, 2020) (last visited October 31, 2020).

information about preventing iatrogenic harm, the system has not had much effect. Whether the system has had positive indirect effects, perhaps through hospitals' presumably more frequent internal reviews of adverse events, remains to be seen.

3 Civil Liability

Although the specter of criminal liability once haunted many in the medical professions and animated considerable political controversy, the prospect of civil liability is a far more frequent concern. The number of civil claims, filed in court, far surpasses the number of prosecutions and the much greater number of out-of-court claims vastly outnumbers the number of criminal investigations.

The quantity of civil claims, filed in court, which rose steadily from the 1970s to the turn of the century, increased rapidly in the years following the notorious cases of 1999, peaked in 2004, declined somewhat for a few years and, in the last decade, resumed its steady upward trend (Fig. 2).

This section of the chapter first sets out the essential doctrinal features of the substantive civil law of compensation for medical injury. This is followed by a discussion of salient aspects of procedural law and practice: the establishment of health care divisions of trial courts in some metropolitan areas, case settlement practices,

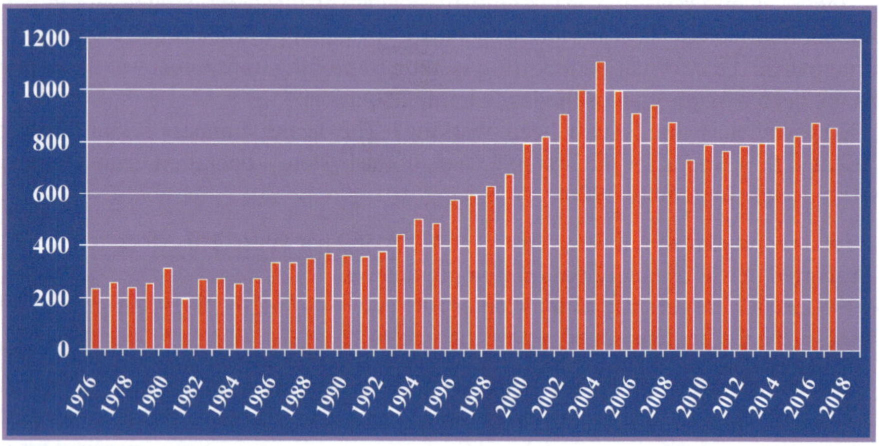

Fig. 2 Medical malpractice cases filed in Japanese district courts, 1976–2018[46]

---

[46] Supreme Court of Japan, Iji kankei soshō jiken tōkei (table 1): Shori jōkyō oyobi heikin shinri kikan (Disposition of Medically Related Litigation and Mean Duration of Proceedings), https://www.courts.go.jp/saikosai/vc-files/saikosai/file1/1905201heikinshinri.pdf (1999–2018 statistics) (last visited September 29, 2020). Pre-1999 statistics are available from the Administrative Office of the Supreme Court.

estimates of the actual total number of malpractice claims including those never filed in court, court filing fees, and practices concerning plaintiffs' attorneys' fees. The chapter concludes with a summary of Japan's system for no-fault compensation of obstetrical injuries.

A. The Substantive Law of Medical Malpractice

1. Theories of Recovery

Either the Civil Code provision governing tort[47] or the provision governing contract[48] can constitute the basis for a civil malpractice claim and both grounds are commonly employed by plaintiffs' attorneys. In contract cases, the plaintiff must prove a breach of the medical provider's obligation, which is equivalent to proving a breach of the applicable standard of care in tort. Since the standards applied under both code provisions are essentially the same, it makes little practical difference which theory is employed in a particular case. Under both code provisions, the plaintiff must prove that the breach caused ascertainable damages, with a few exceptions noted below.

2. Standard of Care

The Supreme Court, in 1982, stated that the legal standard of care to which physicians are held is "*the standard prevailing in clinical medical practice at the time of treatment*."[49] In subsequent cases, the Court recognized that physician custom does not always define the legal standard of care. In a 1996 decision, the Court concluded that when a defendant physician, following general practitioners' common practice of ignoring an anesthetic drug's labeled directions for use, failed to monitor the patient's blood pressure in timely fashion, the physician's conduct breached the legal standard despite his adherence to the custom of average medical practitioners.[50]

Large, sophisticated hospitals and their physicians must perform to a higher standard of care in some respects than physicians in small clinics lacking equivalent resources. In a celebrated 1995 case, involving a premature infant's blindness from retinal injury, the Supreme Court held that in determining the applicable standard of care, the court "*must consider various circumstances such as the nature of the*

---

[47] Civil Code art. 709, Damages in Torts: "A person who has intentionally or negligently infringed any right of others, or legally protected interest of others, shall be liable to compensate any damages resulting in consequence." http://www.japaneselawtranslation.go.jp/law (Ministry of Justice unofficial compilation).

[48] Civil Code art. 415, Damages Due to Default: "If an obligor fails to perform the purpose of its obligation, the obligee shall be entitled to demand damages arising from such failure. The same shall apply in cases it has become impossible to perform due to reasons attributable to the obligor." *Id*.

[49] Judgment of Supreme Court March 30, 1982, 1039 Hanrei Jihō 66, 106.

[50] Judgment of Supreme Court Jan. 23, 1996, 50 Minshū 1, 1571 Hanrei Jihō 57 (perukamin-S case).

(defendant) facility and the distinctive characteristics of the region's medical environment."[51] The standard of care required of a medical facility and its personnel depends on the facility's size and function.[52] The standard of knowledge (*chiken*) expected of physicians, depends on their specialty; non-specialists in a field are not held to the same standard as specialists.[53] If a physician or facility is unable to treat a patient's particular condition, whether due to lack of knowledge, skill or resources, the care provider has a legal duty to transfer the patient to a facility that offers the requisite level of services.[54]

3. Standard of Proof

To establish both breach of duty and causation, plaintiffs must offer evidence proving these elements to "*a high degree of probability*" (*kōdo no gaizensei*).[55] The phrase suggests a level of confidence somewhat higher than the "*preponderance of the evidence*" standard employed in civil cases in common law jurisdictions.[56] In this field of law in which subtle factual matters can be decisive, exact prescriptions of decision criteria are seldom to be found. Regarding causation, the Supreme Court has stated that something less than a scientific standard of certainty will suffice.[57]

---

[51] Judgment of Supreme Court June 9, 1995, 1537 Hanrei Jihō 3, 883 Hanrei Taimuzu 92 (infant retrolental fibroplagia case).

[52] See, e.g., Suzuki et al. (2009) (commentary on infant retrolental fibroplagia case). This approach is analogous to the resource-based locality rule applied in some U.S. jurisdictions. See, e.g., Hall v. Hilbun, 466 So.2d 856 (Miss. 1985).

[53] The Court recognized, however, that the time required for the diffusion of medical knowledge from one field to another is "relatively short." Infant retrolental fibroplagia case, *supra*, 1537 Hanrei Jihō at 7–8, 883 Hanrei Taimuzu at 97.

[54] Iryō Hō (Medical Services Law), Law No. 205 of 1948 as amended, art. 1, para. 4 no. 3; Judgment of Supreme Court November 11, 2003, 57 Minshū 1466, 1845 Hanrei Jihō 63 (acute encephalopathy case); Suzuki et al., *supra* note 52, at 42–43.

[55] Judgment of Supreme Court October 24, 1975, Minshū 1417, 792 Hanrei Jihō 3 (lumbar procedure case, addressing proof of causation). The standard is of judicial rather than statutory origin.

The "high degree of probability" standard is expressed clearly by courts with regard to causation issues, but less clearly with regard to proof of breach of the duty of care. Judges, lawyers, and academics have suggested to the author that in practice, judges actually decide breach-of-duty issues on a basis similar to a preponderance standard, but write their opinions as though the evidence on breach of duty was clearly convincing.

[56] See Kojima (1998) ("[M]ere proof by a preponderance of the evidence is not enough").

Just what "a high degree of probability" means is a matter of debate. Kevin Clermont, while recognizing the existence of controversy, has argued that the standard of proof in Japanese civil cases "requires that facts be proven to a high probability *similar to beyond a reasonable doubt*." Clermont (2004) (emphasis added). He linked the Japanese standard to the *intime conviction* standard employed in French civil law. This writer's interviews with Japanese judges indicate, however, that Clermont's characterization of the Japanese proof standard as "similar to beyond a reasonable doubt" is too stringent.

[57] See Judgment of Supreme Court October 24, 1975, 29 Minshū 1417 (lumbar injection case). Reversing the Tokyo High Court's finding of no proof of causation, the Supreme Court stated:

> Proof of causation is to be established not by the standard of natural science admitting of no doubt, but rather by an overall examination of the totality of evidence informed by

In the author's interviews, with both senior and younger trial judges from several courts, the judges did not express concern about the standard but rather stressed that flexible case-by-case determinations are required.

The ambiguity of the standard of proof also relates to institutional concern with preserving the court system's legitimacy, and to trial judges' personal desire for "cover" when their judgments are reviewed on appeal. Just as American judges, in sending factually controverted cases to juries, may take comfort in the lenient standard of appellate review of juries' factual findings, so Japanese trial judges may rest easier, due to the deference that appellate courts usually allow the trial judges' factual determinations (sometimes written, perhaps, with the same enhanced certainty of an umpire's emphatic call of a close play at the plate) of whether plaintiffs proved their cases to a "*high degree of probability*."[58]

The potential rigor of the "*high degree of probability*" standard is also mitigated in three other ways. A *res ipsa*-like rebuttable presumption of negligence is applied where the facts warrant it.[59] The "loss of chance" doctrine may justify partial compensation in cases where negligence is proven but its causal consequences are difficult to ascertain.[60] Judges commonly pressure attorneys to settle for partial compensation cases in which negligence is established but proof of causation is equivocal.[61]

> common experience (*keikensoku ni terashite*). Where specific facts can be shown to have brought about specific results with a high degree of probability (*kōdo no gaizensei*), such that ordinary people could hold a doubtless assurance of the fact of the (causal) relationship, that constitutes necessary and sufficient proof of causation.

Id. at 1419–1420. The logically muddled nature of this pronouncement is aptly discussed in Shigeto Yonemura, *Runbāru shikō-go no nō-shukketsu to inga kankei* (*Causation and Cerebral Hemorrhage Following Lumbar Procedure*), 183 Juristo 154 (2006) (case commentary).

58 Kevin Clermont has advanced a similar point. See Clermont (2009). Appellate review of lower courts' factual findings, however, is somewhat more rigorous in Japan than in the United States. Japanese appeals courts accept additional evidence on appeal, which may supplement or contradict the trial court's fact findings. See Minsohō (Code of Civil Procedure), art. 296–297; Ramseyer & Nakazato, *supra* note 36, at 145.

59 See, e.g., Suzuki et al., *supra* note 52, at 55, 193–194 (explaining *ichiō no suitei* (rebuttable presumption)); Shintarō Katō, *Iryō kago soshō (I)* (*Medical Malpractice Litigation (I)*), *in* Minji Hō III (Civil Law III) 265, 271–273 (Kaoru Kamata et al. eds., 2005) (same); *cf.* Judgment of Supreme Court Jan. 23, 1996, 50 Minshū 1, 1571 Hanrei Jihō 57 (perukamin-S case) (ignoring drug label indications, absent rational reasons, is basis for negligence finding). See also Judgment of Tokyo Dist. Ct. June 7, 1967, 485 Hanrei Jihō 21, 25–26, *excerpted in* Ramseyer & Nakazato, *supra* note 36, at 67 (early rebuttable presumption case).

60 See *infra* notes 62–65 and accompanying text.

61 Interview with Wataru Murata, C.J. and Nozomu Hirano, J., Tokyo District Ct., 34th Div., in Tokyo (August 10, 2010) (hereinafter Tokyo Judges 2010 Interview); interview with noted plaintiffs' attorney Toshihiro Suzuki and associates, in Tokyo (August 2, 2010). See also Shunko Muto, *Concerning Trial Leadership in Civil Litigation: Focusing on the Judge's Inquiry and Compromise*, 12 Law in Japan 23, 28 (1979), *reprinted in* Milhaupt, Ramseyer & West, *supra* note 8, at 185, 189–190 (2006) (judge's similar advice to trainee judges in 1979).

An augury that Japanese jurisprudence would adopt a less rigorous stance regarding proof burdens was the 2000 Supreme Court decision recognizing a loss-of-chance remedy for negligent failure to diagnose and treat a malady for which timely diagnosis and treatment would have afforded the patient a "*considerable possibility*" (*sōtō no kanōsei*), but not a "*high degree of probability*" (*kōdo no gaizensei*), of survival.[62] Explaining that the preservation of life is a "*fundamental value*" worthy of legal protection, the Court ruled that the value's impairment by acts of medical negligence required a legal remedy.[63] The Court later expanded the loss-of-chance doctrine to encompass cases in which medical negligence was followed not by death, but rather by serious impairment, but the level of impairment the patient would have suffered, absent negligence, was not proven to a high degree of probability.[64] Later cases in the lower courts adopted a principle of proportionate liability, scaling damages in rough accordance with the percentage possibility of survival or full recovery had the defendant acted with due care.[65]

4. Informed Consent and Related Actions

In addition to their duty to provide non-negligent medical care, physicians also have a duty to obtain from patients what has come to be called (for lack of any equivalent expression in standard Japanese) *infōmudo konsento.* Adapting Western concepts of patient autonomy to established customary practices and departing from previous cases granting great deference to medical custom, Japanese courts have come to recognize that, in some circumstances, traditional principles of medical ethics, impelling physicians to preserve human life at any cost, should give way to patients' sometimes contrary personal values.[66] A leading Supreme Court case, recognizing this principle, affirmed a damage award to a Jehovah's Witness who was given a blood transfusion, despite her previously expressed refusal. Although the procedure was medically successful—she survived her cancer far longer than expected—the Supreme Court nevertheless affirmed a solatium (*isharyō*) award for "*emotional suffering*" of the nominal sum of ¥500,000 (US $5,000).[67] This decision recognized—contrary to US informed consent precedents requiring "decision

[62] Judgment of Supreme Court September 22, 2000, 54 Minshū 2574, 1728 Hanrei Jihō 31 (myocardial infarction case).

[63] *Id.* The plaintiff was awarded a solatium (*isharyō*) of ¥2 million (US $18,000).

[64] Judgment of Supreme Court November 11, 2003, 57 Minshū 1466, 1845 Hanrei Jihō 63 (acute encephalopathy and failure-to-transfer case).

[65] Damages may be awarded even if the patient's chance of survival or full recovery was <50%. Tokyo Judges 2010 Interview, *supra* note 61; interview with Yoshio Katō, noted plaintiff's attorney, in Nagoya (July 26, 2010).

These developments are thoroughly discussed in Hatanaka, *supra* note 12, at 118–125.

[66] Detailed examinations of the development of informed consent theory and practice in Japanese medicine can be found in Leflar, *Informed Consent*, *supra* note 7, and Leflar, *Renaissance*, *supra* note 10.

[67] Jehovah's Witness case, *supra* note 8. Excerpts of both the High Court and Supreme Court opinions are translated into English in Milhaupt, Ramseyer & West, *supra* note 8, at 347–356.

causation"[68]—that a dignitary interest apart from physical harm is worthy of legal protection in informed consent cases.

Parallel to physicians' duty to obtain the patient's informed consent before treatment is the physician's obligation to explain accurately the results of treatment, including adverse results. This duty to explain treatment outcomes (*setsumei gimu*) arises from the patient-physician contractual relationship. The principle has been applied in cases in which courts have awarded solatium damages when patients and families were not given honest explanations of adverse outcomes.[69]

5. Damages

Aside from solatium awards for intangible and dignitary injury, damages in Japanese medical malpractice cases are standardized in accordance with injury severity levels as defined in the traffic accident compensation system.[70] Once negligence and causation are determined, the plaintiff is entitled to an award within these rather definite limits. Punitive damages are not available.[71]

Awards for injury, in Japanese medical malpractice cases, do not seem to differ radically in amount from awards in other advanced nations and may exceed them.[72] Mark Ramseyer, drawing on a database of actions filed in 2004, observed that in wrongful death cases, median and mean damage awards were respectively ¥37.5 and

---

[68] The term "decision causation," indicating the requirement that a plaintiff prove that proper risk disclosure would have led the plaintiff to adopt a different treatment course causing less or no physical harm, was coined in Meisel and Kabnick (1980) and popularized in Twerski and Cohen (1989).

[69] For example, in an action for brain damage suffered by a child from heart stoppage due to a medication error and subsequent inadequate resuscitation efforts, the court found that the hospital had engaged in a cover-up of the facts. In addition to awarding damages and costs of ¥243 million (US $2.2 million) plus interest on the malpractice counts, the court awarded ¥1 million (US $9,000) for the contract breach. Judgment of Kyoto Dist. Ct. July 12, 2005, 1907 Hanrei Jihō 112, 124–125. See also, e.g., Judgment of Tokyo High Ct. September 30, 2004, 1880 Hanrei Jihō 72; Suzuki et al., *supra* note 52, at 66.

[70] Oshida et al. (2002). Pain-and-suffering damages in death cases include awards to surviving family members for their grief, and may be adjusted up or down for unusual circumstances. *Id.* Damage amounts for each level of injury severity are set out in publications available not only to judges, lawyers, and liability insurers, but also to the general public. See, e.g., Minji kōtsū jiko soshō songai baishōgaku santei kijun (Computation Standards for Damages in Civil Traffic Accident Litigation) (Japan Federation of Bar Ass'ns ed., 2018) (generally known as "*Akaihon*" ("the Red Book")). For a description of damage calculations using the Red Book, See Feldman (2009c), *originally published as* Feldman (2009a).

Damages of a given level of severity in medical malpractice cases may somewhat exceed those in auto accident cases, taking into account the additional difficulty of proving malpractice liability.

[71] Ramseyer & Nakazato, *supra* note 36, at 89 n. 53.

[72] See Leflar & Iwata, *supra* note 4, at 200 & n. 40 (observing similar scale of damages in Japanese and US wrongful death cases). A caveat: in performing international comparisons over time of malpractice awards (or anything else), one must be alert to year-to-year fluctuations in foreign exchange rates, which can be dramatic.

¥40.6 million (roughly US $350,000 at then-current exchange rates)[73]—recoveries higher in real terms than those observed, on average, during that era in the high-award US jurisdiction of Florida.[74]

Most malpractice claims are not tried to judgment. Most are settled (either extra-judicially or during the litigation process) or dropped.[75] Settlement negotiations depend on assessments, by plaintiff and defense counsel, of the strength of plaintiff's proof of three elements: negligence, causation, and damages. One result of Japan's standardized damages schedule is that negotiations become relatively predictable in respect of the damages element. Not only judges, lawyers, and liability insurers, but also hospital management, patients and families all have access to the formulas for calculating damage amounts.[76] In many US medical malpractice actions, plaintiffs' and defendants' attorneys' widely disparate assessments of the plaintiff's damages obstruct resolution of the case. In Japan, because of the standardized damage schedule, these valuation conflicts are muted. This is a partial explanation for the lower litigation rates for Japanese medical malpractice claims, in comparison with the United States.[77]

Patients' medical and rehabilitation expenses resulting from medical injury are largely covered by the health insurance programs in which virtually all residents of Japan participate. As a legal matter, the insurance programs do have a right of subrogation to patients' claims against providers whose negligence necessitated the expenses. As a practical matter, subrogation claims appear to be rare, although they are not unknown in cases of serious impairment where medical and rehabilitation

---

[73] Ramseyer, *Malpractice Claims, supra* note 19, at 653. Awards ranged from ¥200,000 to ¥189 million (US $2000–$1.6 million). *Id.* Judges arrive at these damage awards by calculating, in addition to out-of-pocket medical and funeral expenses, the present value of the decedent's expected earnings, subtracting almost half of that value for foregone living expenses, and adding a standardized amount for pain and suffering—a method drawn from the standardized evaluation of traffic accident damages, See*supra* note 70. Payments from collateral sources are not included in damage awards. For a helpful summary of the law of damage calculations in tort, See Osaka (2009).

[74] A study of Florida malpractice awards from 1990–2003 found that the median and mean payments for wrongful death claims were $195,000 and $290,000. Vidmar et al. (2005) (tbl. 7); See also Leflar & Iwata, *supra* note 4 at 200 (similar analysis).

[75] Attorneys experienced in medical malpractice have informed the author that the vast majority of settled claims are never filed in court. See Leflar & Iwata, *supra* note 4, at 199–200 n. 35, and interviews, *infra* note 99 (characterizing informally settled claims as "the sunken part of the iceberg"). Of claims filed in court, the percentage litigated to final judgment has diminished from 46% in 2001 to 32% in 2018. Supreme Court of Japan, Iji kankei soshō jiken tōkei (table 2): Shūkoku kubun-betsu gaizai kensū oyobi sono wariai (Medically Related Cases Resolved: Numbers and Percentages of Each Type of Resolution), https://www.courts.go.jp/saikosai/vc-files/saikosai/file1/1905201heikinshinri.pdf (1999–2018 statistics) (last visited September 30, 2020).

[76] Damage calculations are informed to some extent by the circumstances of each case, however, so repeat players such as experienced lawyers will have a better sense of likely damages than members of the general public consulting the "Red Book".

[77] See Mark Ramseyer and Nakazato (1989) (arguing that clear damage guidelines for traffic accident cases promote out-of-court settlements, largely explaining low Japanese litigation rates); Ramseyer & Nakazato, *supra* note 36, at 90–99 (same).

expenses are very high.[78] A reason for their rarity, according to an experienced hospital defense attorney, is that, in settled cases, the release agreement frequently contains a clause prohibiting the parties from disclosing the settlement or its amount to anyone, even the social insurance entity.[79] If the insurer that covered the patient's medical expenses never learns of the claim nor the settlement, and has no inquisitive agent monitoring the case, then its subrogation right never comes into play.

B. Key Aspects of Procedural Law and Practice

1. In General

Japanese civil litigation is conducted by professional judges without juries,[80] in keeping with principles of German law, introduced in the late nineteenth century. Two or three judges hear each case. Trials take place, in sequential hearings, over a span of months or years, and attorneys for all parties submit documentary evidence, testimony and arguments on a scheduled basis during this period.[81] Medical malpractice trials, with their typically complex and controverted facts, are notorious for their prolonged duration. One infamous case required twenty years for its ultimate resolution in the Supreme Court in favor of the injured patient.[82]

Some critics of the medical injury litigation system have pointed to inadequate discovery procedures and the allegedly frequent alteration of medical records by hospital personnel,[83] interfering with plaintiffs' attempts to obtain accurate evidence about adverse events. These criticisms have been largely answered by expansion of discovery procedures, in a 1998 reform of the Civil Procedure Code[84] and by the

---

[78] Interview with Yasushi Kodama, a leading hospital defense attorney, in Tokyo (August 14, 2010) (giving examples of patients left in a vegetative state) (hereinafter "Kodama interview"). However, in catastrophic injury cases the social insurance system limits patients' self-pay burden to 1% of charges over an income-based ceiling (the "high-cost health care expenses system," *kōgaku ryōyōhi seido*). Since collateral source payments (such as those from the social insurance system) are not recoverable under Japanese tort law, patients' recoverable damages—and consequently, the amounts to which health insurers would be subrogated, standing in injured patients' shoes—tend to be much smaller than in most U.S. catastrophic injury cases.

[79] *Id.* Kodama memorably characterized this phenomenon as "the puzzle of the Sphinx".

[80] Non-professional "lay assessors" (*saiban-in*) now sit with professional judges in hearing certain serious criminal cases. Saiban-in no sanka suru keiji saiban ni kansuru hōritsu (Act on Criminal Trials with the Participation of Saiban-in), Law No. 63 of 2004, as amended by Law No. 54 of 2016 (English translation *available at* http://www.japaneselawtranslation.go.jp; input "Saiban-in"). This system does not apply to civil cases.

[81] See Ramseyer & Nakazato, *supra* note 36, at 139–141 (describing discontinuous trial system).

[82] Judgment of Supreme Court January 23, 1996, 50 Minshū 1, 1571 Hanrei Jihō 57 (perukamin-S case). For a moving account of the case by the plaintiff's attorney, See Katō (2003).

[83] See *supra* note 19 and accompanying text.

[84] Minsohō (Code of Civil Procedure) art. 220 (recognizing general principle of discoverability of specifically identified documents, with some exceptions). See Ota (2001).

routine availability on demand of patient charts through evidence preservation (*shōko hozen*) actions,[85] and direct patient requests to the medical facility.[86]

2. Discovery of Peer Review Findings

A concern of many Japanese physicians is the potential availability, for litigation purposes, of peer reviews of adverse events. Such reviews have become somewhat more common pursuant to health ministry guidance[87] and the implementation of the 2014 law.[88] Three legal grounds support at least partial release of peer review documents: national and local Freedom of Information rules applicable to public hospitals,[89] the contractual obligation of hospitals to investigate medical accidents and report the results to patients and families,[90] and liberalized discovery procedures under the revised Code of Civil Procedure.[91] In a leading case interpreting the new discovery rules, the Tokyo High Court ruled that the portion of the hospital report containing fact-gathering interviews with hospital personnel was non-disclosable, in order to protect interviewees' "*free formation of ideas*," but the portion of the report containing "*objective*" conclusions about the patient's course, the causes of death, and proposed corrective measures, must be disclosed.[92] Experienced defense attorneys routinely advise hospital clients to prepare for disclosure of anything that goes into such case reports.[93]

3. Judicial Administration Reforms

Responding to criticisms of excessive delays in medical malpractice litigation, the Supreme Court's administrative office instituted several reforms aimed at improving the speed and efficiency of the judicial process. These reforms delineated time-lines for trials, concentrated evidence gathering, expanded the use of judge-appointed expert witnesses and undertook the creation of health care divisions (*iryō shūchūbu*) in some metropolitan district courts. The first three reforms were launched in 1998, at the time of a reform of the Code of Civil Procedure. The health care divisions began operating in 2001.[94] As Fig. 3 indicates, the duration of civil medical cases had

---

[85] *Id.* art. 234–242 (authorizing and governing evidence preservation actions).

[86] See Nihon Ishikai (Japan Medical Ass'n), Ishi no shokugyō rinri shishin (Physicians' Professional Ethics Guide), Section 2(7) (3d ed. 2016), *available at* http://www.med.or.jp/doctor/rinri/i_rinri/000250.html (recognizing physicians' duty to disclose medical records).

[87] See Leflar & Iwata, *supra* note 4, at 205–206 (citing guidance documents).

[88] See *supra* notes 41–45 and accompanying text.

[89] See Information Disclosure Law, *supra* note 9.

[90] See, e.g., Judgment of Kyoto Dist. Ct. July 12, 2005, 1907 Hanrei Jihō 112, 124–125. See also *supra* note 69 and accompanying text.

[91] See Ota, *supra* note 84; Leflar & Iwata, *supra* note 4, at 206–213.

[92] Judgment of Tokyo High Ct. July 15, 2003, 1842 Hanrei Jihō 57, 1145 Hanrei Taimuzu 298 (Saitama Medical University case).

[93] Tokyo Judges 2010 Interview, *supra* note 61; Kodama interview, *supra* note 78.

[94] For discussions of these reforms, see, e.g., Feldman, *supra* note 70, at 273–275; Leflar (2011).

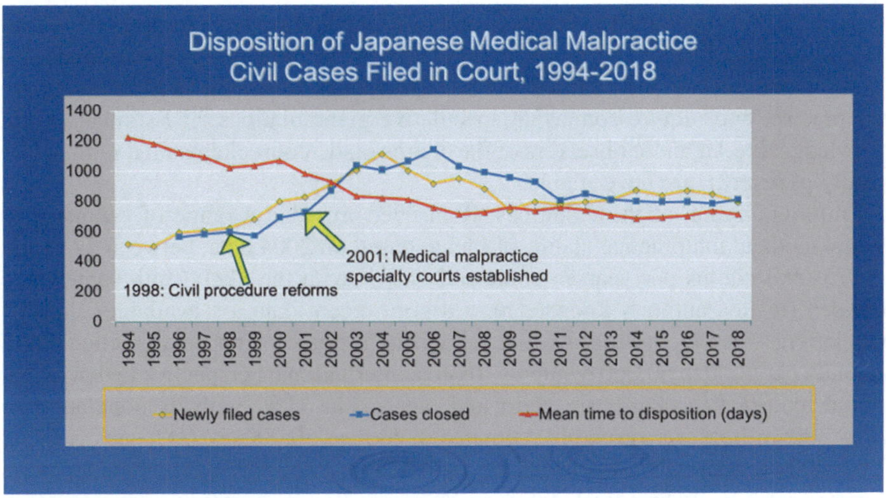

Fig. 3 Disposition of medical malpractice cases filed in court, 1994–2018[95]

already begun to decline, even before these reforms were launched, but the reforms appear to have succeeded in further reducing litigation delays for at least a decade after their implementation.

4. Settlement Practices, Overall Claiming Levels, and Malpractice Insurance Premiums

Malpractice case filings in court, set out in Fig. 2,[96] constitute only a small fraction of all medical injury claims made by patients and paid by medical providers or their liability insurers. Extrajudicial dispute resolution is encouraged both by law[97] and through the activities of entrepreneurial academics.[98] What proportion of all medical injury claims is filed in court is difficult to ascertain, since insurers are famously close with their payout data. Three leading Tokyo attorneys, one representing hospitals, one the Japan Medical Association and the third plaintiffs, all suggested to the author that court-filed claims constitute merely the "*tip of the iceberg*" of all claims.[99]

Mark Ramseyer constructed a useful range of estimates of overall medical malpractice claiming levels, including claims not filed in court, from three sources:

[95] Supreme Court medical malpractice case statistics, *supra* note 46.

[96] *Id.*

[97] Saiban-gai funsō kaiketsu tetsuzuki no riyō no sokushin ni kansuru hōritsu (Act on Promotion of Use of Alternative Dispute Resolution), Law No. 151 of 2004, as amended (English translation available at http://www.japaneselawtranslation.go.jp; input "Alternative Dispute Resolution").

[98] See, e.g., Wada and Nakanishi (2006).

[99] Interviews with Tatsuo Kuroyanagi, in Naha, Okinawa (February 25, 2006), Yoshiharu Kawabata, in Tokyo (July 27, 2009), and Yasushi Kodama, *supra* note 78. Similarly, a 2001 study estimated that only 8% of malpractice claims are litigated. Nakajima et al. (2001) (drawing on JMA closed-claim data from 1973 to 1981).

court statistics, insurance premiums and informed observer estimates.[100] Court claims data are firm: 1110 malpractice claims were filed in court nationwide in 2004, or one lawsuit per 115,000 Japanese residents. Insurance premium data are less precise, and require somewhat speculative manipulations.[101] Estimates, from knowledgeable Japanese observers of the claims made/court claims filed ratio, while worthy of respect, are unverifiable.

Employing each of these sources, Ramseyer provided a range of estimates of annual medical malpractice claims in Japan, based on 2004 data: between 2230 and 13,875 total claims per year, in court and out,[102] with the likely truth somewhere between (to this author's knowledge, no more recent data are available). Japan's population was 127 million, so that represents a range of one malpractice claim annually per 9000 to 60,000 residents. To give international perspective to that range, annual malpractice claims (in court and out) in the U.S., with its population of about 300 million, were credibly estimated in 2006 as 50,000–60,000, one claim per 5000–6000 residents,[103] or between 1.5 and 12 times Ramseyer's estimated Japanese claiming rate. Annual medical malpractice claims, filed in court (not extrajudicially), in 2004 in Canada, with a population of 32 million, amounted to 1,083 claims,[104] or one lawsuit per 30,000 residents, about four times Japan's per capita lawsuit filing rate of one lawsuit per 115,000 residents.[105] A reasonable approximate estimate, for that time period, would be that a Japanese patient was one-fourth to one-sixth as likely to make a claim against a medical provider as a North American patient.[106]

It was once a common practice for physicians and hospitals to offer *mimaikin*, a small gift of money in token of sympathy, to injured patients and families (whether or not they had legal representation) before any lawsuit was filed. See Leflar (1993). That practice has become less common since public distrust of medical skill and probity following the publicized disasters of 1999–2004 made the offering of small *mimaikin* seem "ridiculous." Kodama interview, *supra* note 78.

[100] Ramseyer, *Malpractice Claims, supra* note 19, at 663–668.

[101] Ramseyer estimated that annual malpractice insurance premiums for the year in question totaled about ¥69 billion (US $860 million). Of this sum, roughly 60% was paid out to claimants. Ramseyer, *Malpractice Claims, supra* note 19, at 664. An estimate of annual premiums from Sompo Japan, a major liability insurer, put the total somewhat lower, at ¥41 billion (US $510 million). Sompo Japan Insurance Inc., Ishi baishō_sekinin hoken ni tsuite (Physicians' Liability Insurance) (2011) (on file with author).

[102] Ramseyer, *Malpractice Claims, supra* note 19, at 663–668.

[103] Mello and Studdert (2006), *cited in* Ramseyer, *Malpractice Claims, supra* note 19, at 667.

[104] Canadian Health Services Research Foundation, Myth: Medical Malpractice Lawsuits Plague Canada (2006), *available at* https://www.hhr-rhs.ca/index.php?option=com_mtree&task=att_download&link_id=6845&cf_id=68&lang=en, (last visited October 1, 2020), *cited in* Ramseyer, *Malpractice Claims, supra* note 19, at 667–668.

[105] For an earlier comparison of malpractice claim filing rates in Japan and several Western nations, See Nakajima et al., *supra* note 99, at 1638.

[106] Adding credence to this estimate are statistics from liability insurer Sompo Japan indicating that physician and hospital liability insurance, as a proportion of all casualty insurance, is 0.37% in Japan and 1.52% in the U.S., approximately a 1–4 ratio. See Sompo Japan Insurance Inc., *supra* note 100, at 9 (calculated from figures given in table).

Physicians in private practice obtain malpractice liability insurance to cover these claims, mainly through private insurance plans, run by national and prefectural medical associations. Private and many public hospitals buy insurance from commercial carriers, such as Sompo Japan and Tokyo Marine.[107] Private physicians' standard insurance policies come with a ¥1 million (US $9500) deductible and cover liability up to ¥100 million (US $950,000) but physicians can choose higher coverage levels. Standard hospital policies also offer a choice of coverage levels but typically with no deductible.[108] Hospital-employed physicians receive standard coverage under their hospitals' policies, but some purchase additional personal coverage.[109] Excess liability insurance covering large-claim liability above standard policy limits, considered "*vitally important*" to self-insured hospitals in the U.S.,[110] is available in Japan as well. According to one expert in the field, there are so few large claims that marketing reinsurance for them is generally uneconomical.[111]

Liability insurance does not constitute a significant part of ordinary practitioners' daily concerns, although hospital administrators must keep the issue in mind. Liability insurance is regulated nationally by the Financial Services Agency, which has control over rate-setting. For physicians in private practice, premiums are uniform nationwide: ¥70,000 annually (US $650, tax-deductible), with no differentiation based or practice specialty or location.[112] Hospital-employed physicians pay somewhat less.[113] Hospitals' insurance premiums, once also uniform, now vary depending on their bed count, treatment levels and level of coverage. Hospitals insured by the Japan Hospital Cooperative with more than 500 beds, pay from ¥22,824 (US $215) to ¥28,847 (US $270) per bed per year depending on the level of coverage they choose,

---

[107] Some national hospitals and national university hospitals cover liability costs through taxpayer-funded operating budgets or through a quasi-public entity, Kokuritsu byōin kikō (National Hospital Organization), rather than by purchasing liability insurance from private firms. See http://www.hosp.go.jp (National Hospital Organization website) (last visited October 1, 2020).

For a useful description of the structure and operation of Japanese malpractice insurance systems at the turn of the twenty-first century, See Nakajima et al., *supra* note 98.

[108] See, e.g., Nihon byōin kyōzaikai (Japan Hospital Cooperative, Inc.), Byōin baishō sekinin hokentō no goannai (Introduction to Hospital Liability Insurance) 8 (2020) (premium chart), *available at* https://www.nichibyo.co.jp/pdf/suitable-insuarance-pdf001.pdf (last visited October 2, 2020); Sompo Japan Insurance Inc., *supra* note 101, at 34.

[109] Ramseyer, *Malpractice Claims*, *supra* note 19, at 664–665; Kawabata interview, *supra* note 99.

[110] Sloan and Chepke (2008).

[111] Interviews with Satoko Nishimura, insurance policy specialist, in Tokyo (July 19 and August 3, 2011).

[112] This ¥70,000 premium is charged to JMA members owning clinics or small hospitals. Physicians may also purchase additional insurance to cover the ¥1 million deductible and liability for injuries resulting from non-medical acts, such as slip-and-falls at physician-owned hospitals. This additional insurance sells for ¥8,620 (US $80). Sompo Japan Insurance Inc., *supra* note 101, at 34 (amounts current as of date of 2011 interview).

[113] Non-JMA members (mainly hospital-employed physicians) can purchase a standard policy for ¥55,000 (US $520), and physician trainees for ¥34,000 (US $320). *Id.* These doctors are typically covered by the hospital's liability insurance anyway, so it is unclear to the author why many of them purchase it.

while hospitals with fewer than 100 beds pay ¥12,856 (US $120) to ¥16,211 (US $155).[114] Hospitals' premiums are experience-rated, to some extent[115]; physicians' premiums are not.[116]

5. Plaintiffs' Attorney Fees and Court Costs

One barrier confronting patients considering medical malpractice lawsuits, identified by various scholars and critics of the Japanese court system, has been plaintiffs' attorneys' fee structure.[117] In contrast to the United States, in which pure contingent fee arrangements with no up-front payments are standard, in Japan plaintiffs customarily had to pay lawyers a substantial up-front retainer, according to a standardized schedule enforced by the bar association, plus a filing fee to the court based on the amount claimed. These payments typically amounted to the yen-equivalent of several thousand dollars, closing the courthouse door to most seriously injured patients without substantial means.[118] These barriers are somewhat lower now than they once were: court filing fees in high-damage cases have substantially decreased[119] and the bar association withdrew its attorney fee schedule as contrary to antimonopoly law. Some attorneys, handling malpractice cases for plaintiffs, offer potential clients flexibility in payment arrangements. The attorney may charge a fee for preliminary case evaluation smaller than the standard retainer, and, if the attorney takes the case, a discounted retainer amount may be paid in installments; or the retainer may be decreased while the attorney's share of the recovery, contingent on success, is increased. A contingency arrangement of 15–25% of the total recovery, with various adjustments, is common. Most attorneys are said to work within the basic framework of the former customary fee schedule.[120]

---

[114] Nihon byōin kyōzaikai, supra note 108.

[115] *Id.*

[116] Nishimura interviews, *supra* note 111; Nakajima et al., *supra* note 99, at 1635. Claims experience for individual physicians is too limited to warrant the expense of compiling experience ratings. *Cf.* Sloan & Chepke, *supra* note 110 (explaining limitations of experience rating in the US medical malpractice insurance market). The actuarial difficulty of rating individual physicians' likely future claim exposure is even greater in Japan, with its low litigation rates, than in the U.S.

[117] See, e.g., Maeda et al. (2001), Feldman (2009b), Leflar (2009b).

[118] See Maeda et al., *supra* note 117, at 61 tbl. 9 (noting start-up fees of ¥3 million—then about US $24,000—for cases involving minor plaintiffs claiming lifelong earning deprivation). Occasionally patients do file *pro se* claims, however, and once in a while, they win. Interview with successful *pro se* plaintiff Shunsuke Funase, in Naguri, Saitama-ken (August 9, 2009).

[119] Feldman, supra note 117, at 797 n. 45. Filing a claim for ¥10 million (US $95,000) now requires a filing fee of ¥50,000 (US $470); a claim of ¥100 million (US $950,000) requires a fee of ¥320,000 (US $3,000). For the current filing fee schedule, See https://www.courts.go.jp/vc-files/courts/file3/315004.pdf.

[120] Katō interview, *supra* note 65; Suzuki interview, *supra* note 61; Feldman, *supra* note 70, at 264 & n. 24. Katō and Suzuki are both leaders of cooperating groups of plaintiffs' attorneys specializing in medical malpractice cases.

4 The No-Fault Compensation System for Obstetrical Injury

Japan has a striking history of enacting no-fault administrative compensation systems providing relief for injured persons apart from that available under the civil law, the limitations of which made compensation in circumstances of high social concern difficult or impossible. These compensation systems include schemes aiding people injured by environmental pollution, vaccinations, adverse drug reactions, infections from biological products, blood transfusions and asbestos exposure.[121] The most recent of these no-fault administrative compensation systems provides relief to parents of a limited class of newborn infants with severe brain damage.

Birth injury cases are among the most serious in every legal system. Profound brain injuries, resulting in lifelong rehabilitative needs, add up to enormous potential damages. Obstetricians face the prospect that even 'a minor slip' may subject them and their insurance carriers to vast damage judgments.[122]

Litigation over birth-related injuries has provoked considerable anxiety among Japanese obstetricians. Among civil malpractice actions, suits over obstetrical injuries have apparently resulted in a higher-than-average proportion of plaintiffs' judgments.[123] Prosecutors instituted criminal proceedings in 2006 (intensely publicized, but ultimately unsuccessful) against an obstetrician who lost a patient during a difficult delivery, casting a shadow of fear over the profession and giving impetus to the antiregulatory *iryō hōkai* movement.[124]

At the instigation of the Japan Medical Association, the Japan Society of Obstetrics & Gynecology, and the governing Liberal Democratic Party, the health ministry initiated a no-fault compensation system for a limited class of obstetrical injuries.[125]

---

[121] See Osaka, *supra* note 73, at 400 (listing laws); Takao Tanase, *The Role of the Judiciary in Asbestos Injury Compensation in Japan, in* Fault Lines, *supra* note 70, at 247–248 (noting centrality of administrative compensation rather than private litigation as Japan's "archetype"); Morishima and Smith (1986) (early analysis of development of no-fault systems); Hatanaka, *supra* note 12, at 59–96 (drug and vaccine injury compensation systems). This significant phenomenon has received scant attention in many respected English-language treatises on Japanese law. See, e.g., Milhaupt, Ramseyer & West, *supra* note 8; Ramseyer & Nakazato, *supra* note 36, at 125 & n. 58 (sole mention); Hiroshi Oda, Japanese Law (2d ed., 1999).

[122] The subtleties of the litigation process in a birth-damaged baby case, and their impact on the lives of plaintiffs, defendants, and their attorneys, are set out in memorable fashion in Barry Werth, Damages (first published 1988).

[123] See Uesugi et al. (2010) (69% of sixty-four cases in database of reported birth defect cases resulted in some recovery); *compare* Ramseyer, *Malpractice Claims*, *supra* note 19, at 626–627 (some recovery in 30–40% of all medical malpractice cases litigated to final judgment). It is possible, however, that the publishers' selection of cases to be reported biased the database used by Uesugi et al. in favor of cases in which plaintiffs recovered. See id. at 642–644.

[124] Ohno Hospital case, *supra* note 33 and accompanying text.

[125] Criteria for compensation are rather strict. Infants must be diagnosed with cerebral palsy of the 1 or 2 of severity, must weigh more than 1400 g at birth, and with few exceptions must be born after 32 weeks of pregnancy. Infants who die within six months and those whose anomalies are congenital are excluded from compensation. Eligibility determinations are performed by expert

Launched in 2009, the system is modeled, in some respects, on Florida's neurological injury compensation system.[126] It is administered by the quasi-public Japan Council for Quality Health Care (JCQHC) and is financed through a fixed per-birth levy from the social insurance system, paid to private insurance companies that stand to reap profits (or possibly suffer losses) from the system's operation.[127]

The system's stated goals are to provide prompt compensation, without the need for legal proceedings, to parents of infants suffering cerebral palsy related to brain injuries during childbirth, to analyze the causes of cerebral palsy and help prevent recurrence, and to improve the quality of obstetric care.[128]

Japan's obstetrical injury compensation system was instituted in a manner that required no legislation. It is a voluntary system—no childbirth facility is required to participate. It is operated outside of government by JCQHC. Social insurance funds finance the system and no specific legislative appropriation is needed. Parents still have a right to sue medical providers for negligence, as before the system was instituted.

The system appears to have gained traction. Almost all childbirth facilities in the nation have signed up to participate.[129] For births occurring in 2009–2014, the first six years of operation, the system reviewed 3048 applications for compensation and accepted 2195.[130] This substantially exceeds the proportion of cerebral palsy cases

---

panels. The level of compensation is fixed: a one-time payment of ¥6 million (US $55,000), plus ¥24 million (US $225,000) paid out over the first twenty years of the child's life, for a total of ¥30 million (US $280,000) per child. JCQHC, Sanka iryō hoshō seido ni tsuite: Hoshō naiyō to kakarikin (The Obstetric Compensation System: Compensation and Eligibility), *available at* http://www.sanka-hp.jcqhc.or.jp/outline/system.html (last visited October 2, 2020).

[126] The Florida system, like Virginia's Birth-Related Injury Fund, is a no-fault system for compensation of some serious neurological injuries sustained during or close to child. birth. For an overview of the two systems, See Sloan & Chepke, *supra* note 110, at 280–287.

[127] The cash flow is circuitous. Funding for the system is generated by a levy of ¥30,000 (US $280) on each birth. JCQHC collects this amount from hospitals and maternity clinics that choose to participate, and channels the money to the private insurers. The hospitals and clinics in turn collect an identical amount from each expectant mother. By Cabinet Order, the amount of the lump-sum childbirth subsidy that each mother receives from her health insurance plan was increased by the same ¥30,000 at the time the compensation system was launched. See Tomizuka and Matsuda (2009).

[128] Japan Council for Quality Health Care, The Japan Obstetric Compensation System for Cerebral Palsy: Looking Back over Ten Years 2 (2019) (hereinafter JCQHC, Looking Back).

[129] 3236 of Japan's 3239 childbirth facilities were participating as of June 2018. *Id.* at 3. The high participation rate is chiefly explained by the fact that neither the hospital or clinic, nor the expectant mothers for whose custom the hospitals and clinics compete, bear any financial risk from participation, due to the cost pass-through explained in note 127 *supra*. Interview with Naoki Ikegami, Chair, Dep't. of Health Policy & Management, Keio U. School of Medicine, in Tokyo (August 8, 2011).

[130] JCQHC, Sanka iryō hoshō seido no un'ei jisseki-tō ni tsuite (Obstetric Compensation System Management Results) 6 (June 5, 2020), available at http://www.sanka-hp.jcqhc.or.jp/documents/committee/kentou_meeting1_2.pdf (last visited October 2, 2020) (hereinafter JCQHC, System Results). Results for 2015–2019 are incomplete as of this writing, since not all applicants from that period have received final determinations of eligibility.

compensated by the Florida system.[131] For a recently launched program, the system seems to be capturing a substantial proportion of cerebral palsy cases. It remains to be seen whether the system's financing will suffice, in the long term, but it is running a considerable surplus at present, greatly benefitting participating private insurers (and incurring a substantial cost to the social insurance system).

Another effect of the obstetric compensation system's adoption has been to channel a substantial proportion of injury claims away from the fault-based civil liability arena into the no-fault system. In 2009, the year the system was launched, plaintiffs filed 84 civil actions claiming obstetrical malpractice. By 2016, only 52 such claims were filed—while the number of malpractice lawsuits overall had increased from 732 to 862.[132]

5 Conclusion

Distinctive features of Japanese law and society relating to medical misadventure include the following.

Criminal law: In the early years of the twenty-first century, after a series of publicized errors at hospitals of high repute focused public attention on slipshod practices and dishonesty in the medical world, the criminal justice system, amplified by media reportage, sounded a wake-up call to a medical profession previously lacking in accountability mechanisms. The health ministry and organized medicine responded with various measures to improve patient safety; the extent to which those measures may have been effective is unknown. Prosecutors' sometimes-excessive involvement, in policing medical quality, provoked a reaction from the medical profession, eliciting media and public sympathy, contributing to an unusual string of acquittals of medical defendants, and clipping the prosecutors' wings.

Civil law: Civil Code provisions, governing compensation for medical injury, are fault-based and do not differ greatly in principle from rules applied in North America and Western Europe. The burden of proof of causation is relaxed in informed consent and loss-of-chance cases. Procedural reforms, including the institution of health care divisions of district courts in some metropolitan areas, have helped speed up the

---

[131] The Florida compensation system, and a similar system operating in Virginia, are reported to compensate no more than 2% of cerebral palsy cases in those states. See Sloan & Chepke, *supra* note110, at 282. One estimate placed the annual incidence of cerebral palsy cases in Japan at about 630, Tomizuka & Matsuda, *supra* note 127, although it is unclear whether that estimate is based on a disease definition congruent with the standards for compensation applied in the Japanese system. Supposing the estimate of 630 cases is not far off the mark, and 300–400 of them are accepted for compensation each year, See JCQHC, System Results, *supra* note 130, it is nevertheless obvious that the Japanese system is capturing a far higher percentage of cases for compensation than the Florida system.

[132] See JCQHC, Looking Back, *supra* note 128, at 11 (obstetrical claims); Supreme Court of Japan, *supra* note 46 (overall claims); Hatanaka, *supra* note 12, at 102.

pace of judicial proceedings, once notoriously glacial. Damage awards appear not to differ greatly, on average, from awards in the United States, and are applied on a more consistent, standardized basis. The volume of claims filed in court is considerably lower than North American levels. Claims, in court, declined somewhat after the peak year of 2004 but, in recent years, have been rising steadily. Most compensation payments are made outside, not within, the court system. Overall claiming rates are low, relative to North American practices. Malpractice insurance premiums, uniform nationwide for physicians in private practice without regard to specialty or geography, are far cheaper than in the United States.

Administrative compensation programs: Building on a tradition of no-fault administrative compensation schemes, for people injured by pollution, defective drugs, vaccines, blood transfusions and asbestos, Japan instituted, in 2009, a nationwide no-fault compensation system for infants with severe birth-related brain injuries. Backed by the medical establishment, financed through public funding, administered by a quasi-public entity and offering substantial profit opportunities (as well as a theoretical risk of loss) to private insurers, the obstetrical injury compensation system has achieved almost universal buy-in by childbirth facilities hoping for protection from future litigation.

References

Boling D (1998) Access to government-held information in Japan: citizens' "Right to Know" bows to the bureaucracy. Stanford J Int Law 34:1

Campbell JC, Ikegami N (1998) The art of balance in health policy: maintaining Japan's low-cost. Egalitarian System

Clermont KM (2004) Standards of proof in Japan and the United States. Cornell Int Law J 37:263

Clermont KM (2009) Standards of proof revisited. Vermont Law Rev 33:469, 473

Feldman EA (1999) Blood feuds: AIDS, blood, and the politics of medical disaster

Feldman EA (2009a) Law, society, and medical malpractice litigation in Japan. Washington Univ Global Stud Law Rev 8:257, 266

Feldman EA (2009b) Why patients sue doctors: the Japanese experience. J Law Med Ethics 37:792, 796–797

Feldman EA (2009c) Suing doctors in Japan: structure, culture, and the rise of malpractice litigation. In: Engel DM, McCannM (eds) Fault lines: tort law as cultural practice 233

Fukushima M (1989) The overdose of drugs in Japan. Nature 342:850–851

Hashimoto H, Ikegami N et al (2011) Cost containment and quality of care in Japan: is there a trade-off? The Lancet 378:1174, 1178

Higuchi N (2008) Article 21 of the medical practitioners law. Japan Med Assoc J 51(4):1

Ikeda S (2006) Iryō jiko hassei hindo chōsa kara erareta wagakuni no kanja anzen no genkyō to kadai (Patient safety issues raised by the study of medical accident incidence). Kanja Anzen Suishin Jānaru 14:56

Ishikawa H (2006) Karute kaizan wa naze okiru (Why medical records are falsified)

Katō Y (2003) Kyūsai shisutemu ga jiko bōshi ni kinō suru (Remedial systems prevent accidents). Iji Hōgaku (J Med Law) 18:94, 98–99

Kojima T (1998) Japanese civil procedure in comparative law perspective. Univ Kansas Law Rev 46:687, 708

Komatsu H (2006) Iryō Hōkai (The collapsing health care system)
Kondo M (1988) Kikanu koganzai 3000-oku shijō no kai (The Mystery of a 300-Billion Yen Market of Ineffective Anti-Tumor Drugs), September 1988. Bungei Shunju, pp 278–289
Leflar RB (1993) Personal injury compensation systems in japan: values advanced and values undermined. Univ Hawai'i Law Rev 15:742, 749
Leflar RB (1996) Informed consent and patients' rights in Japan. Houston L Rev 33(1):63–74
Leflar RB (2007) Law and health care in Japan: the renaissance of informed consent. In: Jost TS (ed) Readings in comparative health law and bioethics, 2nd edn., pp 154, 159
Leflar RB (2009a) "Unnatural Deaths," criminal sanctions, and medical quality improvement in Japan. Yale J Health Policy L Ethics 9:1, 6
Leflar RB (2009b) The regulation of medical malpractice in Japan. Clin Orthopedics Related Res 467:443, 445
Leflar RB (2011) Public and private justice: redressing health care harm in Japan. Drexel Law Rev 4:243
Leflar RB (2012) The law of medical misadventure in Japan. Chicago-Kent L Rev 87:79
Leflar RB, Iwata F (2005) Medical error as reportable event, as tort, as crime: a transpacific comparison. Widener L Rev 12:189, 192–195
Lock M (2002) Twice dead: organ transplants and the reinvention of death
Maeda S et al (2001) The problems of medical malpractice litigation in Japan: the significant factors responsible for the tendency of patients to avoid litigation. Legal Med 3:56, 59–61
Mark Ramseyer J (2009) Universal health insurance and the effect of cost containment on mortality rates: strokes and heart attacks in Japan. J Empirical Legal Stud 6:309
Mark Ramseyer J (2010) The effect of universal health insurance on malpractice claims: the Japanese experience. J Legal Anal 2:621, 662–663
Mark Ramseyer J, Nakazato M (1989) The rational litigant: settlement amounts and verdict rates in Japan. J Legal Stud 18:263
Mark Ramseyer J, Nakazato M (1999) Japanese law: an economic approach 178
Meisel A, Kabnick LD (1980) Informed consent to medical treatment: an analysis of recent legislation. Univ Pitt Law Rev 41:407, 438–439
Mello MM, Studdert DM (2006) The medical malpractice system: structure and performance. In: Sage WM, Kersch R (eds) Medical malpractice and the U.S. Health Care System, vol 11, p 13
MHLW (2000) Risuku Maneijimento Manyuaru Sakusei Shishin (Guidelines for the creation of risk management manuals)
Milhaupt CJ, Mark Ramseyer J, West MD (2006) The Japanese legal system: cases, codes and commentary, 347–356
Ministry of Health & Welfare (1998) Karute-tō no shinryō jōhō no katsuyō ni kansuru kentōkai hōkokushō (Report of the study commission on the use of medical charts and information)
Morishima A, Smith (1986) Accident compensation schemes in Japan: A window on the operation of law in a society. Univ Brit Colum Law Rev 20
Nakajima K et al (2001) Medical malpractice and legal resolution systems in Japan. J Am Med Assoc 285:1632, 1635
Nakajima N et al (2009) Interim evaluation of the model project for the investigation and analysis of medical practice-associated deaths in Japan. J Med Saf 34
Oliphant K, Wright RW (eds) Medical malpractice and compensation in global perspective, pp 239–273
Osaka E (2009) Reevaluating the role of the tort liability system in Japan. Arizona J Int Comp Law 26:393, 395–396
Oshida S, Kodama Y, Suzuki T (2002) Jitsurei ni manabu iryo jiko (A real-world view of medical accident cases), pp 20–21
Ota S (2001) Reform of civil procedure in Japan. Am J Comp Law 49:561
Ross Baker G et al (2004) The Canadian adverse events study: the incidence of adverse events among hospital patients in Canada. Can Med Assoc J 170:1678

Sakai H (2006) Iryō jiko no zenkokuteki hassei hindo ni kansuru kenkyū: III (Report on the nationwide incidence of medical accidents: III) 5:18

Sawa R (2008) A healthcare crisis in Japan: criminalizing medical malpractice. Japan Med Assoc J 51:235, 240

Sloan FA, Chepke LM (2008) Medical malpractice, p 247

Suzuki T et al (2009) Iryō jiko no hōritsu sōdan (The law of medical accidents), pp 36–37

Twerski A, Cohen NB (1989) Informed decisionmaking and the law of torts: the myth of justiciable causation. Univ Illinois Law Rev 1988:60

Tomizuka T, Matsuda R (2009) Introduction of no-fault obstetric compensation. Health Policy Monitor, October 2009

Uesugi N et al (2010) Analysis of birth-related medical malpractice litigation cases in japan: review and discussion towards implementation of a no-fault compensation system. J Obstetrical & Gynæcol Res 36:717

Vidmar N et al (2005) Uncovering the invisible profile of medical malpractice litigation: insights from Florida. DePaul Law Rev 54:315, 340

Wada Y, Nakanishi T (2006) Iryō Konfurikuto Manejimento: Medieishon no ronri to gihō (Medical conflict management: mediation theory and skills)

Medical Liability in Macao

Vera Lúcia Raposo

The Special Administrative Region of Macao is an independent jurisdiction within the People's Republic of China. Due to several centuries of Portuguese administration, Macao's legal system is very similar to the Portuguese system.

In Macao, civil medical liability is defined by Law 5/2016, which creates a special regime for healthcare professionals, slightly different from the general rules of the Civil Code. Criminal liability is governed exclusively by the Criminal Code, which provides specific criminal penalties for crimes committed by medical practitioners while they are engaged in their duties, as healthcare workers.

An overall appraisal of medical liability in Macao indicates that it has some good and innovative ideas, but these ideas are not properly executed. Medical liability seems to be something that exists on paper but not in day to day judicial practice, leading to an extremely reduced number of studies and caselaw in this domain.

1 Brief Introduction to the Macanese Jurisdiction

The Special Administrative Region of Macao (Macao SAR or Macao) is a region of China that has autonomy in various matters, including legal matters. For centuries, Macao was under Portuguese administration, an historical incident that strongly influenced Macanese law. Due to its roots in Portuguese law, Macao's legal system is a purely civil law system (while China's civil law system has features that sometimes lead to its categorisation as a mixed system). The main codes—Civil Code, Civil Procedure Code, Criminal Code and Criminal Procedure Code—are almost

V. L. Raposo (✉)
Faculty of Law of Coimbra University, Coimbra, Portugal
e-mail: vera@fd.uc.pt

Faculty of Law of the University of Macau, Macau, China

V. L. Raposo and R. G. Beran (eds.), *Medical Liability in Asia and Australasia*,
Ius Gentium: Comparative Perspectives on Law and Justice 94,
https://doi.org/10.1007/978-981-16-4855-7_9

direct copies of the Portuguese codes, although they have some (sometimes decisive) particularities.

Portuguese influence is also very noticeable in the judicial decisions of the Macanese courts. Due to the similarities between Macanese and Portuguese Law, Portuguese scholars and Portuguese case law are frequently quoted in Macanese judgments.[1] In contrast, legal doctrines and court decisions from mainland China are rarely referred to, which is unsurprising, given the differences between these two jurisdictions, described by the slogan 'one country, two systems'.

In spite of the similarities with Portugal, Macao stands as a jurisdiction with its own particular laws and judicial practices, the result of the confluence between the east and the west.

2 Basic Features of Civil Medical Liability

For many decades, Macao had no specific law to deal with civil medical liability. This is not, *de per se*, a problem.[2] The Civil Code (CC) provides a legal framework for addressing medical conflicts.[3] However, the existence of specific laws, governing the responsibilities of healthcare providers, allow the recognition of the specificities of this domain within the context of general civil liability. Based on these considerations,[4] in 2016, Law n. 5/2016 created a special regime for civil medical liability, different from the one in place in mainland China[5], and came to provide a proper legal ground for some patient's rights.[6]

The subject of Law n. 5/2016 is the improperly designated 'medical error'. Medical errors are irrelevant to the law which is only concerned with fault (culpability)[7] for medical errors (Article 3 Law n. 5/2016).

Its subjective scope refers to 'health care providers' (Article 4 Law n. 5/2016). This term includes, not only doctors of conventional medicine, but also doctors of

[1] For this same reason, this paper will quote Portuguese scholars, especially because in Macao there are very few publications on medical liability.

[2] Arguing the uselessness of such regulation, Associação dos Advogados de Macau (2014), p. 2.

[3] Also to be taken in consideration is Decree-Law n. 111/99/M, of 13 December, which establishes the legal regime for the protection of human rights and human dignity in view of the applications of biology and medicine. This law is essentially a copy of a substantial portion of the Convention for the Protection of Human Rights and Human Dignity with regard to the Application of Biology and Medicine. Portugal is a signatory of this Convention, and the Decree-Law arises from the old days of Portuguese Administration. However, as this Decree-Law only establishes general guidelines, with only a few rules on medical responsibility and patients' rights, it is clearly insufficient to regulate these issues.

[4] About the events leading to the existence of this law see Pessanha (2006), p. 2.

[5] An overview of the model in place in Mainland China in Iong (2017a)

[6] Referring in particular the right to access medical files, Pessanha (2017), p. 63 ff.

[7] Early drafts of the law considered the introduction of a no-fault system, but the final draft rejected this solution. Cf. Cascão (2017), pp. 37–39.

traditional Chinese medicine. This conclusion results from the broad terms of Article 4 of Law n. 5/2016: '*For the purposes of this law, a healthcare provider is considered any natural or legal person carrying out activities of prevention, diagnosis, treatment or rehabilitation of health in the public or private sector*'.[8] In addition, Some regulations, issued to improve the law, expressly refer to traditional Chinese medicine. This solution is a natural consequence of Article 123 of the Macao Basic Law, the highest law of Macao, and the value it grants to this ancient practice: '*The Government of the Macao Special Administrative Region shall, on its own, formulate policies to improve medical and health services and to develop Western and traditional Chinese medicine. Community organizations and individuals may provide various medical and health services in accordance with law.*'

The aims of this law are laudable: it intends to conform to modern legal trends in medical responsibility (notification of adverse events, intervention of multidisciplinary administrative bodies in the resolution of medical conflicts, adverse dispute resolution methods) and to underline the differences between medical responsibility and other types of civil responsibility. However, the methods used to achieve these goals are flawed.

2.1 Contract Liability Versus Tort Liability

Macanese civil liability was developed on the Portuguese model of civil liability. In Portugal, one question that has long divided scholars and judges is whether medical civil liability should follow the rules of contract liability or tort liability.[9] This dilemma is not a purely doctrinal issue, given the practical consequences of this choice for the parties' liability and for the outcomes of a dispute.[10]

A major difference between the two regimes—and the feature that supports the option for one or the other—is related to the burden of proof of culpability. In contractual liability, there is a presumption of the defendant's culpability (in this case, the doctor and/or the healthcare facility). The plaintiff-patient is exempt from proving this element of legal responsibility, consequently easing the burden of proof that falls on him/her (article 788 CC). Moreover, the rules of contract liability offer the plaintiff another advantage: there is a longer prescription period in contract liability than exists in tort liability, 15 years in the former (Article 302 CC) and 3 years in the latter (Article 491 CC). Contract liability is more beneficial for the plaintiff-patient and places more burdens on the defendant-doctor/hospital. For this reason, many authors argue that to protect the patient—considered the weaker party in this

[8] Cf. Iong (2017b), pp. 53–65.

The use of a broad concept of 'health care provider' was advocated by the Association of Doctors of Portuguese Language of Macau (Associação dos Médicos de Língua Portuguesa de Macau 2014).

[9] For a discussion of the differences of these liability regimes in the CC, see Trigo (2014), pp. 237 ff.

[10] For a discussion of the differences between these two regimes in the specific field of medical liability, see Raposo (2013a), pp. 32 ff.

relationship—all medical responsibility cases should follow the rules of contract law.[11]

In Macao, in accordance with the traditional position in Portugal, the Court of Last Appeal established that medical acts performed in State-owned facilities are subject to the rules of tort liability (decision from 18 January 2006, process n. 23/2005).[12] The question was left open for medical acts conducted in private facilities. In a decision from 17 January 2011, the Court of Appeal used contract law (proceeding n. 218/2011), but in general the plaintiffs were allowed to decide which set of rules (contract law or tort law) would be applied to their cases.[13]

Law n. 5/2016 was intended to standardise the regime of medical liability, specifically the issue of the burden of proof.[14] This standardisation ended the existing distinction whereby the practice of medicine in the private sector operated under contractual liability rules (usually the plaintiffs choose contract law, whose solutions are more favourable to them) and the practice of medicine in the public sector operated under tort liability rules. The new law came to establish a general liability regime for all medical acts based on tort liability. The claimant-patient is required to prove all the elements that substantiate the doctors' responsibility. It is up to the claimant-patient to prove, in court, that the doctor acted in a wrongful way, that is, violated medical *leges artis* (wrongfulness); that (s)he did not meet the criterion of the 'reasonable doctor' (culpability)[15]; and that in doing so, caused (causation) injury (damage) to the patient. If the patient fails to demonstrate any one of these four requirements, his/her pretension is dismissed.

The standardisation is a very welcome development. There are differences between medical practice in the public and private sectors which must be recognised by the law, particularly in terms of identifying the person (natural or legal person, namely the doctor or the hospital) who must compensate the patient, but there is no justification for creating different regimes, in terms of proof and the burden of proof, between the two situations.[16]

Rather than choosing between contractual and tort law, the best option would be to create a set of rules that blends the two types of liability. If it is necessary to choose

[11] For the Portuguese context, see Gaspar (1978), p. 341; Rodrigues (2000), pp. 194–198; Sousa (1996), p. 127.

[12] This was a decision intended to standardise case law and its goal was to solve a discrepancy between different court decisions. Until that moment the issue was controversial. For instance, in a decision from 30 October 2003, the Court of Appeal decided that medical acts in public facilities would be assessed under the rules of tort liability (proceeding n. 85/2003); but that same court, in a subsequent decision from 14 July 2005, concluded that the application of tort law rules was suitable in that same scenario (proceeding n. 117/2005).

[13] For instance, see the decision of the Court of Last Appeal, from 13 November 2013, proceeding n. 34/2013, allowing both regimes in a case against a private hospital.

For more on these cases, see Assembleia Legislativa (2016), p. 155.

[14] Cf. Assembleia Legislativa (2016), pp. 31, 35, 44.

[15] These two criteria—medical *leges artis* and the 'reasonable doctor'—correspond to the 'best standard of care' criterion followed in common law. For more on this correspondence, see, Raposo (2019a): 404–405.

[16] A defence of the uniformity of both regimes can be found in Raposo (2017), p. 125.

between the two regimes, tort liability is the most appropriate for governing medical civil liability. This conclusion reflects the conceptual basis of the two regimes: in all medical responsibility cases there is always an injury, suffering and/or unfair loss or harm, which is the core of tort liability. Medical practice, and the responsibility that derives from it, requires a legal regime that does not burden excessively the doctor's position in the judicial dispute. Under a contractual regime, due to the presumption of culpability, the doctor is forced to prove that (s)he has not violated any of the possible duties of care that fall on him/her, but the. The negative proof of a fact is nearly always impossible to satisfy.[17] Moreover, it is necessary to avoid the confluence of multiple presumptions of culpability which are quite common in the field of medical responsibility (presumption related to the obligation of results,[18] presumption connected to simple medical interventions[19] and the presumption *res ipsa loquitur*),[20] that can be added to the legal presumption of culpability typical of contract liability.[21] The exclusion of the presumption of culpability, inherent in contract liability, is counterbalanced by the presence of multiple other presumptions of culpability.[22]

2.2 *Notification of Adverse Events*

There are several possible models for reporting adverse events. The ultimate aim of reporting these events determines the features of each model. If the intended purpose of notification is to ensure that the patient has the information needed for a possible civil or criminal lawsuit against the health care provider, the notification system will be different than if the intention is to reduce future errors. It is necessary to define whether the main intention is to identify and punish doctors who committed medical faults (punitive function) or to detect dangerous behaviours and find a way to avoid them (preventive function).[23]

Law n. 5/2016 imposes the obligation to report medical faults. Only medical faults must be reported. Non-fault errors and adverse incidents are not covered by this obligation. This feature, *de per se*, indicates that the law is more concerned with punishing doctors than protecting patients.[24]

Notification of medical fault is mandatory and disregarding this requirement is a punishable offence. All professionals who are aware of, or even suspect, a medical

[17] *As pointed out by* Dias (1996), p. 225.

[18] Pedro (2008), pp. 98, 102.

[19] Nunes, 2005, pp. 41–42.

[20] Pedro (2008), pp. 341 ff.

[21] On the use of the presumption of culpability in a decision from the Court of Appeal (decision from 1 January 2013, proceeding n. 218/2011), see Raposo (2013b), pp. 110–117.

[22] For a detailed discussion of this question, see Raposo (2013a), pp. 32–42.

[23] For a discussion of these two different models, see Raposo (2018b), pp. 45–59.

[24] Advocating for Macao a solution based on preventive aims, Gonçalves and Rocha (2008), p. 237.

fault, including third parties who have no involvement in the focal incident, are required to notify the Health Services within 24 h. There is an underlying expectation of surveillance: any healthcare provider who does not denounce his/her colleagues' medical fault will be sanctioned with a fine. Medical professionals cannot be made into spies or vigilantes. This creates an undeniable environment of suspicion and mistrust in a hospital. Rules of this type foster a climate of prosecution that any system concerned with patient safety must avoid.

According to Article 9/1 of Law n. 5/2016, the main aim of the notification system is to ensure that the patient is informed of the incident, not because this will mend the relationship between doctor and patient, satisfy the medical duty of candour or promote apologies, but apparently to support a future lawsuit. The number 3 of this provision states that the Health Services must '*inform the patient of the situation and provide him/her with information that can facilitate the defence of his legally protected rights and interests*'.

Article 10/1 of Law n. 5/2016 provides for what the law calls '*accompanying measures*', but this concept refers to '*measures to prevent or reduce the damage caused to the patient's health*'. These measures are provided to the affected patient in case (s)he has suffered an injury but do not prevent another such occurrence in the future.

Article 10/3 of Law n. 5/2016 states that when there are strong indications that a medical fault has occurred, the Health Service can investigate, using measures, such as the sealing and conservation of clinical files, blood supplies, medical instruments and other elements. If this norm is read in conjunction with Article 9 of Law n. 5/2016, (as it should be, according to a harmonious interpretation of the law), it is clear that such investigations are not related to the promotion of patient safety but to the gathering of information to be disclosed to the patient for the objective described in Article 9/3 of Law n. 5/2016.

Article 10/4 of Law n. 5/2016 establishes that '*when there is strong evidence that a medical error is likely to cause a major impact or cause significant risk to public health, the Health Service must adopt the necessary measures for its prevention and monitoring, as well as publicize the respective situation*'. The text of the norm seems to indicate some kind of investigation on the causes leading to the incident. However, given the general framework of this rule, the aim of these investigations does not seem to be discovering the causes of the incident so that it will not reoccur. Nothing in Articles 9 and 10 of Law n. 5/2016 points in this direction. These articles outline a procedure to resolve a specific situation, rather than a mechanism to create measures to prevent future incidents.

The law makes no mention of using the information for preventive aims. It seems that the sole purpose of the notification requirement is to provide the patient with material to initiate a lawsuit and to promote litigation.[25]

[25] For a critique of the Macanese solution, see Raposo (2017), pp. 110–114; and Raposo (2018b), pp. 37–60.

2.3 Medical Error Expertise Commission

Law n. 5/2016 creates a dubious body, the so-called Medical Error Expertise Commission (the 'Commission').[26] This designation seems to describe a group of medical experts (expert witnesses) to be used by the court to clarify medical technical issues. However, the members of this alleged Expert Commission are not all doctors, as specified in its Article 12/1: '*The Commission is composed of seven professionals, five of whom must be in the field of medicine and two in the area of law*'. The Commission's '*technical expertise*' is both medical and legal.

The Commission plays several different roles: it uses its technical expertise (both medical and legal) to: analyse medical faults and assign responsibilities (Article 11/1 and 19 of Law n. 5/2016); investigate the causes of the faults to promote future prevention (Articles 17/3/5 and 17/3/7 of Law n. 5/2016); and evaluate the complaints presented by healthcare providers and users (Article 2 of Administrative Regulation n. 3/2017). The Commission is much more than an expert entity (even though its report is designated '*expert report*'); it is an administrative body that performs multiple legal, ethical and medical functions.[27]

Doubts have been raised as to the binding force of the Commission's reports, that is, whether the court can rule against the Commission's findings. An early legal draft contained a norm stating that '*the conclusions of the investigation and the technical expertise carried out by the Commission serve as a reference for resolving disputes*'.[28] That norm is not included in the current version. This could mean that the reports no longer have the power to serve as reference but, if that is the case, it is worth questioning what is the purpose of those reports. The law is quite ambiguous in a matter that deserves total clarification. There is no way of knowing what is happening in day-to-day judicial practice. Given how the courts operate in Macao, it is likely that they follow, without contesting, the Commission's decisions.

There are also problems related to the process for complaining about the Commission's reports. If the report were a mere expert opinion, disagreements between parties could be solved by requesting a second expert opinion, as outlined in Articles 510 and 511 of the Macanese Code of Civil Procedure. However, the Commission's report is not an expert opinion and, according to Law n. 5/2016, complaints about a report are made to the Commission itself (Article 18/1 of Law n. 5/2016). The Commission may lack impartiality when re-evaluating its own report. The final outcome of a dispute over a report's conclusions is entirely in the hands of the Commission, with no possibility of review or contestation by any other entity. One can speculate that under these conditions any outside medical experts called to the proceeding by the parties (Article 11/3 of Law n. 5/2016) will have a very limited influence on the dispute's outcome.

---

[26] Some hesitations about this entity in Associação dos Médicos de Língua Portuguesa de Macau, pp. 6–9.

[27] It has not been possible to analyse this Commission's reports, because they are not disclosed to the public.

[28] About this expression, Associação dos Médicos de Língua Portuguesa de Macau, p. 11.

In other jurisdictions, the decision to award (or not award) compensation to the injured patient is decided by a multidisciplinary panel.[29] The Expert Commission, created by Law n. 5/2016, bears some resemblance to this model but it mixes the judicial model with the administrative model, creating a muddled system in which the roles of the judiciary and the Commission are poorly defined.[30]

3 Medical Dispute Mediation Centre

One of the most relevant innovations of Law n. 5/2016 is the creation of an entity specifically aimed at resolving healthcare conflicts outside of the judicial system, with the hope of achieving faster, cheaper, friendlier and more effective outcomes.[31] Article 23 of Law n. 5/2016 creates the Medical Disputes Mediation Centre (the Centre), which operates as an alternative to the courts for solving disputes. In spite of the designation ('mediation centre'), the process seems more like a mixture of mediation and arbitration.[32]

It is not mandatory to use this mechanism and the parties may choose to go to court instead. It is not clear whether mediation can go hand in hand with a lawsuit. Law n. 5/2016 is silent on this matter. Article 8/4 of Administrative Regulation n. 4/2017, which regulates the Centre, states that the use of the mediation procedure does not prevent the parties from appealing to the court to resolve the litigation and thus it admits the possibility of a subsequent lawsuit. The existence of a simultaneous lawsuit is not referred to and not forbidden.

The norms of the mediation are also unclear. Will the parties in conflict attend the sessions or only their lawyers? Does mediation take place between the patient and the hospital, between the patient and the doctor or does everyone involved participate in the mediation? Administrative Regulation n. 4/2017 stipulates, in Article 8/3, that both the healthcare provider and the insurer will be present at the mediation, a condition that may prevent the success of the procedure. One can assume that the presence of the insurer may frustrate at least one purpose of the mediation, which is to restore the relationship between patient and healthcare provider. Furthermore, the presence of the insurer increases the risk that the result of the mediation will be unfair to the patient. Article 13 of Regulation n. 4/2017 stipulates that it is not necessary for all of the parties to have a lawyer attending the mediation, arguably to relive the patient of the chore of finding and paying for a lawyer. This would be a reasonable option if only the main parties were present. Given the insurers' particular knowledge of legal issues, their presence at an intervention is likely to

---

[29] On the various possible models and the way in which they have been implemented in other jurisdictions, see Cascão (2005), pp. 59 ff.

[30] For a critique of the Commission's role, see Raposo (2017), pp. 114–117.

[31] For a discussion of the advantages of the alternative dispute resolution methods in the field of healthcare *vide* Raposo (2020).

[32] Cardinal and Peng (2017): 15.

create a wide power imbalance between the parties. Only a mediator with extreme prudence and sensitivity will be able to overcome this counterproductive effect. The Uniform Policy Model (established by Executive Order n. 46/2017) transfers several powers from the insured to the insurer. In practical terms, mediations will effectively take place between the patient and the insurer and not between the patient and the health care provider. This composition prevents the safeguarding of the doctor-patient relationship and the promotion of trust between the two, which is one of the main goals of mediation.

A crucial requirement for the success of this mechanism is that mediators have expertise, not only in mediation techniques, but also in healthcare delivery. Having experts on the matters under discussion to handle a conflict is one of the advantages that alternative dispute resolution mechanisms have over litigation. Such a requirement is absent from the existing regulations in Macao. Macanese lawmakers believe that any mediator is capable of analysing this type of dispute, even if (s)he is not familiar with the matters under analysis; in fact, the current composition of the Centre demonstrates that in Macao this requirement has been disregarded.

The creation of the Medical Disputes Mediation Centre is a praiseworthy effort but its composition and *modus operandi* have prevented it from achieving its many potential benefits.[33]

4 Basic Features of Medical Criminal Liability

Medical criminal liability is regulated by the Macao Criminal Code (CrC). The general norms for any kind of criminal liability apply and the respective crimes apply but there are two norms specific to the medical profession worthy of mention: Article 144 and Article 150 of the CrC.

4.1 An Especially Favourable Legal Framework for Healthcare Professionals

Article 144 of the CrC[34] is a standard designed to define the conditions that exclude the existence of a crime committed by healthcare professionals. This is very unusual in criminal law, as typically its norms define the conditions for the existence of a crime, not for its absence.

[33] This same critique is given in Raposo (2020).

[34] An analysis of this norm, as it exists in the Portuguese Criminal Code, can be found in Andrade (2012b), pp. 601, 607 ff.; Rodrigues (2013), pp. 11–26.

The norm lists four requirements, all cumulative that, when fulfilled, exempt the doctor from liability, even if the patient has suffered harm.[35]

The norm begins by clarifying that it only applies to acts of doctors or '*other person legally authorized*'. It is unclear whether the latter expression refers to doctors of traditional Chinese medicine, as there is no norm making a general equalisation, valid for every scenario, between conventional medicine and traditional Chinese medicine. In what regards medical professionals working for the Government, Law n. 10/2010 expressly includes the practitioners of traditional Chinese medicine in the category of medical professionals. This equalization is only valid for those working in the Macau Health Bureau, so, at least the latter are included in this provision. Doctors of traditional Chinese medicine, working as private practitioners, might be excluded, which makes no sense at all.

These individuals must be acting for a specific purpose: '*preventing, diagnosing, eliminating or mitigating disease, suffering, injury or body fatigue, or mental disorder*', that is, with a general therapeutic intent. The concept of '*therapeutic*' has been widely discussed in Portugal in the context of a legal provision with exactly the same content. Most scholars agree that a purely aesthetic chirurgical intervention does not fit this purpose, because it is not therapeutic. The same argument is made for gender reassignment surgeries or sterilisations.[36] However, all of these medical procedures have (or can have) a therapeutic purpose: they seek to eliminate physiological suffering and even to address mental disorders and thus such exclusions are not accurate.

For liability to be excluded, it is necessary to demonstrate that the medical act was performed '*according to the state of knowledge and experience of medicine*'. This means that the norm only refers to institutionalised medicine, that is, medical practices accepted as common practices, excluding experimental procedures. The same norm exists in Portugal and this segment is interpreted as excluding forms of alternative medicine, including traditional Chinese medicine. For the already referred reasons, this exclusion might not apply in Macao but this issue is unclear.

The last requirement is related to the medical standard of care: the doctor is required to follow the '*rules of the profession*', that is, medical *leges artis*.[37] Compliance with the *leges artis* is equivalent to compliance with the medical standard of care in common law.[38]

---

[35] The norm only expressly refers to cases in which the patient suffered an injury to his/her body, but it has been interpreted as also covering situations in which the patient has died. Accordingly, the norm would exclude liability not only for the crime of bodily harm, but also for the crime of homicide.

[36] These exceptions are listed (in relation to the Portuguese norm, but also valid for the Macanese version) in Andrade (2012a): 465–469.

[37] In contrast, if doctors have not acted as it could be reasonable expected—in other others, if they violate medical *leges artis*—this provision does not apply. That was what happened in proceeding n. 857/2011, from 16.12.2014, where the Court of Appeal convicted two doctors for the crime of bodily harm due to an error in diagnosis that led to injuries to a child.

[38] The equivalence is explained in Raposo (2019a), pp. 404–405.

If there was no such norm (as it happens in most jurisdictions), *prima facie*, a doctor's action that results in harm to a patient would be considered a potential crime but liability would be excluded by means of the so-called clauses excluding the wrongful nature of the conduct or the culpability of the agent. Article 144 CrC immediately determines that any medical act that meets its requirements cannot be considered a criminal act, based on the special value the law recognises to the medical profession.

4.2 *Violation of a patient's Informed Consent*

4.2.1 Prevalence of Self-determination Over Life

Article 150 CrC provides a special legal solution to the violation of a patient's informed consent. It creates a crime, absent in most criminal jurisdictions: the crime of arbitrary medical-surgical intervention or treatment, that is, conducting a medical intervention without the patient's consent.

Medical interventions without the patient's consent (expressed or presumed) are a crime in Macao, whether or not there is any harm to the patient; the medical act might actually ameliorate the patient's health or even save his/her life.[39] If the patient has not properly consented, it is considered that his/her personal freedom has been violated, which explains why this crime is located in the chapter of crimes against personal self-determination. This norm places the value of self-determination over the value of life.

Macanese authors have barely researched this norm but in Portugal the correlated norm (with exactly the same content) has been the subject of several theses.[40] Some authors state that the protection of personal self-determination is limited by the protection provided to human life.[41] According to this interpretation, the doctor is required to intervene, even when the patient has not consented. These authors base their position on the respect for human life as a basic legal principle. This premise is correct but the conclusion is not. In the particular scenario of healthcare delivery, the legislators gave preference to self-determination; otherwise, the limit imposed by the protection of human life would have been included in the norm and it was not. In criminal law, legal interpretation is particularly strict, imposed by the very rigid principle of legality that rules in this domain. If the norm does not state that the criminal responsibility of the doctor is excluded when (s)he intervenes to save the patient's life, the interpreter (legal doctrine, judge) cannot 'make up' this limitation.[42]

---

[39] For the Macanese norm, see Raposo (2015), pp. 59–80.

[40] For more on the equivalent norm in Portugal, with this same content, see Andrade (2012b), pp. 595–631; Raposo (2012), pp. 379–390.

[41] Brito (2002), pp. 403 ff., 408 ff.; Brito (2005), pp. 584; Brito et al. (2007), pp. 58 ff.

[42] This opinion on Portuguese law is given in Raposo (2019b), pp. 250–251.
Regarding Macanese law, see Raposo (2019c).

4.2.2 The Crime of Arbitrary Medical-Surgical Intervention or Treatment

Article 150/1 CrC states that a doctor who performs one of the acts described in Article 144 CrC without the patient's consent can be punished with imprisonment of up to 3 years or with a fine.[43]

There might be cases in which the patient is prevented from providing consent at that moment. Article 150/2 CrC deals with this situation by addressing presumed consent. Presumed consent allows the doctor to act without the patient's prior consent, provided the factual situation corresponds to one of two scenarios described in Article 150/2 CrC. Article 150/2/a CrC refers to cases in which consent can only be obtained through a postponement that carries risk (simple risk) to the patient's life, or serious risk (qualified risk) to his/her body or health. That will be the case when the patient is unconscious and waiting until (s)he regains consciousness would put him/her at risk. Article 150/2/b CrC refers to cases in which the patient has given his/her actual consent for a certain medical act, but during this act the doctor realises that, to prevent harm to the patient's life, body or health, it is necessary to perform a different act that was not authorised by the patient. Suppose that a patient consented to a surgical intervention to treat an infection on the patient's leg but, during the intervention, the doctor concluded that the leg must be amputated, although the patient did not consent to the amputation.

In cases that fit one of these scenarios, a doctor can intervene without the patient's prior consent without risking criminal liability. An additional requirement is needed for both scenarios: there can be no circumstances that would lead the doctor to conclude, with a reasonable degree of certainty, that the patient would have refused consent if (s)he was able to express his/her wishes.[44] The principle of *favor vitae* (in favour of life), which characterises the CrC, is visible in the regulation of presumed consent: the doctor is required to intervene to prevent harm, unless there are sound reasons to believe that consent would be refused.

Article 150 CrC is silent regarding the need for consent to be informed. The subsequent norm, Article 151 CrC, clarifies that, for consent to be relevant, the patient must be informed about the '*diagnosis and the nature, scope and possible consequences of the intervention or treatment*'. The exception is when the information would carry the disclosure of elements which, if known to the patient, would endanger his/her life or would be likely to cause serious harm to his/her physical or mental health. This is called '*therapeutic privilege*' and refers to special circumstances that allow the doctor to medically intervene without informing the patient.[45]

[43] For more on this provision in the Macanese Criminal Code, see Iong (2017b): 26 ff.

[44] For a discussion of presumed consent about the Portuguese norm, see Andrade (2012b), pp. 615–628, and about the Macanese norm, see Raposo (2015), pp. 59–80.

[45] For a discussion of therapeutic privilege in Macanese law, see Raposo (2019c).

4.2.3 A Singularity of Informed Consent in Macao: A Western Law Within a Chinese Culture

Macao has a dual nature: it is both Chinese and Portuguese (Western). This duality has consequences at various levels, including the language and content of medical informed consent.

Macao has two official languages: Chinese and Portuguese. The official Chinese is Mandarin, but in this part of China most people speak Cantonese, and these two versions of Chinese are not mutually understandable. There are three widely spoken languages, to which English must also be added, as a generally understood language.[46] Macao is a real melting pot, with a large proportion of the population coming from other parts of the world and it is not uncommon for healthcare providers and patients to not speak the same language. There is a system of telephonic translations by professional translators but in most cases it is up to health care providers (usually nurses) to act as translators in the language agreed on by the participants in the conversation, even when some or all of the parties do not have sufficient expertise in that language.

In addition to multiple languages, the people in multicultural settings may have different values. The Macanese population is predominantly Chinese and they are used to a specific model of informed consent in which decisions are made by the family (medical familism)[47] and not by the patient. This is due to the influence of Confucianism[48] which suggests that important decisions are taken by the family to support the greater good. This is the reason why, in spite of the very clear language of Article 150 of the CrC, the practice in day-to-day healthcare settings is different, and relatives are frequently asked to sign the informed consent forms.[49]

The Macanese court has never dealt with a complex criminal case involving the lack of informed consent. If called to do so, the courts would probably disregard the lack of patient's consent, especially in the case of life saving medical interventions. A major reason for this assumption is that, even though Macao has its own jurisdiction, distinct from mainland China, Chinese culture and values are dominant. In China, the patient's consent is frequently disregarded.[50] Given this common practice in mainland China,[51] it is expected that the courts in Macao would not condemn medical interventions conducted without the patient's consent but with relatives' consent.

[46] For a discussion of the issue of languages and health communication in Macao, see Raposo (2018c), pp. 386–389.

[47] Cf. Cheng et al. (2012), pp. 431 ff.; Fan (1997), pp. 309 ff.

[48] Cf. Fan and Li (2004), pp. 179–93; Li and Wen (2010), pp. 587–99.

[49] Raposo (2018c), pp. 392–393.

[50] For a description of Chinese law and practice on informed consent, see Du and Rachul (2013), pp. 26–32; Raposo (2018a), pp. 17–30; Raposo (2019c).

[51] An explanation of the influence of Chinese values and laws on Macanese medical (and judicial) practices can be found in Raposo (2018c), pp. 385–396.

An explanation of the Chinese regime on medical liability in Iong (2017b), p. 101 ff.

5 The Absence of Relevant Caselaw in Macao

Medical liability barely exists in Macanese courts. There are no reports of the numbers of incidents and case law in this domain is almost non-existent. Between 1999 and 2016, there were only 25 legal proceedings related to medical malpractice (only 7 were decided in favour of the claimant).

In Macao, medical liability is clearly defined on paper but not in practice. Norms exist but they are rarely used. Most conflicts do not reach the courts and, when they do, they are generally dismissed, as the courts apply all kinds of strategies to avoid making decisions on cases.[52] Even when courts analyse the matters of the cases presented to them, the analysis is very superficial and ignores the particularities of medical liability. This does not favour the creation of caselaw in this domain. Moreover, several decisions are not open to public scrutiny,[53] so there is no way to learn the courts' reasoning.

Medical liability in Macao has one unusual characteristic: it rarely involves litigation.[54] Matters are usually solved extrajudicially, through private agreements between the parties. The reason might be related to money. Most cases involve medical care provided by the Macanese health service; the defendant is the Macao Government, which (unlike most governments around the world) has the financial resources to compensate alleged injured patients and avoid lawsuits. Most injured and allegedly injured patients receive compensation without having to go to court. Easy and speedy extrajudicial '*compensation*' discourages both civil trials and criminal proceedings.

The courts are not used to dealing with these matters and it is clear that they are not comfortable when they are asked to do so. Scholars are not interested in a topic that is barely an issue in Macao and there are very few local legal studies of medical liability. A superficial overview would suggest that medical liability is not a problem in Macao, totally disguising reality.

---

[52] For instance, in proceeding n. 120/2019, from November 19, 2019, the Court of Last Appeal invoked a lack of evidence (since that court cannot ask for more evidence, and must make its decisions based on evidence presented in the lower courts) to avoid providing a legal assessment of the substance of the case.

Likewise, in proceeding n. 327/2018, from January 24, 2019, that very same court also avoided a deep analysis of the matters. The case involved the birth of a baby with brain paralysis, allegedly due to a delay in performing a C-section. Although the case required important, complex and deep considerations, the court solved the legal issues in a simple paragraph.

[53] It is very difficult to perform any kind of serious research on this topic in Macao because several decisions are not publicly available on the website of the Macao courts (http://www.court.gov.mo/pt/).

[54] Most of the few existing lawsuits are related to birth injuries. See, for instance, the decision of the Court of Appeal, from 24 January 2019, proceeding n. 327/2018; the decisions of the Administrative Court, proceedings ns. 220/13-RA, 217/13-RA e 257/16-RA (these decisions are not released to the public and their dates are imprecise but were probably made near the end of 2017 or the beginning of 2018).

References

Assembleia Legislativa (2016) Parecer n.º 3/V/2016, 3.ª Comissão Permanente

Associação dos Advogados de Macau (2014) Análise da Proposta de Lei do Regime Jurídico de Tratamento de Litígios Decorrentes de Erro Médico. https://aam.org.mo/wp-content/uploads/2016/11/Regime_Juridico_Tratamento_Litigios_Decorrentes_Erro_Medico.pdf

Associação dos Médicos de Língua Portuguesa de Macau (2014) 'Opinião da Associação dos Médicos de Língua Portuguesa de Macau'

Andrade MC (2012a) 'Art. 150.º'. in *Comentário Conimbricense do Código Penal, Parte Especial*, Tomo I, 2nd ed., Jorge de Figueiredo Dias (dir.), pp 457–475. Coimbra Editora, Coimbra

Andrade MC (2012b). 'Art. 156.º', in *Comentário Conimbricense do Código Penal, Parte Especial*, Tomo I, 2nd ed, Jorge de Figueiredo Dias (dir.), pp 595–631. Coimbra Editora, Coimbra

Brito TQ (2002) Responsabilidade Penal dos Médicos: Análise dos Principais Tipos Incriminadores. Revista Portuguesa De Ciência Criminal 12:371–409

Brito TQ (2005) Interrupção de Alimentação e Hidratação Artificiais de Pessoa em Estado Vegetativo Permanente. Revista Portuguesa De Ciência Criminal 15:557–607

Brito TQ et al (2007) Crimes Contra a Vida: Questões Preliminares. In *Direito Penal–Parte Especial: Lições, Estudos e Casos,* Teresa Quintela de Brito (coord.). Coimbra Editora, Coimbra, pp 25–68

Cardinal P, Peng CW (2017) 'Lei n.º 5/2016, Regime Jurídico do Erro Médico–Da Proposta de Lei às Páginas do Boletim Oficial: Breve Crónica do Caminho das Diferenças. Legisiuris (Especial Erro Médico) 8:11–30

Cascão R (2005) Prevention and compensation of treatment injury: a roadmap for reform. Boom Juridische Uitgevers, Den Haag

Cascão R (2017) O Regime Jurídico do Erro Médico perante as Grandes Linhas da Responsabilidade Civil Médica Contemporânea. Legisiuris (especial Erro Médico) 8:31–47

Cheng K-Y, Ming T, Lai A (2012) Can familism be justified? Bioethics 26(8):431–439

Dias JÁ (1996) Procriação Assistida e Responsabilidade Médica. Coimbra Editora, Coimbra

Du Li, Rachul C (2013) A brief review on informed consent laws in China. Health Law Review 21(2):26–32

Fan R (1997) Self-Determinations vs. family-determination: two incommensurable principles of autonomy. Bioethics 11:309–322

Fan R, Li B (2004) Truth telling in medicine: the confucian view. J Med Philos 29:179–193

Gaspar AH (1978) Estudo Sobre a Responsabilidade Civil do Médico. *Colectânea de Jurisprudência* III(I):335–355

Gonçalves C, Rocha JP (2008) 'Uma Visão Crítica sobre a Futura Lei do Acidente Médico', *Boletim da Faculdade de Direito de Macau* XIII(26):231–238

Iong MT (2017a) Do Acidente Médico à Responsabilidade Civil Médica no Ordenamento Jurídico da República Popular da China. Cadernos Ibero-Americanos De Direito Sanitário 6(3):101–117. https://doi.org/10.17566/ciads.v6i3.404

Iong MT (2017b) Impactos do Regime Jurídico do Erro Médico Sobre a Medicina Tradicional Chinesa. Legisiuris (especial Erro Médico) 8:53–65

Li E-C, Wen C-F (2010) Should the confucian family-determination, model be rejected? A case study. J Med Philos 35:587–599. https://doi.org/10.1093/jmp/jhq045

Nunes, MR (2005) O Ónus da Prova nas Acções de Responsabilidade Civil por Actos Médicos. Almedina, Coimbra

Pedro RT (2008) A Responsabilidade Civil do Médico: Reflexões sobre a Noção da Perda de Chance e a Tutela do Doente Lesado. Coimbra Editora, Coimbra

Pessanha L (2006) 'Breve Comentário ao Anteprojecto da "Lei do Acidente Médico"' (non published study)

Pessanha L (2017) Direito à Informação Médica – O Acesso ao Processo Clínico pelos Pacientes. Legisiuris (especial Erro Médico) 8:63–103

Raposo VL (2012) To act or not to act, that is the question: informed consent in a criminal perspective. Eur J Health Law 19(4):379–390

Raposo VL (2013a) *Do Ato Médico ao Problema Jurídico (Breves Notas sobre o Acolhimento da Responsabilidade Médica Civil e Profissional na Jurisprudência Nacional).* Almedina, Coimbra
Raposo VL (2013b) O Acto Médico Perante o Olhar Judicial: Breve Apontamento à Decisão Proferida no Processo n.º 218/2011. Legisiuris de Macau em Revista 1(1):110–117
Raposo VL (2015) 'Quando o Paciente diz Não: Sobre o artigo 150.º do Código Penal de Macau (Intervenções e tratamentos médico-cirúrgicos arbitrários). Boletim da Faculdade de Direito da Universidade de Macau, XIX(36):59–80
Raposo VL (2017) Qual o Erro da Lei do Erro Médico? Sobre o Regime Jurídico do Erro Médico no Ordenamento da RAEM. Legisiuris (especial Erro Médico) 8:103–130
Raposo VL (2018a) Lost in 'culturation": medical informed consent in China (From a Western Perspective). Med Health Care Philos 22(1):17–30. https://doi.org/10.1007/s11019-018-9835-0
Raposo VL (2018b) Don't ask, don't tell (adverse events reporting system as a mechanism to punish doctors–the Chinese and Macanese solutions). Med Law 37(1):37–60
Raposo VL (2018c) Macao report: informed consent in a multilingual and multicultural country, a bioethical challenge. Camb Q Healthc Ethics 27(3):385–396
Raposo VL (2019a) Defensive medicine and the imposition of a more demanding standard of care. J Leg Med 39(4):401–416
Raposo VL (2019b) Doctor's criminal liability and medically assisted death – the Portuguese case. Eur J Health Law 26:240–254
Raposo VL (2019c) Informed consent in China and Macao. In: Vansweevelt T, Glover-Thomas N (eds) Informed consent and health-a global analysis. Edward Arnold Publishers, Cheltenham, pp 144–162
Raposo VL (2020) Em favor dos métodos de resolução alternativa de litígios no âmbito dos cuidados de saúde', to be published by the RAEM Goverment
Rodrigues ÁC (2000) Reflexões em Torno da Responsabilidade Civil dos Médicos. *Revista Direito e Justiça* XIV(3):161–252
Rodrigues ÁCG (2013) 'O Artigo 150.º, N.º 1, do Código Penal - Uma Jóia Preciosa no Direito Penal Médico'. Julgar, 21:11–26
Sousa MT (1996) Sobre o Ónus da Prova nas Acções de Responsabilidade Civil Médica' in *Direito da Saúde e Bioética,* António Marques dos Santos et al. (eds.), pp 121–144. AAFDL, Lisboa
Trigo M (2014) Lições de Direito das Obrigações. Faculdade de Direito da Universidade de Macau, Macau

'Medical Negligence in Malaysia: Selected Issues of Liabilities and Damages'?

Sharon Kaur, Charlaine A. Chin, and Mohammad Firdaus bin Abdul Aziz

Abstract This chapter explores selected medico-legal issues within the Malaysian legal landscape. The first issue relates to a medical practitioner's duty of care and whether such a duty ought to extend to a third party, in circumstances where a patient is dependent on a spouse in arriving at a decision or where decisions are made jointly by both spouses, in respect of treatment for one of the spouses. The second issue involves institutional liability within the public and private sectors. Recent developments, within the public sector, dictate that a director of a public healthcare facility may be held personally liable for the negligent act or omission of his/her staff notwithstanding that the tortfeasor is an employee of the Government of Malaysia. With regard to the private sector, the Malaysian apex court has shed judicial light and held that the doctrine of non-delegable duty of care may be imposed on private healthcare facilities in circumstances where the requisite features are met. The third issue deals with aggravated damages and the purpose of such an award in medical negligence suits.

1 Introduction

Healthcare services in Malaysia are primarily provided by a tax-funded public sector together with a fast-growing private sector. Public sector healthcare services are delivered under a civil service structure which is centrally administered by the Ministry of Health through its central, state and district offices.[1] In addition, the Ministry of Higher Education runs university teaching hospitals, the Ministry of Defence runs

[1] World Health Organization. Regional Office for the Western Pacific (2012).

S. Kaur (✉) · M. F. A. Aziz
Faculty of Law, University of Malaya, Kuala Lumpur, Malaysia
e-mail: kaursh@um.edu.my

C. A. Chin
Advocate & Solicitor of the High Court of Malaya, Kuala Lumpur, Malaysia

V. L. Raposo and R. G. Beran (eds.), *Medical Liability in Asia and Australasia*, Ius Gentium: Comparative Perspectives on Law and Justice 94,
https://doi.org/10.1007/978-981-16-4855-7_10

military hospitals and medical centres and the Department of Aboriginal Development provides healthcare services to the indigenous population in collaboration with the Ministry of Health.[2] Private healthcare services are provided through private hospitals and clinics, which are primarily located in urban areas.[3]

The Ministry of Health is the internal regulator of its facilities and staff while the private sector is regulated under the Private Healthcare and Facilities and Services Act 1998 (PHFA)[4] by way of licencing of providers who have fulfilled requisite standards.[5] The Malaysian Medical Council (the Council) set up under the Medical Act 1971,[6] is entrusted with the regulation of the medical profession. All practicing medical practitioners in the country must be registered under this Act. The Council controls entry to and manages the Malaysian Medical Register. The Council also exercises disciplinary jurisdiction[7] over all persons registered under the Act and has the power to impose punishments.[8]

In Malaysia, individuals who have suffered harm as a result of an act and/or omission of an employee, agent and/or representative of a healthcare facility or medical practitioner may commence a civil claim premised upon the tort of negligence. Malaysia, similar to many other Commonwealth countries, is predominantly a common law jurisdiction and the law in respect of medical negligence is derived from judge-made law or case law. Medical liability jurisprudence in Malaysia has evolved along similar lines of other common law jurisdictions such as England, Singapore, and Australia. A notable feature of Malaysian common law is that judgments of other common law jurisdictions are commonly cited in local cases. A survey conducted by Ng and Jacobson notes that 67.1% of Malaysian reported cases cited foreign judgments and that English cases are most frequently cited.[9] Of the cases surveyed, "*93% of Malaysian cases use some or all of the foreign cases cited affirmatively as legal authority in their reasoning*".[10]

Although comprehensive annual statistics on medical negligence claims are not available in Malaysia, Hambali and Khodapanahandeh report some evidence of an upward trend.[11] At the end of 2019, the Minister of Health noted that between the years 2016 to 2018, the number of incidents involving wrong surgery, unintended retention of foreign objects, transfusion and medication errors and patient falls have nearly doubled in both public and private hospitals.[12]

---

[2] World Health Organization. Regional Office for the Western Pacific (2012).

[3] Merican and Yon (2002).

[4] Private Healthcare Facilities and Services Act 1998 (Act 586).

[5] For an overview of the Act and a discussion of its impact on private healthcare providers, see Nik Rosnah and Lee (2011).

[6] Medical Act 1971 (Act 50).

[7] Medical Act 1971, s 29.

[8] Medical Act 1971, s 30.

[9] Ng and Jacobson (2017).

[10] Ng and Jacobson (2017).

[11] Hambali and Khodapanahandeh (2014). at 76.

[12] Zainuddin (2019).

This chapter considers selected issues of medical liability in Malaysia, in relation to personal liability of doctors and highlights the developments relating to duties to third parties. It examines institutional liability of both public and private healthcare institutions and the imposition of a non-delegable duty of care for the negligence of independent contractors. It also touches upon the current trend in awarding aggravated damages in medical negligence cases.

2 Personal Liability

2.1 Duty of Care to Third Parties

The duties which a medical practitioner owes a patient are *(i)* a duty to diagnose and treat a patient and *(ii)* a duty to advise a patient of the material risks of a proposed treatment. To succeed in a claim premised on medical negligence, a claimant is required to prove three elements: that the medical practitioner owed him a duty of care as described above; that the medical practitioner breached this duty by falling below the standard of care; and the breach must cause or materially contribute to the injury and/or loss suffered by the claimant.

There are a number of established categories or relationships where the courts have recognised the existence of a duty of care. The doctor-patient relationship is one of them. Guidance as to how the courts may approach such situations may be obtained from the English case of *Caparo Industries plc v Dickman.*[13] The House of Lords, faced with a series of judgments that appeared to be extending the scope of liability by recognising a *prima facie* duty in most cases, made it clear that courts should not make this general assumption in novel cases, and set out a three-stage test (the Caparo test).[14] The harm must be reasonably foreseeable as a result of the defendant's conduct; the parties must be in a relationship of sufficient proximity; and it must be fair, just and reasonable to impose liability. If any of these criteria is not met, there will be no duty of care owed to the claimant. In most instances, where there is a pre-existing doctor-patient relationship, this duty is easily established.

The question of whether a claimant, who is not a patient, is owed a duty of care is complex. Depending on the circumstances, it is less clear as to how the duty of care of doctors may be extended to third parties based on the Caparo test, as it may be difficult to foresee harm to a third party, it is less likely that there is a relationship of sufficient proximity, and it might be unjust to extend the duty of care of medical practitioners to third parties.

In the case of *Abdul Razak bin Datuk Abu Samah (claimed as a widower to Fatimah @ Rohani bt Zainal, on behalf of the deceased) v Raja Badrul Hisham*

[13] [1990] 2 AC 605.

[14] The Caparo test was affirmed in the case of *Uniphone Sdn Bhd v Chin Boon Lit* [1998] 6 MLJ 441.

bin Raja Zezeman Shah & Ors[15] the High Court considered, among other things, whether a doctor has a duty to obtain consent from a patient's spouse in a situation where the patient is dependent on the spouse to make decisions in respect of the patient's treatment and management. In the *Abdul Razak* case, the patient, a 71-year-old woman, required urgent surgery for a small bowel obstruction. Although the patient consented to the surgery, she repeatedly refused the insertion of a Ryle's tube prior to the induction of anaesthesia.[16] During the induction of anaesthesia, the patient regurgitated a large amount of stomach fluid that entered into her lungs and she subsequently passed away from respiratory failure. The patient's husband commenced a claim against the medical practitioners who treated and managed the patient and the healthcare facility. The patient's husband claimed, *inter alia,* that the defendants breached their duty of care owed to him by failing or neglecting to obtain his consent to proceed with the surgery on the patient.[17]

In considering this claim, against the general principle that a duty of care is ordinarily owed only to a patient, the judge considered two instances of "*exceptions to this general principle.*"[18] First, the case of *Gurmit Kaur a/p Jaswant Singh v Tung Shin Hospital & Anor,*[19] where the High Court held that a patient's consent to a hysterectomy was insufficient without her husband's consent; and, in cases where surrogate consent is required for patients who lack mental capacity. The judge in the *Abdul Razak* case concluded that, "*[s]imilarly, consent of the spouse may be required when it is evident that the patient is dependent on the spouse to make decisions in regards to the proposed medical treatment or when it is evident to the doctor that the decisions are being made jointly by both spouses in respect of the treatment for one of the spouses.*" The judge also found that the medical practitioner who treated and managed the patient in this case "*owed a duty to inform the plaintiff* [the patient's husband] *of the nature of the surgery and the inherent and materials risk of the procedure, especially in light of the patient's refusal to have the Ryle's tube inserted.*"[20]

The decision of the *Abdul Razak* case may be regarded as an exception to the general principle that a medical practitioner owes a duty of care to his patient rather than an extension to the duty of care owed by a medical practitioner. The decision of the *Abdul Razak* case raises several issues.

The decision of the *Abdul Razak* case may be argued to be contrary to the role of consent in the medical decision-making process. The legal basis for the duty to advise of risks and obtaining consent is rooted in the principle of patient autonomy or the protection of the right to bodily integrity. Every person is entitled to have accurate and sufficient information to make their own decisions in respect of their medical

[15] [2013] 10 MLJ 34.

[16] The insertion of a Ryle's tube to pump out stomach fluid before surgery reduces the risk of aspiration during the induction of anaesthesia.

[17] [2013] 10 MLJ 34, at 40.

[18] [2013] 10 MLJ 34, at 53.

[19] [2012] 4 MLJ 260.

[20] [2013] 10 MLJ 34, at 53.

treatment. A medical practitioner, therefore, is duty bound to advise of material risks and do so in a manner that is comprehensible to each patient. The harm occasioned by a breach of the duty to advise is the violation of a patient's right to make an autonomous and informed decision. This duty cannot be transferred to a third party as no one can be said to have any claim over the autonomy of another competent person or have suffered any harm as the result of the violation of someone else's autonomy. To argue otherwise would be to endorse a form of 'spousal paternalism'. Furthermore, a distinction ought to be drawn between cases involving proxy consent of incapacitated individuals and cases similar to the *Abdul Razak* case where the patient was a competent adult. If the claimant's wife had the capacity to make her own decision regarding the insertion of the Ryle's tube, requiring her husband's consent as well would be a fundamental violation of her right to bodily integrity.

The exceptions to the general principle that a medical practitioner owes a duty of care to his patient arguably adds uninvited complexity to the treatment and management of patients. Medical practitioners may find it difficult to identify situations "*when it is evident that the patient is dependent on the spouse to make decisions in regards to the proposed medical treatment or when it is evident to the doctor that the decisions are being made jointly by both spouses*". Moreover, domination may be interpreted as dependency and requiring spousal consent in such situations would have the perverse result of exacerbating relationships where there is an imbalance of power or autonomy.

It would appear to be an unfair extension of the duty of care and not in keeping with the ways in which courts in other common law jurisdictions have developed the jurisprudence on duties to third parties.[21]

The *Abdul Razak* case raises an important question about the role of third parties in the decision-making process and more importantly, where to draw the line between a case which falls within the general principle and one which ought to be regarded as an exception to the general principle. In *the Abdul Razak* case, the court was presented with evidence demonstrating that the patient was reliant on her husband in many ways. At the outset of her illness, it was the husband who decided that the patient be transferred from a rural healthcare facility to a tertiary healthcare facility in the city. The patient's husband selected the hospital and made the necessary arrangements for the patient to be treated and managed specifically by the first defendant. When informed of the need for surgery, the patient called her husband and asked the first defendant to speak to him. In the circumstances, the judge found that the first defendant had "*full personal knowledge that the Plaintiff was the one who made decisions with regards to the medical treatment of the patient.*"[22] If the duty of care should be confined solely to the patient in a case such as this, then perhaps the more appropriate question is whether the scope of this duty should be extended in

[21] See the following cases: *ABC v St George's Healthcare NHS Trust* [2020] EWHC 455 (QB), *Paul v Royal Wolverhampton NHS Trust* [2020] EWHC, *Taylor v A Novo (UK) Ltd* [2013] EWCA Civ 194, North Glamorgan NHS Trust v Walters [2002] EWCA Civ 1792.

[22] *Abdul Razak bin Datuk Abu Samah (claimed as a widower to Fatimah @ Rohani bt Zainal, on behalf of the deceased) v Raja Badrul Hisham bin Raja Zezeman Shah & Ors* [2013] 10 MLJ 34, at 50.

certain circumstances to include a duty to ensure that patients are supported in the decision-making process, which might include a duty to determine who should be part of the conversation. Any such consideration must be mindful of the importance of respecting the autonomy and wishes of the patient.

2.2 *Standard of Care*

In 2007, following the decision of the Federal Court[23] in *Foo Fio Na v. Dr Soo Fook Mun & Anor*,[24] there was some uncertainty regarding the test that should be applied in regard to the standard of care in medical negligence cases. There were a number of conflicting decisions of both the High Court and the Court of Appeal in Malaysia. In 2017, the Federal Court in *Zulhasnimar Hasan Basri & Anor v Dr Kuppu Velumani P & Ors,*[25] clarified the position in Malaysia in respect of the tests that should apply in determining the standard of care expected of medical professionals. The Federal Court in *Zulhasnimar* held that, "*The test propounded by the Australian case in Rogers v Whitaker and followed by this Court in Foo Fio Na in regard to standard of care in medical negligence is restricted only to the duty to advise of risks associated with any proposed treatment and does not extend to diagnosis or treatment. With regard to the standard of care for diagnosis or treatment, the Bolam test still applies, subject to qualifications as decided by the House of Lords in Bolitho.*"[26] In *Zulhasnimar,* the Federal Court made a clear distinction between the duty to diagnose and treat a patient, and the duty to advise of risks.

In respect of the duty of a medical practitioner to diagnose and treat, the applicable test is the one articulated in the English case, *Bolam v Friern Hospital Management Committee,*[27] (the Bolam Test) which states that "*A doctor is not guilty of negligence if he has acted in accordance with a practice accepted as proper by a responsible body of medical men skilled in that particular art ... Putting it the other way round, a doctor is not negligent, if he is acting in accordance with such a practice, merely because there is a body of opinion that takes a contrary view.*" Reflecting on the fact that the practice of medicine does not admit to scientific precision and that medical experts frequently and genuinely differ in opinion on diagnosis and treatment, the Federal Court in *Zulhasnimar* concluded that it was not equipped to resolve these differences. The Federal Court held that "*the Bolam test makes good sense. It requires the court to accept, not just the views of medical experts simpliciter, but the views of a responsible body of men skilled in that particular discipline. It removes from the courts the responsibility of resolving a dispute that is not equipped to resolve.*"[28]

---

[23] The Federal Court is the s the highest court and the final appellate court in Malaysia.

[24] *Foo Fio Na v. Dr Soo Fook Mun & Anor* [2007] 1 MLJ 593.

[25] [2017] 8 CLJ 605.

[26] [2017] 8 CLJ 605.

[27] [1957] 1 WLR 583.

[28] [2017] 8 CLJ 605 at 642, paragraph 95.

The Bolam Test is subject to qualifications as described in the English case of *Bolitho v. City and Hackney Health Authority,*[29] (the Bolitho qualification) where the House of Lords "*calls upon the court to analyse the logic and reasonableness of the conflicting medical opinion advanced by the defence before accepting the same. The court should not accept an opinion put forward by the defence as being "reasonable", "respectable" or "responsible" without first assessing whether such opinion is susceptible to logical analysis.*"[30]

In the case of *Dato' Dr V Thuraisingam & Anor v Sanmarkan a/l Ganapathy & Anor,*[31] the Court of Appeal set aside the judgment of the High Court based on, *inter alia*, the fact that the trial judge discounted the medical expert evidence of two defence witnesses. The trial judge had specifically highlighted the fact that one of the expert witnesses was a member of the same indemnifier as the defendant medical practitioner and as such, the said expert witness could not be relied upon to provide an impartial opinion. The Court of Appeal found this to be a "*grave misdirection on the part of the learned judge to disregard the medical expert opinion on the subject in issue*".[32] In the case of *Ahmad Zubir bin Zahid (suing by himself and as the administrator of the estate of Fatimah bt Samad, deceased) v Datuk Zainal Abidin Abdul Hamid & Ors,*[33] the Court of Appeal expressed rather strong partial views on the development and application of the Bolam Test in other jurisdictions by describing the decisions in the following ways: "*a successful attempt was made to increase the doctor's liability*",[34] "*attempts to extend the duty of care principle between the doctor and patient to new heights to the detriment of the doctors..*",[35] "*further assault on the medical professions*",[36] and "*has placed doctors as well as experts to be severely cross-examined with a view to discredit their evidence and to establish liability as well as quantum.*"[37]

In respect of the duty of a medical practitioner to advise of risks, the applicable test is the one propounded by the Australian case *Rogers v Whitaker*[38] which states that "*the Law should recognise that a doctor has a duty to warn a patient of a material risk inherent in the proposed treatment: a risk is material if, in the circumstances of the particular case, a reasonable person in the patient's position, if warned of the risk, would be likely to attach significance to it or if the medical practitioner is or should be reasonably aware that the particular patient, if warned of the risk,*

---

[29] *B* [1996] 4 All ER 771.

[30] Dr Hari Krishnan & Anor v. Megat Noor Ishak Megat Ibrahim & Anor And Another Appeal [2018] 3 CLJ 427 at 455.

[31] [2016] MLJ 227.

[32] [2016] MLJ 227 at 262.

[33] [2019] 5 MLJ 95.

[34] [2019] 5 MLJ 95 at 106, referring to *Bolitho v City and Hackney Health Authority* [1988] AC 232.

[35] [2019] 5 MLJ 95 at 106, referring to *Rogers v Whitaker [1993] 4 Med LR 79.*

[36] [2019] 5 MLJ 95 at 106, referring to *Naxasis v Western General Hospital* (1999) 197 CLR.

[37] [2019] 5 MLJ 95 at 107, referring to *Montgomery v Lanarkshire Health Board* [2015] UKSC 11.

[38] 1993] 4 Med LR 79.

would be likely to attach significance to it." A different consideration is given to this aspect of a doctor's duty as a recognition that this duty is rooted in the right of self-determination. The courts do not look at the usual practice of the profession as the yardstick to govern the standard of care in this context. This is a welcome development, both in terms of the clarification of the law as well as the discarding of the Bolam Test in respect of providing advice and information. Significantly, the Federal Court remained silent on the issue as to whether a medical practitioner ought to advise a patient of the material risks in respect of treatment options as propounded in the English case of *Montgomery v Lanarkshire Health Board*[39] and the Singapore case of *Hii Chii Kok v Ooi Peng Jin London Lucien and another.*[40]

3 Institutional Liability

3.1 Public Sector

In *Pengarah Hospital Selayang & Ors v Ahmad Azizi bin Abdullah James & Ors,*[41] a pregnant woman presented to the emergency department of a government hospital with severe vaginal bleeding. Later that night, her husband was informed that she had passed away. Her family were not able to ascertain the identities of the doctors who treated her prior to her death and, therefore, brought an action against the Director of the Selayang Hospital (the Hospital). The defendants applied to strike out the claim on three main grounds. First, the defendants argued that the claimants had failed to name the tortfeasors and were in error in naming the Director of the Hospital as a defendant, as he had not personally treated the deceased. Second, the defendants asserted that the claim failed to comply with the provisions of the Government Proceedings Act 1956,[42] specifically Sect. 6(1), which states that "*no proceedings shall lie against the Government ... in respect of any act, neglect, or default of any public officer, unless proceedings for damages in respect of such act, neglect or default would have lain against such office personally*"; and finally, that the claim constituted an abuse of the court process.

The court rejected all three arguments, noting that the Director was, at all times, in charge of all doctors and nurses in the hospital and they were his agents at that material time. The Director owed the deceased patient a duty of care for the negligent acts of the doctors and nurses working in the hospital, individually and collectively. This was viewed by the court as a form of vicarious liability in that any breach of duty of care by an employee is vicariously imputed to the director of that hospital.

---

[39] *Montgomery v Lanarkshire Health Board* [2015] UKSC 11.

[40] *Hii Chii Kok v Ooi Peng Jin London Lucien and another* [2017] SGCA 38.

[41] [2012] 5 MLJ 679.

[42] Government Proceedings Act 1956 (Act 359).

Given that it may be difficult for claimants to identify the exact persons involved in the treatment and management of a patient in public healthcare facilities, a strict and literal interpretation of the statute and the principle of vicarious liability would have unfairly denied a claimant access to the justice system. Following the decision in *Pengarah Hospital Selayang,* the director of a public healthcare facility is now personally liable for the actions of his staff, despite the fact that the actual employer is the Government of Malaysia.

3.2 Private Sector

As noted earlier, the private healthcare sector in Malaysia is a fast-growing industry. Experts attribute the success of the private healthcare sector to a number of factors such as an ageing population, rising affluence, increasing life expectancy, increase in medical tourism backed by highly competitive charges and hospitalisation costs, a generally English-speaking population and various government incentives.[43] One of the more interesting developments in relation to the institutional liability of private healthcare facilities is the development of the non-delegable duty of care doctrine in Malaysia. In the case of *Dr Kok Choong Seng & Anor v Soo Cheng Lin and Another Appeal,*[44] the Federal Court considered, *inter alia,* whether the doctrine of non-delegable duty of care as expounded in *Woodland v Swimming Teachers Association and others,*[45] should apply to private healthcare facilities in Malaysia.

In *Woodland*, Lord Sumption identified two board categories in which non-delegable duties have been long recognised in English Law. First, where the defendant engages an independent contractor to perform an inherently hazardous function and second, where the common law imposes a duty upon the defendant. In the second category,[46] this duty is imposed based not on the negligent character of the act, but rather on the antecedent relationship between the defendant and the claimant. The duty is a positive duty to protect a particular class of persons against particular types of risk. The work that is carried out may be delegable but the duty itself remains the defendant's duty. Lord Sumption went on to set out five defining features of this duty.

(1) The claimant is especially vulnerable or dependent on the protection of the defendant against the risk of injury.
(2) There is an antecedent relationship between the claimant and the defendant, independent of the negligent act itself,

---

43 *Healthcare sector sees positive long-term growth prospects, says AmInvestment*, The Star, 2019, https://www.thestar.com.my/business/business-news/2019/07/15/healthcare-sector-sees-positive-long-term-growth-prospects-says-aminvestment

44 [2018]1 MLJ 685.

45 [2014] AC 537.

46 The application of this doctrine to private hospitals would fall under the second category of cases.

a. which places the claimant in the actual custody, charge or care of the defendant, and
b. from which it is possible to impute to the defendant the assumption of a positive duty to protect the claimant from harm, and not just a duty to refrain from conduct which will foreseeably damage the claimant.

(3) The claimant has no control over how the defendant chooses to perform those obligations.
(4) The defendant has delegated to some third party some function which is an integral part of the positive duty which he has assumed towards the claimant.
(5) The third party has been negligent in the performance of the very function assumed by the defendant and delegated by the defendant to him.

The defendants in *Dr Kok Choong Seng* argued that the doctrine should not apply given that private healthcare facilities were not providers of medical services but mere providers of hospital facilities. They highlighted the fact that in this case, the claimant had specifically chosen Dr Kok to perform the service whereas the hospital merely provided the facilities and back-up services for the operation. The plaintiffs maintained that because private healthcare facilities choose to engage in the commercial enterprise of providing healthcare for profit, they should not escape liability for harm caused in pursuance of that enterprise by delegating its performance to an independent contractor. The Federal Court considered the line of English cases leading up to the decision in *Woodland* and noted that the common law had long rejected the view that hospitals merely provide facilities and staff selection, it observed that such a notion was incongruent with current societal expectations of private hospitals as healthcare service providers. The Federal Court ultimately rejected both arguments that private hospitals are either always or never under a non-delegable duty to patients. It averred that the extent and scope of the hospital's duty must be ascertained from the facts and circumstances of each case as applied to the *Woodland* features.

In applying the circumstances of the case to the *Woodland* features, the court accepted that the patient, who was admitted to the hospital for surgery, was in an especially vulnerable position and dependent on the Hospital for protection against the risk of injury. When considering the second feature, the court focused on the question of whether in the given circumstances, it was possible to impute an assumption of a positive duty by the hospital to protect the patient from harm. Reference was made to the fact that in the present case, the patient had originally consulted Dr Kok at his private clinic and was subsequently admitted to the hospital pursuant to Dr Kok's advice. At first instance, the High Court and later, the Court of Appeal, both rejected the relevance of the claimant's own choice in engaging Dr Kok's services and opined that liability should depend on which party is in a better position to evaluate Dr Kok's competence. The Federal Court was of a different opinion. Based on the understanding that non-delegable duties are based on an assumptions of responsibility, and not relative resources or vested interests, the Federal Court found that the personal choice of a patient is a relevant factor in applying the second *Woodland* feature, that is, in determining whether there is an antecedent patient-hospital relationship from which to impute an assumption of responsibility by the hospital. Given that the claimant in this case had selected Dr Kok, the private healthcare facility was not in breach of its non-delegable duty to the claimant.

The fact that private healthcare facilities in Malaysia may be subject to a non-delegable duty of care to patients is a positive development. Although the Federal Court declined to consider the importance of relative resources, it is undeniable that unlike individual members of the public, most private healthcare facilities have the resources to ensure that the medical practitioners providing services in their facilities have the necessary expertise and are competent medical practitioners. Following this line of reasoning, the imposition of this duty should not be contingent on whether the patient has made a personal choice. If the assumption of responsibility is tied to the fact that an institution chooses to provide healthcare services within its premises and accordingly, assumes a positive duty to protect individuals in its charge. It should not matter whether that individual chooses the hospital or the doctor because the assumption of the responsibility is connected to the provision of healthcare services within its premises and not the individual patient. To assume otherwise would be unjust as this would create two classes of patients in private hospitals who are owed two different duties of care, However, it should also be borne in mind that a patient's choice of doctor should be regarded as an important factor. If a patient chooses a particular doctor, it would be a heavy duty to impose a non-delegable duty of care on the hospital as the hospital would have no prerogative in turning the patient away or diverting the patient to a different doctor.

4 Aggravated Damages

In tort, a claimant is entitled to be restored to the position that (s)he would have been in if the tort had not been committed, in so far as this is achievable by payment of money. There are two kinds of damages, general damages, which are awarded for pain and suffering and loss of amenity; and special damages, which are awarded for pecuniary losses incurred by the claimant arising from an injury caused by the negligent act or omission of the defendant which have to be specifically proved. In recent years, there appears to be an upward trend in the amount of damages awarded in medical negligence cases.[47]

In *Rookes v Barnard,*[48] Lord Devlin held that *"it is very well established that in cases where the damages are at large, the jury (or the judge if the award is left to him) can take into account the motives and conduct of the defendant where they aggravate the injury done to the plaintiff. There may be malevolence or spite or the manner of committing the wrong may be such as to injure the plaintiff's proper feelings of dignity and pride."* Lord Devlin believed that the punitive principle ought logically to belong to criminal law.[49] He nevertheless felt constrained by precedent

---

[47] Anbalagan (2020), Mazlina (2018), Astro (2014).

[48] [1964] 1 All ER 367 at 407.

[49] Law Commission No. 247, *Aggravated, Exemplary and Restitutionary Damages,* 1997.

from abolishing punitive damages altogether and therefore, sought to narrow their ambit. In his analysis, Lord Devlin extracted those words which were explicable in compensatory terms and renamed them "*aggravated damages*".[50]

In *Dr Hari Krishnan & Anor v. Megat Noor Ishak Megat Ibrahim & Anor And Another Appeal,*[51] the Federal Court recognised that aggravated damages may be awarded as a separate head of damage in tort. The Federal Court affirmed the award of the High Court of aggravated damages in the sum of RM1 million. The likely facts in *Dr Hari Krishnan* which were material to the finding of aggravated damages include, among others, the fact that the patient was not informed that his right eye was beyond salvation at an earlier instance and the patient was given false hope that he would regain sight in his right eye.

In *Nur Syarafina bt Sa'ari v Kerajaan Malaysia & Ors,*[52] the High Court found that the suppression of the claimant's medical records and internal inquiry report in breach of an earlier consent judgment in pre-action discover findings, warranted an award of RM200,000 for aggravated damages.

In *Dato' Stanley Isaacs (suing by himself as administrator of the estate of To'Puan Suzanne Thomas, deceased) v The Government of Malaysia & Ors,*[53] the High Court awarded the sum of RM500,000 for aggravated damages for what the court described as "*defendant's words and conduct which are disturbing, appalling and an insult to his profession and to the plaintiff and his family.*"[54] In determining a fair amount, the court considered the motive of the defendants, the claimant's status, position and character and the purpose of aggravated damages. In its decision, the court held that the purpose of awarding aggravated damages in this case was not to punish but to compensate the plaintiff for "*injuries affecting feelings arising out of the tortious act of the defendants*".[55]

Aggravated damages are meant to compensate for the aggravation of an injury arising from a negligent act or omission of a tortfeasor, and not an "*arbitrary top-up unrelated to the desire of the court to compensate the plaintiff for the aggravation*".[56] Aggravated damages should also not be used to punish the tortfeasor for the extent or severity of the injury caused given that a claimant ought to be compensated for pain and suffering through an award for general damages. Ultimately, the objective of aggravated damages is to compensate and not to punish.[57]

---

[50] Ibid.

[51] [2018] 3 CLJ 427.

[52] [2019] 12 MLJ 741.

[53] [2019] 8 MLJ 331.

[54] [2019] 8 MLJ 331 at para 88.

[55] [2019] 8 MLJ 331 at para 111.

[56] *Sambaga Valli a/p KR Ponnusamy v Datuk Bandar Kuala Lumpur & Ors and another appeal* [2018] 1 MLJ 784 at 799.

[57] Law Commission No. 247, *Aggravated, Exemplary and Restitutionary Damages,* 1997.

References

Anbalagan V (2020) Court Awards Myanmar refugee RM1.7 mil in medical negligence suit, FMT News. https://www.freemalaysiatoday.com/category/nation/2020/01/28/court-awards-myanmar-refugee-rm1-7-mil-in-medical-negligence-suit/

Astro A (2014) Medical negligence: Court awards girl, 9, RM2.78 million. http://english.astroawani.com/malaysia-news/medical-negligence-court-awards-girl-9-rm2-78-million-37314

Hambali SN, Khodapanahandeh S (2014) Review of medical malpractice issues in Malaysia under tort litigation system. Global J Health Sci 6(4):76

Mazlina M (2018) Husband awarded over RM735k for wife's death by negligence at Hospital KL, TheStar. https://www.thestar.com.my/news/nation/2018/08/06/husband-awarded-damages-hkl-wife-death

Merican I, Yon B (2002) Health care reform and changes: the Malaysian experience. Asia Pacific J Public Health 14(1):17

Nik Rosnah WA, Lee KH (2011) Impact of the private healthcare facilities and services act 1998 (act 586) & regulations 2006 on the medical practice in corporate private hospitals in Malaysia. OIDA Int J Sustain Dev 2(9):89

Ng KH, Jacobson B (2017) How global is the common law? A comparative study of Asian common law systems–Hong Kong, Malaysia, and Singapore. Asian J Comp Law 12(2):209

World Health Organization. Regional Office for the Western Pacific (2012) Malaysia health system review. WHO Regional Office for the Western Pacific, Manila. https://apps.who.int/iris/handle/10665/206911

Zainuddin A (2019) Cases on medical negligence on the rise, Health Ministry's data shows. The Malaysian Reserve. https://themalaysianreserve.com/2019/09/18/cases-on-medical-negligence-on-the-rise-health-ministrys-data-shows/

Medical Liability in New Zealand

Fiona McDonald

Abstract This chapter examines the framework for medical liability in New Zealand. From European settlement, until 1974, New Zealand's system for medical liability was based on the common-law. Persons who sustained injuries, as the result of negligent actions by a healthcare provider, could bring proceedings to be compensated for that harm. Major legislative reforms, in 1974, introducing a no-fault insurance system for personal injuries, significantly limited the ability to sue for medical malpractice in New Zealand. This chapter examines New Zealand's Accident Compensation scheme relating to compensation for medical injury and the residual ways in which claims for medical liability may be brought.

1 Introduction

This chapter examines the framework for medical liability in New Zealand. From European settlement, until 1974, New Zealand's system for medical liability was based on the common-law. People who sustained injuries, as the result of negligent actions by a healthcare provider, could bring proceedings to be compensated for that harm. Major legislative reforms, in 1974, introducing a no-fault insurance system for personal injuries, significantly limited the ability to sue for damages for medical malpractice in New Zealand. This chapter examines New Zealand's Accident Compensation scheme (the ACC scheme) in respect of claims relating to compensation for medical injury and the residual ways in which claims for damages for medical liability may be brought.

F. McDonald (✉)
Australian Centre for Health Law Research, Queensland University of Technology, Brisbane, Australia
e-mail: fiona.mcdonald@qut.edu.au

Department of Bioethics, Dalhousie University, Halifax, Canada

New Zealand Centre for Public Law, Victoria University of Wellington, Wellington, New Zealand

V. L. Raposo and R. G. Beran (eds.), *Medical Liability in Asia and Australasia*,
Ius Gentium: Comparative Perspectives on Law and Justice 94,
https://doi.org/10.1007/978-981-16-4855-7_11

2 Accident Compensation

In 1967, a Royal Commission of Inquiry Into and Report upon Workers' Compensation, chaired by Hon Justice Woodhouse (the Woodhouse Report), focused on examining tort actions for damages, primarily in the context of motor vehicle accidents and workplace accidents.[1] It strongly critiqued the existing tort based system finding that, as the Court of Appeal later described it, such actions had "*uneven and inadequate scope … as a means of securing compensation for personal injury in a modern society*".[2] The Woodhouse Report argued that the focus on the individual, as the locus of fault, no longer reflected community norms and should be replaced with community responsibility for managing the costs of personal injury.[3] It also noted long delays with high costs diminishing the ambit of awards, liability insurance reducing any deterrent effect and that the system created impediments to prevention and rehabilitation. The Woodhouse Report recommended that negligence proceedings, for personal injury, be replaced by a no-fault compensation scheme based on insurance principles.

In 1972, the *Accident Compensation Act 1972* (NZ) was passed and from 1 April 1974 extinguished the capacity to bring proceedings seeking compensation for personal injury. Glazebrook J stated:

> …At the broadest level of generality, [the] aim [of the accident compensation scheme] is to promote distributive rather than corrective justice by spreading the economic consequences of negligent conduct over the whole community and to provide compensation for injury (regardless of fault)…[4]

In its most recent iteration, the *Accident Compensation Act 2001* (the 2001 Act), the statutory bar is set out in s 317. It is essentially unchanged since the first legislation came into effect, in 1974. Section 317 states that no person may bring proceedings, under any rule of law (namely the common-law) or enactment, for damages arising, directly or indirectly, out of a personal injury, covered by the 2001 Act or any previous Acts.[5] A foetus is not considered a person for the purposes of this legislation.[6]

A person may bring proceedings, relating to damage to property, breach of most forms of contracts or proceedings relating to a contract of service,[7] but no court, tribunal or other body hearing these proceedings may award compensation

---

[1] Royal Commission to Inquire into and Report Upon Workers' Compensation, *Compensation for Personal Injury in New Zealand: Report of the Royal Commission of Inquiry,* (Government Printer, 1967) (*Woodhouse Report*).

[2] *Donselaar v Donselaar* [1982] 1 NZLR 97 (CA) at 104.

[3] *Woodhouse Report,* supra note 1.

[4] *Accident Compensation Corporation v Ambros* [2007] NZCA 304, [2008] 1 NZLR 340 (CA) at [25].

[5] *Accident Compensation Act 2001* (NZ) s 317(1) [2001 Act].

[6] *Harrild v Director of Proceedings* [2003] 3 NZLR 289 (CA).

[7] 2001 Act, *supra* note 5 at s 317(2).

for personal injury.[8] A person may bring proceedings for other remedies, such as declaratory relief, injunctions or exemplary or punitive damages. Proceedings may still be brought, pursuant to section 50 or 51 of the *Health and Disability Commissioner Act 1994*, or if the cause of action is liability for damages in relation to any international convention relating to the carriage of passengers.[9]

The 2001 Act provides cover for a personal injury sustained in New Zealand that meets the definition of personal injury.[10] Personal injury is defined in s 26 of the 2001 Act as:

(1) Personal injury means—

  (a) the death of a person; or
  (b) physical injuries suffered by a person, including, for example, a strain or a sprain; or
  (c) mental injury suffered by a person because of physical injuries suffered by the person; or
  (d) mental injury suffered by a person in the circumstances described in section 21 [cover for mental injury caused by certain criminal acts]; or
  (e) work-related mental injury that is suffered by a person in the circumstances described in section 21B [directly experiencing, seeing or hearing a sudden event or its outcome in the workplace that could reasonably be expected to cause mental injury to people generally]; or
  (f) damage (other than wear and tear) to dentures or prostheses that replace a part of the human body.[11]

It is further defined in s 20(2) to include:

(a) personal injury caused by an accident to the person;
(b) personal injury that is treatment injury suffered by the person;
(c) treatment injury in circumstances described in section 32(7);
(d) personal injury that is a consequence of treatment given to the person for another personal injury for which the person has cover;
(e) personal injury caused by a work-related gradual process, disease, or infection suffered by the person;
(f) personal injury caused by a gradual process, disease, or infection that is treatment injury suffered by the person;
(g) personal injury caused by a gradual process, disease, or infection consequential on personal injury suffered by the person for which the person has cover;
(h) personal injury caused by a gradual process, disease, or infection consequential on treatment given to the person for personal injury for which the person has cover;

[8] Id at s 317(3).
[9] Id at s 317(4) and (5).
[10] Id at s 20(1).
[11] Id at s 26(1).

(i) personal injury that is a cardiovascular or cerebrovascular episode that is treatment injury suffered by the person;
(j) personal injury that is a cardiovascular or cerebrovascular episode that is personal injury suffered by the person to which section 28(3) applies.[12]

Outside of the above definitions, the 2001 Act does not cover injury attributed to the aging process, gradual processes, disease, infections, damage to teeth or dentures caused by usage or cardiovascular or cerebrovascular episodes.[13] Blanchard J, writing for the majority in the Supreme Court (New Zealand's highest court), noted that the expression 'personal injury' should be interpreted in an expansive way.[14]

What about personal injury sustained as the result of medical treatment? This has been covered from 1974, although for a period of time the definition of medical misadventure included a fault element which was out of step with the no-fault nature of the scheme.[15] From 1 July 2005, the fault element was removed to increase fairness and remove arbitrary decisions for claimants and to reflect a systems approach to patient safety that seeks to move from a blame culture to a learning culture.[16] The terminology also changed from 'medical misadventure' to 'treatment injury'. Treatment injury is defined in the 2001 Act as:

(1) Treatment injury means personal injury that is—

  (a) suffered by a person—
    (i) seeking treatment from 1 or more registered health professionals; or.
    (ii) receiving treatment from, or at the direction of, 1 or more registered health professionals; or
    (iii) referred to in subsection (7) [the injury is an infection that is passed on to a spouse, partner, child or third party]; and
  (b) caused by treatment; and.
  (c) not a necessary part, or ordinary consequence, of the treatment, taking into account all the circumstances of the treatment, including—
    (i) the person's underlying health condition at the time of the treatment; and
    (ii) the clinical knowledge at the time of the treatment.[17]

It also includes treatment provided in the course of a clinical trial if either the person did not agree in writing to participate or it was approved by an approved ethics committee that was satisfied that the trial was not being conducted principally for the benefit of the manufacturer or distributor of the item being trialled.[18]

---

[12] Id at s 20(2).

[13] Id at s 26 (1A), (1B), (2), (3), (4).

[14] *Allenby v Hannam* 3 NZLR 425 (SC) per Blanchard J at [68].

[15] Manning (2015a).

[16] Id.

[17] 2001 Act, *supra* note 5 s 32(1).

[18] Id s 32(4)-(6).

Treatment includes: diagnosis; the giving of treatment; decisions to provide or not to provide treatment; failing to provide treatment or to provide it to a timely manner; not obtaining informed consent; providing a prophylaxis; the failure of any tool or device or equipment used during treatment (including implants and prosthetics during or after treatment unless failure caused by wear and tear); and any support systems directly used by the organisation or person to support the treatment.[19]

As with the definition of personal injury, the definition of treatment injury excludes personal injury, caused wholly or substantially by a person's underlying health condition.[20] It also excludes injury, solely attributable to a resource allocation decision, or an injury caused by a person unreasonably withholding or delaying their consent to undergo treatment and notes that the fact that a treatment did not achieve the desired result does not constitute a treatment injury.[21]

A still-birth, arising from a treatment injury, is considered as a personal injury to the pregnant woman and is covered by the ACC scheme.[22] The courts have also considered so-called wrongful birth claims.[23] In *Allenby v Hannam*,[24] the Supreme Court (New Zealand's highest court) considered whether a pregnancy, arising from a failed sterilisation, was covered under the *Injury Prevention, Rehabilitation and Compensation Act 2001* (the Act in force prior to the 2001 Act). The Court was unanimous that the pregnancy constituted a personal injury pursuant to s 26(1)(b) (physical injury) arising from s 20(2)(b) (medical misadventure).[25] The Chief Justice also considered cover was available under s 20(2)(g) (as a gradual process personal injury) and s 20(2)(f) (as a gradual process injury caused by treatment injury).[26] Blanchard J concluded:

> ...If ... the purpose of the medical treatment is to prevent pregnancy from occurring and by reason of medical error that purpose is not achieved, it does not seem to us that, just because the pregnancy then occurs as a biological process, there should be no cover for the consequences. The development of the fetus following impregnation occurs because of the medical error, just as in the case of the undetected tumour. It causes significant physical changes to the woman's anatomy, which of course occur naturally but still cause discomfort and, at least ultimately, pain and suffering...[27]

---

[19] Id s 33(1).

[20] Id s 32(2)(a).

[21] Id at s 32(2)(b), (c) and 32(3).

[22] *Harrild,* supra note 6. It is possible that the spouse of the woman could bring proceedings for compensation for mental injury under the common-law, although not under the *Health and Disability Commissioner Act 1994* (NZ).

[23] In this chapter wrongful birth includes wrongful conception (unwanted conception) and wrongful birth (a child born in circumstances where there would have been a lawful termination or conception would not have occurred). In *Groom v Selby* [2001] EWCA Civ 1522 (Unreported, Broker LJ, Hale LJ and Steele J, 18 October 2001). Hale LJ stated at [28] that 'the principles applicable in wrongful birth cases cannot sensibly be distinguished from the principles applicable in wrongful conception cases'. See discussion in Thomas (2003).

[24] *Allenby, supra* note 14.

[25] Id per Blanchard J at [71] and Elias CJ at [9].

[26] Id per Elias CJ at [30 and 31].

[27] Id per Blanchard J at [80].

Wrongful birth was further considered by the Court of Appeal, in *Cumberland v Accident Compensation Corporation,* under the 2001 Act.[28] In that case, the treatment provider had failed to identify that a foetus had indications of spina bifida, at the 20 week ultrasound scan. Without this diagnosis, the pregnant woman did not have the opportunity to terminate the foetus and the baby was born with spina bifida. Experts were of the view that indications of the disease, in the scan, were overlooked. *Allenby* was applied and the continuance of the pregnancy was held to constitute personal injury, under s 26(1)(b) (physical injury) and s 20(2)(b) of the 2001 Act (treatment injury). The Court was satisfied that the treatment injury arose in respect of failure to diagnose, the woman not having the information to decide about further treatment, and a failure to provide treatment in a timely manner.[29] The Court determined that it was necessary to show, on the balance of probabilities, that a termination would have taken place.[30] The case was remitted to the District Court for determination. While it was accepted, on the balance of probabilities, that the woman would have sought a termination, if properly advised, it was unclear whether she would have been able to make such a choice, under New Zealand's abortion law at that time raising a question of causation.[31] The question of wrongful life has not been considered.

Section 371 of the 2001 Act also applies to bar proceedings for compensatory damages for conduct that occurred outside New Zealand but where the treatment injury (in this case from a defective hip implant) was sustained within New Zealand.[32]

Cover, under the 2001 Act, may include the costs of medical treatment, necessary aids or equipment, home help, child-care, contribution to transport costs, travel costs if necessary for treatment, counselling and therapy and retraining for work. It will also include 80% of earnings if the person is unable to work. There is also provision for one-off lump sum payments or ongoing payments, if the injury is permanent, the level of which depends on the degree of impairment. If a person dies, support may be provided to the family for funeral costs, loss of income, childcare and a one-off payment dependent on the circumstances.[33] There are provisions to appeal any determination by the Accident Compensation Corporation, the body that administers the ACC scheme.[34]

---

[28] *Cumberland v Accident Compensation Corporation* [2014] 2 NZLR 373 (CA).

[29] Id at [42].

[30] Id at [45].

[31] Id at [55].

[32] *McGougan v DePuy International Ltd* [2017] 2 NZLR 119 (HC).

[33] 2001 Act, *supra* note 5 Pt 4.

[34] Id at Pt 5.

3 Psychiatric Injury

The ACC scheme covers some forms of 'mental injury'. The 2001 Act defines mental injury as: "*a clinically significant behavioural, cognitive, or psychological dysfunction*", namely not damages to feelings or emotional harm.[35] It is clear that mental injury, directly connected to physical injury, is covered,[36] as is mental injury from directly witnessing a workplace accident or its immediate aftermath[37] and mental injury arising from certain types of criminal acts.[38]

The courts have examined the meaning of the phrase "... *indirectly out of a personal injury* ..." related to the statutory bar in s 317 of the 2001 Act in two cases. In *Queensland Lakes District Council v Palmer*,[39] the plaintiff brought a proceeding for compensatory damages for mental injury, after watching his wife drown in a rafting accident. Her death was covered under the ACC scheme but he sustained no physical injury and so his mental injury was not covered. The question that needed to be resolved, by the courts, was whether the mental injury that he sustained arose indirectly from his wife's personal injury and therefore was caught by the statutory bar. The Court of Appeal found the statutory bar did not preclude the plaintiff from bringing a case for compensatory damages, as Mr Palmer did not sustain a personal injury covered by the Act. It interpreted the relevant provision as requiring personal injury "*covered by this Act*", also suggesting that this was consistent with the then long title of the Act. The Court also noted that it would be unjust to deny a person a remedy under the ACC scheme and under the common-law.[40]

In a further case, patients brought a negligence action against a hospital for damages for mental injury, after a pathologist failed to carefully examine tissue biopsies.[41] If analysed properly, the samples would have established malignancy, instead of being reported as benign. The Court considered that the patients had suffered physical injury, in the form of progression of the illness, due to misdiagnosis. The claim for mental injuries related to the period of uncertainty between discovery of the issue and reanalysis of the samples (period 1) and second after diagnosis in relation to the loss of trust and concerns about the impact of the delayed treatment (period 2). The Court held, in relation to period 1, that there was no causal connection between the mental injury and the personal injury as the personal injury was suspected but not yet established.[42] A proceeding for compensatory damages, in relation to period 1, was not barred. In relation to period 2, the Court held that the mental injury arose, at least indirectly, out of the physical injury, even though it was not an outcome of the injury, and was therefore not covered by compensation scheme. Because it was

[35] Id at s 27.

[36] Id at s 26(1)(c).

[37] Id at s 21B.

[38] Id at s 21.

[39] *Queenstown Lakes District Council v Palmer* [1999] 1 NZLR 549 (CA).

[40] Id at 556.

[41] *Brownlie v Good Health Wanganui Ltd* [2005] NZAR 289 (CA).

[42] Id at [14].

held that any mental injury, incurred during period 2, was indirectly connected to the personal injury, a proceeding for compensatory damages, in relation to period 2, was barred by statute. This was considered justifiable as it was a necessary consequence of limits imposed on cover.[43]

These cases created an inconsistency in approach which has yet to be resolved by the Court of Appeal or the Supreme Court. Pending this, the High Court has applied *Brownlie* to cases involving primary victims and *Palmer* to cases involving secondary victims.[44] The Court of Appeal suggested that the distinction, between primary and secondary victims, seen in the common-law,[45] was helpful in *van Soest v Residual Health Management Unit* but it also noted the Law Commission had raised concerns about this distinction.[46] At present, secondary victims can bring an action for compensatory damages for psychiatric injury, provided they meet the requirements of the cause of action, usually through a negligence action. Primary victims may be able to bring proceedings if they have sustained no physical injury and/or sustained a psychiatric injury, as the result of specified criminal acts or witnessing workplace accidents.

Once the issue of s 317 of the 2001 Act has been addressed, New Zealand's approach is similar to other common-law jurisdictions. The first requirement is that the claimant has a recognised psychiatric illness. In *van Soest v Residual Health Management Unit*[47] family members of patients who died, after negligence during surgery, brought proceedings. The majority of the Court of Appeal concluded that a recognised psychiatric illness is required to bring proceedings for psychiatric injury. Mental distress or emotional harm which was what the family members suffered is not covered.[48]

There have been few cases, in the health context, involving primary victims. In *L v Robinson,*[49] the plaintiff who was being treated for prior sexual abuse had a consensual sexual relationship with her treating psychiatrist. The consequent mental injury was not covered by the accident compensation scheme because it was 'consensual' sex so was not a sexual offence, the consequences of which would be covered.[50] It was accepted that the doctor had a duty of care to the patient and that, having a sexual relationship with this patient, was considered to breach the standard of care. It was also foreseeable, given the patient's history, that the conduct could cause her mental injury. The plaintiff was awarded $50,000 in compensatory damages for psychiatric injury.[51]

---

43 Id at [12]–[13].

44 *Sivasubramaniam v Yarrall* [2005] 3 NZLR 268 (HC).

45 *White v Chief Constable of the South Yorkshire Police* [1999] 1 All ER 1 (HL).

46 *van Soest v Residual Health Management Unit* [2000] 1 NZLR 179 (CA) at [21].

47 Id.

48 Id.

49 *L v Robinson* [2000] 3 NZLR 499 (HC).

50 2001 Act, *supra* note 5 s 21.

51 Id s 21.

There have also been few successful cases, in the health context, involving secondary victims. In *van Soest* the plaintiffs were unsuccessful.[52] The Court required 'relational proximity' while indicating it may consider relaxation of the 'direct perception' rule, by leaving open the question of whether hearing of a death or injury, from another, was sufficient.[53] In *Hobson v Attorney-General,* the majority of the Court of Appeal required actual presence at an accident, or its immediate aftermath, for the husband of the primary victim to recover damages for psychiatric injury.[54] This is consistent with the requirements of s 21B(2)(a) of the 2001 Act which addresses mental injury due to a workplace accident. To receive cover, under the ACC scheme for a mental injury, a person must directly experience, see or hear a single event workplace accident which does not include seeing it through a secondary source, such as television or hearing about it from another person.[55]

4 Exemplary Damages

In 1982, the Court of Appeal determined that the statutory bar in the Accident Compensation legislation, in force at that time, only related to proceedings where the plaintiff was claiming compensatory damages for personal injury; it did not apply to claims for exemplary damages.[56] The rationale for this was that the purpose of exemplary damages is not to compensate but to punish and any award of exemplary damages does not undermine the ACC scheme. An action claiming exemplary damages can be brought despite compensatory damages not being awarded.[57] This view that exemplary damages are available was explicitly confirmed in the 2001 Act.[58] The *Law Reform Act 1936 (NZ)* states that exemplary damages are not available to deceased persons.[59]

A cause of action must first be established. The leading case *Couch v Attorney-General*[60] involved a claim for exemplary damages for alleged negligence by the Department of Corrections in managing an offender on probation who went on to murder three people and seriously injure another during a robbery. The majority of the Supreme Court held that, in addition to reasonable foreseeability, a relationship of sufficient proximity is required.[61] Policy issues (such as congruence with the

[52] *van Soest, supra* note 45.

[53] Id.

[54] *Hobson v Attorney-General* [2007] 1 NZLR 374 (CA).

[55] 2001 Act, *supra* note 5 at s 21B(2)(a) and 21B(6). It must also be an event of the type expected to cause mental injury to people generally s21B(2)(b).

[56] *Donselaar, supra* note 2.

[57] *Couch v Attorney-General (No 2)* [2010] NZSC 27, [2010] 3 NZLR 149.

[58] 2001 Act, *supra* note 5 at s 319(1).

[59] *Law Reform Act 1936 (NZ)* s (2)(a).

[60] [2008] 3 NZLR 725 (SC).

[61] Id at [80]-[81].

ACC scheme) must also be examined and the issue of causation addressed. In terms of proximity, the majority of the Supreme Court suggested two relationships were critical:

- The control relationship between the defendant public authority and the person who caused the harm
- The proximity relationship between the defendant and the plaintiff.

Control relates to the ability of the defendant to have sufficient control to manage or eliminate the risk. Proximity relates to the defendant's knowledge of the nature of the risk to others. Tipping J expressed the test for proximity as:

> ...To establish a duty of care [the plaintiff] must demonstrate that, either as an individual or as a member of an identifiable and sufficiently delineated class, she was or should have been known by the defendants to be the subject of a distinct and special risk of suffering harm of the kind she sustained ..... The necessary risk must be distinct in the sense of being clearly apparent, and special in the sense that the plaintiff's individual circumstances or her membership of the necessary class rendered her particularly vulnerable to suffering harm of the relevant kind ...[62]

In *S v Middlemore District Health Board (No 2)*,[63] the plaintiff was raped by a co-patient with a known history of sexual misconduct, including rape, of female patients and women more generally. The plaintiff sought exemplary damages from the hospital, arguing that the clinicians had a duty of care as she was a patient.[64] Proximity was established, on the basis of her being in an identifiable and delineated group (female patients) of people who could be reasonably foreseen to be at particular, and heightened risk, different in its level from the risk posed to women in general. The co-patient was under a compulsory treatment order so, despite being on leave, was subject to control.

In *Ellis v Counties Manukau District Health Board*,[65] the High Court considered the issue of control. The plaintiff killed his father. Before this, the plaintiff and had been admitted to the hospital for compulsory assessment and treatment, for a five-day period mandated under the *Mental Health (Compulsory Assessment and Treatment) Act 1992* (Mental Health Act). The plaintiff sought statutory review of this decision. The judge consulted with the treating doctor who had not yet examined the plaintiff. The plaintiff was released after agreeing to being examined and assessed. The doctor diagnosed a psychotic disorder but did not consider the plaintiff a risk to self or others and thus could not 're-section' him under the Mental Health Act and he was treated as a voluntary outpatient. The family repeatedly expressed concerns to the hospital, about the plaintiff's behaviour, but no action was taken. The court held there was no control as the Judge had released the plaintiff and the doctor had not re-sectioned him, even though the doctor had the power to do so, and thus the plaintiff was a voluntary patient over whom the hospital had no control.

[62] Id per Tipping J at [112].

[63] (2013) 24 FRNZ 435 (HC).

[64] As she was raped psychiatric injury would have been covered under the 2001 Act.

[65] [2007] 1 NZLR 196 (HC).

The issue of control was not considered in detail by the Supreme Court, in the subsequent case of *Couch.* Tipping J considered it was possible that the plaintiff, in that case, could establish that the probation officer "*had sufficient power and ability to control Bell in a way that would have prevented the harm.*"[66] Manning suggests that the term 'sufficient' may mean that actual and full control is not required, arguing that the probation officer in *Couch* had less legal power and practical ability to control Bell than the doctor in *Ellis.*[67]

The position on when exemplary damages may be awarded has evolved. *A v Bottrill*[68] involved a pathologist who misread a cervical smear, leading to the plaintiff developing invasive cancer. Treatment included a radical hysterectomy and extensive radiotherapy that removed her capacity to have children. A previous line of cases had refused to award exemplary damages for simple negligence. The majority of the Privy Council (at that time New Zealand's highest court) held that the rationale for exemplary damages was to punish 'outrageous' conduct for which compensation was an inadequate response.[69] This would require intentional conduct or conscious (subjective) recklessness that is considered 'outrageous', but exceptionally:

> ...There may be the rare case where the defendant departed so far and so flagrantly from the dictates of ordinary or professional precepts of prudence, or standards of care, that his conduct satisfies this test even though he was not consciously reckless...[70]

Subjective recklessness involved the defendant being subjectively aware of the risk of his /her conduct but proceeding with reckless indifference.[71] The case was sent back for further consideration of new evidence.

In *Couch v the Attorney-General (No 2),*[72] the majority of the Supreme Court overturned this precedent. The Court determined that exemplary damages are only available, in New Zealand, where the conduct was intentional or subjectively reckless and considered to be 'outrageous'.[73] Exemplary damages are not available for inadvertent negligence, even when such negligent conduct is outrageous. Tipping J (in the majority) suggested this was necessary as:

> ...There is an ever-present danger, if exemplary damages were available for outrageous but inadvertent negligence, that they would be perceived as a means of obtaining extra compensation outside the accident compensation system when the negligence was bad enough...[74]

McGrath J concluded that the Privy Council's broader test would "*be destructive of the exceptional nature of the remedy*" pointing to increased claims for exemplary

---

[66] *Couch, supra* note 60 per Tipping J at [84].

[67] Manning (2015b).

[68] *A v Bottrill* [2003] 2 NZLR 721 (PC).

[69] Id at [20].

[70] Id at [26].

[71] Id at [23].

[72] *Couch (No 2), supra* note 57.

[73] Id.

[74] Id per Tipping J at [135].

damages post 1992 reforms to the accident compensation legislation that eliminated lump sum payments for non-pecuniary loss.[75]

It was also noted that the purpose of exemplary damages is to punish the defendant so as to deter that person, and others, from the conduct in question, thus the focus should be on the character of the defendant's conduct and not the plaintiff's suffering.[76] This interpretation makes it more difficult to bring claims against organisations for systemic negligence although in *obiter* comments Tipping J considered it was possible that an organisation's systems, resources and priorities could be subjectively reckless, but noted a danger in the case of public authorities that this could lead to an examination of government policies somewhere where "*the legal system should be very reluctant to go*."[77] In the context of hospitals, New Zealand courts have not considered the issue of a non-delegable duty of care.[78] Exemplary damages are not available for vicarious liability as the courts consider it unfair to inflict punishment on someone who was not party to the wrongful conduct and it could create an avenue to provide additional compensation, undermining the ACC scheme.[79]

Successful proceedings, for exemplary damages in the health context in New Zealand, outside of proceedings under the *Health and Disability Commissioner Act 1994*, relate primarily to sexual abuse by a health provider. In *L v Robinson*, the plaintiff was also awarded $10,000 in exemplary damages.[80] Some cases have related to the release of psychiatric patients into the community where they have harmed or killed others or allegations of a failure to supervise them on release or to warn identifiable potential victims.[81]

The quantum of damages must be considered in regard to the 2001 Act which specifies that, in determining whether to award exemplary damages or the amount of them, the court may consider whether a penalty has been imposed for an offence and the nature of that penalty.[82] Assessment is discretionary but consequences to the victim are irrelevant, except as they go towards assessing the gravity of the conduct that is being punished. The courts are guided by the principle of moderation, in making such awards, and, for health related cases, they tend to be under $20,000, although pre-trial settlements may be somewhat larger.[83] The small quantum of damages may operate as a disincentive to bring proceedings.

---

[75] Id per McGrath J at [241].

[76] Id per Blanchard J at [58] and Wilson J at [254].

[77] Id per Tipping J at [161].

[78] Manning, *supra* note 67.

[79] *S v Attorney-General* [2003] 3 NZLR 450 (CA). See also *Couch (No 2), supra* note 57 per Tipping J at [158].

[80] *L, supra* note 49. See also *R v Eade* DC Auckland NP3604/97, 12 May 2000—award of $27,000 in exemplary damages for breach of fiduciary duty by a primal healer who had a sexual relationship with a client with a prior history of sexual abuse.

[81] For example, *Van de Wetering v Capital Coast Health Limited* HC Wellington CP368/98, 19/05/2000; 6 *Maulolo v Hutt Valley Health Corporation Limited* HC Wellington CP212/99, 20/07/2001 where the courts found insufficient proximity. See also *S, supra* note 79.

[82] 2001 Act, *supra* note 5 at s 319(2).

[83] Manning, *supra* note 67.

5 Proceedings before the Human Rights Review Tribunal

Despite the commencement of the ACC scheme, it was still considered important to assess the safety and quality of care provided and to provide accountability mechanisms. A Royal Commission of Inquiry in 1988, examining the 'unfortunate experiment' at National Women's Hospital, concluded that there was a gap in accountability mechanisms in a system where financial accountability of health providers was affected by the ACC system.[84] The *Health and Disability Commissioner Act 1994* (the HDC Act) was enacted:

> ... to promote and protect the rights of health consumers and disability services consumers, and, to that end, to facilitate the fair, simple, speedy, and efficient resolution of complaints relating to infringements of those rights...[85]

The Health and Disability Commissioner may take several actions on receipt of a complaint. It may take no further action or may refer the matter: back to the health or disability services provider to resolve; for low level resolution through advocacy or mediation; or to another agency. It also may investigate complaints that health or disability services providers breached the Code of Health and Disability Services Consumers' Rights (the Code) when providing care to a health or disability services consumer.[86] The Code sets out health and disability services consumers' legal rights, when receiving health or disability services, and are the basis of the expected standard of care. While complaints focus on whether the expected standard of care is breached, not all complaints will have resulted in personal injury. If, after investigation, a breach of the Code has been established, one of the discretionary remedies, available to the Health and Disability Commissioner, is to refer the matter to the Director of Proceedings[87] (DP) for consideration as to whether proceedings (disciplinary or before the Human Rights Review Tribunal[88] (the Tribunal)) should be brought.[89] In deciding whether to refer a matter to the DP, the Health and Disability Commissioner must consider: the wishes of the complainant and/or the aggrieved person; any comments about the referral by the person or organisation against whom

---

84 Committee of Inquiry into Allegations Concerning the Treatment of Cervical Cancer at National Women's Hospital and into Other Related Matters, *The report of the Committee of Inquiry into Allegations Concerning the Treatment of Cervical Cancer at National Women's Hospital and into Other Related Matters*, (Government Printing Office, 1988) at 172 (*Cartwright Report*).

85 *Health and Disability Commissioner Act 1994* (NZ) s 6.

86 The Code is a regulation (*Health and Disability Commissioner (Code of Health and Disability Services Consumers' Rights) Regulations 1996* (NZ)) issued pursuant to the *Health and Disability Commissioner Act 1994* (NZ).

87 The role of the Director of Proceedings is established under the *Health and Disability Commissioner Act 1994* (NZ) s 15 and is to act independently of the Health and Disability Commissioner. The functions of the Director are set out in section 49 and include a decision as to whether to bring disciplinary proceedings or proceeding before the Human Rights Review Tribunal and to institute the proceedings.

88 The Human Rights Review Tribunal considers human rights, privacy and Health and Disability Commissioner cases.

89 *Health and Disability Commissioner Act, supra* note 84 s 45(2)(f).

a breach finding(s) are made; and "*the need to ensure that appropriate proceedings are instituted in any case where the public interest (whether for reasons of public health or public safety or for any other reason) so requires.*"[90]

The DP may bring proceedings, before the Tribunal, if a health care or disability services provider has been investigated and referred to the DP by the Health and Disability Commissioner for any action found to be in breach of the Code.[91] Neither the complainant (if any) nor the aggrieved person (if not the complainant) will be a party to or join the proceedings unless ordered by the Tribunal.[92] There is a limited ability for an aggrieved person (or their agent if they lacked capacity) to bring proceedings of their own volition but only if the Health and Disability Commissioner has found that there was a breach of the Code but has not referred the matter to the DP or the DP has not taken proceedings.[93] A secondary victim, such as a family member, may not bring proceedings before the Tribunal.[94] The ability to bring proceedings, by the DP or the aggrieved person, is limited by the Health and Disability Commissioner undertaking an investigation and/or finding a breach of the Code. Manning has noted: "*In recent years approximately four per cent of complaints (approximately 80 of about 2,000 complaints closed annually) are formally investigated.*"[95] Manning also notes:

> ...Referral to the DP and prosecution is an exceptional step; less than one per cent of all providers complained about per annum are referred to the DP, which amounts to, on average, 10 providers each year in the last three years. The DP took disciplinary or HRRT proceedings in 10% (on average) of investigations concluded each year over the last five years...[96]

The Tribunal considers the matter afresh and is not bound by the Commissioner's finding of a breach(s) of the Code. The plaintiff bears the onus of proof and the standard is the balance of probabilities 'flexibly applied'.[97]

If the Tribunal is satisfied there has been a breach of the Code it may: issue a declaration; issue a restraining order; issue an order requiring the performance of specified actions; award punitive damages; award costs; or any other relief that the Tribunal thinks fit, but must have regard to any penalty imposed during disciplinary proceedings.[98] Any proceedings before the Tribunal are impacted by the 2001 Act

---

[90] Id s 44(3).

[91] Id s 50.

[92] Id s 50(4).

[93] Id s 51. There have been few cases brought by aggrieved persons or their agents see for example, *ABC v XYZ* [2013] NZHRRT 25 and *Marshall v Idea Services Limited* [2020] NZHRRT 9.

[94] *Health and Disability Commissioner Act supra* note 84 at s 56; *Marks v Director of Health and Disability Proceedings* [2009] NZCA 151, (2009) 3 NZLR 108 (CA). See also *P v Iyengar* [2011] NZHRRT 2 and *P v Iyengar* [2012] NZHRRT 9. While the Court of Appeal in *Marks* left open the possibility that a father of a baby injured during the birth process could be an aggrieved person, the Court of Appeal subsequently rejected this in *P v F* [2015] 3 NZLR 758.

[95] Manning (2018) at 636.

[96] Id at 639.

[97] *Z v Dental Complaints Assessment Committee* [2009] 1 NZLR 1.

[98] *Health and Disability Commissioner Act 1994, supra* note 84 at s 54.

in that, if the aggrieved person has sustained personal injury within the meaning of that Act, no damages (other than punitive damages) may be awarded, arising directly or indirectly from that injury may be sought or awarded, except punitive damages.[99] Subject to the bar on the award of compensatory damages the Tribunal may award damages: for pecuniary loss; loss of benefit; humiliation, loss of dignity and injury to the feelings of the aggrieved person; or any action that was in flagrant disregard of the rights of the accused.[100] The Tribunal is also required to take into account the conduct of the defendant or an officer, employee or member of the defendant, when deciding whether to grant a remedy and what remedy to grant.[101]

Awards of damages, under s 57(1)(c) for humiliation, loss of dignity and injury to feelings are compensatory, not to "*punish or convey disapproval*".[102] These awards can be made for feelings of humiliation, shock, grief, anxiety, emotional, spiritual or cultural distress and are "*measured by the individual characteristics of the individual.*"[103] This class of damages does not require the aggrieved person to have a recognisable psychiatric disorder,[104] nor does it need to be equated with "*clinically significant behaviour, cognitive, or psychological dysfunction*" per the definition of mental injury in the *Accident Compensation Act 2002.*[105] Loss of dignity does not necessarily have to involve the subjective experience of emotional harm, but is grounded objectively in the "*normative concept of human dignity*".[106]

Section 57(1)(d) of the *HDC Act* (any action in flagrant disregard of the rights of the accused) does not directly refer to this form of damages as punitive, but it is considered as such.[107] The Court of Appeal has suggested that this form of damages is different from exemplary damages under the common-law as, it is a statutory head of damages with the threshold of "*flagrant* disregard".[108] The High Court has noted "*'[f]lagrant' is a strong word. It connotes 'outrageous' behaviour or 'glaring, notorious or scandalous' acts or omissions.*"[109] It also stated that this form of damages can only be awarded if the statutory test is met and awards should be requested for truly outrageous conduct which cannot be punished in any other way.[110] The Tribunal has stated: "*[c]aution must be exercised to ensure that every serious breach of the Code is not for that reason alone stigmatised as outrageous or flagrant.*"[111]

---

[99] Id at s 52(2).

[100] Id at s 57.

[101] Id at s 54(4).

[102] *Director of Proceedings v Emms* [2013] NZHRRT 5 at [104].

[103] Id at [106].

[104] Manning, *supra* note 67.

[105] *Director of Proceedings v Emms, supra* note 102.

[106] *Marshall, supra* note 93 at 85.

[107] *Marks, supra* note 94.

[108] Id.

[109] *Director of Proceedings v O'Neil* [2001] NZAR 59 (HC) at [39].

[110] Id at [40].

[111] *Director of Proceedings v Emms, supra* note 102 at [111].

The quantum of damages, under either 57(1)(c) or (d) of the *HDC Act,* is at the discretion of the Tribunal but common-law factors, such as moderation, are relevant.[112] Awards for proceedings, coming out of breaches of the Code of Rights, are in the low tens of thousands.

6 New Zealand Bill of Rights

Despite the *New Zealand Bill of Rights Act 1990* having no remedy provision, the Court of Appeal confirmed that remedies for rights violations were available.[113] A public law proceeding, claiming a breach of a right(s) in the *New Zealand Bill of Rights Act 1990,* is also subject to the s 371 statutory bar in the 2001 Act.[114] A monetary award may still be available for the affront to the right, rather than to compensate for any personal injury.[115] The *New Zealand Bill of Rights 1990* includes rights that directly relate to the provision of medical and health treatment: Right 10—the right not to be subjected to medical or scientific experimentation; and Right 11—the right to refuse to undergo medical treatment.

7 Discussion

Medical malpractice claims focus on harm to individuals, resulting from negligent medical treatment. In the New Zealand context, it is important to emphasise that Māori have brought many health-related claims before the Waitangi Tribunal, in respect of the Crown's obligations to Māori, under Te Tiriti o Waitangi (*The Treaty of Waitangi*).[116] In respect of Stage 1, of the Waitangi Tribunal's Inquiry into Health Services and Outcomes Kaupapa, its overarching conclusion was that the primary health care framework in New Zealand "*does not recognise and properly provide for tino rangatiratanga and mana motuhake of hauora Māori*".[117] Some degree of compensation, by the Crown to Māori or Māori health organisations, may be an outcome of this process.

New Zealand's approach, of replacing individual responsibility for causing personal injury, including some forms of mental injury, with community responsibility, and prohibiting the award of compensatory damages, for injuries covered under the ACC scheme, significantly changed the medical liability landscape in New Zealand. The approach by the New Zealand courts to issues of liability focuses on

---

[112] Manning, *supra* note 67.

[113] *Simpson v Attorney-General* [1994] 3 NZLR 667 (CA).

[114] *Wilding v Attorney-General* [2003] 3 NZLR 787 (CA).

[115] Manning, *supra* note 67.

[116] Tribunal (2019).

[117] Id at xv.

the primacy of the ACC scheme and is cognizant of the need not to undermine it. This acts as a significant limit on the capacity to bring proceedings for medical liability in New Zealand. The courts have been careful to keep any damages, arising from most of the available forms of proceedings, such as for exemplary damages, moderate. This also creates a disincentive to bring such cases as the associated costs of bringing them can be high, unless, as is the case for some proceedings under the *Health and Disability Commissioner Act 1994*, the costs are bourne by a state actor.

8 Conclusion

Major legislative reforms, in 1974, that introduced a no-fault insurance system for personal injuries, significantly limited the ability to bring proceedings for medical malpractice in New Zealand. The ACC scheme precludes individuals bringing claims for compensatory damages for personal injury. The remaining possibilities, for proceedings for medical liability, include, in some circumstances, claims for psychiatric injury, claims for exemplary damages, proceedings for damages for humiliation, loss of dignity and injury to feelings and flagrant disregard of rights pursuant to the *Health and Disability Commissioner Act 1994,* and claims for affronts to rights that are recognised in the *New Zealand Bill of Rights Act 1990.*

References

Manning J (2015a) Treatment Injury. In: Skegg P, Paterson R (eds) Health law in New Zealand 997

Manning J (2015)b Civil proceedings in personal injury cases. In: Skegg P, Paterson R (eds) Health law in New Zealand 1061

Manning J (2018) Fair, simple, speedy and efficient"? Barriers to access to justice in the Health and Disability Commissioner's Complaints Process in New Zealand 4 NZ LRev 611

Thomas C (2003) Claims for wrongful pregnancy and damages for the upbringing of the child. UNSW LJ 125 26(1):125–126

Tribunal W (2019) Hauora: Report on stage one of the health services and outcomes Kaupapa Inquiry WAI 2575. https://waitangitribunal.govt.nz/news/report-on-stage-one-of-health-services-and-outcomes-released/#:~:text=The%20Waitangi%20Tribunal%20today%20released,health%20inequities%20experienced%20by%20M%C4%81ori

Medical Negligence Law in Papua New Guinea

Ian Freckelton AO QC

Abstract The law on medical negligence is evolving gradually in Papua and New Guinea. It is influenced by the law in both England and Australia. Litigation in relation to the right to health has not yet taken place. Disregard of a patient's entitlement to prompt and sound care has been found to be negligent and has been visited by significant sums in damages. While Papua New Guinea courts have exhibited some reluctance to award exemplary damages where the relevant conduct is conduct for which the State may be vicariously liable by reason of what has been done by an individual health practitioner, a trend of increasing awards of damages can be identified over the past 20 years, including the award of exemplary damages.

1 Introduction

Papua New Guinea is a sovereign South Pacific nation that gained independence from Australia in 1975 (*Papua New Guinea Independence Act 1975* (Aust Cth)). It is a constitutionally based democracy (see Griffin and Katter 2015; Kwa 2011; Jessep et al. 2001; Chalmers 1984) with a rapidly growing population approaching nine million people. It has a unicameral Parliament and courts that apply Papua New Guinea's common law (see Weisbrot et al. 1982) which has evolved since the state of the law on 16 September 1975, the date it gained independence. Its statutes are largely adapted from overseas jurisdictions, in particular England and Australia.

As of 2016, life expectancy at birth for men was 64 years and for women 68 years (WHO 2016). Still in 2018, 27 per cent of women between 20 and 24 years of age were married or in a union (UNICEF 2018). Maternal and neonatal malnutrition as

I. Freckelton AO QC (✉)
Castan Chambers, Melbourne, Australia
e-mail: i.freckelton@vicbar.com.au

Supreme Court of Nauru, Yaren, Nauru

Law and Psychiatry, University of Melbourne, Melbourne, Australia

Krieger School of Arts and Sciences, Johns Hopkins University, Baltimore, USA

V. L. Raposo and R. G. Beran (eds.), *Medical Liability in Asia and Australasia*,
Ius Gentium: Comparative Perspectives on Law and Justice 94,
https://doi.org/10.1007/978-981-16-4855-7_12

a cause of death remains high, accounting for more than 50% of all deaths in some provinces (Kiture et al. 2019; Aipit et al. 2015). Church health services are a major provider of healthcare (Mapira and Morgan 2011).

HIV posed very serious difficulties for a time but less so latterly, with the improving availability of anti-retroviral drugs (see Luker and Dinnen 2010). The country has been very hard hit by COVID-19 although the available figures for its incidence are not reliable. Papua New Guinea is considered one of the most dangerous countries in the world for females and there is limited access to services such as healthcare, especially for women and children (Klaver and Coe 2018).

Papua New Guinea has developed distinctive criminal trial processes, incorporating customary law (see Matui 2017). A range of law and order issues exists for Papua New Guinea (Dinnen 2001), as well as issues of corruption (see Harris 2018), violence (see Jolly et al. 2012) and human rights abuses (see United States Department of State 2018). Retribution for what is perceived to be sanguma (sorcery) and witchcraft remains a significant law and order issue (Forsyth and Gibbs 2020).

The preamble to the Papua New Guinea Constitution calls for "*improvement in the level of nutrition and the standard of public health to enable our people to attain self fulfilment*" and Articles 35 and 36 provide broadly for the right to life and freedom from inhuman treatment. However, there is no provision guaranteeing a right to the highest attainable standard of health.

There is a significant corpus of Papua New Guinea law in relation to medical negligence as a component of civil law (see Katter 2015). It is closely influenced by English law but cultural issues (see Corrin 2013) also affect matters, such as assessment of damages. In *Albert v Aine* (2019) at [32] Kandakasi DCJ observed that:

> …having more children in PNG is a form of insurance for parents. In advanced countries like Australia, New Zealand and elsewhere, there are better superannuation and aged care for the old. Such services are not available in PNG. Children in PNG are expected to grow up and as the parents become more advanced in life, they become the dependants of their children. In the present case, having only one child comes with the risk of that child dying before his or her parents, which exposes the parents to the risk of no one in their family living and able to support them. This in some cases, unfortunately, leads to the parent's premature deaths…

While there can be many reasons why patients may take medico-legal action (see Graham et al. 2019), in Papua New Guinea a number of logistical factors impact upon the quality of health care that is provided. These include the absence of high quality medications (see Hetzel et al. 2014) and a range of cultural issues which can render women and children, in particular, vulnerable to substandard provision of care. This renders the comparatively rare phenomenon of medical negligence litigation an important mechanism for imposing leverage for the quality of healthcare to be of a suitable standard, given resourcing and other logistical limitations.

2 Duty of Care in Negligence

Under Papua New Guinea negligence law, a medical practitioner is required to exercise reasonable skill and judgment, taking into account all the circumstances in which a doctor provides medical services (*Laki v Gawi* (2018) at [20]). This includes a distinctive environment, such as an emergency department in a public hospital where a doctor is expected to do what is reasonable in such a setting, but not "*to perform miracles*" (*Laki v Gawi* (2018) at [20]). A delineation between conduct that is negligent, as against that which is not, is that a doctor has been held to be expected not to be reckless or lackadaisical or to disregard standard and accepted medical practices. (*Kembo Tirima v Angau Memorial Hospital Board and The State* 2005).

In *Laki v Gawi* (2018), where a patient was brought to an accident and emergency department in a public hospital in Madang, she was found to have received inadequate care and attention, resulting in her death. Expert evidence concluded that the patient died as a result of continuous bleeding from one of her pulmonary arteries which had burst, most likely due to active lung tuberculosis or lung scarring from a previous tubercular infection. Cannings J concluded that the defendant, Dr Gawi, was culpable for neglecting to see his patient until 4.00 pm, although she had arrived at the accident and emergency department at about 8.00am: "*Dr Gawi failed to exercise reasonable skill and judgment, taking into account all the circumstances in which he was working, due to his failure to attend to the deceased in a timely manner. I find that he disregarded standard and acceptable medical practice in an emergency department*" (*Laki v Gawi* (2018) at [22]).

3 The Test for Causation

A "but for test" is applied in Papua New Guinea (*Laki v Gawi* (2018)) in determining whether the tort of negligence is established on the evidence. Although a doctor may be shown to have had a duty of care toward his/her patient and to have breached it, if the patient would have died anyway, causation will not be found proved and the plaintiff will lose their case. In *Laki v Gawi* (2018) at [24], for instance, Cannings J of the National Court of Justice applied *Barnett v Chelsea and Kensington Hospital Management Committee* (1969) and observed that:

> …A man felt ill and went to a hospital accident and emergency department in England. He was told by the nurse, who consulted the duty medical officer, to go home to bed. He did that, then died five hours later. His widow sued the hospital for negligence. She proved the first two elements of negligence: the hospital owed a duty of care and it was negligent, as the duty officer did not see, examine, admit or treat the deceased. But the plaintiff failed to establish the element of causation. The Court held that the deceased had been poisoned with arsenic and, even if he had been given proper medical treatment, he would have died anyway. The plaintiff lost the case and received no compensation…

4 Vicarious Liability

For vicarious liability to be established against the State, such as for conduct in a hospital, the following elements must be proved:

a. An employer-employee relationship existed between it and the first defendant (the tortfeasor).
b. The tort of negligence was committed by the first defendant.
c. The tort was committed in the course of the employee's employment. (*Roka Coffee Estate Pty Ltd v Gerebi* (1973); *Laki v Gawi* (2018) at [24]).

Papua New Guinea courts have exhibited some reluctance to award exemplary damages where the relevant conduct is conduct for which the State may be vicariously liable by reason of the conduct of an individual (see *Goria v Simewa* 2001).

5 Damages

Damages in the form of general and special damages and aggravated and exemplary damages can be awarded in medical negligence cases in Papua New Guinea. English law, as to the purpose of damages being to restore a person as nearly as possible to the position in which they were before the tort is applied as a measure of compensation (*Albert v Aine* (2019) at [16]; *Motor Vehicles Insurance Ltd v Kol* (2007) at [6]), taking into account the prevailing circumstances, especially the economic conditions at the time of the assessment of damages, as well as the views of the community as to what is fair and reasonable compensation, and awards in previous similar or comparable cases (*Motor Vehicles Insurance Ltd v Kol* (2007) at [8–9]). There is no mathematical formula which is applicable (*Oresi v Marjen* (1998); *Jack v Mola* (2008) at [33]).

Aggravated damages, as a form of compensatory damages, follow the model established in Australia. Thus, in *PNG Aviation Services v Somare* (2000) the Supreme Court applied Australian authority that:

1. Aggravated compensatory damages are awarded where either the circumstances of both the publication or the defendant's conduct then or subsequently make the injury to the plaintiff worse.
2. They are usually only awarded in relation to the injury to the plaintiff's feelings but may also be awarded in respect of conduct which has the effect of increasing injury to the plaintiff's reputation.
3. Conduct relevant to the issue of aggravated damages must be capable of amounting to conduct which was in some way unjustifiable, improper or lacking in bona fides.

In terms of an award for pecuniary loss:

> …a plaintiff must establish his economic loss, before the Court can make an award for any such losses. This is not a difficult thing to do. If the plaintiff was engaged in an income

> earning activity as at the time of his or her sustaining the injuries, he or she must produce evidence of both the income generating activity and its monetary value, the amounts he or she has lost and stands to lose as a result of the injuries and the disabilities. Where a plaintiff produces such evidence, the Court is duty bound to assess the plaintiff's past and future economic losses. On the other hand, if a plaintiff fails to produce any such evidence, the Court can either make no award or make a nominal award having regard to the reduction in the plaintiff's income earning capacity to support him or herself and his or her dependants... (*Motor Vehicles Insurance Ltd v Kol* (2007) at [26]).

The award of damages is specific to the particular case and the harm suffered by a plaintiff. In *Oresi v Marjen* (1998) two surgical instruments were negligently left inside the plaintiff, resulting in a permanent disability and the inability to have a full term pregnancy. That resulted in the award of K10,000,[1] as general damages.

In Papua New Guinea, exemplary damages can be awarded as an incident of a court's discretion, and the court can decide whether the State is vicariously liable to pay (*Tomba v The State* (1997); *Bellawa v Tasing* (2021) at [37]). They are regarded as punitive in nature as their purpose is to punish the wrongdoer. They have been held to be relevant in cases where there has been a continuing breach and disregard of a plaintiff's rights and are a reflection of a court's condemnation of outrageous and illegal actions by a defendant (*Kakipa v Nikilli* (2002) at [55]) or infringements of constitutional rights. The question is whether the defendant's conduct is "*sufficiently outrageous to merit punishment, as where it discloses malice, fraud, cruelty, insolence or the like.*" Such damages are also intended to be deterrent (*Enei v Rimbunan* (2011), at [72]). Courts have a wide discretion in deciding whether to order exemplary damages and as to their quantum. The discretion must be exercised judicially and properly.

Different factors need to be incorporated in the calculation of general damages. Two decisions by the National Court of Papua New Guinea are particularly instructive.

Jack v Mola. In *Jack v Mola* (2008) the plaintiff, Julie Jack, underwent a tubal ligation to prevent her from conceiving and bearing children. She was married and aged 30 at the time of the assessment of damages. While in her fifth month of pregnancy, she attended the ante-natal clinic at Port Moresby General Hospital, on 20 January 2000, and, in February she was advised that she was HIV-positive. She was told that if she wanted to live longer, given her HIV status, she should seriously consider tubal ligation surgery after the birth of her child—the operation would prevent her from conceiving further children and passing on the virus to any child she might have later. She was given a consent for sterilisation form in which a name had been crossed out and hers had been substituted and she was wrongly referred to as unmarried. Her husband was informed of her blood test result and he was advised to have a blood test. He tested HIV-negative. After the birth of the child, the plaintiff and her husband signed a consent form for sterilisation but she requested another test. It did not proceed and the tubal ligation surgery was performed. Further blood testing showed the plaintiff, her husband and her daughter to be HIV-negative.

[1] As of 12 September 2021, 1 PNG Kina = $US0.28.

When the plaintiff sued, she claimed not to be in a position to reverse the surgery because of its cost and, in any event, had been advised there was only a 50–70% of chance of a reversal. A psychiatric report, from Dr Tienang, the Chief Psychiatrist of the Department of Health, attested to the fact that Ms Jack had no previous history of psychiatric illness or any chronic physical illness. However, after the relevant events she had become very depressed and anxious and had lost considerable weight. She wept most of the night. After informing her relatives of her HIV status, she and her daughter had to live with considerable stigma and, when she delivered her daughter, she received substandard treatment on the labour ward because of what was believed to be her HIV status. The assessing psychiatrist recorded that the plaintiff's marriage had come under increasing strain due to her inability to conceive and deliver children and her husband had become progressively more estranged from her and beat her due to his frustration at her inability to conceive. She felt less complete as a woman and a failure as a wife. She was preoccupied by her infertility and, when alone with her daughter, wept when thinking about her inability to bear children to keep her daughter company. She had suffered considerably decreased enjoyment of her personal life and her marital relationship as a result of her inability to conceive children and her relationships with teachers, schoolmates and family members had deteriorated. Dr Tienang concluded that Ms Jack was suffering from symptoms of moderate depression and anxiety, caused directly by the trauma of wrongly having a permanent sterilisation procedure performed on her, after an incorrect result from an HIV test. A psychologist's report also attested to her suffering.

Sevua J commented that the emotional stress or the psychological effect of the traumatic experience and sufferings endured by Ms Jack were demonstrated at the trial on assessment of damages: "*During the plaintiff's counsel's submissions, I observed that there was a woman sitting at the back of the Court weeping as Ms Sawanga was making her submissions and referring to the evidence and the reports of the psychiatrist and the psychologist. I later learnt that the woman was the plaintiff*." (*Jack v Mola* (2008) at [29]). He emphasised that the initial diagnosis of HIV was conducted in a "*highly unprofessional manner and in circumstances where little or no regard for professional care and attention was given to the plaintiff especially in a situation where the defendants' servants and agents were dealing with a very dangerous and volatile disease, namely, HIV and AIDS. More proper care should have been given to the plaintiff in this case*." (*Jack v Mola* (2008) at [40]). He had no difficulty in concluding that the results were due to negligent procedures, negligent attitude, negligent doctors and negligent medical staff. He observed that the wrong HIV + result may have been for the person whose name had been crossed out on the consent form given to Ms Jack.

Sevua J observed that no amount of money could compensate Ms Jack for the wrong and permanent damage that rendered her sterile and emotionally and/or psychologically affected, although she had continued to be employed. He assessed general damages at K100,000, K75,000 for loss of fertility, K50,000 in aggravated damages for the negligent sampling of Ms Jack's blood sample and K50,000 "*because the conduct of the servants and agents of the second and third defendants was not only negligent, but outrageous, malicious and done without due regard to the plaintiff's rights. Legally and medically, the plaintiff was not infected with HIV. virus as several tests after delivery of her child resulted in HIV negative results*" (*Jack v Mola* (2008) at [57]).

Albert v Aine. The decision of the National Court in *Albert v Aine* (2019) is the most contemporary judgment on damages for medical negligence. It also provides an extensive analysis of medical negligence law and the award of damages in Papua New Guinea.

The plaintiff, Jacinta Albert, claimed damages for suffering a ruptured uterus resulting in a loss of fertility and inability to conceive on the basis of negligence by Dr Aine and his medical team. The case was not defended by the health practitioners and the contest arose at the stage of assessment of damages against the State. Ms Albert attended at Port Moresby General Hospital as she was in labour with her second child. She sat on the floor for more than an hour before a midwife saw her. She continued to wait for medical attention and approached Dr Aine and asked him to carry out a caesarean section on her because that was how she had previously given birth. He did not carry out any medical check on her and told her that it was a woman's natural ability to give birth and paid no more attention to her. She was left unattended and received no form of care but commenced to suffer more pain and bleeding until some hours later she lapsed into a state of unconsciousness. She was seen nearly 10 hours after presenting at the hospital and diagnosed with a rupture of her uterus with foetal death. A hysterectomy was performed.

Three days after the surgery, Ms Albert was visited by the obstetrics and surgical team whose members informed her about the surgery and told her she would never again be able to experience her menstruation cycle and would not be able to conceive or bear children. They encouraged her to adopt if she wanted more children. She went into great distress and became emotionally unstable. Deputy Chief Justice Kandakasi classified the gross carelessness or negligence on the part of Dr Aine and his medical team as bordering on criminal negligence—there were:

> ...several hours of anguishing pain and suffering right before the eyes of the medical doctors and other medical staff on duty at the relevant time. No human being should be allowed to suffer unnecessarily under the eyes or the nose of a medical doctor or a nurse in a hospital. The Plaintiff required immediate medical attention, given her medical history and her worsening condition. She did not have to go looking for a doctor or a nurse. It was their duty and responsibility to attend to her the moment she entered the door of the Hospital... (*Albert v Aine* (2019) at [18]).

He observed that:

> ...A professional doctor, nurse or a medical staff who is true to the medical calling as a profession, would have immediately attended to the patient until the patient received the correct and appropriate level of medical attention, care and treatment. Instead of treating the Plaintiff as a high-risk patient, Dr Aine and his medical team treated her like any other person with no serious medical condition warranting immediate attention and left her unattended for a very long time. The situation would have worsened with the Plaintiff's own death, had it not been for the other doctors who came on the next shift and attended to her. Unfortunately,

> by that time, she had already raptured her uterus and lost her child. Then due to lack of appropriate medical attention and treatment, she also lost her ability to conceive, become pregnant and give birth to children as a normal young mother of only one child… (*Albert v Aine* (2019) at [18]).

Deputy Chief Justice Kandakasi observed that there was no doubt that the medical operations to which Ms Albert was subject and the resultant loss and disabilities had exercised a serious mental and emotional impact upon her, aside from the imposition of strains for her marriage, because of her inability to conceive again and bear children. There was some uncertainty about what occurred during the operation which was claimed to have removed the plaintiff's ruptured uterus and possibly her cervix, ovaries, fallopian tubes and other surrounding structures. She subsequently experienced her monthly period but she was unable to conceive again. He found the pain, suffering, loss and grief of Ms Albert to be far worse than those of Julie Jack.

He reflected on the fact that the level of damages awarded in Papua New Guinea was significantly lower than in countries such as the United States and Australia. He noted the justification proffered for this, that the differential in economic status was a legitimate explanation, but rejected the argument, concluding, interestingly and to some degree counter-intuitively, that awards for damages should be far greater than those awarded in developed jurisdictions. His explanation was:

> …For in the developed jurisdictions, there are well developed and functional welfare services and health and other facilities even to get disabled persons to function normally in society and indeed live longer. These kinds of services and facilities are non-existent in PNG and other third world countries. A person who is injured and left with a disability in PNG will have a much more difficult time adjusting to get back to living a good life and is often made to suffer for the rest of his or her life. This in my view calls for higher awards then the kinds of awards the Courts have been making to date to adequately compensate the victims of careless, reckless or negligent conduct. Substantially increasing awards will indeed, deliver on the law's object of awarding damages which is to "nearly as possible. put the party who has been injured, or who has suffered, in the same position as he would have been in if he had not sustained the wrong for which he is now getting his compensation." Those engaging in negligent conduct such as medical doctors, nurses and other medical workers, drivers of motor vehicles or persons in possession of things that would cause others harm, damage and loss should be warned that damages for any injury, loss or damage they cause, will result in substantially increased awards of damages… (*Albert v Aine* (2019) at [29]).

He awarded Ms Albert K200,000 in general damages for pain and suffering and K350,000 for loss of fertility, commenting:

> …I know that an award of K350,000.00 could sound a lot of money. But in my view, this in no way equates the unwarranted loss of a child and being rendered infertile for life for a young woman with one child. Having children is a big deal for women and families in PNG. The Plaintiff has been and will continue to face the challenges of not being able to have a child. On top of that, she stands the risk of having no children to look after her in her old age. The amount I decided to award is at least in my view something that will enable the Plaintiff to feel vindicated and give her the opportunity to make the necessary adjustments and face the challenges brought upon her by her uncalled-for infertility at the hands of Dr. Aine and his team and the Hospital… (*Albert v Aine* (2019) at [29]).

In addressing the issue of exemplary damages, he noted that in prior cases there had been failures on the part of doctors, nurses and other staff in State-owned hospitals to attend to patients competently and effectively in a timely manner but that awards of exemplary damages had failed to produce a change in the medical culture or attitudes. He commented, "*Many patients who could otherwise be spared from dying are unnecessarily caused to die or are ending up with lifelong losses as in this case, by the plain and inexcusable failures of doctors and other medical professionals.*" (*Albert v Aine* (2019) at [29]). He stated that he had not seen any evidence of the State taking meaningful and effective steps to ensure that health practitioners "*discharge their duties professionally and in a timely, diligent and most competent and effective manner.*" He commented that:

> ...Every human life is precious. Medical doctors and other professionals within hospitals or medical establishments be it, public like the Port Moresby General Hospital or, private like the Pacific International Hospital or any other medical establishments have a duty to appropriately attend to patients who get to their hospitals for treatment. Payment of fees and meeting of other requirements are secondary to a doctor or a medical establishment's duty to save lives. Until there is a due recognition and appropriate change of attitude to promptly, diligently and competently attend to patients as they enter medical establishments, the Courts have a social and moral duty as part of a legal duty to award damages in a way that it serves the dual purposes of, those who fail in their duties being punished and serve as a deterrent to other doctors and medical professionals and establishments in the discharge of their duties and responsibilities... (*Albert v Aine* (2019) at [38]).

This led him to the conclusion that it was necessary for exemplary damages to rise substantially "*until the medical profession wakes up and makes serious improvements in its current level of failures.*" (*Albert v Aine* (2019) at [39]). He commented:

> ...In PNG, negligent and incompetent doctors and other medical professionals appear to get away easily without any form of punishment or discipline. I am yet to hear or see a medical doctor being disciplined for professional negligence and am certainly, not aware of the existence of a functional disciplinary process. Until we get to that point, the Courts must and have a duty to award more and more exemplary damages... (*Albert v Aine* (2019) at [38]).

This led him to award K100,000 in exemplary damages to the plaintiff, observing:

> ...Hopefully, by virtue of this award, doctors, nurses and other staff in our hospitals will be caused to become diligent, attentive and competent and enable them to promptly attend to their patients' needs instead of letting them suffer as they did with the Plaintiff in this case... (*Albert v Aine* (2019) at [38]).

Taking into account that K50,000 in aggravated damages were awarded to Julie Jack, he doubled the amount and awarded K100,000 to recognise that Ms Albert's medical history and request for a caesarean section were ignored by Dr Aine for no good reason and the level of suffering that she was likely to experience for life.

The damages awards in *Albert v Aine* constitute an important and illustrative example of Papua New Guinea's modern quest to fix damages at a level which is genuinely restorative of a plaintiff's situation after medical negligence and effectively recognises particularly adverse aspects of such conduct. It remains to be seen how this precedent will be implemented and the extent to which awards of damages in medical negligence cases will rise.

6 Conclusion

The law on medical negligence is evolving gradually in Papua and New Guinea. It is influenced by the law in both England and Australia. Litigation in relation to the right to health has not yet taken place. Disregard of a patient's entitlement to prompt and sound care has been found to be negligent and has been visited by significant (and rising) sums in damages. While Papua New Guinea courts have exhibited some reluctance to award exemplary damages where the relevant conduct by a health practitioner is conduct for which the State may be vicariously liable, a trend of increasing awards of damages can be identified over the past 20 years, including the award of exemplary damages.

References

Aipit S, Aipit J, Laman M (2014) Malnutrition: a neglected but leading cause of child deaths in Papua New Guinea. Lancet Glob Health 2(1):e568. https://doi.org/10.1016/S2214-109X(14)70302-X

Albert v Aine [2019] PGNC 34; N7772

Auka R, Gore B, Koralyo PR (2015) Sorcery-and witchcraft-related killings in Papua New Guinea: the criminal justice system response. In: Forsyth M, Eves R (ed) Talking it through: responses to sorcery and witchcraft beliefs and practices in Melanesia. ANU press, Canberra http://press-files.anu.edu.au/downloads/press/p316611/pdf/13.-Sorcery-and-Witchcraft-Related-Killings-in-Papua-New-Guinea-The-Criminal-Justice-System-Response.pdf

Baledrokadroka J (2002) The interface of law and medicine in the South Pacific. J S Pac Law 6:JSPL 14. http://www.paclii.org/journals/fJSPL/vol06/9.shtml

Barnett v Chelsea and Kensington Hospital Management Committee [1969] 1 QB 428

Bellawa v Kasing [2021] PGNC 111; N8860

Chalmers DRC (1984) An introduction to the law in Papua New Guinea. Law Book Co

Chalmers DRC, Weisbrot S, Injia S (2009) Criminal law and practice of Papua New Guinea. University of Papua New Guinea Press

Corrin J (2013) Getting down to business: developing the underlying law in Papua New Guinea. J Leg Plur Unoff Law 46(2):155–171. https://doi.org/10.1080/07329113.2014.893126 Accessed 12 April 2020

Dinnen S (2001) Law and order in a weak state: crime and politics in Papua New Guinea. University of Hawaii Press

Enei v Rimbunal Hijau Ltd [2011] PGNC 142; N4402

Forsyth M, Gibbs P (2020) Contagion of violence: the role of narratives, worldview, mechanisms of transmission and contagion entrepreneurs. Int J Crime, Justice Soc Demo 9(2):37–59

Goria v Simewa [2001] PGNC 142; N2066

Graham D, Kelly B, Richards D (2019) Why patients sue doctors: lessons learned from medical malpractice cases. Elsevier

Griffin JA, Katter DH (2015) Criminal procedure in Papua New Guinea. LexisNexis Butterworths
Harris H (2018) The global anti-corruption regime: the case of Papua New Guinea. Routledge
Hetzel MW, Page-Sharp M, Bala N (2014) Quality of anitmalarial drugs and antibiotics in Papua New Guinea: a survey of the health facility supply chain. PLoS ONE. https://doi.org/10.1371/journal.pone.0096810
Injia S (2013) Injia on criminal offences in Papua New Guinea and the Pacific. University of Papua New Guinea Press
Jack v Mola [2008] PGNC 309; N3537
Jessep O, Regan AJ, Kwa EL (2001) Twenty years of the Papua New Guinea constitution. Lawbook Co
Jolly M, Stewart C, Brewer C (2012) Engendering violence in Papua New Guinea. ANU EPress
Kakipa v Nikilli [2002] PGNC 146; N5689
Katter D (2016) Civil procedure in Papua New Guinea: National Court of Justice. LexisNexis Butterworths
Kitur U, Adair T, Riley I, Lopez AD (2019) Estimating the pattern of causes of death in Papula New Guinea. BMC Public Health. 19:1322. https://doi.org/10.1186/s12889-019-7620-5
Klaver R, Coe JR (2018) Barriers to healthcare for female patients in Papua New Guinea. BMJ case reports. https://casereports.bmj.com/content/2018/bcr-2017-224005
Kwa EL (2011) Constitutional law of Papua New Guinea. University of Papua New Guinea
Laki v Gawi [2018] PGNC 57; N7146
Luker V, Dinnen S (2010) Civic insecurity: law, order and HIV in Papua New Guinea. ANU E Press
Mapirea P, Morgan C (2011) The contribution of church health serevices to maternal health care provision in Papua New Guinea. P N G Med J 54(3/4):139–146
Matui M (2017) Trial practice and criminal procedure in Papua New Guinea. University of Papua New Guinea
Motor Vehicles Insurance Ltd v Kol [2007] PGSC 38; SC902
Oresi v Marjen [1998] PGNC 106; N1784
PNG Aviation Services v Somare [2000] PGSC 18; SC 658
Roka Coffee Estate Pty Ltd v Gerebi [1973] PNGLR 486
Tirima v Angau Memorial Hospital Board and the State [2005] PGNC 165:N2779
Tomba v The Independent State of Papua New Guinea [1997] SC 518
UNICEF, Data Warehouse (2018) Papua New Guinea. https://data.unicef.org/resources/data_explorer/unicef_f/?ag=UNICEF&df=GLOBAL_DATAFLOW&ver=1.0&dq=PNG.PT_F_20-24_MRD_U18.&startPeriod=1970&endPeriod=2020
United States, Department of State (2018) Country reports on human rights practices for 2018. https://www.state.gov/wp-content/uploads/2019/03/PAPUA-NEW-GUINEA-2018.pdf Accessed 12 April 2020
Weisbrot D, Paliwala AH, Sawyer A (1982) Law and social change in Papua New Guinea. LexisNexis Butterworths
World Health Organization (2020) Papua New Guinea. https://www.who.int/countries/png/en/ Accessed 7 Aug 2021

Medical Liability in Qatar

Barry Solaiman

Abstract Qatar's healthcare system is developing substantially. World-class facilities are opening at a rapid pace in a country which boasts a comprehensive public health system, alongside a robust offering of private facilities. Clinicians are drawn, from around the world, to work within this system. For lawmakers, the challenge of creating medical liability regulations is stark. Qatar must develop bespoke regulations which balance religious and cultural expectations while harmonising best practices applied by established medical systems abroad. To unpack these issues, this chapter undertakes a three-part evaluation. First, legislation and case law are examined to determine the principles underlying criminal and civil law which underpin medical liability provisions. There is a focus on infectious disease control, organ transplantation, mental health and abortion. Second, the opportunities for alternative means of dispute resolution are analysed and their limitations considered. Third, there is an analysis of how this diverse system encourages an inclusive method of law creation. Despite that emphasis, challenges of harmonisation persist, and questions about the impact of criminal law on medical practice remain undetermined, requiring further research.

1 Introduction

Qatar's healthcare system is undergoing substantial change. The country's not-for-profit healthcare provider, 'Hamad Medical Corporation' (HMC), is at the heart of the public health system. There are also numerous private hospitals and facilities. Investment is significant, with the country's per capita health spending being one of the highest in the Middle East and North Africa Region.[1] In recent years, Hamad

[1] Demand for health services rises in Qatar Oxford Business Group (2019).

B. Solaiman (✉)
College of Law, HBKU, Doha, Qatar
e-mail: bsolaiman@hbku.edu.qa

V. L. Raposo and R. G. Beran (eds.), *Medical Liability in Asia and Australasia*,
Ius Gentium: Comparative Perspectives on Law and Justice 94,
https://doi.org/10.1007/978-981-16-4855-7_13

Medical City has been inaugurated in Doha.[2] There are state of the art facilities, such as the Women's Wellness Research Center and the Ambulatory Care Center, amongst others. There is also the world's leading specialised orthopaedic and sports medicine hospital (Aspetar) and the sprawling Sidra Medicine facility, providing care to women and children. Medical practitioners are drawn from across the globe to work within the many facilities. This paradigm influences how laws are made. Qatar looks outward to international best practices to develop its internal legal expertise, but it must also heed local expectations.

This is a complex challenge in a country which balances three legal systems. There is Sharia law, the principal source of legislation; civil law arising from the Napoleonic Code which was adopted into parts of the Arab World by Egypt; and the common law applied within the Qatar Financial Centre.[3] Medical liability cases are heard in the criminal and civil courts in Arabic. Judgments of the Court of Cassation (QCC) (the highest court in Qatar) are analysed in this chapter.[4] The courts consider the Penal and Civil Codes, as well as an array of other legislation regarding healthcare law created under the purview of the Ministry of Public Health (MOPH).

This chapter examines those laws and their application by the courts. Several matters are illuminated, including the prevalence of criminal sanctions and the principles underlying negligence. While negligence standards are influenced by countries in the Anglosphere, the burden of proof for civil disputes has a higher threshold than is applied in those countries. Alternative complaint mechanisms are analysed. These can lead to additional sanctions which are distinct to those found in legislation. There is a discussion about the broader insights which can be derived concerning the liability system in Qatar. While it is challenging to make laws in a system with competing expectations, this creates an incentive for an inclusive approach to law creation. Nevertheless, questions linger about the prominence of criminal liability and its impact on practice, a matter which requires further research.

---

[2] Hamad Medical Corporation (2017).

[3] The Permanent Constitution of the State of Qatar (2004), Article 1; Roy Georgiades, The Court Structure in Qatar, Al Tamimi & Co. (2012), https://www.tamimi.com/law-update-articles/the-court-structure-in-qatar/visited 29 May 2020; The Qatar International Court and Dispute Resolution Centre hears cases pertaining to the Qatar Financial Centre. It is comprised of judges mainly from common law jurisdictions. See, The Court Overview, Qatar International Court and Dispute Resolution Centre (2020), https://www.qicdrc.gov.qa/the-courts/overview last visited 29 May 2020.

[4] Full judgments are not provided in Qatar in English. Instead, summaries are provided by the official legal portal and/or Lexis Nexis. This chapter relies on the available English summaries of cases from the official Al Meezan Qatari Legal Portal or Lexis Nexis Middle East. The courts give precedence to the Arabic language version of the law. The analysis in this chapter should be understood with the disclaimer that the English sources relied upon may not represent the accurate interpretations given to the Arabic laws by the courts.

2 Liability and the Law

This section provides a comprehensive outline of the law on medical liability as well as case law which gives context to the legislation. It will be seen that criminal sanctions are a consistent feature of the law.

2.1 *Criminal Law*

Where a patient is harmed, they may seek redress through both the criminal and civil courts. A civil court cannot reconsider the findings of a criminal court. However, the judgment of a criminal court is deemed to be '*conclusive evidence*' for a civil claim by which the civil courts must abide. In this regard, the findings of a criminal court can form the basis for both claims.[5] It is more beneficial, from a patient's perspective, to seek redress through the criminal courts first. At the same time, a term commonly found in legislation is that sanctions apply '*without prejudice to any more severe sanction provided by another law*'. Usually being more severe, criminal penalties will take precedence.

The starting point for such claims is the Penal Code because there is no self-contained medical liability law.[6] Article 312 states that anyone accidentally harming another, due to negligence, may be imprisoned for up to 6 months and receive a fine not exceeding 1,000 Qatari Riyals. Where negligence leads to a 'deformity', the sanction is increased to 1 year in prison and a fine not exceeding 5,000 riyals.[7] Article 313 of the Penal Code doubles the above penalty where:

> …the crime is the result of a transgression of the offender's occupation, profession or job … or the offender fails to help or seek help for the victim despite having the capability to do so…

In the first instance, a clinician could be imprisoned for up to 2 years and be fined up to 10,000 riyals, depending on the circumstances. Criminal law also covers breach of confidentiality. Article 332 stipulates that anyone acting in an official capacity, trade or profession who divulges a secret entrusted them shall be liable up to 2 years imprisonment and/or a fine not exceeding 10,000 riyals.

Below, specific laws are analysed which stipulate for harsher criminal penalties than the Penal Code. The Penal Code will apply where they do not, and vice versa. The victim may also pursue a claim in the civil courts. Where criminal liability is established, a case may be transferred to the civil courts where appropriate compensation can be determined.

---

[5] Case QCC 84/2008; Law No.13 of 1990 Civil and Commercial Procedure Law, Article 301; Law No. 23 of 2004 Regarding Promulgating the Criminal Procedure Code, Article 319.

[6] Law No. 11 of 2004 Issuing the Penal Code; Analysing the payment of '*blood money*' or '*Diyya*' under Sharia law (and the related provisions in the Penal Code) is beyond the scope of this chapter.

[7] *Id*. Article 312.

2.2 Negligence

In terms of the standard of negligence applied, the relevant provisions are found in Law No. 2 of 1983 (Practice of Medicine)[8]:

> ...The doctor shall not be liable for poor patient outcomes following treatment if it is found that due care had been afforded and if the doctor behaved in a reasonable and professionally orthodox or evidence-based manner in his approach to the diagnosis and management of the patient...[9]

The law goes on to determine where a doctor will be liable '*to a claim for compensation or a charge of negligence*'[10]:

(a) If the error was as a result of ignorance of technical or basic scientific matters that every doctor should be familiar with both in terms of medical diagnoses or in dispensing the relevant treatment.
(b) If the cause of harm to the patient was through negligence or the lack of affording due care.[11]

These provisions provide the broad underpinnings of the liability regime. The terms '*due care*' and '*reasonably*' pertain to the standard of care expected of clinicians, and whether a doctor is negligent will depend on whether they fall short of those standards. Case law provides further insight into the application of the law.[12] In Case QCC 84/2008, it was held that there must be fault, causation and damage established.[13] Fault is established by reference to the provisions concerning '*due care*' and the standard of care. There are no particular rules outlined on causation, but in Case 84/2008, it was held that the act must occur in '*such a way*' as to be causally connected to the damage. In that case, the harm caused the patient a '*loss of chance*' at being cured, which illustrates that causation analyses extend beyond '*but for*' causation. It is unclear whether (and what) percentage thresholds are applied. Damage is simply established by identifying some harm.

There is a high burden of proof for establishing these elements. In Case QCC 3/2009, it was emphasised that fault should be '*clearly and positively*' established through acts or omissions, demonstrating that the doctor '*undoubtedly*' violated the '*established, undisputed principles and basic scientific rules of the medical profession*'.[14] That case involved a negligence claim which is significant because it imposed what would be considered a criminal law standard of proof in countries like the UK

---

[8] Law No. 2 of 1983 with respect to the Practice of the Profession of Medicine and Dental Medicine and Surgery.

[9] *Id*. Article 18.

[10] *Id.*

[11] *Id.*

[12] Qatar is not a common law system but precedent is important. Judges refer to previous decisions where relevant. See, e.g., Case QCC 3/2009 where the Court held that a judgment of the lower court was erroneous because it departed from established jurisprudence.

[13] Case QCC 84/2008.

[14] Case QCC 3/2009.

and US (*'beyond reasonable doubt'*) rather than a lower threshold that is more typically applied in civil courts (*'more likely than not'*). On omissions, there is liability where doctors refuse to come to the aid of injured people or to treat a patient unless the patient's condition is outside of their area of specialisation.[15] The law actively requires doctors to take action in those circumstances and penalises those who omit to assist. There are a range of civil sanctions set out in Law No. 2 of 1983 (Practice of Medicine). These range from fines, warnings and suspensions to the withdrawal of licences.[16] A clinician omitting to act may also be criminally liable to both imprisonment and a fine under Article 313 of the Penal Code (failing to help or seek help for the victim despite having the capability to do so). Four other matters are important to highlight.

As is common in other jurisdictions, negligence will arise where the clinician has not acted in accordance with *'basic scientific matters that every doctor should be familiar with'*, namely, where the doctor is not acting in accordance with the standards expected of the profession. In case QCC 3/2009, relying on the findings of an expert report, the court held that the duty of care of a doctor must be delineated by having regard to the average knowledge and expertise of doctors in the same circumstances, the traditions of the profession, established principles and basic scientific rules of the medical art.[17] It appears that the expert report in that case (which was subsequently applied by the QCC), applied the English case of *Bolam*[18] setting the standard of care as to whether a doctor *'has acted in accordance with a practice accepted as proper by a responsible body of 'medical men skilled in that particular art''*.[19] In QCC 3/2009, it was held that liability could be ascertained by the opinions of *'more than one medical authority'*. This alludes to the standard of care applied in *Bolam,* which would be satisfied by a few experts finding the conduct acceptable.[20]

The courts place significant weight on expert testimony, in line with Part 8 of the Civil and Commercial Procedure Law.[21] Almost every published case either refers to an expert report or raises some related procedural issue. From a liability perspective, the courts will not hold a doctor liable where the expert determines that there are disparities between doctors' opinions concerning the matter at hand.[22] From a procedural perspective, the parties and experts must conduct their role precisely in accordance with the law. In QCC 180/2009, it was held that a lower court had erred in not appointing an expert to determine the mental health of the appellant, even when the appellant had made such a request.[23] In QCC 136/2008, it was held that the lower court had erred in applying the law because it relied upon a nullified expert

---

[15] Law No. 2 of 1983, Article 20(6).

[16] *Id.* Articles 22 & 23.

[17] Case QCC 3/2009.

[18] Bolam v Friern Hospital Management (1957).

[19] Id. at 587.

[20] See also, Defreitas v O'Brien (1993) 4 Med LR 281.

[21] Law No. 13 of 1990, Articles 333–361.

[22] Case QCC 3/2009.

[23] Case QCC 180/2009.

report. The expert committee had not followed proper procedures when it failed to summon the litigants.[24] Therefore, the courts are inflexible where procedure is not followed, which can have a significant impact on liability outcomes for both sides.

The courts have held that employers will usually be held vicariously liable for the conduct of doctors.[25] This is in accordance with Article 209 of the Civil Code, which holds employers liable for the conduct of their employees acting in the course and scope of their employment. The employer must exercise some control over their employee, whether directly or indirectly.[26] In practice, the insurer or hospital will pay compensation. The doctor may also be subject to other sanctions by their employer or by the MOPH.

In terms of damages, Article 201 of the Civil Code stipulates that compensation is limited to the loss incurred and profit forfeited by the victim. Under Article 202, damages are payable for mental harm that results from the wrongdoing, including physical or mental harm to the spouse and relatives up to the second kin where the victim is deceased.

Through an examination of legislation and case law, one can piece together the crucial facets of the general liability regime in Qatar. An assessment of negligence is conducted in congruence with recognised standards, but there are particularities of the system, such as the burden of proof. The next section examines how liability arises within specific fields of medicine and how the law is shaped around the particular experiences of Qatar.

2.3 Liability in the Specialities

Once the analysis ventures away from the general law on medicine and practice, and into the specialised fields, one begins to find more severe sanctions. The focus here is on legislation regarding the prevention of infectious diseases, organ transplantation, mental health and abortion.[27]

2.3.1 Infectious Diseases

Qatar is not unfamiliar with the challenge of controlling infectious diseases which account for about 8% of all deaths in the country.[28] It has a dedicated Communicable Disease Center (the first to open in the region) operating within the auspices of HMC

---

[24] Case QCC 136/2008.

[25] Case QCC 129/2009;Case QCC 241/2013.

[26] Law No. 22 of 2004 Regarding Promulgating the Civil Code, Article 209(1) & (2).

[27] End-of-life care and medical research are beyond the scope of this chapter.

[28] Communicable diseases, Ministry of Public Health (2017).

that catered for 120,000 outpatient visits in 2018.[29] The primary laws in this area are the Penal Code and Law No. 17 of 1990 on the Prevention of Infectious Diseases which was amended by Law No. 9 of 2020 following the COVID-19 Pandemic.

For the most serious cases, Article 252 of the Penal Code stipulates that any person intentionally committing an act which '*might cause the spread of an infection or an epidemic*', may be imprisoned up to 15 years in jail, rising to capital punishment where any person dies as a result. For other cases, the Infectious Diseases law will apply.

A recurring challenge for health authorities is the transmission of disease by pilgrims leaving the country for the *Hajj* pilgrimage who may return to Qatar with an infectious disease. Under Article 16 of the law, pilgrims should be vaccinated before leaving the country. The spread of disease, from pilgrimages, can also contribute to or exacerbate acute threats, such as the Middle East Respiratory Syndrome (MERS-CoV) and the novel coronavirus (COVID-19). The number of confirmed MERS infections has been low, but the Covid-19 pandemic led to amendments to the law premised on a collective responsibility to stem the spread of the virus.

To achieve this, there were important changes to liability provisions during the 2020 pandemic. The measures reflect the seriousness with which the state took the spread of the disease. A 'Health Prosecution' was created, headed by the Public Prosecutor to dispose of all health-related crimes.[30] Some provisions of the law go beyond those typically found elsewhere, with an emphasis on collective responsibility. Article 3 of the law requires that the nearest medical centre or hospital must be notified '*immediately*' if someone is diagnosed or suspected of having a listed infectious disease. Article 4 (as amended in 2020) states that the burden of reporting is on:

> …Any physician who has examined the Infected Person or the Person Suspected to be suffering from an Infectious Disease, as well as the responsibility of the Infected Person himself, the head of the family or the person who receives him into his house. It is also the responsibility of the director of the university, institution or school or his representative, as well as the responsibility of the immediate superior if the infection has occurred or suspected to have occurred during work, or the expatriate's recruiter, whether the Infected or Suspected Person is found inside the country or abroad, when such matter has come to the knowledge of either one…

The law creates a wide burden on doctors and those in society who have some formal relationship with the person to report a suspected infection. The duty extends to guardians, university and school representatives, direct managers and employers. Article 6 gives the health authority the power to isolate and quarantine infected individuals or those suspected of having an infectious disease with surveillance measures. The same article was amended in 2020 to stipulate that those placed in isolation or quarantine must '*stay in the Isolation area specified by the said authority, and*

---

[29] *120,000 outpatients visit Communicable Disease Centre last year*, Gulf Times, 2019, https://gulf-times.com/story/622587/120-000-outpatients-visit-Communicable-Disease-Centre-last-year.

[30] Resolution No. 46 of 2020.

comply with Isolation and surveillance measures'.[31] Article 7 states that individuals are forbidden from returning to work until the health authority grants permission. The responsibility of implementing the suspension is on the person's '*immediate superior, employer or chief director*'. These provisions illustrate a legal approach premised on collective responsibility, placing a burden on several parties to report an infection.

Underpinning the provisions are broad powers of adjudication and strict penalties for violations. Article 20 gives powers to managers and staff of the health authority to act as '*judicial officers to report any violations of the provisions of this law*'. This includes the power, at any time and with police assistance if necessary, to enter houses or other premises to take the necessary measures to stem the spread of an infectious disease. For those in violation of the law, there is a maximum sentence of three years in prison and a fine not exceeding 200,000 riyals.[32] Prior to the 2020 amendments, the maximum penalties ranged from one to two months in prison and a fine of 2000 riyals. The seriousness of the Covid-19 pandemic has resulted in broader powers underpinned by harsher penalties for both clinicians and members of the public more widely. It also reveals distinctive features of Qatar's law, such as vaccination requirements for pilgrims.

2.3.2 Organ Transplantations

For organ transplantations, the country is developing a strong reputation, backed by a robust legal regime, to safeguard standards. The key principle, underlying the law, is that '*neither citizenship nor financial status plays a determining role in policy governing the allocation of organs*'.[33] This approach is known as the '*Doha Model of Organ Donation and Transplantation*' which has involved specific impacts on legal provisions concerning liability.[34] Law No. 15 of 2015 on Regulating the Human Organs Transfer and Transplantation, creates a strict prohibition on the trade of organs and of the donor or their heirs acquiring financial or in-kind benefits.[35] The concern of the law can be seen in an article published by the Director of the Qatar Organ Donation Center, which preceded the law.[36]

> ...Incentive payments not only greatly exacerbate the risks of coercion, exploitation, and physical and psychosocial harm to organ providers and recipients, they also impair efforts to promote deceased donation as the laudable fulfilment of an ethical responsibility...[37]

---

[31] Law No. 17 of 1990 on the Prevention of Infectious Diseases, Article 6 (as amended by Article 6bis of Law No. 9 of 2020).

[32] *Id.* Article 21 (as amended by Article 2 of Law No. 9 of 2020).

[33] Dominique Martin and Riadh A S Fadhil (2014).

[34] *Id.*

[35] Law No. 15 of 2015 on Regulating the Human Organs Transfer and Transplantation, Article 10.

[36] Martin & Fadhil, *supra* note 33. Dr. Fadhil played a leading role in developing the Doha Donation Accord and subsequent law.

[37] *Id.* 312.

Particular care is taken, under the law, to ensure the donor freely consents and to identify any potential economic imbalances between the donor and donee. The frequent mention of consent, in various provisions, underscores its significance within the law.[38] The way consent applies highlights particular features of familial hierarchies in the country and the provision of medical care. Under Article 6, for deceased donors, it must be verified that there is kinship with the donor up to the fourth degree. A donation to someone who is not family requires the consent of a Medical Ethics Committee. The approach of these provisions is underlined by how donors are recognised. Article 16 grants a '*medal of altruism*' to donors at an annual awards ceremony (or the family of the donor where they are deceased). The award also emphasises that donations ought to be given as one's ethical responsibility rather than for economic benefit.

The response to violators sits at the opposite extreme. Violating Article 6, by fraud, would draw a maximum sentence of 10 years in prison and/or a 1 m riyal fine.[39] Another example is Article 7, which requires that a donor is informed in writing by a '*specialized medical team*' of '*all potential and certain medical consequences resulting*' from donating. A violation of this article may result in a three-year prison term and or a 100,000 riyal fine.[40] Underlying the seriousness of such provisions is Article 24 under which the court may, amongst other things, promulgate the judgment in '*two daily newspapers at the expense of the convict*'. This gives judges the power to '*name and shame*' offenders in addition to the punishments above.

The law concerning organ transplantation is premised on incentivising altruistic behaviour and punishing exploitation. This has clearly been successful. In 2009, approximately 95% of patients travelled abroad to seek an organ transplantation.[41] By 2019, the number travelling abroad had reduced by 85%, with the vast majority obtaining donations in Qatar.[42] The strict provisions of the law have raised standards and enhanced medical provision.

2.3.3 Mental Health

Another area which has seen changes in recent years is mental health. There is a growing recognition of the importance of dealing with mental health issues at the primary and community care levels.[43] The main legal approach remains hospital admission and treatment under Law No. 16 of 2016 on Mental Health. Liability is strongly premised on criminal, rather than civil, sanctions.[44] Under Article 28, there

[38] Law No. 15 of 2015, Articles 4, 6, 8, 12 & 13.

[39] *Id.* Article 19.

[40] *Id.* Article 20.

[41] Fazeena saleem (2019)

[42] *Over 400,000 register for organ donation*, Gulf Times 2019 https://www.gulf-times.com/story/647302/Over-400-000-register-for-organ-donation.

[43] (Barry Solaimand and Suhaila Ghuloum – DOI https://doi.org/10.1192/bji.2021.21

[44] Although, there are also provisions for Community Treatment Orders.

is a penalty of 3 years imprisonment and a fine not exceeding 60,000 riyals where a patient is mistreated by staff, causing pain, damage, disease, injury or disability. Beyond this, there are specific penalties pertaining to some noteworthy provisions.

The law divides the relevant rights into four areas, with two areas drawing specific penalties. A patient's right to be informed about their health condition, under Article 3(1), requires that patients or their guardians receive '*detailed*' and '*understandable*' explanations of their rights, diagnoses and treatment. The term '*detailed*' means that doctors must tread a fine line when upholding the law. The stigma of the diagnosis of a mental health condition may cause some families to refuse the information from a doctor because of the perceived social harm arising from a diagnosis. Doctors must explain the health condition to the patient, and failing to fulfil this obligation may lead to one-year imprisonment and a fine of up to 50,000 riyals.[45] This tension, between the legal requirement to give explanations and the aversion of some families to receive it, appears to be an unresolved issue and would benefit from greater guidance and clarity. Such guidance could be premised on respecting the wishes of patients who do not want to know, in detail, about their condition or treatment but ensuring they receive the information necessary for giving consent. Patients refusing even that basic information must understand the consequences of not having the information, including that their consent may be invalid.[46] Guidance in the UK notes that the risk of a patient becoming 'upset' or refusing treatment is not an excuse for not giving information.[47] In Qatar, similar guidance may be needed but which takes into consideration local sensitivities.

The second area drawing specific penalties is on the rights related to a patient's independence and privacy (confidentiality). These rights highlight a unique aspect of the law because of the social stigma associated with mental health in the country. There is a concern that clinicians or others may try to seek information about a patient. This may occur where someone is getting married and a family member investigates the potential spouse for mental health issues. If such confidential information is leaked, it can lead to significant social stigma in the local community. The law deals with this matter in different ways. Article 3(4) protects the patient from threats, physical or moral punishments, for whatever reason. The law explicitly upholds the rights of patients to reject visits which do not conflict with their treatment plan. The law states that it will:

> …Protect his privacy and personal belongings and protect the confidentiality of information related thereto, and prohibit any access to such information unless by the members of medical team or the employees in charge of the medical registers, unless by a written permission of the Psychiatric Patient or his Legal Guardian or by an order from the Competent Entity. This commitment shall remain valid even after the Patient's recovery...[48]

[45] Law No. 16 of 2016 on Mental Health, Article 29(1).

[46] See, *Reference Guide to Consent for Examination or Treatment*, Department of Health (UK), 13–14 (2 ed, July 2009).

[47] Consent Patients and Doctors Making Decisions Together (2008).

[48] Law No. 16 of 2016, Article 3(4)(4).

A doctor may be imprisoned for up to one year and receive a fine of up to 50,000 riyals where they disclose '*any confidential information*'.[49] Liability may also arise under Article 20 of Law No. 2 of 1983 (Practice of Medicine) which prohibits doctors from disclosing confidential information about a patient which s/he discovered on account of his/her profession (except where permitted). The penalty for a breach is either a warning, a fine or a withdrawal of a licence upon consideration by a committee.[50] These apply '*without prejudice to any more severe sanction provided by another law*'.[51] It is conceivable that a doctor would be punished first under Article 332 of the Penal Code.

For the mental health law, it is unclear whether divulging information may also potentially constitute '*damage*' or '*pain*' to the patient and draw additional liability under Article 28 (although, Article 28 is likely referring to physical rather than mental harm when read in context). The provisions on confidentiality are premised, to a great extent, on the risk of information being leaked. The law seeks to prevent professionals from divulging information, give the patient control over their information and protect them from corporal or moral punishment.

Beyond the provisions concerning patient rights are those pertaining to voluntary and involuntary admission to the hospital. One important section of the law is Chap. 5 on judicial placement or '*civil commitment*'. A public prosecution, court order or judgment can require that an individual is placed in a government institution for a mental and psychological examination.[52] The dominant role of the family and extended families should be emphasised. This may have positive aspects because families may take responsibility in actively helping the practitioners to manage the patient's condition. That familial influence and support can be crucial in recovery. However, the inverse may also be true where false claims are made by one member of the family to a GP concerning the aggression or abnormal behaviour of another family member. In practice, this may lead to a GP writing an order of detention for 48 hours which is renewable. This is processed through the general prosecution, which results in enforced hospital detention. The risk is not only of a patient being involuntarily detained, owing to an unfair complaint but also the stigma that arises with a person being officially '*registered*'.

In terms of leaving the hospital, much will depend on whether it is a civil or a forensic case (known as a '*police case*'). For civil cases, once an assessment is carried out, and a report is produced, the competent authority must approve any leave to return home.[53] Forensic cases are those in which the patient is brought to the facility by the police.[54] Only the General Prosecutor or the courts can admit a patient or authorise a discharge or temporary return home.

---

[49] *Id.* Article 29(2).

[50] Law No. 2 of 1983, Article 23.

[51] *Id.* Articles 22 & 23.

[52] Law No. 16 of 2016, Article 16.

[53] *Id.* Article 17.

[54] *Id.* Article 18.

Underpinning these provisions are strict penalties of 3 years imprisonment and or a fine not exceeding 200,000 riyals for '*any physician who has deliberately included in his report any false information about the psychiatric condition of any person, for the purpose of his admission to or discharge from the Institution*'.[55] There are additional penalties of one-year imprisonment and/or a fine up to 50,000 riyals where anyone enables a patient to escape, assists in the escape or hides the patient.[56]

The law on mental health has familiar provisions on voluntary and involuntary detention that can be found in other jurisdictions. The distinction is the emphasis on matters specific to the challenges faced in the country surrounding social stigma and confidentiality. There are also risks of the system being used to process unfair complaints and the detention of a patient until they are assessed and deemed fit to be discharged.

2.3.4 Abortion

On abortion, the laws are congruent with similar restrictions in other countries which have more conservative abortion regimes. Abortion is permitted where the pregnancy has reached less than four months' gestation. It may be performed to save the woman's life, where the continuation of the pregnancy would cause certain and serious harm to the mother's health, or where there is evidence that the foetus would be born suffering from serious and incurable physical malformations or mental deficiency.[57] These provisions are broader than the laws that had existed in the Republic of Ireland and Northern Ireland before 2019 but are narrower than the provisions in England that have existed since 1967.

A woman seeking an abortion, for reasons other than those stipulated in the law, will not be able to obtain it in Qatar. It is necessary to highlight the crossover with criminal law under the Penal Code.[58] Although there are stringent punishments for rape (death or life imprisonment), abortions are not permitted on the grounds of rape or incest under the law.[59] It is an offence for a consenting male and female to copulate outside of marriage, and doing so carries a maximum sentence of 7 years in prison for both.[60] It is unclear what would happen where doctors do not report pregnancies in which the woman is not married.

Beyond these cases, where the woman is married, doctors must comply with the circumstances in which abortions are allowed. An abortion must be performed in a government hospital after recommendation from a specially formed medical

---

[55] *Id.* Article 27(1).

[56] *Id.* Article 29(3).

[57] Law No. 2 of 1983, Article 17.

[58] Law No. 11 of 2004.

[59] *Id.* Articles 279 & 286; On rape and incest, see *CEDAW Examines the Report of Qatar*, United Nations Humans Rights Office of the High Commissioner (2 July 2019),https://www.ohchr.org/EN/NewsEvents/Pages/DisplayNews.aspx?NewsID=24789&LangID=E.

[60] Law No. 11 of 2004, Article 281.

commission. That commission comprises three medical specialists, including one from gynaecology and one from obstetrics.[61] Penalties for giving abortions, outside this process, carry severe penalties. Article 316 of the Penal Code stipulates a sentence of 7 years imprisonment for those intentionally aborting a pregnant woman, rising to 10 years if the said person works in the fields of medicine or pharmacy.[62] Women who, without medical necessity, have an abortion shall be 'punished with imprisonment up to three years'.[63]

Such provisions highlight particular features of abortion laws one would find in socially conservative countries, namely, narrow circumstances in which abortion is permitted and severe penalties for those who act outside the law. There is a multidimensional aspect of liability influenced by criminal and civil laws.

3 Resolving Disputes Through Hospitals and the Ministry

Outside the legal system, patients may also seek to resolve disputes internally, through a hospital's own dispute resolution mechanism or through the MOPH. In practice, lawyers representing a patient will submit a claim to the courts at the same time as an application to the MOPH. A clinician will be subject to both a legal claim and an internal disciplinary investigation with separate sanctions. The Qatar Council for Healthcare Practitioners (QCHP) and the Permanent Licensing Committee *(PLC)* operate under the MOPH to regulate all healthcare practitioners in the country. There is also a Fitness to Practice Department (FTP) of the QCHP which hears complaints from those dissatisfied with the care received.

Underpinning this mechanism is the Patients' Bill of Rights and Responsibilities which details rights to respectful care, safety, information, informed decision-making, privacy and confidentiality and complaints.[64] All hospitals are subject to licensing requirements, imposed by the Ministry, as well as the Bill of Rights, which are displayed in licenced facilities. In addition to those requirements, the major hospitals often seek accreditation from major international bodies which impose further requirements concerning patient care. HMC, consisting of the main public hospitals, has accrued a plethora of accreditations, becoming the first hospital system globally to have all its hospitals accredited by the Joint Commission International (JCI) under the Academic Medical Center Accreditation program.[65] Other hospitals, such as Aspetar, Sidra Medicine, Al-Ahli and Al Emadi, amongst others, have also attained accreditations from various international bodies which will raise standards for patients. Any potential breaches of accreditation standards concerning patient care must be dealt with per those standards to maintain accreditation. Patients may

---

[61] Law No. 2 of 1983, Article 17.

[62] Law No. 11 of 2004.

[63] *Id.* Article 317.

[64] Protecting the Public and Promoting High Standards of Practice (2020).

[65] our accreditations (2020).

complain directly to the hospital or, in some cases, the international body directly, such as the JCI.

Where attempts have failed to resolve a dispute directly with the facility, the FTP can receive complaints from anyone who is '*aggrieved or hurt*' by the conduct of a health practitioner.[66] The FTP will especially consider whether there have been poor standards of clinical care or unethical behaviour.[67] Little information can be found regarding the standards which are applied by the Committee when assessing a complaint, but it will collect evidence, reports from the practitioners and an independent expert report if necessary.[68] If the Committee determines that there has been some breach, then it will liaise with the PLC which can impose a range of sanctions. Those sanctions do not involve financial compensation to the aggrieved patient. Instead, the PLC can give verbal or written warnings, require further education, change the scope of the practitioner's practice, suspend the registration of a practitioner or facility, revoke their licence and blacklist a practitioner among the Gulf-Cooperation Council (GCC) to ensure that the practitioner is not able to obtain work within the region.[69] The PLC may refer a practitioner to the public prosecutor, but only where they are found to have practised without a licence.

In most cases, patients seek an apology and recognition that something has gone wrong with their care. They want to ensure that mistakes are not repeated. However, the lack of compensatory powers of the PLC will push some to seek redress through the courts where harsher penalties and compensation can be imposed through legislation. Nevertheless, the powers of the PLC, concerning revocation of licences and blacklisting, form an essential part of the liability toolkit in Qatar and help to raise standards of health provision in the region.

4 Discussion

An analysis of the specific laws would be incomplete without a discussion of broader insights that can be derived about the liability system in Qatar. In this section, three factors are posited which are pertinent to that discussion.[70] First, the challenge of creating medical law within a hybrid system consisting of competing expectations. Second, how those challenges encourage an inclusive method of law formation. Third, the potential consequences of that system for the provision of medical care, in light of the retention of criminal sanctions in the law. This chapter is the first systematic analysis of Qatar's medical liability regime in English. The discussion

---

[66] QCHP, *supra* note 63, 18.

[67] *Id.* at 7.

[68] Information for Public and Practitioners (2020).

[69] *Id.*

[70] Some of these insights arise from the author's experience of collaborating with various governmental and medical entities in the country.

points may be debated, but the purpose is to lay the foundation for future discussions of the issues and to highlight where further research is required.

Qatar not only has a hybrid legal system but also a hybrid medical system. There are the main public hospitals, under HMC, which all residents and citizens are entitled to use and private hospitals which are more accessible to those with private health insurance. Medical practitioners come from different parts of the world, each with unique legal approaches and standards of training. The rosters of hospitals and clinics are a true melting pot of nationalities. Some reflect specific nationalities. There is the Cuban Hospital which opened in 2012, as a joint project between Qatar and Cuba, to provide patient care. It is operated under the auspices of HMC and is staffed by 400 Cuban medical professionals.[71] One also finds many private medical or dental clinics bearing the names of certain countries, such as Germany or America, staffing professionals trained in those countries.

This amalgam is controlled through strict licensing and training requirements by QCHP. These different backgrounds can lead to different philosophies and understandings about the law. This may not be a problem for the many specific laws that exist. Anecdotally, it seems that most medical practitioners are not aware of the specifics of most laws. Instead, a few practitioners (usually those leading the respective departments) tend to take leadership in working with the MOPH to develop new laws. Many practitioners seem to have an intuitive realisation of the strict legal environment within which they operate. Proposed laws, with criminal sanctions, do attract attention and criticism of doctors trained in systems where such sanctions are not the norm.

Those developing laws must also be cognisant of treading a line between creating laws which are congruent with international scientific norms, but which also heed religious expectations. In the Arab World, medical issues are debated by religious scholars who issue legal opinions called *Fatwahs*. On the issue of abortion, *Fatwahs* have focussed on the duration of pregnancy and the seriousness of the defect of the foetus, with most holding that abortions can be permitted within 120 days where the disorder is extreme and incurable.[72] For organ transplantations, religious scholars agree that no compensation should be given for donated organs because the human body is on trust from God, rather than being one's own property.[73] The laws in Qatar are congruent with such *Fatwahs*, and indicate why penalties are significant. That is not to say that *Fatwahs* are not informed by science.

Ghaly argues that the systematic and frequent involvement of Muslim biomedical scientists into the whole process of independent legal reasoning: '*has blurred the borders between the informative role that should be assigned to the biomedical scientists on the one hand and the normative role of religious scholars on the other hand*'.[74] This poses challenges because the vast majority of Muslim religious scholars

[71] *The Cuban Hospital*, Hamad Medical Corporation. https://www.hamad.qa/EN/Hospitals-and-services/The-Cuban-Hospital/About/Pages/default.aspx.

[72] Mohammed Ghaly (2010).

[73] *Id.* at 289.

[74] Mohammed Ghaly (2015).

have almost exclusively theological and religious educational backgrounds where little English is used and where '*no attention*' is paid to biomedical sciences.[75] To remedy this, Muslim religious scholars look to Western scientific academies for answers where there are conflicting biomedical opinions.[76] Over time, collective bioethical deliberations have become standardised and systematised.[77] Balancing adherence to *Fatwahs* and international scientific standards is a unique challenge for the MOPH. For the main hospitals, their pursuance of numerous accreditations by internationally recognised bodies indicates where they believe the balance tilts.

The MOPH do take an open and collaborative approach to forming law and policy. Committees are set up consisting of representatives from hospitals, academia and elsewhere to discuss potential laws. Comments are invited and taken seriously. It is telling that proposals are often informed by the standards applied in other leading medical systems, such as the US, UK, Canada, and Australia, amongst others. Draft laws often reference laws or guidelines from those countries. The need for consensus is paramount because of the different expectations, and it seems that this motivates this process. It seems that the process is also simply driven by the fact that certain laws do not exist yet in the country. While some have existed for decades, much work is still needed in several areas. A standalone medical liability law, medical research law and more are required. There is little legal precedent in the country, so committees look to local expertise and international best practices to progress. There is no standalone law on genomic research, but the MOPH has issued guidance which was drafted in collaboration with the Qatar Genome Project and the Qatar Biobank for Medical Research.[78] International best practices inform the work of those bodies. The hybrid environment seems to encourage a collaborative, inclusive and consensus-driven approach to law-making. In the same vein, the outcome of that process cannot satisfy everyone.

The above raises questions about what impact this entire legal and policymaking paradigm has on medical practice. On a positive note, the country has developed laws and guidelines which are in line with international best practices. Criminal sanctions remain a key feature of the law. The main question is whether such sanctions have a chilling effect on medical practice and whether it encourages a '*blame culture*'. Further research is needed to determine whether this is so and whether some doctors may feel pressure to act (or omit to act), in a certain way, to avoid liability (all of which may have adverse outcomes for patient safety). In the UK, doctors highlight significant concerns about a blame culture which may affect patient safety.[79] To

---

[75] *Id.*

[76] *Id.* at 298.

[77] *Id.* at 310.

[78] *Guidance for the Design, Ethical Review, and Conduct of Genomic Research in Qatar*, Ministry of Public Health (2017–2018),https://www.moph.gov.qa/Admin/Lists/Services%20Attachments/Attachments/36/Guidance%20for%20the%20Design,%20Ethical%20Review,%20and%20Conduct%20of%20Genomic%20Research%20in%20Qata.pdf last visited 23 May 2020; *Phase One*, Qatar Genome, https://qatargenome.org.qa/node/43 last visited 23 May 2020.

[79] Jacqui Wise (2018).

remedy this, there have been calls for a move towards a '*just culture*'.[80] This emphasises personal responsibility for medical errors, within a systems approach which also protects those who come forward. The aim is to learn about systemic failures that led to errors and to resolve those system-wide problems, rather than blaming one individual.[81]

The same conversations have taken place in Qatar, which reference those in the UK. Qatar regularly hosts a major conference on quality and safety.[82] Recent conferences have specifically considered the issue of moving from a blame culture to a just culture, and there appears to be agreement that this is desirable.[83] Despite these intentions, it seems that such proposals may not have much impact on practice, as long as criminal sanctions remain. A just culture could be implemented when investigating and resolving disputes at a hospital level, but the law would also require amending so as not to undermine those aims.

5 Conclusion

One is left with a complicated picture of the medical liability system in Qatar. At its heart are standards on negligence, familiar to those in other established systems, but venturing into the specialities illuminates specific challenges that the law has had to anticipate and for which it must make provision. These include a collective responsibility approach to controlling the spread of infectious diseases, the social stigma of mental health, the confidentiality of such information, encouraging organ transplantations locally, ensuring that economic imbalances do not lead to abuses in obtaining organs and more. Beyond the courts, alternative means of resolving disputes are possible through the hospitals, the MOPH or international accreditation bodies. These lack compensatory powers which may lead patients to pursue resolutions through the courts. Together, these matters raise normative questions about what the liability regime should look like. Competing expectations do encourage inclusive approaches to law-making, but criminal liability is an ever-present feature of the law. Further research is required to determine the effects, if any, on medical practice, and how best lawmakers can balance those expectations for the benefit of the medical community and patients.

[80] David Oliver (2018).

[81] *Learning, Candour and Accountability*, Care Quality Commission (UK) (December 2016); *The Future of NHS Patient Safety Investigation*, NHS Improvement (March 2018); *Learning Not Blaming*, Department of Health (UK) (July 2015).

[82] See *Middle East Forum on Quality and Safety in Healthcare*, Hamad Medical Corporation, https://www.hamad.qa/EN/All-Events/mefqsh2020/Pages/default.aspx last visited 27 May 2020.

[83] Although detailed research determining the views the medical community is required.

References

Bolam v Friern hospital management (1957) 1 WLR:582

Communicable diseases ministry of public health (2017) https://www.moph.gov.qa/english/strategies/Supporting-Strategies-and-Frameworks/QatarPublicHealthStrategy/Pages/Communicable-diseases.aspx last visited 4 May 2020

Consent: patients and doctors making decisions together (2008) General Medical Council, 11–12, 2 June 2008

Demand for health services rises in Qatar oxford business group (2019) https://oxfordbusinessgroup.com/overview/keeping-pace-private-sector-set-play-more-important-role-demand-medical-services-continues-rise last visited 29 May 2020

David Oliver (2018) Accountability-individual blame versus a Just Culture. BMJ:361

Defreitas v O'Brien (1993) 4 Med LR:281

Dominique Martin, Riadh AS Fadhil (2014) The Doha model of organ donation and transplantation: thinking beyond citizenship. Griffith J Law Hum Dign 2(2):293–295

Fazeena Saleem (2019) Doha becomes model for organ transplant. The Peninsula https://thepeninsulaqatar.com/article/01/01/2019/Doha-becomes-model-for-organ-transplant

HH the emir officially opens HMC's new medical city hospitals (2017) Hamad medical corporation. https://www.hamad.qa/EN/news/2017/December/Pages/HH-The-Emir-Officially-Opens-HMCs-New-Medical-City-Hospitals.aspx last visited 1 June 2020

Information for public and practitioners (2020) QCHP. https://www.qchp.org.qa/en/Pages/FTPComplaints.aspx last visited 12 May 2020

Jacqui Wise (2018) Survey of UK doctors highlights blame culture within the NHS BMJ:362

Mohammed Ghaly (2015) Biomedical scientists as co-muftis: their contribution to contemporary islamic bioethics, 55 Die Welt des Islams, 286–289

Protecting the public and promoting high standards of practice (2020) Qatar council for healthcare practitioners (QCHP). https://sehanafsia.moph.gov.qa/English/Resources/Documents/Bill%20of%20Rights-Booklet-ENG-AW_LR.pdf last visited 12 May 2020

The permanent constitution of the state of Qatar (2004) Article 1 Roy Georgiades the court structure in Qatar. Al Tamimi & Co (2012). https://www.tamimi.com/law-update-articles/the-court-structure-in-qatar/ last visited 29 May 2020.

Our Accreditations (2020) Hamad medical corporation. https://www.hamad.qa/EN/About-Us/Our-Accreditations/Pages/default.aspx last visited 12 May 2020

Negligence in Russia: Expert Legal Analysis of Adverse Outcomes of Medical Care

Svetlana I. Pospelova, Natalia A. Kamenskaya, Yulia V. Pavlova, and Sergey V. Erofeev

If we are demanding of ourselves, then not only success, but also error will become a source of knowledge.
—Hippocrates

Abstract This chapter provides an historical analysis of the evolution, in the past 30 years, of the issue of medical professionals' and organizations' liability for providing improper medical care. The specificities of forensic and legal assessment of medical negligence are identified. The distinctive features of the activities of the Russian Investigative Committee, over the past 3 years, are described. The statistics of the growing number criminal cases, against medical professionals, over the recent years, is given. The challenges of classifying negligence and specifics of criminal sentencing of medical professionals are analysed. The basic civil-liability principles and procedure for medical professionals are specified. Typical criminal and civil court cases, concerning medical negligence in the past 5 years, are given.

S. I. Pospelova (✉) · N. A. Kamenskaya · Y. V. Pavlova
Medical Law Department, Sechenov First Moscow State Medical University (Sechenov University), Moscow, Russia
e-mail: medpravo.pospelova@mail.ru

N. A. Kamenskaya
e-mail: privet.03@mail.ru

Y. V. Pavlova
e-mail: 08101967@list.ru

S. V. Erofeev
Department of Forensic Medicine and Medical Law, Ivanovo Medical Academy, Chief of the Bureau of Forensic Medicine, Honored Health Worker of the Russian Federation, Ivanovo, Russia
e-mail: esv384@mail.ru

V. L. Raposo and R. G. Beran (eds.), *Medical Liability in Asia and Australasia*, Ius Gentium: Comparative Perspectives on Law and Justice 94,
https://doi.org/10.1007/978-981-16-4855-7_14

1 Introduction

The problem of improper medical care (hereafter negligence) and the inextricably linked issues of liability are among the most socially significant and complex in medical and legal practice in both today's Russia and worldwide.

The complex system of medical care, quality assessment and recognition of its 'improper' nature, includes: clinical; organizational; economic; deontological; expert; sociological; and legal aspects.

This is extremely relevant because 'medical errors' remain in the top ten most frequent causes of death. According to experts of the World Health Organization, one of the most significant problems, for national healthcare systems, is that of wrongful deaths or injuries to patients, through negligence. As per, World Association for Medical Law (WAML) Honorary President, Professor A. Carmi's apt words, the problem of 'medical errors' has long since become a 'silent epidemic.'[1]

There is a growing number of negligence cases, making it necessary to: constantly analyse and systematize the most frequent medical care deficiencie, review the specifics of evidence evaluation in such cases; and improve the current healthcare legislation.

In recent years, Russia has seen a steady increase in the number of criminal cases brought against medical professionals, due to the growing number of applications concerning negligence, filed by the public to the Investigative Committee of the Russian Federation (hereafter the IC RF). Most criminal cases concern obstetrics and gynaecology, surgery, anaesthesiology and intensive care, paediatrics, traumatology and cardiology.[2]

The IC RF received 4947 such complaints in 2016; 6,050 in 2017; 6623 in 2018; and 6500[3] in 2019 (3 times the number of 2012). In 2019, the number of in-person complaints alone about doctors' actions was 4373, which is almost twice as many as in 2018.[4]

In 2019, of 6500 complaints about doctors' actions, 2100 criminal cases were opened, of which only 15% reached the courts (332 cases together with the bills of indictment were brought to court). The remaining cases are justifiably dropped because of the identified non-criminal nature of the medical error. The majority

---

[1] Sergeyev Yu (2016).

[2] Data provided by an IC RF meeting on iatrogenic crime investigation on October 4, 2017. http://sledcom.ru/press/events/item/1168957/.

[3] The IC RF Brings to Court Only One-Sixth of all Medical Error Cases (in Russian). https://medvestnik.ru/content/news/Sledstvennyi-komitet-napravlyaet-v-sudy-lish-shestuu-chast-del-o-vrachebnyh-oshibkah.html. Accessed 29 June 2020.

[4] Medical Complaints to Investigate Committee Double in 2019 (in Russian). https://medvestnik.ru/content/news/Chislo-jalob-grajdan-v-Sledstvennyi-komitet-na-deistviya-vrachei-v-2019-godu-vyroslo-vdvoe.html. Accessed 29 June 2020.

of forensic examinations, of iatrogenic crimes, have not confirmed deficiencies of medical care.[5]

These statistics do not fully reflect all medical negligence cases in Russia. To obtain a comprehensive picture, one needs to include the complaints lodged with the public prosecutor's office, law enforcement bodies, local branches of the Compulsory Medical Insurance Fund, healthcare authorities and human rights advocacy groups. Many criminal cases 'migrate' into civil proceedings.

2 Expert Legal Assessment of Negligence

2.1 Forensic Examinations of Negligence Cases

Medical care historically has been associated with negative consequences, which may be caused by both erroneous and correct actions and/or inaction of medical professionals. Forensic examination, commissioned in criminal and civil negligence cases, plays a key role in evaluating quality of care and identifying possible deficiencies.

Forensic examinations of medical professionals' misconduct have always been considered to be most complex and sensitive. This area of patient-doctor conflicts affords a valuable insight into medical wrongdoing prevention, to be used to improve litigation and investigation practices, and to amend clinical, expert and organizational healthcare activities.

Forensic physicians have always participated directly in the analysis of 'medical' criminal and civil cases, so they were the first to pay attention to growing number of 'medical misconduct' cases and the qualitative changes in the investigation of medical incidents. Hundreds of Russian doctors and lawyers are now united in this community of professionals who are interested in unfavourable outcomes of medical care. In the past 30 years, professional communication has facilitated changes in expert legal assessment of medical incidents. These changes are underpinned by the growing public proactivity and legal awareness together with increased activity of the courts and investigation bodies. Different Russian regions experienced similar changes that can be divided into several periods.

In the early 1990s, there was a surge in medical-care forensic examinations: numbers grew 3–13 times in 5 years. Concurrently, there was an increase in the number of civil suits for compensation, for death or injury, caused by negligence. This was observed mainly in large cities. The final version of the Criminal Code of the Russian Federation (1996) which was updated at that time did not contain any dedicated articles on causing death and injury through negligence.

In 2000–2010, the number of criminal and civil cases against doctors rose, exceeding the 1990 figure by multiples. They weare still initiated mainly by patients

[5] No Proof of Deficient Medical Care Found by Most IC RF Forensic Examinations (in Russian). https://medvestnik.ru/content/news/Bolshinstvo-ekspertiz-v-Sledstvennom-komitete-pokazalo-otsutstvie-defektov-okazaniya-medicinskoi-pomoshi.html. Accessed 29 June 2020.

or their family. In some Russian regions, civil lawsuits equalled criminal cases, while the amount of settlement reached RUB 5–22 million (1 USD = 73 RUB) which is much higher than in premeditated murder cases.

The third period began after 2010, and in those 9 years, the IC RF paid close attention to cases of adverse outcome of medical care.

This resulted in forensic examinations being commissioned for all pre-investigation probes, not restricted to criminal cases, and criminal proceedings or examinations initiated, with or without victims' complaints, on the initiative of investigating authorities.

In 2016, the IC RF established its own expert groups, separate from national forensic service, at regional IC RF offices, specificaly for expert review of 'medical incidents.' Within a year, the IC RF analysed the experience of these expert units and, in 2017, it recommended to scale up this initiative to a national level. For more than 90 years, the country's national forensic service successfully conducted expert negligence reviews in good faith. In recent years, the general public has formed a strong opinion about medical corporatism, with mass media playing an active role. Patients and investigators mistrust the opinion of national forensic experts, working in the healthcare system. Law enforcement introduced a new term: 'iatrogenic crimes.'

The IC RF now pays special attention to ensuring the qualification of investigators, dealing with 'iatrogenic crimes',[6] and the Academy of Investigative Committee of the Russian Federation has increased investigator training on medical incident investigation methods. Similar workshops have been introduced for investigator training programmes in all regions of the country.[7]

A bill has been drafted to amend the Criminal Code, introducing a special provision on liability for harm to health, caused by negligence. This suggests growing public attention to adverse outcomes of medical care. This presents one of the few areas that has attracted the focus of the law enforcement.

The WAML first appeared due to the 'claims epidemic' against doctors in the 1960–70s, in Western Europe and the United States. Excessive law enforcement, combined with the prosecutorial bias of the investigation and the courts, have damaged the prestige of the medical profession, causing a significant understaffing of emergency specialities and the development of defensive medicine. Superficial examination of such consequences has identified negative impact on the healthcare system and public health.

---

[6] Bastrykin (2017).

[7] Alexeev (2017).

2.2 *Prevention of Adverse Consequences for the Healthcare System*

The papers co-authored by Yuriy Sergeyev (2001),[8] state that experienced and responsible doctors with spotless reputation are more likely to be prosecuted in civil and criminal cases than those who are inexperienced because they are obliged to make decisions in the most difficult cases. This is also confirmed by international medico-legal practice.

To prevent negative consequences for medical professionals, and the entire healthcare system, it is necessary to implement the following measures, to establish an unbiased system of assessment of negligence cases and preclude violations, in this area.

This includes the development and revision of treatment standards, clinical recommendations that accomodate modern clinical practice and mandatory monitoring of adverse outcomes of medical care, at the national level. The most illuminating insights, into patient conflict resolution, building a medical risk management system and correctly designing forensic practice inexcusably, currently are underused.[9]

The establishment of a mandatory monitoring system, for negligence cases, will enable the identification of: the most common medical risks, among doctors and healthcare providers of various specialities; specific traits of their manifestation; causes; and conditions of their occurrence.

The analysis of judicial and investigative practice, in negligence cases, is equally important for the law enforcement system[10]:

- to systematically eliminate the defects in the commission and organization of expert negligence reviews;
- to identify typical signs and categories of a special legal case, negligence and other legal case characteristics;
- to train investigators in the methods of multifactorial influence analysis of medical care provision.

For monitoring, there is Medi, a software suite, adapted to the needs of modern medical and legal practice. It allows the recording, analysis and storage of unlimited information about medical incidents, using 290 parameters.[11]

---

[8] Sergeyev Yu and Erofeev (2001).

[9] Erofeev et al. (2015).

[10] Sergeyev Yu and Erofeev (2001).

[11] Sergeyev Yu and Erofeev (2013).

2.3 Concept of Negligence

Experts argue that 'improper' in 'improper medical care,' or negligence, by default, is similar to 'a deficiency' and is interpreted as 'something imperfect.'[12] The current laws and established law enforcement practice have made it possible to form the concept of negligence, namely provision of medical care, in breach of accepted medical procedures and standards, approved by the Russian Ministry of Health, and recommendations developed and approved by professional medical non-profit organizations, which include technical, therapeutic and diagnostic errors, made while providing care to a patient.[13]

Violations of regulatory requirements, including clinical recommendations and medical care procedures and standards, are a mandatory characteristic of negligence. A proper legal assessment of the actions (or inactions) of a medical professional, in a given medical situation, can be completed by pretrial investigation authorities and a court, only if expert evaluation has been methodologically correct and has followed established procedures for such assessment.

The examination of a medical professional's actions, as proper or improper, performance of their professional duties, must be based on an evaluation of their actions' correctness, in providing medical care, according to the current law.

3 Negligence Liability of Medical Professionals

3.1 Characterizing Negligence

Criminal liability, of a medical professional who has improperly performed professional duties, is governed by various articles of the Criminal Code of the Russian Federation[14] (hereafter the CC RF), depending on the type of consequences: art. 118, Section 2 governs infliction of grave injury to health[15]; art. 109, Section 2 governs infliction of death on a patient[16]; and art. 109, Section 3 governs infliction of death by negligence on two or more persons (for example, death of a woman and her newborn). The CC RF provides for maximum penalties, in the form of imprisonment for up to

[12] Tsypina (2019).

[13] Kovalyov (2017).

[14] Criminal Code of the Russian Federation No. 63-FZ of June 13, 1996.

[15] Grave injury to health includes, inter alia, life-threatening injury; loss of an organ or loss of its functions; termination of pregnancy. See Order of the Ministry of Health and Social Development of the Russian Federation No. 194n of April 24, 2008.

[16] Vast majority (about 90%) of criminal cases are brought under art. 109, Section 2 of the CC RF.

1 year,[17] up to 3 years[18] and up to 4 years,[19] with or without forfeiture of the right to hold certain posts or engage in certain activities for up to 3 years. The CC RF does not criminalize the inflicting of medium and/or light injury, through negligence.

'Medical' crimes include the improper performance of professional duties, by a medical professional, resulting in a patient's death or grave injury to his/her health. This may include: late hospitalization; treatment and diagnosis errors; insufficient preparation for, and careless performance of, diagnostic or therapeutic manipulations; and careless drug administration.

The onset of adverse consequences, for a patient's life or health, should be directly connected with a medical professional improperly performing of professional duties.[20] Absence of such connection is the basi of refusal to initiate criminal proceedings.

After proper investigation, law enforcement bodies refused to initiate criminal proceedings once it was established that the actions of medical professionals were not directly connected to the death of a patient who had sought medical attention but died in the admissions unit of the hospital. The direct cause of the patient's death was a disease known to cause fatality even when treated properly.[21]

The subjective side of these crimes is characterized by guilt of carelessness, manifested in recklessness and negligence. Most often, death caused by carelessness is a result of criminal negligence, namely when a medical professional fails to foresee socially dangerous consequences for the patient, even though s/he could and should have foreseen said consequences, with requisite care and prudence. Examples include: surgical instruments and materials being left in the abdominal cavity; S. aureus contamination due to sanitary violation; drug dosage violation; or diagnostic shortcomings.

An obstetrician-gynaecologist, through criminal negligence, caused the death of a pregnant patient who was hospitalized with 'pregnancy, aggravation of pancreatitis, possibly caused by food.' During the examination of the patient (H), the on-duty obstetrician gynaecologist (R) underestimated her condition, namely R performed an incomplete set of diagnostic procedures and did not order Chest X-ray; R also underestimated the severity of H's condition, based on the results of ultrasound examination, and did not consult with a surgeon (given the absence of vesicular murmur in the left side of the chest).

Due to the lack of dynamic monitoring, the disease was diagnosed late (pinched hernia of the left diaphragmatic cupula with the displacement of abdominal organs to the left pleural cavity, complicated by the perforation of the stomach wall and the large intestine wall with subsequent development of fibropurulent pleuritis and

[17] Article 118, Section 2 of the CC RF of June 13, 1996 No. 63-FZ.

[18] Article 109, Section 2 of the CC RF of June 13, 1996 No. 63-FZ.

[19] Article 109, Section 3 of the CC RF of June 13, 1996 No. 63-FZ.

[20] Kovalyov (2017).

[21] Appellate decision of the Judicial Collegium on Civil Cases of the Supreme Court of the Republic of Bashkortostan of April 24, 2016 on case No. 33–17,941/2019.

peritonitis and further septic shock) resulting in delayed surgical treatment, the only life-saving method, not being administered in time.[22]

R was found guilty of committing a crime, under art. 109, Section 2 of the CC RF, and was sentenced to up to 1 year of restriction of freedom without forfeiture of the right to practice medicine.[23]

If the doctor, in this case, R, had foreseen the possibility of socially dangerous consequences, but presumed they would not occur, without sufficient grounds for such presumption, the crime is recognized as reckless. Recklessness poses a greater public danger than does negligence, since it implies conscious violation of safety regulations and anticipation of the possible occurrence of socially dangerous anticipating a safe outcome without adequate reasoning to contemplate same. A combination of recklessness and criminal ignorance of the part of a doctor is far from being an isolated case in medical practice.[24]

The following is an example of criminal recklessness. In pretrial investigation, authorities charged two obstetrician gynaecologists with choosing a wrong delivery strategy, having improperly performed their professional duties, in the presence of combined surgical indications which resulted in the death of the newborn, invoking negligence. The doctor, acting recklessly and hoping for a favourable delivery outcome, knowing that caesarean section should be performed in a timely fashion, did not perform the procedure and decided to continue conservative labour management. She completed her shift and handed the patient over to a colleague, indicating that there were no grounds for surgical intervention. The court found that the cause of death of the newborn (V) was associated with acute foetal hypoxia, due to impaired placental blood circulation, as a result of an obstetric situation: a clinically narrow pelvis with a complication in the form of a shoulder dystocia. The obstetrician gynaecologist who was to provide appropriate medical care, at that time, did not perform timely, correctly, consistently and fully the shoulder dystocia procedures. There was determined a direct causal link, in the error made by the delivering doctor, in following the shoulder dystocia procedure in case of a clinically narrow pelvis, while there was no such link in the actions of the attending doctor: her actions were not directly connected with the consequences, as they were a condition and not the cause of their occurrence. The delivering doctor was convicted, under art. 109, Section 2 of the CC RF, and sentenced to 18 months of restriction of freedom with a number of duties and restrictions imposed but without forfeiture of the right to practice medicine. The court of appeal left the sentence unchanged.[25]

Case law leads to the conclusion that in the overwhelming majority of cases, the courts take into account the nature and degree of danger of the crime, personality of

---

[22] The correct diagnosis was made when the patient was treated in another hospital to which she was transferred in critical condition. However, due to late diagnosis, non-performance of surgery and severity of the condition, the patient died.

[23] Verdict No. 1–151/2019 of September 5, 2019 in the case No. 1–151/2019.

[24] Sergeyev Yu et al. (2014).

[25] Ruling No. 22–1975/2016 of April 21, 2016 in the case No. 22–1975/2019.

the guilty person and mitigating circumstances[26], to impose a non-custodial sentence: restriction of freedom or suspended imprisonment (often involving forfeiture of the right to practice medicine). Such convicted individuals receive a criminal record, showing that they have committed a crime and received a punishment, which entails certain adverse social or penal consequences. Those, with a criminal record, cannot take certain jobs or adopt children; having a criminal record is taken into account when imposing a sentence; it impedes a person's exemption from criminal liability in connection with active repentance.

A court decision, in a criminal case that has gone into effect, has preclusive effect[27] for the court reviewing a case concerning civil and legal consequences of said medical professional, in whether these actions happened and whether they were committed by this person.[28]

3.2 Matters of Classification

There has been a tendency towards unjustified prosecution of medical professionals, for negligence, under the articles of the CC RF that establish heavier penalties, which clearly violate their rights and legitimate interests. Article 238, of the CC RF, provides for the punishment for deliberate fulfilment of works or rendering of services which do not meet safety standards. Delays in investigation are often connected with unlawful initiation of criminal prosecution under this article, when the statute of limitations on crimes, under art. 109, Section 2 and art. 118, Section 2 of the CC RF, has expired. Reclassification, to art. 238, allows continued investigation and reference of the case to the prosecutor. The objectives of the offence, in art. 238 of the CC RF, are legal relations ensuring protection of life and health of the people, namely an undetermined number of people rather than an individual patient, during the provision of medical care. In order to classify a medical professional's actions, under art. 238, it must be established that s/he violated regulatory requirements of safe service.

Not all healthcare regulations contain provisions ensuring safe service. Among the norms that establish the safe service requirements are sanitary and epidemiological instructions, labour safety and fire safety rules. Art. 238 of the CC RF can apply in cases where medical services are provided to a patient:

- without a license

[26] The courts recognize as mitigating circumstances the absence of a criminal record, the existence of minor dependants, actions aimed at mitigating the harm caused to the victim, etc.

[27] *Issue preclusion* means that 'once a court has decided an issue of fact or law necessary to its judgment, that decision … preclude[s] relitigation of the issue in a suit on a different cause of action involving a party to the first case' https://en.wikipedia.org/wiki/Collateral_estoppel. Accessed 26 June 2020.

[28] Article 61 of the Civil Procedural Code of the Russian Federation No. 138-FZ dated November 14, 2002.

- by professionals lacking the necessary training
- in violation of the requirements for the operation of medical devices and equipment (malfunctioning, unregistered or not maintained)
- using unsafe medication (expired, improperly stored, falsified, of poor quality or counterfeit) or a prohibited method of treatment (squeezing out the fetus during childbirth), medical practice in violation of safety requirements (vaccination at home, anesthesia without primary resuscitation equipment)

It is not necessary for consequences for the life or health of patients to ensue; they are only an element essential to a crime.

This article can be applied to the provision of medical care, only in case of deliberate violation of safety requirements: namely the perpetrator must fully understand the nature of his/her actions and the non-compliance with safety requirements and choose to violate them. If improper provision of medical care results from negligent actions or inaction, there are no elements of a crime under art. 238 of the CC RF.[29] Taking into account the nature of violations, only a person entrusted with compliance with safety requirements (licensing requirements and sanitary and epidemiological norms) can be a perpetrator. This may only be a medical director or a private medical practitioner.

Law enforcement practice also sometimes misclassifies negligence under art. 124 of the CC RF 'Failure to Render Aid to a Sick Person'. Cases of incomplete medical care are classified as failure to render aid, while the crime of failing to render aid, to a sick person, implies complete inaction. This article subjectively stipulates a double form of guilt: a medical professional deliberately refuses to render aid to a sick person, negligently affecting their life or health (causing medium injury, grave injury or death).

The next classification issue is the separation of negligence and neglect of duty by an official, which constitutes malfeasance in office. Article 293 of the CC RF 'Neglect of Duty' is sometimes incorrectly applied in cases of improper performance of professional duties by a doctor who is also an official (such as a chief physician or a head of department in a medical organization). When reviewing a criminal case, against a head of an intensive care unit, who wrongly transfused blood to two maternity patients, the Supreme Court of the Russian Federation emphasized that he was acting as a doctor and not as an official and during the blood transfusion he did not perform any organizational or business duties in respect of the patient.[30] The Supreme Court overturned the sentence and reclassified the doctor's actions, from art. 293, Section 2 to art. 118, Section 2 of the CC RF, since the case file showed that the guilty party had committed the offence due to improper discharge of his

---

[29] According to art. 8 of the CC RF, only persons committing a deed containing all the elements of a crime: an object, an objective side, a subject and a subjective side, can be held criminally liable. Absence of at least one element of the crime precludes case proceedings, and therefore a case cannot be opened and those opened must be dropped.

[30] Judgement of the Supreme Court of the Russian Federation of May 21, 2007 No. 5-D06-166.

professional duties. The sanction was reduced by 3 times and the ban on medical activity as a medium-grade medical professional was lifted.

3.3 Circumstances Excluding Criminality of an Act

Negligence should be distinguished from a doctor's bona fide mistake which has adverse effects on the patient's health. The list of such circumstances was compiled by Professor Sergeyev in 1988, and it is still relevant today:

- insufficient, limited medical knowledge of diagnostics, treatment and prevention of certain diseases and complications;
- imperfection of certain instrumental medical methods of diagnostics and treatment;
- extreme atypicality, rarity or malignancy of a certain disease and its complications;
- disparity between the actual scope of rights and obligations of a medical professional and the performance of the required diagnostic and treatment actions;
- inadequate conditions for appropriate medical care for a patient with a certain disease (injury) in a particular medical facility (availability of diagnostic and therapeutic equipment);
- exceptional specificities of a patient's body;
- patient's or their legal representatives' improper actions (late request for medical assistance; refusal to be hospitalized; avoidance of and opposition to treatment and diagnostics and violation of the treatment and rehabilitation regime).
- particular psychophysiological state of the medical professional (illness, extreme fatigue).[31]

Such circumstances exclude criminal liability, as they fall under art. 28 Innocent Infliction of Harm, art. 39 Extreme Necessity and art. 41 Justified Risk of the CC RF.[32]

3.4 Grounds for Release from Criminal Liability

The CC RF provides several grounds for release from criminal liability that can be applied to 'medical' criminal cases.

A medical professional can be released from criminal liability in connection with:

- active repentance (art. 75): if after the perpetration of the offence s/he has admitted the offense, assisted in the exposure and investigation of a crime, compensated for the damage inflicted or, in any other way, effected restitution, for the damage caused as a result of the crime, which has ceased to be socially dangerous;

---

[31] Sergeyev Yu et al. (2014).

[32] Criminal Code of the Russian Federation of June 13, 1996 No. 63-FZ.

- reconciliation with the victim (art. 76): if s/he has reconciled with the victim and restituted any damage inflicted;
- imposition of a court fine (art. 76, Section 2) if s/he repaired the damage or otherwise undid the harm caused by the crime. This article was introduced into the CC RF in 2016[33] in order to humanize criminal law measures;
- expiration of statutes of limitation (art. 78).[34]
  Russian criminal law also provides for the possibility of releasing medical professionals from criminal liability or punishment by an amnesty act, since negligence is classified as a minor offence.[35]

4 Specific Aspects of Civil Liability in Negligence Cases

4.1 Basic Principle of Civil Liability

The most common type of legal liability, for medical organizations and medical professionals, for causing injury or death, is civil liability. The main principle of civil liability is full compensation for the damage caused. The conditions and procedure for compensating, for injury and death, including cases of negligence, are determined by thc provisions of Chapter 59 of the Russian Civil Code (hereafter the Civil Code).[36] These norms concern obligations resulting from causing damage, or so-called delictual obligations (from Latin *delictum*: offence), which were put in a separate group already encompassed in Roman law. These obligations arise from violation of absolute subjective civil rights of the victims and aim to compensate for material or moral damage. The obligation to compensate the caused damage is a measure of civil liability which applies to the offender, as a rule, in the presence of *corpus delicti*, including the infliction of damage, the unlawfulness of the offender's conduct, the causal link between their conduct and the infliction of damage, and guilt.[37] Applying the provisions on obligations, in connection with damage, courts developed a common legal position on the application of the articles of the Civil Code. Several features of modern law enforcement practice, emerging in the field of civil liability in negligence cases, can be defined.

---

[33] Federal Law of July 3, 2016 No. 323-FZ.

[34] Since art. 109, Section 2 and art. 118, Section 2 of the CC RF refer to minor offences, the statute of limitation is just 2 years.

[35] Amnesty (from Greek *amnestia*: obliteration, forgiveness) falls under the jurisdiction of the Russian State Duma. The amnesty act applies to an undefined group of persons meeting the criteria specified in the act itself. Usually the amnesty is timed to significant national dates.

[36] Part Two of the Civil Code of the Russian Federation of January 26, 1996 No. 14-FZ.

[37] Judgement of the Constitutional Court of the Russian Federation of October 4, 2012 No. 1833-O.

4.2 *Presumption of Offender' Guilt*

The presumption of the offender's guilt, established by the Civil Code, implies that the defendant has to prove innocence. The burden of proving the fact of inflicting damage, its extent and the fact that the defendant is the offender rests with the injured party; the offender's guilt is presumed. The victim provides evidence of injury, or other harm to health, its extent, and evidence that it was the defendant who caused the damage or is legally obliged to compensate for it.[38] Law enforcement practice sometimes requires an additional judgement, by the Supreme Court, for the correct application of this provision.

The husband, of a deceased patient, filed a civil lawsuit against the central district hospital to recover compensation for moral damages and legal expenses, in connection with his wife's death. She came to the hospital admission room with high blood pressure and headaches. For the next three weeks, she was treated in outpatients, diagnosed with arterial hypertension. Despite the lack of improvement and continuing complaints, she was not seen by a neurologist and was not offered hospital admission for examination. Three weeks later, the patient died while at home. According to the forensic report, the cause of death was cerebrovascular disease with a ruptured cerebral aneurysm in the main artery of the brain, haemorrhage under the soft cerebral membranes on the main surface of the brain and cerebral oedema.

Forensic medical examination revealed deficiencies in medical care, including: during her first visit, the patient's complete medical history had not been illicited and complete physical examination not performed; a neurologist consultation had not been arranged; in violation of the standard of primary medical care for hypertension, the necessary examinations had not been ordered.[39] In considering the claim, the court of first instance concluded that there was no evidence of a causal link between the deficiencies in medical care, provided by the hospital, and the patient's death, and therefore no grounds to hold the hospital responsible for the damage caused, nor to recover compensation for moral damages in the husband's favour. Appellate judgement, by the regional court, left the ruling of the court of first instance unchanged.[40]

The cassation appeal lodged with the Supreme Court asked for annulling these court rulings as unlawful. The Judicial Collegium on Civil Cases declared the complaint to be admissible, due to a substantial breach of the law by the lower courts.[41] Under the current legal regulation, the hospital must prove that it was not

[38] Resolution of the Plenum of the Supreme Court of the Russian Federation of January 26, 2010 No. 1 On Courts' Application of Civil Legislation Governing Relations under Obligations in Connection with Damage to the Life or Health of a Citizen.

[39] Order of the Ministry of Health of the Russian Federation of November 9, 2012 No. 708n On the Standard of Primary Medical Care in Case of Primary Arterial Hypertension (Hypertensive Disease).

[40] Appellate judgement of the Judicial Collegium on Civil Cases of the Kaliningrad Regional Court of June 20, 2018 on case No. 33–2725/2018.

[41] Judgement of the Judicial Collegium on Civil Cases of the Supreme Court of the Russian Federation of February 18, 2019 No. 71-KG18-12.

guilty of causing moral damage to the, in connection with the death of his wife, who had received improper medical care. The courts placed, on the plaintiff, the burden to prove the circumstances of negligence, concerning his wife and the causal link between the committed deficiencies and the death. Concurrently, the hospital (defendant) did not provide evidence confirming that it was not guilty of providing the patient with substandard medical as approved by the Russian Ministry of Health.

4.3 Employer's Liability for the Damage Caused by an Employee

The defendant, in a claim for compensation for damage caused by negligence, is usually a medical organization. This is due to the Civil Code norms establishing that an employer compensates for damage caused by its employee. Liability for damage occurs when there is a causal connection between the conduct (action or inaction) of employees of a medical organization (regardless of the form of ownership) and the resulting consequences for the patient.

The employer is civilly liable, regardless of whether the employee causing the damage is held criminally or administratively liable.

A St. Petersburg district court found an obstetrician gynaecologist (B) guilty in a criminal case of committing an offence, under art. 109, Section 2 of the CC RF, negligent murder, owing to the improper discharge by a person of professional duties, specifically, of the improper discharge of professional duties which had resulted in the death of a newborn, from the application of obstetric forceps. The court of first instance, decided in favour of compensation for moral damages to be recovered from the maternity hospital where B worked.[42] The court of appeal supplemented the decision and levied an additional fine, in the amount of 50% of the amount awarded to the victim for failure to comply with the voluntary procedure for meeting the consumer's requirements.[43]

In the event of compensation for damage, an employer is entitled to make a recourse claim, against its employee, in the amount of the damages paid and to demand reimbursement of all amounts paid by the employer as compensation. Legal relations between an employee and an employer are governed by the Labour Code of the Russian Federation which establishes only a few exceptions for the employee to compensate for damages caused to the employer (such as intentional damage or alcohol intoxication). It is extremely rare for a medical organization to obtain a reimbursement from an employee who has caused damage by negligence.

The Supreme Court received a cassation appeal from a doctor (E) against the decision of the lower courts to fully reimburse damages in regress. The hospital paid the

[42] Decision of the Smolninskiy District Court of St Petersburg of May 22, 2017 on civil case No. 2–996/17.

[43] Appellate decision of the Judicial Collegium on Civil Cases of the St Petersburg City Court of December 19, 2017 on case No. 33–25,217/2017.

patient compensation for moral damages, caused by doctor E's negligence (leaving a foreign object in the patient's body during surgery) which caused adverse consequences for her health. The regressive claim, filed by the hospital to recover the full amount of compensation from doctor E, was satisfied in the court of first instance.[44] The appellate ruling left this decision unchanged.[45] The Judicial Collegium on Civil Cases of the Supreme Court concluded that the first instance and appellate courts had committed significant violations of the law. The Court noted that Chapter 39 of the Labour Code of the Russian Federation regulates material liability, imposed on an employee who caused property damage to the employer, setting the limits of such liability.[46]

It follows from the above norms that the main type of an employee's liability is limited material liability. The employee's obligation is to reimburse the employer for the direct actual damage caused but not exceeding the maximum limit established by law. This maximum limit is the employee's average monthly salary. The employee's limited liability rule applies in all cases, except when the law expressly provides for a higher liability of the employee, in particular, full liability. According to the Plenum of the Supreme Court's explanation, when considering a case for full compensation for damages, the employer must provide evidence showing that the employee can be held liable in full, according to the law.[47] There were no grounds, provided by the Labour Code of the Russian Federation or other federal laws, for imposing full liability on doctor E when the case was considered by the first instance and appellate courts. The Supreme Court referred the case for another consideration to the court of first instance.[48]

4.4 *Compensation for Injury to Life and Health*

In accordance with the norms of the Civil Code, damage caused to a citizen, or their property, is subject to full compensation by the offender. It is the court's prerogative to assess the amount of damage to be compensated and the validity of the stated claims. When determining the amount of compensation, the courts specify the principle of full compensation for the damage caused, established by the Civil Code[49]:

---

[44] Decision of the Volodarskiy District Court of the Astrakhan oblast' of January 29, 2019 on case No. 2–33/2019.

[45] Appellate decision of the Judicial Collegium on Civil Cases of the Astrakhan Regional Court of April 24, 2019 on case No. 33–1271/2019.

[46] Labour Code of the Russian Federation of December 30, 2001 No. 197-FZ.

[47] Decision of the Plenum of the Supreme Court of the Russian Federation of November 16, 2006, No. 52 On Courts' Application of Legislation Governing the Material Liability of Employees for Damage Caused to the Employer.

[48] Judgement of the Judicial Collegium on Civil Cases of the Supreme Court of the Russian Federation of February 10, 2020 No. 25-KG19-12.

[49] Decision of the Constitutional Court of the Russian Federation of June 5, 2012 No. 13-P.

- in case of maiming an individual or of any other injury to their health, compensation shall be extended to the earnings (income) which has been lost by the injured person and which they had, or could definitely have, and also to the expenses incurred by injury to their health, if it is found that the injured person is in need of aid of these kinds and care and cannot receive them free of charge;
- the court has the right to refuse to recover additional costs, caused by the injury to health, if the plaintiff has not provided evidence that the costs have actually been incurred or will be incurred in the future;
- in order to reimburse the victim, for the additional costs, two conditions must be met simultaneously, which they must prove: the need for additional services and the absence of right to receive them free of charge;
- if the victim, entitled to free assistance and care, has been deprived of the possibility to receive such assistance, in a qualitative and timely manner, the inflictor of damage will bear the actual costs incurred[50];
- the Civil Code's list of additional expenses incurred is not exhaustive.

By enshrining in the Civil Code the right to compensation for moral damage, namely, compensation for physical and moral suffering, the legislator leaves it to the court's discretion to decide on its award. The legislative criteria for determining the amount of monetary compensation for moral damage are (art. 1101 of the Civil Code):

- the nature of physical and moral suffering with due account of the actual circumstances under which the moral damage was inflicted and of the victim's individual features;
- the degree of guilt of the inflictor of damage in cases when guilt is a ground for the redress of injury;
- requirement of reasonableness;
- requirement of justice.

Neither existing legislation nor officially generalized legal precedents offer any other guidance. This inevitably poses a serious challenge to both complainants and courts in determining the amount of moral damages to be claimed and awarded. The courts, when determining the amount of compensation for moral damage, proceed from the assumption that the victim, in connection with the harm to their health, in all cases suffers physically or emotionally, the fact of inflicting moral damage is assumed. The courts establish the following grounds for compensation for moral damage, in cases of negligence:

- emotional stress due to loss of relatives (the fact of kinship with the victim is not in itself an unconditional basis for moral damage compensation; concurrently, in cases involving compensation for moral damage, caused by the victim's death, to other people, particularly members of the victim's family and dependants, the

[50] Resolution of the Plenum of the Supreme Court of the Russian Federation of January 26, 2010 No. 1 On Courts' Application of Civil Legislation Governing Relations under Obligations in Connection with Damage to the Life or Health of a Citizen.

court takes into account the circumstances which testify to the physical or moral suffering inflicted on such individuals)[51];
- emotional stress due to not being able to maintain an active social life;
- emotional stress due to loss of employment;
- emotional stress due to the breach of doctor-patient confidentiality.

The issue of determining the fair amount of compensation for moral damage has been discussed repeatedly.[52] Since 2007, the Rosgosstrakh Centre for Strategic Studies has been conducting sociological research into the 'value' of human life. The sociological approach to value assumes that the amount of compensation, paid to victims and their families, should be perceived by Russians as fair and sufficient. The research shows slight fluctuations in the average 'value' of human life between 3 and 4.5 million roubles over the decade.[53] The issues with calculating the amount of compensation for injury and death, according to experts, can be reduced to three main conisderations:

- the amount of compensation awarded varies by hundreds of times (from RUB 5000 to 20 million[54] for death of a person);
- even an expert will not be able to predict the amount of compensation for loss of life or health in a particular case;
- compensations usually do not correspond to the notions of justice.

There is a need to formalize a methodology for calculating the amount of compensation for moral damage. Most experts agree that the best way to do it would be by a resolution of the Plenum of the Supreme Court of the Russian Federation. The Supreme Court already recommends that the amount of compensation, awarded under similar circumstances by the European Court of Human Rights, should serve as a reference point.

5 Discussion

Analysis of the legislation and law enforcement practice in 'medical cases' poses the following questions for discussion:

- Are the concepts of 'negligence' and 'deficiency of medical care' identical?

---

[51] Resolution of the Plenum of the Supreme Court of the Russian Federation of January 26, 2010 No. 1 On Courts' Application of Civil Legislation Governing Relations under Obligations in Connection with Damage to the Life or Health of a Citizen.

[52] Round table discussion Determining the Amount of Compensation for Moral Damage: https://m-logos.ru/mlogos_publication/nauchno-prakticheskij-blagotvoritelnyj-kruglyj-stol-opredelenie-razmera-kompensaczii-moralnogo-vreda/. Accessed 29 June 2020.

[53] The Value of a Human Life: [website of the Rosgosstrakh Centre for Strategic Studies, in Russian]. https://www.rgs.ru/pr/csr/index.wbp. Accessed 29 June 2020.

[54] 1 USD = 69 RUB, www.cbr.ru/eng/currency_base/daily/. Accessed 29 June 2020.

- Should criminal liability for 'negligent crimes' by medical professionals be abolished and should they came under the rubric of civil, administrative and disciplinary liability?
- Is it expedient to formalize the methodology of determining the amounts of compensation for moral damage by the current legislation?
- Can legal norms provide for compensation of damage directly by a medical professional who was negligent in their professional duties by excluding the medical organization from the subjects of liability?
- Is it acceptable to apply consumer right protection laws to medical legal matters in cases where medical care was provided to a patient free of charge?

6 Conclusions

Deficiencies in the provision of medical care usually occur during diagnosis and treatment. Only few cases have a direct causal link between deficiencies and a patient's death. A deficiency in medical care is often due to the insufficient professional training of medical professionals and organizational issues (medical professionals' heavy workload, errors in patient referral).

Recently there has been a trend towards unjustified prosecution of medical professionals for negligence, under the articles of the CC RF, that provide for heavier penalties and towards misclassification of negligence, which violates the rights and legitimate interests of medical professionals.

The issue of classification of criminal offences for negligence might be solved by the well-founded initiative of the Investigative Committee to include, in the CC RF, a separate article entitled Improper Provision of Medical Care with a medical professional being its specific subject. The Plenum of the Supreme Court of the Russian Federation needs to develop recommendations, for the courts, explaining the disputed points of prosecuting medical professionals for negligence under healthcare legislation, which will harmonize the law enforcement practice.

The existing system for determining the amount of compensation claimed, and the amount of moral damages awarded, does not generally corresponds to the notions of justice and does not ensure the implementation of the principle of full reparation to the injured party.

In the fight against negligence, the prevention of professional crimes by medical workers has an important place, which mainly consists of: an in-depth special analysis and synthesis of such cases; and identification and stimulation of professionals' awareness of the specific circumstances, causes and conditions that contributed to their commission.

Taking into account territorial specificities, of the Russian Federation, to prevent cases of negligence, healthcare authorities, in each region, must monitor transport accessibility, population density and climatic and geographical characteristics of the regions, in order to develop regulatory acts that take into account special regional requirements. The establishment of a mandatory monitoring system, for negligence cases, will make it possible to identify the most common medical risks, among doctors and healthcare providers of various specialities; specific traits of their manifestation; causes; and conditions of their occurrence.

There is a need to develop and introduce medical-law training programmes for judges and law enforcement officers and to provide compulsory basic legal education to doctors, at all stages of professional training and retraining. Since criminal and civil liability is most often connected with providing medical care, in such specialities as obstetrics and gynaecology, surgery, anaesthesiology, intensive care, paediatrics, traumatology and cardiology, it calls for additional requirements for the training and retraining of medical professionals in these specialities, taking into account the increased risks involved.

Acknowledgements Legal and medical practice shows that the higher the legal culture of doctors, the more faithfully they discharge their professional duties and the more rigorously the healthcare rights and legitimate interests of citizens are enforced. This fair statement belongs to our mentor and colleague—the founder of the first in Russia Department of Medical Law at Sechenov University (1995), National Association of Medical Law (2000), National Institute of Medical Law (2009), World Association for Medical Law (WAML) Honorary BoG, corresponding member of the Russian Academy of Sciences, Honoured Lawyer of Russia, MD, Professor Yuriy Sergeyev. He is the first Russian researcher, medical doctor, forensic expert and lawyer who has devoted his career to studying the medical and legal aspects of medical negligence. We hope that our collective study will serve as an appreciation of Professor Sergeyev's determining our career path in legal and medical science.

References

Alexeev P (2017) What is behind iatrogenic crimes. Medical errors presented as criminal offences' (in Russian). Meditsinskaya gazeta 79:5

Bastrykin A (2017) Countering crimes committed by medical professionals: challenges and solutions (in Russian). IC RF Bulletin 1:11–14

CB RF, Central bank (2021)

Criminal Code of the Russian Federation No 63-FZ of June 13, 1996 (1996)

Erofeev S, Malakhov N, Timofeev D (2015) Monitoring of present-day capabilities of complex expert reviews in negligence cases (in Russian). Abstracts presented at the 14th Healthy Moscow Assembly, 19–20 November 2015, pp 111–113

Kovalyov A (2017) Forensic examination and fact-finding procedure in case of non-provision or improper provision of medical care: methodological recommendations (revised and enlarged 2nd edition, in Russian). Moscow, p 29

Medical complaints to investigative committee double in 2019 (in Russian). https://medvestnik.ru/content/news/Chislo-jalob-grajdan-v-Sledstvennyi-komitet-na-deistviya-vrachei-v-2019-godu-vyroslo-vdvoe.html. Accessed 29 June 2020

No proof of deficient medical care found by most IC RF forensic examinations (in Russian). https://medvestnik.ru/content/news/Bolshinstvo-ekspertiz-v-Sledstvennom-komitete-pokazalo-otsutstvie-defektov-okazaniya-medicinskoi-pomoshi.html. Accessed 29 June 2020

Sergeyev Yu D (2016) Negligence and ways of preventing it are extremely relevant for theory and practice (in Russian). Meditsinskoye parvo, no 2, March/April 2016

Sergeyev Yu D, Erofeev SV (2001) Adverse outcome of medical care (in Russian). Moscow, pp 97–157, 245–265, 264–268, 268–276

Sergeyev Yu D, Erofeev SV (2013) Modern Russia in legal and forensic medicine. In: Beran RG (ed) Forensic Medicine and Medical Law, 3, vol Springer. Verlag. Berlin, Heidelberg, pp 553–570

Sergeyev Yu D, Pavlova Yu V, Pospelova SI, Kamenskaya NA (2014) Textbook jurisprudence. Medical Law (in Russian). Sergeyev Yu D (ed), Moscow, p 552

The IC RF brings to court only one-sixth of all medical error cases (in Russian). https://medvestnik.ru/content/news/Sledstvennyi-komitet-napravlyaet-v-sudy-lish-shestuu-chast-del-o-vrachebnyh-oshibkah.html. Accessed 29 June 2020

Tsypina E (2019) Medical cases (in Russian). Advokatskaya gazeta, no 13, July 2019

The Patient-Centric Turn in Medical Liability in Singapore

Calvin Wai-Loon Ho

Abstract The basis of medico-legal claims against a doctor may occur in contract law, tort law or criminal law. This chapter focuses on the ethical and legal requirement of informed consent, which in tort law relates to two legal actions, namely trespass to persons (or battery) and negligence, as they give effect to a patient's right to autonomous decision-making on matters relating to her or his medical treatment and care. These legal actions have been central in defining legal expectations of the doctor's responsibility to the patient which, apart from the provision of medical advice, includes medical diagnosis and treatment. Where medical advice is concerned, an important change in the legal standard of care, from one that was profession-centric to a more patient-centric formulation, is also considered. This development has been codified into statutory law, and is instructive in a number of ways. From a jurisprudential angle, it shows the law to be normatively open, as the change occurred interactively with the norms of medical ethics, and the practical realities of professional medicine. Developments since this change suggest that the courts may be more open to look beyond the doctor-patient relationship in addressing institutional and systemic deficiencies. If medical jurisprudence should advance in this direction, it may be fair to say that medical liability is likely to acquire a more prominent role in sustaining quality of medical care.

1 Introduction

The basis of medico-legal claims against a doctor may occur in contract law, tort law or criminal law. From a medico-legal perspective, the obligations of a doctor under contract and her or his liability in tort are central concerns in medical practice.[1] This chapter focuses on two legal actions in tort law, namely trespass to persons

[1] Chew (2004, p. 26).

C. W.-L. Ho (✉)
Faculty of Law, The University of Hong Kong, Hong Kong, People's Republic of China
e-mail: cwlho@hku.hk

V. L. Raposo and R. G. Beran (eds.), *Medical Liability in Asia and Australasia*,
Ius Gentium: Comparative Perspectives on Law and Justice 94,
https://doi.org/10.1007/978-981-16-4855-7_15

(or battery) and negligence. Where the provision of medical advice is concerned, these legal actions seek to give effect to a patient's right to autonomous decision-making on matters relating to her or his medical treatment and care. Generally known as the requirement of informed consent, these legal actions have been central in defining legal expectations of the doctor's responsibility to the patient in the provision of medical diagnosis and treatment, aside from medical advice. This account is incomplete without understanding how legal requirements relate to professional self-regulation, especially in the context of Singapore where doctors continue to enjoy professional privileges that have been eroded in other common law jurisdictions, like Australia and the United Kingdom (UK). The Singapore Medical Council (SMC) has had a critical role in steering the law towards a more patient-centric approach, through its dialectical relationship with the medical profession and the Supreme Court of Singapore. A recent decision on medical negligence illustrates this in its extensive discussion on the scope of respect for autonomy in the relationship between consent-taking as a professional (and regulatory) requirement and the legal duty of doctors to inform their patients.[2]

In the section that follows, an overview of the Singapore legal system is provided. Readers who are already familiar with this may wish to proceed to Sect. 3, which sets out the key legal features of professional self-regulation for doctors, as registered medical practitioners in Singapore. In Sect. 4, the relationship between professional regulatory requirement on informed consent and its legal corollary in trespass to persons (or battery) is considered. It is the recognition of a patient's right to information on material risks, associated with medical tests, treatments or procedures in medical professionalism that has contributed to a monumental shift in the legal standard of care on the provision of medical advice, which is discussed in Sect. 5. Recent developments in the legal elements of medical negligence (particularly on the disclosure and/or discussion of material risks) and related statutory amendments are also discussed in this section.

2 Overview of the Legal System of Singapore

The Constitution of Singapore is the supreme law of Singapore and any law enacted after the effective date of the Constitution is void to the extent that it is inconsistent with the provisions of the Constitution.[3] The institution of law (principally, the judiciary) is one of the key organs of state, under the Constitution, together with the legislature (namely Parliament) and the executive. Under Article 93 of the Constitution, judicial power is vested in the Supreme Court. The Constitution further requires that judicial power be exercised independently of the Executive and the Legislature. The Supreme Court consists of the High Court and the Court of Appeal. The Court

---

[2] Goh Guan Sin v Yeo Tseng Tsai [2019] SGHC 274.

[3] Constitution of the Republic of Singapore, Revised Edition 1999.

of Appeal comprises the Chief Justice and two Judges of Appeal. The Chief Justice and the other Judges of the Supreme Court are appointed by the President, acting on the advice of the Prime Minister.

The Court of Appeal is the final appellate court of Singapore with jurisdiction over any judgment or order of the High Court, in any civil matter whether made in the exercise of its original or appellate jurisdiction. It hears appeals from decisions of the High Court in the exercise of its original criminal jurisdiction and determines questions of law reserved for its decision by the High Court. The High Court comprises Judges and Judicial Commissioners, although the Chief Justice and the Judges of Appeal may also hear cases in the High Court. Judges are appointed by the Prime Minister, in consultation with the Chief Justice. A Judicial Commissioner has the powers of a High Court Judge and is appointed for such period(s) as the President deems fit. This judicial office was created to alleviate the workload of the Judges. The Supreme Court is supported by the State Courts (previously known as Subordinate Courts), which also form the first tier in the judicial hierarchy in the administration of justice. State Courts is a general reference to the District Courts, Magistrates' Courts, Coroner's Court, Employment Claims and Small Claims Tribunals and the Court Mediation Centre. In 2014, the Family Justice system was established as a specialised body of courts, comprising the Family Division of the High Court, the Family Courts and the Youth Court.

Singapore has a unicameral (one chamber) legislature. A piece of legislation or statute is usually first introduced by a Minister concerned as a Bill. Under the Interpretation Act,[4] every Act must be a public Act affecting the whole community. A Bill in Singapore must be subject to three readings. The first reading occurs when the Bill is introduced to Parliament. The objects and reasons of the Bill are then explained by the Minister at the second reading. A debate on the Bill may follow and a Bill with important implications may be sent to a Select Committee for further study. The Select Committee is required to report its findings to Parliament. At the final reading, amendments may be proposed for the Bill. The Bill becomes law when it is published in the Gazette. There are a number of statutes relating to the medical profession and the practice of medicine in Singapore. Examples that are of relevance to the healthcare context include, but are not limited to, the Medical Registration Act (MRA),[5] the Private Hospital and Medical Clinic Act (PHMC),[6] the Infectious Diseases Act,[7] the Mental Capacity Act,[8] Health Products Act[9] and even the Penal Code where serious injury or death might have occurred due to negligent practice.[10] Subsidiary or delegated legislation usually takes the form of regulations, issued by a Minister or such people or entities, authorized by an Act of Parliament,

[4] Chapter 1 of Singapore, Revised Edition 2002.

[5] Chapter 174 of Singapore, Revised Edition 2014.

[6] Chapter 248 of Singapore, Revised Edition 1999.

[7] Chapter 137 of Singapore, Revised Edition 2003.

[8] Chapter 177A of Singapore, Revised Edition 2010.

[9] Chapter 122D of Singapore, Revised Edition 2008.

[10] Chapter 224 of Singapore, Revised Edition 2008.

to do so. Under the Interpretation Act, an Act of Parliament is intended to provide the basic legal framework, leaving delegated or subsidiary legislation to deal with detailed regulations that may be required for day-to-day implementation. Subsidiary legislation also allows Parliament to function more efficiently, without being caught up in inconsequential details. Subsidiary legislation has relatively greater flexibility in that it may be modified, from time to time, without the need for Parliament to pass a new Act of Parliament.

The legal system in Singapore follows the common law tradition owing to its historical link with the United Kingdom. The common law of England (including principles and rules of equity) that has been part of the law of Singapore before 12 November 1993 continues to be in force in Singapore through the Application of English Law Act,[11] provided that it is applicable to the circumstances of Singapore and subject to such modifications as those circumstances require. The common law is judge-made law, where the law is based on legal principles laid down from past cases (precedence). Judges thereby play a key role in defining and making the law. A judge would decide a case, in accordance with a statute or based on an earlier decision or precedent. In the absence of a precedent, the judge may extend the law through analogy or otherwise create a new law in order to resolve the dispute, in a fair and equitable manner. The body of law that emerges through the accumulation of precedents is known as the common law.

When deciding a case, the judge may set out a principle that represents what the law, in relation to a particular legal issue, is. Analogous cases will be decided the same way, under the doctrine of binding precedent. Under this doctrine, a judge is bound to follow a precedent of courts above him or her, in judicial hierarchy, if the case cannot be distinguished from a prior case. The judge may also be constrained to follow a precedent of courts at his or her level. As the highest court of the land, the Court of Appeal may decline to follow a precedent on very limited occasions. The doctrine of binding precedent does not limit the judge's choice of precedent and typically applies only when the judge disagrees with a prior decision. Only the reasons or rationale by which that decision was made (ratio decidendi) is binding as a precedent. It is not uncommon for a judge to make additional observations or considerations in a decision, but these are not binding. There are some rationales behind this doctrine which includes uniformity within the legal system, consistency in application and certainty in outcome. The law relating to day-to-day issues, arising from medical practice, is drawn, in large part, from tort law which is mainly based on common law.

[11] Chapter 7A of Singapore, Revised Edition 1994.

3 Profession Self-regulation

The MRA sets out the requirements (including academic qualifications) for a person to be registered as a "medical practitioner" and the legal privileges of this person, after having been so registered.[12] Only registered medical practitioners are allowed to practise medicine in Singapore. It is an offence to advertise or represent oneself as a medical practitioner, unless registered under the Act. There is also a system of registration for specialists, so that a registered medical practitioner may not assume the title of a specialist unless he or she is registered as such. In enabling professional self-regulation, the MRA establishes and empowers the SMC with extensive statutory authority to discipline and regulate the medical profession, especially through its power over the register. The SMC is a statutory board, under the Ministry of Health, and a majority of the board members of the SMC is drawn from the medical profession. The functions of the SMC, as prescribed by law, are to: (1) keep and maintain registers of registered medical practitioners; (2) approve or reject application for medical registration under the MRA or to approve any such application subject to such restrictions as it may think fit; (3) issue practising certificates to registered medical practitioners; (4) make recommendations to the appropriate authorities on the courses of instructions and examinations leading to the Singapore degree; (5) make recommendations to appropriate authorities for the training and education of registered medical practitioners; (6) determine and regulate the conduct and ethics of registered medical practitioners; and (7) do all such acts and matters and things as are necessary to be carried out under the MRA. The MRA has been amended in 2020 to improve quality and consistency of processes, reduce delays and facilitate faster resolution of complaints, protect patients more effectively, and encourage the amicable resolution of complaints.[13]

The SMC has statutory jurisdiction over disciplinary proceedings and health proceedings for registered medical practitioners (or doctors). Proceedings may be initiated against a doctor for any:

(1) Complaint touching on the conduct of a doctor in his or her professional capacity or on his or her improper act or conduct which brings disrepute to his or her profession;
(2) Information on the conviction of a doctor of any offence implying a defect in character which makes him or her unfit to practise as a doctor;
(3) Complaint that the professional services provided by a doctor are not of the quality which is reasonable to expect of him or her; or
(4) Information touching on the physical or mental fitness to practise of a doctor.

---

[12] For more background details on professional regulation in Singapore, see: Kaan (2004).

[13] Hwee-Min Ang and Cindy Co, MPs debate new statutory test for informed consent, changes to medical disciplinary process, *ChannelNewsAsia*, 6 October 2020. Available at: https://www.channelnewsasia.com/news/singapore/doctors-informed-consent-singapore-medical-counsel-laws-13212732.

The initiation and conduct of disciplinary and health proceedings are subject to a set of rules that can be quite complex. A simplified outline is provided in the explanatory notes to the 2020 amendments to the MRA[14]: (a) Any complaint or information (collectively called complaints) that is not made or provided by the SMC first proceeds to the Inquiry Committee stage; (b) any complaint that is made by the SMC does not need to go through the Inquiry Committee stage and proceeds instead to the Complaints Committee stage; (c) any complaint that relates to the physical or mental fitness of a registered medical practitioner to practise medicine may proceed directly to the Health Committee stage; (d) any complaint that involves a serious threat to patient health and safety may proceed directly to the Disciplinary Tribunal stage; (e) any complaint that is time-barred cannot proceed unless the President of the Disciplinary Commission is of the opinion that it is in the public interest to do so despite the expiration of the limitation period, and if he or she is of that opinion, the complaint will proceed directly to the Complaints Committee stage[15]; (f) any aggrieved party may request a review of a Complaints Committee's direction or decision; (g) at the Inquiry Committee or Complaints Committee stage, the inquiry may be suspended if parties are engaged in mediation; (h) at any stage, the relevant Committee or Disciplinary Tribunal may appoint an investigator to investigate into the complaint; (i) at any stage, an immediate interim order or interim order may be made against the registered medical practitioner where necessary, pending the final resolution of the complaint; (j) only a decision by the Disciplinary Tribunal or an Interim Orders Committee is subject to an appeal to the High Court.

Where a Disciplinary Tribunal is concerned, the doctor is entitled to be represented by a lawyer at hearings before the Tribunal. Disciplinary Tribunals are independent from the SMC and are appointed by the President of the Disciplinary Commission (which is appointed by the Minister for Health), each comprising 2 registered medical practitioners of at least 10 years' standing and one legal professional who are all members of the Complaints Panel.[16] For complex or novel cases, the President of the Disciplinary Commission may apply to the Chief Justice to appoint a Judge or Judicial Commissioner of the Supreme Court as the chairman of the Disciplinary Tribunal.[17] At the end of the inquiry, it may dismiss the complaint if the Tribunal finds that it has no basis. Otherwise, the doctor may be found to have[18]:

(1) Been convicted in Singapore or elsewhere of any offence implying a defect in character which makes him or her unfit for his or her profession;

[14] Medical Registration (Amendment) Bill (hereafter, MRAmBill), Bill No. 30/2020, at p. 82. At the time of writing, the Parliament of Singapore has just passed the MRAmBill as law. Available at: https://sso.agc.gov.sg/Bills-Supp/30-2020/Published/20200903?DocDate=20200903.

[15] MRAmBill, at p. 13. Subsections (1) and (2) of Sect. 41 of the MRAmBill set the limitation period of complaints as 6 years after the date of the act, conduct of occurrence that is the subject matter of the complaint or information; or 6 years after the earliest date on which the complainant (or the SMC, as the case may be) had knowledge of the act, conduct or occurrence, or could with reasonable diligence have 20 discovered it.

[16] Sections 57 and 58 of the MRAmBill.

[17] Section 59 of the MRAmBill.

[18] Section 59D of the MRAmBill.

(2) Been guilty of such improper act or conduct which, in the opinion of the Disciplinary Tribunal, brings disrepute to his or her profession;
(3) Guilty of *professional misconduct* (emphasis added); or
(4) Failed to provide professional services of the quality which is reasonable to expect of him or her.

The SMC's Ethical Code and Ethical Guidelines (ECEG) have a central role in the determination of professional misconduct as it posits important values within a doctor–patient relationship, including requirements relating to standard of care, conflict of interest, advertisements, consent, truth-telling, confidentiality and patient privacy.[19] The professional standards that the SMC requires of doctors may exceed those required in law. In *Low Cze Hong v Singapore Medical Council* ('*Low Cze Hong*'),[20] the Supreme Court of Singapore held that the ECEG serves a crucial role in providing an ethical "compass" to guide doctors on what constitutes the acceptable standards from which a departure might amount to professional misconduct. Professional misconduct could be made out in at least two situations: where there was an intentional, deliberate departure from standards observed or approved by members of the profession of good repute and competency; or where there had been such serious negligence that it objectively portrayed an abuse of the privileges which accompanied registration as a medical practitioner.

Where any of the above-mentioned conviction, improper act or conduct, professional misconduct or failure to provide professional service of reasonable quality is found, the Disciplinary Tribunal is able to exercise one or more of the following powers, including[21]:

(1) By order remove the name of the doctor from the appropriate register;
(2) By order suspend the registration of the doctor for a period of not less than 3 months and not more than 3 years;
(3) By order impose on the doctor a penalty not exceeding $100,000;
(4) By writing censure the doctor;
(5) By order require the doctor to give such undertaking as the Disciplinary Tribunal thinks fit to abstain in future from the conduct complained of; or
(6) Make such other order as the Disciplinary Tribunal thinks fit, including any order that a Complaints Committee may make.

The strongest sanctions that the SMC can impose are fines or suspension or even revocation of the doctor's licence to practice. As opposed to a tortious claim, where any award against the doctor goes to the party taking action, fines by the SMC revert to the SMC. An appeal from the order of a Disciplinary Committee is to the High Court, with the appeal to be heard by three Judges of the High Court. The decision of the High Court is final and no further appeal is permitted. The disciplinary process

[19] Singapore Medical Council, Ethical Code and Ethical Guidelines, 2016. Available at: https://www.healthprofessionals.gov.sg/docs/librariesprovider2/guidelines/2016-smc-ethical-code-and-ethical-guidelines---(13sep16).pdf (Last visited: 17 August 2020).

[20] [2008] 3 SLR(R) 612.

[21] Section 59(D)(2) of the MRAmBill.

has recently been reviewed by an expert body that has been commissioned by the Ministry of Health (MOH), and procedural changes are expected to follow in the foreseeable future.[22]

Other statutes (other than the Civil Law Act (as amended) to be discussed below) have less direct impact on the professional conduct of doctors or the doctor-patient relationship. The PHMC Act establishes a framework to regulate (through licensing) all private hospitals and medical clinics and mandates the establishment of a quality assurance committee in all private hospitals. The governance of healthcare facilities will not be discussed in this chapter but more details are available from the website of the Ministry of Health.[23]

4 Informed Consent and Trespass to Persons

The requirement of consent arises from the recognition in law that a patient should be able to exercise autonomous choice in making decisions about his medical care. Obtaining consent is a communicative process that could occur at different points in the relationship between the doctor and her or his patient. It is not limited to accepting a proposed treatment but can relate to a patient's choice of different treatment options and/or refusing treatment. In order for consent to be legally valid, it must have been obtained: from a patient with the requisite capacity or from another person legally empowered to make decisions on behalf of the patient; after the patient has been provided with information that is sufficient for decision-making within the specific circumstances; and voluntarily, in that the patient should not have provided consent under conditions of coercion, duress or manipulation. A clear articulation of the principle of informed consent was made in the case of *Mary E. Schloendorff v The Society of New York Hospital*[24] and subsequently advanced in *Canterbury v Spence*.[25] This principle was endorsed by the High Court of Singapore in *Re LP*,[26] where it indicated that a person who is sufficiently mature is entitled to give or withhold consent to any medical treatment and doctors are usually obliged to respect that patient's decision. No one else, however close by reason of kinship or friendship, is legally entitled to make the decision for the patient. This case relates to a legal dilemma over whether the patient's refusal of a proposed amputation, prior to being comatosed, was adequately informed as she was not told that death would be

[22] Report on Recommendations of the Workgroup to Review the Taking of Informed Consent and SMC Disciplinary Process, 28 November 2019. The Workgroup's recommendations have contributed to statutory changes introduced in the MRAmBill, and additional institutional and procedural changes are expected to follow. The Report is available at: https://www.moh.gov.sg/docs/librariesprovider5/default-document-library/wg-report.pdf (Last visited: 17 August 2020).

[23] See: https://www.moh.gov.sg/hpp/all-healthcare-professionals/guidelines (Last visited: 17 August 2020).

[24] Court of Appeals of New York 211 N.Y. 125; 105 N.E. 92 Decided April 14, 1914.

[25] 464 F.2d. 772, 782 D.C. Cir. 1972.

[26] [2006] SGHC 13.

inevitable unless the procedure was performed. The Court held that where doctors did not have a clear and expressed consent of their patient, their only course was to act in the best interests of the patient. It would not have been unreasonable for the doctors to regard the proposed amputation, which was the only hope of saving the patient's life, to be in her best interests.

Treating a patient without his or her consent is a civil wrong that is actionable in law as battery or trespass to persons. A failure to adequately inform the patient, when obtaining consent, could amount to negligence which is also actionable in law. There are some exceptions to this requirement, such as during an emergency when treatment must be administered immediately in order to save the patient's life or to prevent serious harm that the patient would have reasonably wanted to avoid. Other exceptions to the consent requirement include a waiver by the patient (whether implicit or explicit), incompetency, and other exceptions provided by law. For instance, the law legislates for certain individuals who are assessed as a danger to self or others to be provided institutionalised care.[27] Under the MCA, there are legal requirement for medical care to be provided in ways that advance the best interests of these patients who are deemed to not have the capability of exercising individual autonomy.

In addition, a failure to obtain informed consent violates professional requirements under the SMC's ECEG, which requires a doctor to ensure that her or his patient is adequately informed of the medical condition, as well as treatment options, so that the patient is able to participate in decisions about treatment. A doctor could be brought before the SMC Disciplinary Committee for failing to obtain adequate consent. Apart from the crucial role that the ECEG has in the regulation of professional conduct, its provisions on patient's right to information and on informed consent have also been pivotal to the change in standard of care on provision of medical advice that was introduced by the Court of Appeal in the landmark case of *Hii Chii Kok v Ooi Peng Jin London Lucien and another* ('*Hii Chii Kok*').[28] This will be discussed later in this chapter.

The ECEG provides that patient autonomy is a fundamental principle in medical ethics and must be respected.[29] Patients are entitled to have accurate and sufficient information to be able to make decisions about medical management. Respecting patients' autonomy means that they must be provided with adequate information in a manner that they can understand so as to allow them to make informed choices. Doctors must accept their patients' decisions on management options, even if there is no agreement between them, but doctors must ensure that patients have sufficient information to understand the consequences of decisions. Patients must also not be deliberately deceived on any aspect of their diagnosis or management. Doctors must ensure that the information given is presented in terms and at a pace that allows patients to assimilate, thereby enabling informed decisions about management. If family members request withholding of information from patients, this must not be

[27] See: Mental Health (Care and Treatment) Act, Chapter 178A of Singapore, Revised Edition 2012.
[28] [2017] SGCA 38.
[29] See: Section C5 on "Patients' right to information and self-determination"; ECEG at page 36.

done unless the patients are assessed to react in an extreme way which would cause them serious harm.

Where consent is concerned, the ECEG indicates that an important part of patient autonomy involves ensuring that patients give valid consent (if able to do so) to any treatment or procedure, prior to undergoing such treatment or procedure. This involves the patients making voluntary decisions about medical care after having known and understood the benefits and risks involved. In Section C6 of the ECEG, consent-taking requirements are set out in detail, although it is these first 13 provisions that have a profound impact on the Supreme Court's decision in *Hii Chii Kok*.[30] For many years prior to the issuance of the 2017 edition of the revised and updated ECEG, the SMC has held doctors to an ethical/professional standard of consent-taking higher than what has generally been perceived to be legally required under the *Bolam* test. In the case of *Low Cze Hong*, the High Court upheld the decision of the SMC that the appellant doctor failed to inform his patient of alternative treatment options and the risks, side-effects and nature of a surgical intervention. While information provided by the appellant doctor in this case would have cleared the *Bolam* test and thereby prevent a legal claim in medical negligence, the SMC considered it to have fallen short of the standards prescribed by the ECEG. In the case of *Eu Kong Weng v Singapore Medical Council*,[31] the suspension order imposed by the SMC against a doctor, for failing to obtain adequate informed consent from his patient, was upheld by the High Court. Where medical negligence was concerned, the High Court in *D'Conceicao Jeanie Doris (administratrix of the estate of Milakov Steven deceased) v Tong Ming Chuan* held that the defendant doctor was not legally negligent for recommending a particular treatment as his recommendation was supported by a respectable body of medical opinion (reflecting the law on standard of care as it was then).[32] Based on this body of medical opinion, the doctor could decide, as a matter of medical judgment, whether it was appropriate for particular risk to be disclosed to the patient. If risk disclosure is made, the Court held that risk should be communicated in relative terms, although it accepted that under certain conditions, risk could be communicated in (quantitative) percentage terms. The Court further indicated that in most cases, it should be sufficient to inform a patient of the main (or material) risks. It warned against a non-evaluative categorical approach to risk disclosure and recognised that there may be cases where a doctor could be negligent for not disclosing a particular risk that was substantial and where there was no cogent clinical reason for not making the disclosure. The 2017 edition of the ECEG continues in this normative trajectory, with paragraph 3 of Section C6 clearly indicating the requirement for doctors to

[30] See: Section C6 on "Consent"; ECEG at pp. 37–39. For instance, paragraph (3) provides: "You must ensure that patients are made aware of the purpose of tests, treatments or procedures to be performed on them, as well as the benefits, significant limitations, material risks (including those that would be important to patients in their particular circumstances) and possible complications as well as alternatives available to them.".

[31] [2011] SGHC 68.

[32] [2011] SGHC 193.

discuss material risks with their patients. This in turn contributed to a change in the legal standard of care on the provision of medical advice by doctors in Singapore.[33]

5 Medical Negligence

Medical negligence is a specialised area of law concerned with standard of medical conduct that is considered acceptable in law. It imposes a duty on doctors to take reasonable care to avoid injury to those under their care. An action for negligence against a health care provider is available to an injured patient when there has been a failure of the health care provider to exercise the reasonable and ordinary care that a similarly qualified practitioner would exercise under the same or similar circumstances. A claim in medical negligence will require the claimant to prove, on balance of probability, that: there is a legal duty of care between the claimant and the respondent; the respondent has breached that duty by acting below the requisite standard of care; and that the breach of that duty caused harm to the claimant.

a. Duty of Care

Duty of Care is an essential element in what is known as the law of negligence under a broad class of legal action for civil wrongs known as tort law. It grew out of a 1932 case in which a snail had been left in a bottle of soft drink (ginger beer).[34] The person who drank the contents sued successfully for compensation from the manufacturers even though there had been no direct contract between the purchaser of the drink and the soft-drink manufacturer. The broad legal obligation (or otherwise referred to as the "neighbour principle" which arose from that case) is for a person to take reasonable care to avoid injury to those whom one could reasonably foresee would be likely to be injured if due care was not taken. Since the time that the notion of duty of care was first introduced on the premise of the "neighbour principle", courts in Singapore and other common law jurisdictions have sought to clarify circumstances under which a duty of care would be imposed. Different tests have been applied in the determination of duty of care, depending on the type of the damages claimed. There was one test for a claim for damages arising from bodily injury and another test for one arising from economic loss. The Court of Appeal in Singapore, in the case of *Spandeck Engineering (S) Pte Ltd v Defence Science & Technology Agency*,[35] considered all these complexities and simplified the law so that a single test would be used to determine the imposition of a duty of care in all claims arising out of negligence. It held that the test to determine the imposition of a duty of care was to first consider if there was factual foreseeability and then to apply a two-stage test comprising of proximity and policy considerations. Regarding proximity, the focus was on the closeness of the relationship between

---

[33] Kumaralingam Amirthalingham, Medical Negligence and Patient Autonomy—Bolam Rules in Singapore and Malaysia (2015) 27 *Singapore Academy of Law Journal* 666.

[34] *Donoghue v Stevenson* [1932] All ER Rep 1; [1932] AC 562; House of Lords.

[35] [2007] SGCA 37.

the parties, including physical, circumstantial and causal proximity, and to consider whether there had been a voluntary assumption of risk and reliance. Concerning policy considerations, a court would take into consideration a number of factors, including the presence of a contract and the relative bargaining positions of the parties. The Court of Appeal made clear that a duty of care could be imposed if it was just and fair to do so, taking into account the relevant policy considerations.

A legal duty of care generally exists between a doctor and patient, the latter being someone who has relied on the former's expertise. In medical negligence, the contentious aspects of medical care broadly relate to: (a) diagnosis, or the means of establishing what the patient's medical condition is; (b) treatment; and (c) advice, which involves presenting information regarding what should be done (namely treatment options), reasonable alternatives and the risks attendant on the various options. Previously, the Supreme Court of Singapore had applied the *Bolam-Bolitho* test to adjudicate the standard of care required in all three aspects of medical care, in order to determine whether there was medical negligence on the part of the doctor. In 2017 a new patient-centric standard was introduced for the provision of medical advice in the *Hii Chii Kok* case, while the *Bolam-Bolitho* test continues to apply to diagnosis and treatment. It first considers the legal standard of care for diagnosis and treatment and then the more recent change in standard of care on medical advice.

b. Standard of Care

The Singapore Court of Appeal decision in *Dr. James Khoo and Another v Gunapathy d./o Muniandy and Another* ('*Gunapathy*') is the authority for the legal standard of care for diagnosis and treatment in an action on medical negligence.[36] A doctor is not guilty of negligence if s/he has acted in accordance with a practice accepted as proper and responsible by a responsible body of medical practitioners skilled in that particular art, subject to the test of logical reasoning. Broadly referred to as the '*Bolam-Bolitho* test', this legal standard of care is primarily based on the test formulated by the English High Court in *Bolam v Friern Hospital Management Committee* ('*Bolam*'),[37] and subsequently qualified by the House of Lords decision in *Bolitho v City and Hackney Health Authority* ('*Bolitho*'). In the *Bolam* case, the plaintiff sustained fractures when electroconvulsive therapy was administered on him for his mental illness on the advice of a consultant attached to the defendant hospital. Among those skilled in the profession and experienced in this form of therapy, there were two bodies of opinion on whether relaxant drugs should be administered during the therapy in order to reduce the risk of fracture. One body of opinion favoured the use of relaxant drugs (usually with manual control) as a general practice while the other preferred limiting the use of relaxant drugs to cases where there were particular reasons for their use, because of concerns about the risk of death that such drugs presented. During the plaintiff's treatment, no relaxant drugs were used, but a male nurse stood by each side of the treatment couch throughout the treatment. Although he signed a consent form, the plaintiff was not warned of the risk of fracture, which

36 [2002] 2 SLR 414.

37 [1957] 2 All ER 118.

was very small (of the order of one in ten thousand). The plaintiff sued the defendant hospital for negligence in the administration of the treatment in not using the relaxant drugs, or some other form of manual control, and in failing to warn him of the risk involved before the treatment was given. Justice McNair's direction to the jury was: "a doctor is not negligent, if he is acting in accordance with a practice accepted as proper by a responsible body of medical men skilled in that particular art, merely because there is a body of such opinion that take a contrary view."

The scope of the Bolam test was restricted in the *Bolitho* decision, in terms of when the court is not bound to apply medical opinion. In that case, the plaintiff sued the defendant health authority for medical negligence resulting in the death of her son, who suffered total respiratory failure and a cardiac arrest, and consequently severe brain damage. The defendant contended that the cardiac arrest would not have been avoided if the defendant authority's physician had attended to the plaintiff's son earlier than had been the case. It was common ground that intubation which was performed to provide an airway would have ensured that respiratory failure did not lead to cardiac arrest and that such intubation would have had to have been carried out before the final episode. Although the views of expert witnesses of the plaintiff and defendant were diametrically opposed, both represented a responsible body of professional opinion espoused by distinguished and truthful experts. The court indicated that a doctor could be liable for negligence, in respect of diagnosis and treatment, despite a body of professional opinion sanctioning his conduct where it had not been demonstrated to the judge's satisfaction that the body of opinion relied on was reasonable or responsible. In rare cases, if it could be demonstrated that the professional opinion was not capable of withstanding logical analysis, the judge would be entitled to hold that the body of opinion was not reasonable or responsible. As the plaintiff failed to show that the body of opinion that the defendant relied on was unreasonable or irresponsible, and that a breach of duty by the defendant had caused the injury which occurred to the plaintiff, the ruling in favour of the defendant authority was upheld. Lord Browne-Wilkinson emphasised in his judgment that it is very seldom that the court would consider a body of opinion to be unreasonable or irresponsible: "I emphasise that in my view it will very seldom be right for a judge to reach the conclusion that views genuinely held by a competent medical expert are unreasonable. The assessment of medical risks and benefits is a matter of clinical judgment which a judge would not normally be able to make without expert evidence…it would be wrong to allow such assessment to deteriorate into seeking to persuade the judge to prefer one of two views both of which are capable of being logically supported. It is only where a judge can be satisfied that the body of expert opinion cannot be logically supported at all that such opinion will not provide the benchmark by reference to which the defendant's conduct falls to be assessed."

In the *Gunapathy* decision, the Court of Appeal in Singapore has made clear that the acceptable level of professional skills is similarly to be determined on the basis of the *Bolam* test. The Court of Appeal further clarified the ways in which it considered the *Bolam* test to have been modified as a matter of Singapore law. The Court of Appeal has made clear that the *Bolam* test, as supplemented by the Bolitho addendum, applies to the determination of acceptable professional standards in diagnosis and treatment. Under the *Bolam-Bolitho* test, a doctor would not be legally negligent for a diagnosis or treatment if it is supported by a respectable body of medical opinion, so long that opinion can be logically defended.

Where the provision of medical advice is concerned, the Singapore Court of Appeal has, in the *Hii Chii Kok* decision, replaced the *Bolam-Bolitho* test with what it considers to be a more patient-centric standard of care.[38] The Court explained that its main motivation for changing the standard of care, in relation to the provision of medical advice, has been due to growing emphasis on shared medical decision-making, whereby a patient is actively involved in making choices and decisions about her or his treatment and care. It follows that a doctor's role would be to empower the patient to do so through the provision of relevant and material information. From the standpoint of medical ethics, the court observed that the shift in emphasis, from the principle of beneficence to the principle of autonomy, was most evident in the changes introduced in the revised edition of the SMC's ECEG, which came into force on 1 January 2017. Unlike its earlier 2002 version, the court noted that revised ECEG reflects the fact that the "*nature of the doctor-patient relationship has evolved together with the level of education and access to knowledge of the ordinary Singaporean*", and the provision of medical advice should be "*now best seen as a collaborative process involving the doctor and the patient*". As the *Bolam* test was observed to "*not allow any room for the patient's perspective*", the Court considered it to be best consigned to history.

The Court of Appeal was also influenced by jurisprudential developments elsewhere, notably in the decision of the UK Supreme Court in *Montgomery v Lanarkshire Health Board* ('Montgomery') which was discussed at some length.[39] The UK Supreme Court departed from its earlier decision in *Sidaway v Board of Governors of Bethlem Royal Hospital*,[40] where the *Bolam* test was considered as not limited to medical diagnosis and treatment, but also applied to the amount of information that a doctor must give to a patient about the risks involved in a proposed course of treatment. In *Montgomery*, the court rule against the obstetrician for failing to disclose the increased risk of complications that could arise in vaginal delivery by the claimant who was diabetic and of small statute. This was not withstanding the fact that the claimant asked if her baby's size could present any problem and she would have requested for a caesarean section if she had known of this. Complication did arise from shoulder dystocia, which resulted in her son developing cerebral palsy. The ruling makes clear that there is a legal duty, on the part of doctors, to warn of material risks, even if they were to disagree with the decision that the patient is likely to make with the disclosure of such information. What constitutes a material risk is to be determined, based on whether a reasonable person in the patient's position would be likely to attach significance to the risk or the doctor is, or should reasonably be, aware that the particular patient would be likely to attach significance to it.

---

[38] [2017] SGCA 38.

[39] [2015] UKSC 11.

[40] [1985] AC 871.

In *Hii Chii Kok*, the claimant sought to rely on *Montgomery* in the legal action against the defendants, for failing to provide proper medical advice. In 2010, tests that were performed on the claimant produced inconclusive findings as to whether the pancreatic nodules found in him were cancerous. Due to the position of one of the nodules, a complex surgery known as the Whipple procedure had to be performed. This involved removing the head of the pancreas along with parts of the bile duct, gallbladder, duodenum and stomach, and then joining up the remaining parts of the pancreas, bile duct and stomach to keep the gastrointestinal tract intact (referred to as anastomosis). The claimant was advised of the risk of post-operative anastomotic breakdown, but he decided to proceed due to the risk that further investigations would not resolve the uncertainty and delayed intervention could result in cancerous spread. After the surgery, his anastomosis broke down which resulted in the need for further surgery to remove more of his pancreas, as well as his spleen. The High Court and the Court of Appeal ruled against the claimant, both holding that he had been provided with proper advice on the uncertainty of the diagnosis, the treatment options that were available and associated risks. The Court of Appeal also took the opportunity to introduce a '*modified-Montgomery*' standard of care, for the provision of medical advice, as it considered the materiality test in *Montgomery* to be too general to provide adequate guidance to the medical community. Under this revised standard, a doctor is required to disclose information that the doctor knows is important or would be reasonably relevant and material, which is to be determined from the particular patient's standpoint. A doctor would fall below this standard of care if s/he possessed information that is important or reasonably relevant and material to the patient, and failed to inform that patient without any legal justifications. The legal justifications for non-disclosure of information in medical advice include waiver by the patient, emergency treatment and therapeutic privilege. This revised standard may be applied as a 3-stage test applicable to determine the standard of care on the provision of medical advice to the patient[41]:

(1) Would a reasonable patient have expected to be given that information?

The first stage assesses the sufficiency of information given to the patient from the patient's perspective. The patient is required to identify the exact nature of the information that was allegedly omitted and explain why it would have been relevant and material, either from the standpoint of a reasonable patient situated in the particular patient's position or on the basis that the doctor should have known that the information was important to that patient. Information that should be disclosed includes diagnosis, prognosis (both with and without treatment), nature of the proposed treatment, risks and alternatives. It would ordinarily not be necessary to disclose remote

[41] See: Siang-Pheng Lek and Seow-Hwei Mar, Medical Negligence—The new legal test in Singapore to determine the standard of a doctor's duty in advising his patient. Available at: https://dentons.rodyk.com/en/insights/alerts/2017/may/31/medicalnegligence-the-new-legal-test-in-singapore (Last visited: 17 August 2020); Louise V Austin, Hii Chii Kok v (1) Ooi Peng Jin London Lucien; (2) National Cancer Centre: Modifying Montgomery (2019) *Medical Law Review* 27(2):339–351.

risks, with minor consequences, or very severe consequences with very low chances of occurring as they would generally be deemed immaterial. Similar to the UK Supreme Court in *Montgomery*, the Court of Appeal made clear that the patient should not be overwhelmed with information but should be empowered with the provision of information that is customised to her/his needs and concerns and at an appropriate pace that allows the information to be assimilated. While a doctor should be sensitive to the context within which medical advice is provided, s/he does not have an "*open-ended duty to proactively elicit information from the patient and will not be at risk of being found liable owing to idiosyncratic concerns of the patient unless this was made known to the doctor or the doctor has reason to believe it to be so*".

(2) Would it be reasonable to expect the doctor to have given the information, no matter how seemingly inconsequential, taking into account what is unique about the patient or her/his circumstances?

It must then be asked if the doctor was in possession of relevant and material information. If the doctor does not have the information, at the material time, a separate inquiry may arise in respect of any negligence in diagnosis or treatment (but not advice) because s/he did not conduct the procedure which would have discovered that information or because s/he lacked the factual or technical knowledge to realise that a particular risk or alternative treatment existed.

(3) Is there sound legal justification for the doctor not to disclose the information?

If the doctor possessed information that is relevant and material to the patient but did not disclose it, the doctor has the burden to justify why s/he chose to withhold the information. The Court will decide if the doctor was justified to withhold the information having regard to the doctor's reasons for withholding the information and then considering whether this was a sound judgment, having regard to the standards of a reasonable and competent doctor. Three instances whereby the withholding of information may be justified: (i) waiver situation, where the patient expressly indicated that s/he does not want to receive further information about the proposed treatment or alternatives; (ii) emergency situation, where life-saving treatment is required and the patient temporarily lacks decision-making capacity and no appropriate substitute decisionmaker can be found; and (iii) therapeutic privilege, where although the patient has mental capacity, her/his decision-making capabilities are impaired to an appreciable degree such that the doctor reasonably believes that the very act of giving particular information would cause the patient serious physical or mental harm.

In 2020, the patient-centric principle encapsulated in the *Hii Chii Kok* decision has been codified as statutory law. Under the Civil Law Act (as amended), doctors providing medical advice must satisfy two legal requirements[42]: (1) they must act in

[42] Section 37 of the Civil Law (Amendment) Bill, Bill No. 33/2020. Available at: https://www.parliament.gov.sg/docs/default-source/default-document-library/civil-law-(amendment)-bill-33-2020.pdf.

a logical manner that is accepted by a body of their peers (referred to as peer professional opinion); and (2) they must give information that a patient would reasonably inquire, or that is material to a patient in making an informed decision. Statutory determination of whether information is material to the patient (from the patient's perspective) for the purpose of making an informed decision about whether to undergo a treatment or follow a medical advice must be based on the patient's specific concerns or queries about the treatment or medical advice: (i) which the patient expressly communicates to the healthcare professional; or (ii) which are not expressly communicated by the patient to the healthcare professional but which ought to be apparent to the healthcare professional from the patient's medical records that the healthcare professional has reasonable access to and ought reasonably to review.[43]

It is beyond the scope of this chapter to analyse and reconcile subtle differences that could arise in the various formulations of materiality by Parliament (in the Civil Law Act, as amended), the Supreme Court (in the *Hii Chii Kok* decision) and the SMC. Since legislative intervention is not intended to substantially alter professional self-regulation,[44] it bears repetition that the SMC could still institute a higher professional standard for a doctor to ensure that her or his patient is aware of the purpose of a recommended test, treatment or procedure. A doctor who fails to inform her/his patient of material risks in relation to a procedure could be subject to disciplinary action by the SMC, even if she or he has not fallen below the legal standard.

c. Causation

The Supreme Court of Singapore has recently had the opportunity to consider the element of causation in medical negligence in two decisions.[45] In *Noor Azlin bte Abdul Rahman v Changi General Hospital Pte Ltd* ('*Noor Azlin*'), the appellant sued a hospital and its doctors in negligence, for having failed to diagnose her as having cancer when she presented at the accident and emergency (A&E) department in 2007, 2010 and 2011 for chest pain and breathlessness. In 2007, the appellant was referred by her A&E doctor to the hospital's respiratory doctor for follow-up when her X-ray image revealed an opacity in the right region of her chest. She was discharged after the health concern was considered to have resolved on its own. In 2010, the opacity in the X-ray image was again noticed but the appellant was discharged from A&E care, without follow-up, as the doctor was not aware of her medical history. In 2011, the A&E doctor did not notice the opacity as the appellant had complained about pain in the other side of her chest. It was only in 2012 that she was diagnosed with cancer in another hospital after further investigations were

---

[43] Section 37(2)(a)(ii) of the Civil Law (Amendment) Bill. The Bill provides non-exhaustive illustrations on the determination of materiality. See Explanatory Notes (at p. 7) to the Civil Law (Amendment) Bill.

[44] Timothy Goh and Salma Khalik, Informed Consent: Doctors must answer any question patients ask, *The Straits Times*, 7 October 2020. Available at: https://www.straitstimes.com/singapore/politics/informed-consent-doctors-must-answer-any-question-patients-ask.

[45] For a background discussion of the element of causation in a medical negligence claim in Singapore, see: Tong (2004).

ordered. At first instance, the High Court dismissed the claim, even though the hospital and respiratory doctor were found to be negligent, as the appellant had failed to prove that she had cancer by 2011 and that the negligence had caused the damage. The Court of Appeal reversed the judge's decision in relation to the hospital. In its review of the evidence, it was of the view that the appellant had proved, on balance of probabilities, that she developed lung cancer by 2011. The A&E doctor failed to notice this, due to the failings of the hospital's information system, which the hospital had the evidentiary burden of showing to be effective. The hospital failed to do so, as the patient's information could not be consolidated to ensure that there was an uninterrupted flow of complete information (including past medical history) to all professionals involved in the patient's care. There was also no means for A&E doctors to document their reasons for not ordering any follow-up. The hospital's information routing system was also found to be inappropriate, as radiologists should send their reports directly to specialist outpatient clinic for review, rather than the A&E department, unless the radiologist was unable to determine which specialist should follow-up on the finding. These failings led to a delay in the diagnosis and treatment of the appellant's condition, and consequently caused her harm.

The Court of Appeal agreed with the lower court in its decision concerning the doctors. While the respiratory doctor was found to have been negligent for having failed to order a follow-up, to confirm that the opacity had resolved, it did not cause the appellant harm as the nodule was likely to have been benign in 2007. It also agreed that A&E doctors have not been negligent. While A&E doctors were to be judged under the *Bolam/Bolitho* standard for negligence, in relation to diagnosis and treatment, the special conditions under which emergency medicine is practiced need to be taken into account. As A&E doctors have to deal with medical emergencies, it would be reasonable for them to adopt a targeted approach to resolve specific medical complaints, make quick decisions and ensure proper handover in team-based care. They would not be expected to perform holistic medical examination or be involved in long-term follow-up with patients. A&E doctors have a legal duty to take proper medical histories of patients and to refer patients to appropriate outpatient department for more thorough investigations or follow-up.

In *Armstrong, Carol Ann v Quest Laboratories Pte Ltd* ('Armstrong'), the Court of Appeal upheld the High Court's decision that the pathologist was negligent in reporting the tissue slides to be non-malignant without further testing. In 2009, a biopsy was done on the mole of the deceased's back and the specimen was sent to the respondents (these being the laboratory and its pathologists). The respondents' pathology report stated that there was no malignancy but re-examination, by a different pathologist, of the slides indicated a malignant melanoma. The respondent pathologist also found the same after a deeper examination was performed on the specimen collected in 2009. The Court of Appeal agreed with the High Court that the respondents' misdiagnosis was a straightforward breach under the *Bolam* test. It did not consider it necessary to apply the *Bolitho* addendum as there was no material difference in opinion between any of the experts, regarding the state of the primary tumour in the original slide, and none of them was prepared to conclusively state that the tumour was benign.

On the issue of causation, the Court of Appeal rejected the respondents' argument that the *Bolam-Bolitho* test to be applicable. The appellant needs to show, on balance of probabilities, that a necessary physical connection between the defendant's wrongful conduct and the damage caused; or that, "*but for*" the wrongful conduct, the damage would not have occurred. The Court of Appeal agreed with the trial judge that the misdiagnosis was a straightforward breach and that "*if a pathologist could not rule out the worst-case scenario, they should have stated so in their report*".[46] Some scholars have observed that this is an implicit endorsement of the "*absolute confidence*" test in *Penney v East Kent Health Authority*,[47] and more recently applied by the Supreme Court of Ireland in *Morrissey v Health Service Executive*,[48] although neither of these decisions were considered by the courts in Singapore.[49]

It did not address the issue of loss of chance, which was applied by the lower court, following the dissenting (and minority) decision in *Gregg v Scott*.[50] In that case, loss of chance claims were argued to be applicable when the plaintiff is unable to prove, on balance of probabilities, the likelihood of survival but is able to prove that the chance of survival was reduced. It was proffered, in that case, that the loss of chance was 17%, this being the difference between the initial likelihood of survival, when the cancer was missed (42%), and the likelihood of survival when the cancer was subsequently detected (25%). While English and Australian courts have rejected loss of chance claims, in medical negligence, the position remains unclear in Singapore.

For completeness, a brief mention is made that the eggshell skull rule applies to medical practice so that a patient is to be taken in the condition in that s/he is found to be whyen seen by the doctor. If a doctor negligently injures a patient who is in a vulnerable or weakened state, due to a medical condition, the doctor is responsible for all the consequences, whether they were foreseeable or not. The doctor could, in some cases, be excused if the harm suffered by the patient was inevitable and the negligent act only had a minimal effect on the already deteriorating condition of the patient.

d. Damages

In the *Armstrong* case, the plaintiff (being the deceased's spouse) set out four heads of claims: (1) dependency claims, or the benefits the dependents (namely the deceased's spouse and their two daughters) would have received; (2) the loss of inheritance; (3) the loss of appreciation in the value of the family home; and (4) the estate claims, comprising medical, funeral, out-of-pocket and probate expenses and bereavement, pain and suffering. In first instance, the dependency claim was allowed, based on the

---

46 [2020] 1 SLR 133, at Paragraph 67.

47 [2000] PNLR 323 at 27.

48 [2019] IEHC 268.

49 Kumaralingam Amirthalingam and Gary Kok-Yew Chan, Tort Law, *Singapore Academy of Law Journal* (2020): e-First (July 2020). Available at: https://journalsonline.academypublishing.org.sg/e-First/Singapore-Academy-of-Law-Annual-Review-of-Singapore-Cases/ctl/eFirstPDFPage/mid/570/ArticleId/1270?Citation=Published+on+e-First+6+July+2020 (Last Visited: 17 August 2020).

50 [2005] 2 AC 176.

trial judge's estimation that the deceased would have lived four more years, if his condition was properly diagnosed. The loss of inheritance claim was also allowed. The claims for loss of appreciation of the value of the home and the estate claims were rejected based on the assumption that the deceased would have lived out his natural life. On appeal, the court stated that damages should be assessed, based on the finding that, but for the respondents' negligence, the deceased would have been cured of his melanoma and would have lived out his expected natural life of 82 years. On this basis, it reversed the trial judge's assessment of the deceased annual income and remitted the determination of future salary increment back to the High Court. Determination of the dependency claim, loss of inheritance claim and estate clams were also remitted to the High Court for determination.

6 Conclusion

In this chapter, we considered how the legal standard of care on medical advice for a claim in medical negligence became broadly aligned with professionalism standards on consent-taking in the context of Singapore. This change came about, not only (or even primarily), due to the change in legal trend, conspicuously reflected in the landmark ruling in *Montgomery* by the UK Supreme Court, but may perhaps be more attributable to the gradual patient-centric turn in medical practice and profession expectations that occurred over several decades. This development is further instructive on a jurisprudential point: the change in legal norm did not occur, purely within the institutional confines of law, but interactively with the norms of medical ethics and the practical realities of professional medicine. In *Noor Azlin*, the inquiry into institutional and systemic deficiencies by the Supreme Court may reflect a new trajectory where redress for civil wrongs could extend well beyond the doctor-patient relationship. This too reflects the changing nature of medical practice, where many more doctors are now employees of healthcare institutions, rather than independent practitioners. If medical jurisprudence should advance in this direction, it may be fair to say that medical liability is likely to acquire a more prominent role in sustaining quality of medical care.

References

Chew L (2004) Principles of medical law. In: Yeo K-Q, Chew L, Goh L-G, Kaan T, Kuah B-T, Tong E (eds) Essentials of medical Law. Sweet & Maxwell Asia, Singapore, pp 17–63

Kaan T (2004) Professional regulation. In: Yeo K-Q, Chew L, Goh L-G, Kaan T, Kuah B-T, Tong E (eds) Essentials of medical law. Sweet & Maxwell Asia, Singapore, pp 289–310

Tong E (2004) Causation of Damage. In: Yeo K-Q, Chew L, Goh L-G, Kaan T, Kuah B-T, Tong E (eds) Essentials of medical law. Sweet & Maxwell Asia, Singapore, pp 145–205

Medical Liability in South Korea

Hyuna Bae

Abstract The main statutes that govern medical practice in South Korea (hereinafter "Korea") are the Medical Service Act, the Emergency Medical Service Act, and the National Health Insurance Act. But the medico-legal system in Korea refers to all the legal areas related to medical practice, including administrative, civil and criminal law. The legal basis of medico-legal claims against a medical practitioner or medical institution is mainly contractual liability, such as non-performance of obligations and tortious liability. Liability attaches for torts or non-performance of contractual terms when there is a breach of the duty of care in medical treatment, a generation of damage and a causal relationship between the breach of the duty of care and the damage caused. In recent years, a patient's right to self-determination and a doctors' duty of explanation have become increasingly more important. Violations of a doctor's duty to explain are independently becoming a large part of medical liability. The Act on Remedies for Injuries from Medical Malpractice and Mediation of Medical Disputes was enacted. This Act stipulates the matters related to mediation and arbitration of medical disputes, so as to promptly and reliably relieve damages caused by medical accidents and to create a stable medical environment for health care workers. To understand the medical liability in one country, it is necessary to consider the medical community, the historical and cultural background and the medical technology. It is also necessary to apply and interpret the rules while considering the medical, legal and social status of Korea.

H. Bae (✉)
School of Law, Ewha Womans University, Seoul, Republic of Korea
e-mail: sincerebae@ewha.ac.kr

V. L. Raposo and R. G. Beran (eds.), *Medical Liability in Asia and Australasia*,
Ius Gentium: Comparative Perspectives on Law and Justice 94,
https://doi.org/10.1007/978-981-16-4855-7_16

1 Introduction

1.1 Medico-Legal System in Korea

South Korea's (hereinafter "Korea") legal system is the continental law system. Unlike the common law system, congressional or legislative bodies, such as the Ministry of Health and Welfare enact rules known as statutory law. The main statutes that govern the medical practice in Korea are the Medical Service Act, the Emergency Medical Service Act and the National Health Insurance Act. The medico-legal system in Korea refers to all legal areas related to medical practice, including the Civil Act and the Criminal Act, and does not mean specific statues.

The legal basis of medico-legal claims, against a medical practitioner or medical institution, is mainly contractual liability, such as non-performance of obligations, and tortious liability. In the context of the medical practice, criminal liability could also be relevant to the Criminal Act which creates offenses that apply to medical doctors, such as Article 233 (Preparation of False Medical Certificate) and Article 270 (Abortion by Doctor or Abortion without Consent). The Criminal Act includes crimes related to general medical practice, such as death and injury from professional (occupational) negligence. The Korean medico-legal system is characterized by an abundance of criminal liability provisions for medical practitioners.

Medical liability related to medical practice in Korea, along with the administrative regulations by the government, including licensure, result in civil liability and criminal liability.

Specific medical liability will be reviewed based on precedents and by considering the specific nature of the Korean medico-legal system.

1.2 Health Care Providers Responsible for Medical Liability

Under the Korean Medical Service Act, the providers of medical services in Korea are medical personnel and medical institutions. Medical personnel and medical institutions are mainly regulated by the Medical Service Act. There are actually many types of medical practitioners. Per the framework Act of Health and Medical Services, the term *health and medical services personnel* means any person who acquires qualifications or licenses or who is allowed to engage in providing health and medical treatment services, under statutes related to health and medical services. Health and medical services personnel include medical service technologists and emergency medical technicians among others as well as medical personnel. The Medical Service Act requires five kinds of medical professionals to hold a license, granted by the Ministry of Health and Welfare. The term *Medical Personnel* (의료인, 醫療人), as used in the act, refers to a medical doctor, dentist, oriental medical doctor, midwife, or nurse.[1] Each medical person has his/her own mission and different scopes of practice, as required by the act. Although the act stipulates that medical personnel shall not perform medical procedures, other than those for which they licensed,[2] the problem is that the Medical Service Act defines the mission of the medical personnel and the scopes of medical practice quite broadly and indeterminately.

The medical acts and subordinate statutes neither define the content of licensed medical acts nor provide a classification criterion for doctors, or others. The mission and scope of practice may overlap and do not have clear-cut borders between various medical personnel. Conflicts occur among medical personnel about the mission and the scope of practice.

The following holdings, of the Supreme Court and the Constitutional Court, involve the definition and the scope of medical practice. The Supreme Court defines the practice of medicine as "*acts of prevention of disease or cure by means of diagnosing, examining, prescribing, medicating, or operating based on medical professional knowledge, and other acts unless performed by an authorized person might endanger the public health and hygiene.*"[3]

Interpreting and applying the statutory definition of the practice of medicine, to a particular set of activities, is often required in litigation with respect to violations of the prohibition against the unauthorized practice of medicine. The court may use its discretion in determining whether ***criminal liability*** occurred, such as through unlicensed medical practices.

The issue of whether the actions include "*medical acts other than those licensed*" should be decided reasonably, in each specific case, considering the social norms and the following as a whole: the legislative purpose of **the two-tier medical system** in Korea[4]; the provision and purport of the Acts related to the pertinent medical act; the academic principle underlying the pertinent medical act; the pertinent medical act's circumstance, purpose, and mode; and whether expertise of the pertinent medical act can be secured through a medical curriculum or the national exam of the school of medicine and the school of oriental medicine. "*Medical practices outside the scope of their license*" should be determined on a case-by-case basis, considering the generally accepted notions and a variety of factors, such as the legislative purport of the Medical Service Act, which distinguishes the following: the license of medical doctors and dentists as well as the regulatory provisions on practicing medicine; the academic principles that form the basis of the relevant medical practice; the details, purpose,

[1] Medical Service Act Article 2.

[2] Medical Service Act Article 27 (1).

[3] Supreme Court Decision 2011Do16649 Decided Jan 16, 2014 et al.

[4] Regarding these issues, the Korean Supreme Court addressed that the legislative purport lies in: (a) providing better medical services to the public by having medical personnel specialize in one particular field and encouraging them to develop competency in their area of expertise; and ultimately, (b) improving public health by preventing occurrence of risks to human life and public health in cases where medical doctors, dentists, and traditional Korean medicine doctors who received education in their area of expertise, gained initial qualifications, and obtained license after passing the relevant national exam provides medical treatment outside the scope of their respective license.

and type of the relevant medical care provided; and whether certain qualifications (such as completing educational courses at medical colleges or passing national exams) are sufficient to assure a satisfactory level of medical care.[5]

Health care providers also include medical institutions. In Korea, all medical institutions are compulsorily designated as health care institutions which may not refuse to provide health care benefits without a justifiable ground recognized by the National Health Insurance Act.

There are regulations related to the establishment of medical institutions under the Medical Service Act. In Korea, only medical personnel (excluding nurses) may establish medical institutions. Under this Act, the ability to establish medical institutions in Korea is also limited to public institutions or non-profit corporations, such as medical corporations. As a result, medical personnel, or those establishing medical institutions, are liable for medical activities.

2 Medical Liability and Medical Malpractice

Medical malpractice lawsuits in Korea are based on contractual liability and tortious liability. These are due to civil liability.

In Korea, criminal suits are often filed separately from civil liability in medical malpractice. In criminal liability, to acknowledge a medical doctor's negligence in a medical accident, it is necessary to review for negligence in failing to anticipate and avoid the occurrence of a consequence, where it is possible to anticipate and avoid such consequence. The standard for determining the existence of negligence is from the perspective of the ordinary person's duty of care who is in the same field of work and performing the same duties. The court must consider the level of ordinary medical science, at the time of the medical accident, the medical environment and conditions, the medical treatment's special nature, and other factors.[6]

In principle, criminal law punishes intentional offenders, negligent offenders are exceptionally punished and the severity of the punishment is different. Civil law treats the same intention or negligence equally, in terms of compensation for damages caused by unlawful acts. In many cases, criminal liability and administrative liability could arise, at the same time, due to unlawful acts under the Civil Act.

This chapter will discuss civil liability only. The legal basis of medical liability (civil liability) is possible through contractual liability, such as from non-performance of an obligation and tort. According to the current rules and precedents, the claimant may claim either of them or select both claims selectively.

Injured patients (plaintiffs) can file a lawsuit in a way that is beneficial to them, by considering the burden of proof. In a tort lawsuit, the plaintiff must prove the negligence. To ask for contractual liability, the plaintiff (patient) must prove the non-performance of an obligation. Considering the court's attitude, such as the recent

[5] Supreme Court Decision 2013Do850 Decided July 21, 2016.

[6] Supreme Court Decision 2010Do10104 Decided April 14, 2011.

easing and shifting of the burden of proof, in medical malpractice cases, medical malpractice lawsuits mainly consist of tort, rather than contract liability, because of the patient's family's right to claim consolation money for the mental pain, suffered by the patient or his/her family. The burden of proof may shift to the defendant physician.

2.1 Contractual Liability

Contractual liability, in medical liability, is based on Article 390 of the Civil Act. The narrow meaning of medical liability includes civil liability for which monetary compensation is requested. Such civil liabilities are based on 390 of the Civil Act (non-performance of obligations and compensation for damages).

If an obligor fails to effect performance, in accordance with the tenor and purport of the obligation, the obligee may claim damages; provided this shall not apply where performance has become impossible and where this failure is not due to the obligor's intention or negligence.

Liability for non-performance of obligations is based on the medical contract. Korean civil law does not stipulate an explicit definition of a medical contract.

The Supreme Court has ruled on *medical contracts* as follows.[7] If a patient asks a health care provider (namely a medical doctor or medical institution in the context) for treatment and the medical practitioner begins treatment, a *medical contract* is concluded between the medical practitioner and the patient. Under this agreement, the medical practitioner is responsible for treating patients, based on his/her medical knowledge and the medical technology, and patients are required to pay medical expenses for receiving the treatment.

The content and the scope of the medical contract is comprehensive and abstract because the medical treatment tends to vary, depending on the progress of the disease and the changes in a patient's condition. The treatment depends on several factors (such as the diagnosis, the patient's condition and natural changes and the biological response to treatment). A medical practitioner has considerable discretionary power to select the proper treatment methods, depending on the patient's health condition, the level of medical care at the time and his/her knowledge and experience.[8]

The medical obligation, under the medical contract, is an instrumental obligation not a resulting obligation that must achieve the complete results such as cure of a disease. Unlike other contracts, achieving results is not necessarily an essential requirement in medical contract.[9] This is also related to the issue of the burden of proof. The Korean Supreme Court also held that a medical obligation is *the obligation*

---

[7] Supreme Court Decision 2009Da17417 Decided May 21, 2009.

[8] Supreme Court Decision 91Da23707 Decided May 12; Supreme Court Decision 2005Da5867 Decided May 31, et al.

[9] Jun (2005).

de moyens and the plaintiff has the burden of proof in principle.[10,11] The obligation moyens theory derived from French contract law that a doctor has a duty of reasonable care to perform his or her medical obligation.[12] So a patient as a plaintiff has to prove the doctor's negligence not presumption in the medical malpractice lawsuit.

For a medical contract, a medical doctor owes a duty of care to take the best action necessary to prevent any risk associated with the patient's specific symptoms or circumstances, in light of the nature of the profession, which concerns human life, the body and health.

2.2 *Tortious Liability and Medical Negligence*

A medical practitioner may be liable for torts, based on Article 750 of the Civil Act, for damages to patients due to medical accidents. The Civil Act defines torts by noting that any person who causes losses to, or inflicts injuries on, another person, by an unlawful act, intentionally or negligently, shall be bound to compensate that person for damages arising therefrom.

The provisions of Articles 751 and 752 of the Civil Act state that civil liability may also arise for physical injuries and other mental distress in which the responsibility for damages, caused by the unlawful acts, applies to more than property and it may extend to the families of the victims, if their lives are affected. Article 751 of the Civil Code (Compensation for Non-Economic Damages) states that a person who has injured the person, liberty or fame of another or who has inflicted any mental anguish to another person shall be liable to compensate for the damage arising therefrom. Article 752 of the Civil Code (Consolation Money in Case of Violation of Life) notes that a person causing the death of another person shall be liable for damages to the lineal ascendants, lineal descendants and spouse, even if no economic damage resulted.

Tortious liability is based on its constituent elements: negligence (a breach of duty of care), unlawful act; damages resulting from a breach of that duty of care; and causation between the unlawful act and damage. To hold a medical practitioner (medical doctor) liable for breaching the duty of care in the medical practice, the damages and the causation between them should each be proved. Under a theory of negligence, the injured patient (plaintiff) must prove each of the following essential elements by the preponderance of the evidence: duty; breach of duty; causation; and damages.

Medical negligence is a breach of the physician's duty to behave reasonably and prudently, under the circumstances, which causes foreseeable harm to a patient where the harm is avoidable. In engaging in medical practices, such as diagnosis and

---

[10] Supreme Court Decision 2007Da76290 Decided March 27, 2008; Supreme Court Decision 2001Da52568 Decided Nov 9, 2001; Supreme Court Decision 92Da15031 Decided Jul 27, 1993.

[11] OhSik (2007).

[12] id.

treatment, a medical doctor owes a duty of due care to take the best action necessary to prevent any risk associated with the patient's specific symptoms or circumstances, in light of the nature of the profession, which concerns human life, the body and health.[13] Courts use this when judging negligence.

To hold medical personnel liable, for a breach of the duty of care, the plaintiff must prove a breach of the duty of care attributable to medical acts, accrual of loss and the existence of causation between them. Considering the nature of a medical practice, medical personnel are under **a duty of care** to adopt the best measures required to prevent risks, depending on the patient's concrete symptoms or circumstances.[14] In a case where medical personnel fail to do their best, in treating a patient,—in violation of the patent's expectations—they should be deemed to have violated the duty of care in the profession. In a case where no substantial causation is acknowledged, between such breach of the duty of care and the unfavorable result inflicted on the patient, it is impossible to seek damages in relation thereof. In a case where the degree of violating the duty of care reached a level where an ordinary person would believe that a significantly unfaithful treatment was made, beyond the tolerable limits, such an act constitutes a tort, and it is possible to order payment of consolation money for the mental pain suffered by the patient or his/her family.[15]

The standard for such a duty of due care, owed by a medical doctor, is the level of medical practice, as exercised in the field of clinical medicine, including at medical institutions, at the time of engaging in the given medical practice. Such a level of medical advancement means one that is generally known and acknowledged, by ordinary doctors at the time, of engaging in the given medical practice. The level of medical advancement should be understood as a normative level, accounting for such factors as the treatment environment, condition and the uniqueness of a given medical practice.[16]

In determining any negligence in the diagnosis,[17] although a completely flawless clinical diagnosis may be impossible to attain, the court should at least investigate whether the doctor fulfilled the duty of best possible care, necessary to anticipate the risks of any dangerous consequences and to avoid these risks by prudently and accurately examining and diagnosing the patient based on medical ethics, knowledge and experience, as professionally demanded of him/her, within the bounds of the level of diagnosis, as exercised in the field of clinical medicine.[18]

---

[13] Supreme Court Decision 2016Da26606,26613 Decided November 29, 2009.

[14] Supreme Court Decision 2004Da61402 Delivered on September 28, 2006.

[15] Supreme Court Decision 2004Da61402 Delivered on September 28, 2006.

[16] Supreme Court Decisions 2004Da 65121, March 10, 2005.

[17] Diagnosis is an important medical practice as a starting point of clinical medicine and a basis for selecting the specific means of treatment, including by discerning any existence of a disease based on the results of the patient interview, ocular inspection, palpation, stethoscopy, and various clinical tests and by identifying the type, character, and the extent of progression of a given disease.

[18] Supreme Court Decisions 2002Da 3822, Jan. 24, 2003; 2010Da76849, Sept. 13, 2012.

A physician's foregoing duty of care is determined by the standard of a medical practice in clinical medicine, like in medical institutions, at the time of a medical practice. The standard refers to common medical knowledge that is generally known and recognized by ordinary physicians, at the time of a medical act. It is the norm determined in light of the medical examination environment, conditions and characteristics of the medical practice.[19]

A physician may administer a treatment by selecting a method that is regarded as proper according to a patient's circumstances, the current medical standard and his/her knowledge and experience. Unless a physician's judgment, about the treatment method selection, deviates from a reasonable scope, **medical negligence** cannot be directly acknowledged merely because a specific treatment method brings about bad results.[20]

The court held that doctors had substantial discretion to choose adequate treatment methods based on a patient's status, the level of medical care available at the time and his/her knowledge and experience. The court also held that, unless such discretion exceeded the reasonable scope, it would not constitute medical malpractice based on the results of treatment.[21]

2.3 Filing of Medical Malpractice Lawsuit Against Medical Practitioner: Burden of Proof

To determine whether liability exists, for a tort or non-performance of contractual terms during medical treatment, there should be a breach of the duty of care, generation of damage and a causal relationship between the breach of the duty of care and the damage caused.

Medical practice requires highly sophisticated expertise. It is extremely difficult for a layman to determine whether a doctor breached the duty of care during medical procedures or to assess the causal relationship between a breach of the duty of care and the damage therefrom.

Because medical practice requires a high level of expertise, it is considerably difficult for the general public to determine whether doctors violated the duty of care in treating patients or whether causation exists between the violation of the duty of care and damages.[22]

---

[19] Supreme Court Decision 2004Da13045, October 28, 2005, etc.

[20] Supreme Court Decisions 91Da23707, May 12, 1992; Supreme Court Decisions 2010Da95635, June 14, 2012.

[21] Supreme Court Decision 2005 Da5867, May 31, 2007.

[22] Damage is divided into property damage and non-property damage. Property damages are divided into active and passive damages. Active damages refer to the loss of existing property and the victim's expenses and debts. Frequently, in malpractice lawsuits, treatment costs, care costs, funeral expenses, and attorneys' fees are included. Passive damage includes a case where an increase in property is hindered. In the case of life infringement, it is the amount of profit equivalent to the

Due to the disproportion of information in the medical field, it is difficult to prove the defendant's intention, negligence and causality in a medical malpractice lawsuit. The plaintiff must prove the imputable causes, such as intention or negligence, the occurrence of the damage and the causation between the act and damages.

In most medical malpractice cases, these factors are highly technical, and witnesses with special medical qualifications must provide information for the judge. In nearly all cases, the standard for medical care of a prudent physician must be determined based on expert medical testimony. In some cases, it is permissible to presume medical negligence by proving indirect facts, suggesting that there is no other reason except for medical negligence.

In a medical malpractice lawsuit seeking compensation, the burden of proof is eased to make **assumptions** regarding the causal relationship between medical negligence and the consequence and to impose liability for damages.[23] In cases, where a symptom that leads to serious problems occurs in a patient during a surgery, this may prove indirect factual matters that show no causes—other than medical malpractice—led to such symptoms, and this may lead to the presumption that such symptom was caused by the medical malpractice. Even in such a case, courts prohibit imposing a burden of proof of non-negligence on a doctor by making a groundless assumption about the causal relationship between a considerable outcome and a doctor's negligence, solely based on circumstances that do not ensure probability sufficient to predict that the outcome arose from the doctor's negligence.

Similar to the Supreme Court, even when tort damage liability is found to have arisen from a medical doctor's violation of a duty of due care in his/her medical practice, if the injury from an error in medical practice concurrently arose from, or was aggravated by, factors attributable to the victim, then courts, in setting the level of compensation, may consider such factors that contributed to causing or aggravating the injury by applying **the legal doctrine of comparative negligence**, even when those factors are irrelevant to the victim's liability, such as his/her physical, constitutional disposition or the fatality of disease, in as much as it is contrary to the ideals of equity to hold the wrongdoer liable for the entire damages amount given the features, pattern and extent of the disease. The fact-finding or ratio-setting, on the limitation of liability, shall not be manifestly unreasonable, in light of the principles of equity and fairness.[24]

To overcome this, the proving through indirect facts and the mitigation of the burden of proof is being discussed in Korea; shifting the burden of proof is also being considered.[25]

---

available period of work, and in the case of disability due to physical infringement, the difference in realistic income becomes the net profit.

[23] Supreme Court Decision 2017Da203763 Decided February 14, 2019.

[24] Supreme Court Decision 2014Da16968, Decided Jul. 10, 2014.

[25] Bin (2008).

3 Right to Self-determination and Duty to Explain

Under the Framework Act on Health and Medical Services, Article 12 (Right to Decide on Health and Medical Treatment Services), all nationals shall have the right to receive full explanations from health and medical services personnel on the methods for treating their diseases, including whether they are subject to medical research or require organ transplants, and the patient must decide whether to agree, or reject the aforementioned.

This is an explicit and declarative statement about the patient's right to self-determination. In practice, the doctor's duty to explain is based on the constitutional rights of a patient and the medical contractual obligations.

The patient's consent aims at guaranteeing "*the right to self-determination,*" which is protected by the rights to personality and the pursuit of happiness under **Article 10 of the Constitution.**[26] Because the patient decides how to maintain his/her life and body functions and selects the treatment, the details of the treatment, offered under the **medical contract,** are specified by the medical practitioner's explanation and the patient's consent.[27] The content and the scope of treatment are comprehensive and abstract because medical treatment tends to vary depending on the progress of the disease and changes in a patient's condition.

In the case of invasive treatments, such as an operation, a medical practitioner should provide an explanation, including about the disease symptoms, treatment method and necessity and foreseeable risks, in light of the level of medical care at the time, and the patient should weigh the risks against the necessity and give **consent** to the selected treatment. The physicians' duty of explanation to the patient is not limited to the operation. It occurs at every stage of the care, including tests, diagnosis and treatment. The informed consent to the procedure in every stage of the medical practice makes the content and the scope of the medical contract more specific.

The recently revised medical Service Act explicitly stipulated the Explanation about Medical Practices. Under the Article 24–2 (Explanation about Medical Practices), where a physician, dentist, or oriental medical doctor performs a surgery, blood transfusion or general anesthesia that might cause serious harm to a human life or body, he/she shall explain the matters to the patient (referring to a legal representative, where the patient lacks decision-making ability; hereafter the same shall apply in this Article) and obtain written consent (including an electronic document; hereafter the same shall apply in this Article). This does not apply where the patient's life might fall into danger or the patient might fall into serious mental incapacity, due to the delay of treatment. caused by explaining the procedures and obtaining consent.

Under the Medical Service Act, the following matters are required in giving an explanation to, or receiving consent from, a patient: diagnosis of a symptom that has

[26] Article 10 of the Constitution of the Republic of Korea states, "All citizens shall be assured of human worth and dignity and have the right to pursue happiness. It shall be the duty of the State to confirm and guarantee the fundamental and inviolable human rights of individuals".

[27] Supreme Court Decision 2009Da17417 Decided May 21, 2009.

occurred in or which might occur in the patient; necessity, methods, and details of the treatment.; the name of the physician, dentist, or oriental medical doctor who gives the explanation to the patient; the name of the principal physician, dentist, or oriental medical doctor who participates in the procedures.; sequelae or side effects expected to occur, typically following such treatment; and matters to be observed by the patient before and after the intervention.

Where the methods and details of the treatment or the principal physician, dentist, or oriental medical doctor who will participate in it are changed, among the matters on which consent is obtained, the patient shall be informed of the ground for and details of the change in writing. This is a provision prepared for the recently emerging *ghost surgery or shadow doctor* that performed by unauthorized substitute surgeon.[28] Under Article 92 of the Act, a person who fails to make explanations to, or to obtain written consent from, a patient, and a person who fails to inform a patient of the ground for, and details of the change, shall be punished by an administrative fine not exceeding three million won.

The legal basis of the duty to explain affects the scope of compensation for damages caused by the violation of that duty. Physicians may owe solatium for violating the duty of explanation, thus compensating the patient for emotional suffering from the loss of an opportunity for self-determination, based on the occurrence of a significant consequence from the pertinent medical act. This applies where a physician conducted an operation, without explaining to a patient in advance, about a disease's symptoms, treatment or diagnosis method or the necessary and foreseeable risks of the treatment and negative consequences occurred. The physician's explanation does not apply to all medical processes but only to medical acts where patients are required to choose by self-determination, such as an invasive treatment like an operation with the probability of bad results or significant consequences like death. Where significant consequences to a patient are not due to a physician's invasion, or where a patient's self-determination right is not at issue, a violation of a duty of explanation cannot be a ground for liability for solatium.[29] This consolation money refers to damages that generally reimburse victims for mental damage, such as pain, shock, and despair. This is based on Article 751(1) of the Civil Act.

A physician could have triggered a patient's treatment opportunity loss[30] but also invaded a patient's self-determination right in violation of a duty of explanation.[31] The Supreme Court recognizes both compensation for total damages and solatium for violations of the duty to explain.

In addition to civil liability for damage compensation, if a medical doctor administered a medical treatment, in violation of a duty to explain, and the victim suffered an injury, a causal relationship must exist between the victim's injury and the medical doctor's violation of a duty to explain or fault when determining whether a medical doctor should be held liable *criminally* due to occupational negligence. It is hard

---

[28] Man-Seong (2015).

[29] Supreme Court Decision 94Da27151, April 25, 1995, etc.

[30] Bok-Hyun (2020).

[31] Supreme Court Decision 2011Da36848, Decided April 25, 2013.

to acknowledge a causal relationship between the defendant's (medical practitioner) violation of the duty to explain and the victim's injury. Only the burden of proof of the duty to explain is on the defendant (health care provider). This is because it is disadvantageous to doctors when they fail to prove it.

In special cases, the duty to explain is waived, such as the Emergency Medical Service Act Article 9 (Informed consent to emergency medical treatment). This Act indicates that emergency medical personnel shall provide explanations of emergency medical services to an emergency patient and obtain his/her consent thereto, except in any of the following cases: where the emergency patient is incapable of making decisions; and where a delay in emergency medical services due to the procedures for providing explanations and obtaining consent could endanger the patient's life or cause severe bodily or mental harm to the patient.

If an emergency patient is incapable of making decisions and the patient is accompanied by a legal agent, emergency medical personnel shall explain the emergency medical services to the legal agent and obtain his/her consent. Where the patient is not accompanied by a legal agent, the emergency medical personnel shall provide such explanations to whomever accompanies the patient, before giving first aid and may administer an emergency medical examination and treatment according to the medical judgment of a physician. This emphasizes the duty to provide emergency medical services even without consent. It enhances the obligation to provide emergency medical services and is an exception to informed consent. Except in special cases, like emergency medical treatment, the medical practitioner's duty to explain is very important in medical liability.

4 Medical Dispute Resolution System of Korea

The Act on Remedies for Injuries from Medical Malpractice and Mediation of Medical Disputes was enacted in 2011. It was enacted to promptly and fairly redress injuries caused by medical malpractice and to create a stable environment for medical treatment by medical professionals, by providing for matters relating to the mediation and arbitration of medical disputes.

This Act established the Korea Medical Dispute Mediation and Arbitration Agency, as an independent body. This agency was tasked with establishing a Medical Malpractice Appraisal Board (hereinafter the "Appraisal Board") to settle medical disputes promptly and fairly. Under Article 25, the Appraisal Board's appraisal processes are the most important proceedings under this system because investigating the facts necessary for the mediation or arbitration of medical disputes and causation relieves the parties of the burden of proving the existence of medical negligence and a causal relationship.

The Medical Dispute Mediation Act has a program that provides compensation for unavoidable medical misadventure, in the course of childbirth. Compensation is provided for injuries caused by medical accidents, in the course of childbirth, if the Committee for the Deliberation on Compensation for Medical Malpractice determines that such injuries were unavoidable, although public health or medical professional fulfilled their duties of care (Article 46). This Act also provides patients with compensation for medical misadventures caused by other *force majeure* in other exceptional cases. It is also politically related to Korea's low birth rate problem.

Because doctors cannot completely control the outcome of a medical procedure, there could be unavoidable medical misadventures. The compensation is paid only based on the principle of fault due to liability and remedies for injuries may not be satisfactory for both patients and doctors.[32] This program is one of the attempts at no-fault liability for compensation in the medical field.

The Minister for Health and Welfare may also partially subsidize expenses incurred in the program to compensate for medical accidents within budgetary limits. This system is being implemented to relive the victims (patients) of medical accidents of the burden of litigation costs and to create a stable medical environment for medical personnel.[33]

One merit of the medical Dispute Mediation Act is saving time and costs by introducing a mediation and arbitration system for medical malpractice cases as an alternative dispute resolution (ADR) method to time-consuming and costly lawsuits. The medical dispute mediation and arbitration system in Korea is a prompt, simple and low-cost dispute resolution system, compared with litigation.

A lawsuit may be filed regarding a medical dispute without undergoing mediation proceedings under this Act (Article 40). Mediation proceedings must commence when the respondent on whom a mediation petition is served notifies the Mediation and Arbitration Agency of his/her intention to accede to mediation. If the respondent fails to notify the Mediation and Arbitration Agency of his/her intention to accede to mediation, within 14 days from the day on which the petition for mediation is served, the president will reject such a petition for mediation (Article 27).

Notwithstanding the above, the president will commence mediation procedures without delay when medical malpractice, for which a petition for mediation has been filed, results in death or other conditions that result in unconsciousness for at least one month and severe disabilities. In such cases, the date that the respondent is served with the petition for mediation shall become the commencement date of the mediation procedures.

After the mediation and arbitration process, where mediation is successfully concluded or a mediation statement is prepared, under an agreement, while mediation proceedings are pending pursuant to Article 37, the public health or medical professional who negligently conducted the business, under Article 268 of the Criminal Act, will not be publicly prosecuted against the victim's express intent. The foregoing shall not apply to cases where a victim's life is threatened or a victim becomes disabled or suffers from a fatal or incurable disease as a consequence of a bodily injury.

If a victim, in a medical malpractice case, fails to receive money, if he/she falls under any of the following categories, he/she may file a claim for vicarious payment

---

[32] Soo et al. (2013).

[33] Min (2011).

of the money receivable with the Mediation and Arbitration Agency: (1) where mediation has been concluded successfully, an arbitral award has been granted or a mediation statement has been prepared under an agreement, pursuant to Article 37(1), while mediation proceedings are pending; (2) where a mediation statement has been prepared, pursuant to Article 67(3) of the Framework Act on Consumers; or (3) where a court has prepared a deed of assignment for execution that orders the operator or public health or medical professional of a public health or medical institution, or any other person who is found to be a party, to pay money in civil proceedings. The last category only applies where the judgment of a court in the Republic of Korea is final and conclusive.

The ADR system is good for saving time and costs in a medical malpractice lawsuit.

5 Discussion: Recent Changes in Medical Liability in Korea

The characteristics and changes in medical liability in Korea include a rapid increase in medical disputes and litigation. This increase has led to rising health care costs due to defensive care and avoidance of high-risk patients by medical institutions.

The Medical Dispute Mediation Act was enacted and implemented, and, accordingly, the role of the Medical Dispute Mediation Arbitrator has been increasing. A lawsuit may be filed regarding a medical dispute, without undergoing mediation proceedings under this Act. Because mediation is not an essential step, litigation is still preferred to this ADR procedure.

Even criminal charges, against medical practitioners, are often filed in Korea. It is one of the characteristics of Korea's medical liability.

Another change, in medical liability in Korea, is the transformation of the standard for such a duty of care, owed by a medical doctor. The court is increasingly upgrading the standard of judgment for a doctor's violation of his/her duty of care. This is due to the specialization, segmentation of medical practices and the enlargement of medical institutions.

These changes, in the medical community, create other problems, such as joint liability among health care providers. Health care providers, in medical institutions, each have their own scopes of practice, as required by the Medical Service Act. In a case where multiple health care providers were involved in medical care and where it is not clear who actually caused the medical accident, it is proper to deem that all of the healthcare providers, involved in the series of medical care, should be held liable to compensate for the damage as joint tortfeasors, per the Civil Act in Korea.

In some cases, conflicts in the scope of practice could arise among doctors and other doctors, doctors and nurses, medical personnel and medical technicians, and emergency paramedics. These conflicts become disputes, but as a result, the scope of practice becomes concrete through those precedents.

To understand medical liability in Korea, when medical law is applied and interpreted, social changes should be reflected in a timely fashion. The medical community should be not only sensitive to advances in medical science and technology but also to these changes in society. Although the Korean legal system does not specify and explicitly define the legal concept of medical practice, it is also true that the concept of flexible medical practice has recently expanded and new technologies are being introduced and activated in the medical field, such as digital healthcare. Due to the rapid development of biomedical technology, the definition and scope of medical practice must also be expanded and must be embraced by the legal concept in a timely manner. A balanced direction of medico-legal policy is needed.

Korea has been responding to potential, future changes to society by providing a legal basis for digital health care, such as artificial intelligence in medicine, digitalization of the health information exchange and big data. It is necessary to introduce a legal concept of new medical practice.

The right to health information is also important, along with the patient's right to self-determination. After several Supreme Court decisions, related to the withdrawal of life-sustaining treatment, Korea enacted the Act on Hospice and Palliative Care and Decisions on Life-Sustaining Treatment for Patients at The End of Life. These issues also arise from the development of medical technologies, such as intensive and critical care medicine, including artificial ventilators. The purpose of this act is to prescribe matters necessary for hospice and palliative care and life-sustaining treatment for patients at the end of life, the determination to terminate such life-sustaining treatment and the implementation thereof—thereby protecting the dignity and value of human beings by assuring the best interests of the patients and by respecting their self-determination.

The importance of exercising the patient's right to self-determination has been increased. The doctor's duty to explain is further emphasized. Violations of a doctor's duty to explain are becoming a large part of medical liability. A violation of the duty to explain, without a breach of the duty of care, may result in liability for damages as well as solatium.

6 Conclusion

The debate on medical liability is ultimately based on the judgment of the judiciary. Medical liability should consider the health care system and the medico-legal system. The medical environment of the country, its historical characteristics, the degree of development of medical technology and the atmosphere of the medical community should be considered.

To understand the country's medical liability, it is necessary to understand the background rules from institutional, legal, cultural and problematic situational elements that form the background of legal interpretation.

References

Bin KY (2008) The meaning and criterion of medical malpractice(negligence) from moderating the burden of proof in a medical malpractice Suit. 9 Med Law 57

Bok-Hyun E (2020) Legal interest in damages regarding loss of treatment chance. 20 Med Law 83

Jun KB (2005) Malpractice and standard of care. 12 J Comparat Private Law 187

Man-Seong H (2015) Criminal liabilities of ghost surgery. 16 Med Law 27

Min JC (2011) A review on the proxy payment for damage in the medical dispute mediation law. 34 Chonbuk Law Rev 219

OhSik S (2007) An examination on 'the obligation Moyens Theory' for medical obligation 31 Chung-Ang J Legal Stud 201

Soo PH, Young OS, Ahm K (2013) The issues in obstetric no fault compensation act and suggestions for the improvement. 24 Korean J Perinatol 65

Medical Malpractice in Taiwan

Kevin Chien-Chang Wu and Ching-Ting Liu

Abstract Around 2012, the insufficient supply of physicians in internal medicine, surgery, gynecology/obstetrics, pediatrics and emergency medicine became an important policy problem in Taiwan. Increasing numbers of medical disputes and medical malpractice were recognized as one of the contributing factors. Several bills, intending to systematically manage medical malpractice problems, failed. The government (at both the central and local levels) and professionals (including medicine and law) continued to work together to incrementally modify the laws, regulations and practices of medicine, to manage the problems. The trend of increasing risk of medical disputes and medical malpractice seems to have subsided. The recruitment of residents also improved. This chapter aims to describe the main development of the systems of managing medical disputes and medical malpractice in Taiwan. Although it is difficult to ascertain the causes for the above trend, the chapter provides some insight into what might have facilitated the development. In the following, Sect. 2 briefs the basic legal principles of medical malpractice in Taiwan. Section 3 addresses the procedures and characteristics of medical malpractice in Taiwan before the year of 2012. Section 4 describes the alternative medical disputes resolution mechanisms, in Taiwan, about a decade ago. Section 5 presents the attitudes of the public in Taiwan, towards medical malpractice which could be used as a check on the medical malpractice policy. Section 6 depicts the current no-fault and quasi-no-fault compensation programs in Taiwan. Only vaccine injury (no-fault), drug injury (quasi-no-fault) and childbirth incidents (no-fault) are covered now. Section 7 reviews the failed bills intending to systematically address medical disputes and medical malpractice in Taiwan. Section 8 depicts the later development of legislation related to medical malpractice and Sect. 9 the later development of

K. C.-C. Wu (✉)
Department/Graduate Institute of Medical Education and Bioethics, National Taiwan University College of Medicine, No. 1 Sec 1 Ren-Ai Road, Zhongzheng Dist., Taipei City 10051, Taiwan
e-mail: ccwu88@ntu.edu.tw

Department of Psychiatry, National Taiwan University Hospital, No. 1 Changde Street, Zhongzheng Dist., Taipei City 10048, Taiwan

C.-T. Liu
College of Law, Fu Jen Catholic University, Taipei City, Taiwan

V. L. Raposo and R. G. Beran (eds.), *Medical Liability in Asia and Australasia*, Ius Gentium: Comparative Perspectives on Law and Justice 94,
https://doi.org/10.1007/978-981-16-4855-7_17

mechanisms of alternative medical dispute resolution in Taiwan. Taiwan currently does not have a full-scale no-fault medical malpractice liability system. Through reforms in law, mediation procedure reconciliation procedure and cooperation among governments at different levels and different professionals may continue to facilitate the development of a better medical malpractice system in the future.

1 Introduction

In 1995, Taiwan created its national health insurance (NHI) that covers the health care of almost all the people (99.6% in 2016) in Taiwan. Healthcare accessibility improved as 93% of the medical facilities in Taiwan were NHI-contracted in 2016 (Health Promotion Administration of the Ministry of Health and Welfare 2015). As the use of health care increased, medical malpractice gradually became a serious health policy challenge. The number of criminal cases, referred for medical dispute review, increased to a historical high point in 2012, based on the data of cases reviewed by Taiwan's Medical Review Committee (MRC) in the central government (Fig. 1) (https://dep.mohw.gov.tw/DOMA/cp-2712-7681-106.html, in Chinese, accessed on August 20, 2020). Around 90% of medical malpractice complaints would be referred for the MRC review (Liu 2011). According to a review of criminal medical malpractice cases, at the level of district courts in 2000–2010, the leading three medical disciplines, having the highest proportions in the case pool of criminal medical malpractice litigation were surgery (32.4%), internal medicine (19.7%), and gynecology/obstetrics (16.1%). The majority (75.7%) of the defendants were sentenced not guilty or not liable (Liu 2011). It was reported that more and more physicians adopted practices of defensive medicine and/or avoided entering the medical specialties with high litigation risks. Some even earned law degrees as a way to protect themselves (Lin 2018). This was a lose-lose situation for both physicians and patients. Physicians were afraid of malpractice litigation all the

Fig. 1 Annual numbers of cases referred for the MRC medical dispute review in Taiwan

time and patients could not obtain the best health care. In 2012, the Executive Yuan (the highest administrative entity in Taiwan) was officially corrected by the Control Yuan (the highest auditing entity in Taiwan) for the failure to manage the insufficient supply of doctors in internal medicine, surgery, gynecology/obstetrics, pediatrics and emergency medicine. According to the official correction document, among others, medical disputes drove these physicians away (https://www.cy.gov.tw/CyBsBoxContent.aspx?n=133&s=3593, in Chinese, accessed on September 1, 2020). Around the end of 2012, the Executive Yuan proposed a bill that emphasized medical dispute mediation and quasi-no-fault medical incident compensation. The bill did not pass through the legislative process, mainly due to a lack of consensus on what share medical facilities and healthcare professionals should afford to set up the compensation fund (Hung 2017).

The government and the professionals have continued to work together both at the central and local levels, to modify the laws, regulations and practices of medicine to promote and implement some ideals and measures in the above failed bill. The public images of physicians, as high rank laborers vulnerable to verbal, physical and legal threats from patients and their family members gradually consolidated. According to Article 24 of the Medical Care Act in Taiwan, criminal penalty has been strengthened against those who threaten or attack medical professionals while the professionals are performing their duties. The harsh criminal penalty against medical malpractice has been lessened. A no-fault remedy system for birth injury incidents was adopted. More and more medical facilities adopted the litigation and dispute risk management system under the support of the government. Furthermore, through the collaboration of medical and legal professionals, a paradigmatic institution of medical dispute mediation was developed in Taiwan. After 2012, the annual number of civil cases referred for the MRC has been increasing slowly, but the annual number of criminal cases decreased (https://dep.mohw.gov.tw/DOMA/cp-2712-7681-106.html, in Chinese, accessed on August 20, 2020). Overall, as the indictment rate was about 9%, the annual numbers of criminal medical malpractice litigation were in general lower than those of civil ones (Chen 2019).

This chapter describes the main development of the systems managing medical disputes and medical malpractice in Taiwan. Although it is difficult to ascertain the causes for the above trend, the chapter provides a rough picture of what might have facilitated the development.

Section 2 briefs the basic legal principles of medical malpractice in Taiwan. Section 3 addresses the procedures and characteristics of medical malpractice in Taiwan before the year of 2012. Section 4 describes the alternative medical disputes resolution mechanisms in Taiwan about a decade ago. Section 5 presents the attitudes of the public in Taiwan towards medical malpractice. This could be used as a check on the medical malpractice policy. Section 6 depicts the current no-fault and quasi-no-fault compensation programs in Taiwan. Only vaccine injury (no-fault), drug injury (quasi-no-fault) and childbirth incidents (no-fault) are covered now.

Section 7 reviews the failed bills intending to systematically address medical disputes and medical malpractice in Taiwan. Section 8 depicts the later development of legislation related to medical malpractice and Sect. 9 the later development in mechanisms of alternative medical dispute resolution in Taiwan. Taiwan currently does not have a full-scale no-fault medical malpractice liability system. Through reforms in law, mediation procedure, reconciliation procedure and cooperation among governments at different levels and different professionals may continue to facilitate the development of a better medical malpractice system in the future.

2 Basic Legal Principles of Medical Malpractice in Taiwan Before 2012

Taiwan has a two-pronged system of medical malpractice litigation. The patients and/or family members could seek justice both from the civil courts and the criminal courts. In the traditional fault based medical malpractice litigation in Taiwan, the courts have to consider four elements to determine whether the sued healthcare facilities and/or practitioners are liable for the damage: negligence, injury, causation and healthcare relationship. Since this chapter's focus is on the trend of medical malpractice policy in Taiwan, it will only describe briefly the principles of determining negligence, causation and harm. The complicated legal theories of medical malpractice will not be covered.

If a healthcare professional failed to fulfill the duty of care, (s)he will be deemed negligent. According to paragraph 1 of Article 14 of the Criminal Code in Taiwan, a conduct is committed negligently if the actor fails, although not intentionally, to fulfill the duty of care to the extent that (s)he could exercise and should have exercised in the circumstances. Based on paragraph 2 of the same article, a conduct is considered to have been committed negligently if the actor is aware that his/her conduct would, but firmly believes it will not, accomplish the element of an offense. A healthcare professional has to fulfill two kinds of duties: one is to reasonably predict the bad outcome based on science and professional knowledge; the other is to reasonably avoid the bad outcome by taking preventive measures or avoiding risky practices. These formal definitions are also taken up by the civil courts. The "could" in the above definition is prima facie determined based on the objective criteria, such as a reasonable expectation of quality care towards professionals holding medical licenses. The contents of reasonable prediction and avoidance of bad outcome are determined based on medical custom or what an ordinary healthcare professional with due diligence and caution would do in the circumstances (Chen 2014). Before their revisions on May 10, 2019, according to Articles 276 (negligent homicide) and 284 (negligent harm and severe harm) of the Criminal Code in Taiwan, all people in the course of conducting business (including healthcare professionals) were required to bear a higher business/occupational duty of care and harsher penalty than laypeople when their negligent practices lead to a victim's death, harm or severe harm.

In civil cases, healthcare professionals could be liable for tortious behavior or failure to fulfill a healthcare contract. Negligence has been interpreted as the failure of a healthcare professional to perform as a good administrator (Taiwan Supreme Court, 42 Tai-Appeal No. 865 (1953)). Since healthcare contract is interpreted to be similar to the contract of mandate, healthcare professionals are required to perform as a good administrator who according to the common conception has reasonable experience, caution and diligence in healthcare practices. If a healthcare professional does not disclose adequate information to the patient party or, among others, fail to realize the goal of the contract without justified causes, (s)he must bear the liability for contract violation. The formulation of the duty of care by a good administrator is also adopted when malpractice is raised in tort litigation. Those healthcare professionals who fail to fulfill such duty will be deemed negligent. In some rare occasion, based on the Hand formula (burden of precaution should be less than the loss times its probability) a court ruled that a healthcare professional was negligent in prescribing Vitamin B1 that not only brought no definite treatment benefit but also induced severe allergy that led to a patient's fatality (Taiwan Supreme Court, 98 Tai-Appeal No. 656 (2009)).

The Consumer Protection Act came into force in Taiwan in 1994. It covers the no-fault liability of enterprise products and services. Since it does not provide a definition of service, healthcare service could be covered by the Act. There were reports that some patients sought resolution of their medical malpractice disputes through a consumption disputes process (Liu et al. 1997). Following a milestone court ruling on a case of birth injury due to shoulder dystocia (Taiwan Taipei District Court, 85 Litigation No. 5125 (1996)), some courts in Taiwan charged physicians or medical facilities with no-fault liability in medical malpractice cases. According to Article 7 of the Act then, service enterprise operators have to be liable for the safety or health risk caused by their services. The damage amount awarded to the patients may be reduced if the operators could prove the services were not negligently provided. This innovative but hasty application of the Act to medical malpractice aroused fierce legal debates among legal scholars and roars from medical professionals. Although the majority of court decisions did not deem healthcare practices as covered by the Consumer Protection Act (Liu and Wu 2019), there was no consensus among the courts in the following years, until the revision of the Medical Care Act in 2004. Article 82 of the Act stipulated that physicians or medical facilities were liable only for intentional or negligent medical malpractices. Even now, there remain debates on whether cosmetic surgery, not aiming at treating injuries, diseases or deformities, may be construed as services covered by the Consumer Protection Act (Liu and Wu 2019; Wei 2017).

In Taiwan, informed consent has become a standard practice required both in statutes related to general and specific healthcare practices such as end of life care. Informed consent is a collateral obligation for the healthcare professionals in their healthcare encounters with the patient parties, no matter interpreted from the lens of contract or tort. Healthcare professionals will be liable for negligence in obtaining informed consent from the patient party, even if they were not negligent in offering the technical treatment to their patients. In more than a decade ago, healthcare professionals tended to use the informed consent form to obtain the consent of the patients or their legal representatives, spouses, relatives or significant others. In 2005 the Taiwan Supreme Court ruled that a healthcare professional must verbally explain the benefits and risks of the medical procedures before obtaining consent of the qualified parties (Taiwan Supreme Court, 94 Tai-Appeal No.2676 (2005)) (Yang 2005). It means that a signed consent form could still be challenged in the court for lacking appropriate informed consent. With some exceptions such as emergency or civil commitment, violation of the duty of informed consent is interpreted as infringement of patients' autonomy. It is construed as civil negligence in tort or medical contract law, but not as criminal negligence (Lu et al. 2018).

In Taiwan, courts adopt the theory of adequate causation in determining healthcare malpractice. To conclude that negligent healthcare practices led to injuries, the courts have to be convinced: (a) but for the negligent healthcare practices, injuries would not have happened; (b) the negligent healthcare practice usually would lead to the injuries in the circumstances of the malpractice. An adequate cause needs not to be a proximate or direct cause, but the causal process could be interrupted by other intervening events. After a court determines that the malpractice caused an injury, it has to determine the extent of harm in order to rule on the civil damage or criminal penalty (Chen 2014). The healthcare professional will be punished or liable for the damage of a harm to the extent that the harm has an adequate causal relationship with the malpractice. In some cases, the court will use the theory of loss of chance of survival to determine the amount of the damage based on a consideration of the value of human life (Chen 2014).

In civil medical malpractice, a healthcare professional (or facility) may be required to bear the burden of proof if a court determines that (a) the professional (facility) has a major fault (similar to *res ipsa loquitur*), (b) the professional (facility) has the total control of the domain of injury risk, or (c) there is prominent inequality in the plaintiff's access to relevant evidence and knowledge (Chen 2014). Based on the principle of fair trial, Article 277 of the Taiwan Code of Civil Procedure stipulates that "*a party bears the burden of proof with regard to the facts which he/she alleges in his/her favor, except where the law provides otherwise or where the circumstances render it manifestly unfair.*" The shift of the burden of proof could be related to negligence, causation and even the extent of harm. The proviso of this article allows the court the discretion to shift the burden of proof from the complaining plaintiff to the defending medical facilities or healthcare professionals. Many scholars have argued for specification of the basis and conditions for the shift of the burden of proof and recommended the German legal framework that the use of the principle should be restricted to the dispute regarding a serious medical fault. It is hoped that the restricted interpretation could lessen the uncertainty in legal conception and lessen the feelings of anxiety and insecurity of healthcare professionals in their practices (Liu 2020).

3 Medical Malpractice Litigation in Taiwan

The injured patients and/or their family members could use the criminal litigation to force the healthcare professionals to negotiate for paying the damage. The presumed victims of medical injuries and/or their qualified family members may append their civil actions for damage to the criminal medical malpractice litigation. One procedural benefit is that the plaintiff in an ancillary civil action does not need to pay litigation fees to the court as their counterparts in pure civil litigation do. Since prosecutors are in charge of investigation, indictment and litigation, the plaintiff's need to hire a lawyer in criminal medical malpractice litigation is much reduced.

Criminal medical malpractice complaints had the following four characteristics: high investigation rate, low indictment rate, low conviction rate and low prison sentence rate (Lin 2015). Although the annual numbers of formally indicted cases of medical malpractice were low compared to those of civil cases, the numbers of criminal complaints against healthcare personnel and those of referral to the MRC review were not low (Chen 2015). Around 80% of the MRC review cases came from the criminal medical malpractice procedure (Lin 2014). As the number of formal criminal complaints of medical malpractice increased, the rates of indictment in the investigated complaints decreased from 36.7% in 2002 to 9.1% in 2011 (Chen 2015). From January 2002 to June 2012, among the 2,526 medical malpractice complaints handled by prosecutors in Taiwan, only 8.31% led to the indictment (Yang and Huang 2015).

In the 277 criminal medical malpractice cases, from January 2000 to June 2010, there were 380 physicians indicted. Among the indicted physicians, 35% worked in medical centers, outnumbering those in other facilities. Almost all cases were referred for medical professional review (95.7%) and 28.9% of the reviews opined that physicians were negligent in the concerned practices. 75.5% of the indicted professionals were sentenced not guilty. It implied that the criminal courts adopted the review opinions most of the time (Liu 2011). A study in 2014 found that in the criminal cases (N = 365) with final and binding court decisions, 61.7% (N = 245) went to appeal. In 93.5% of those sentenced not guilty in the district court (N = 174), the sentences were maintained. Only 61.0% of the guilty decisions were maintained during the appeal. On average, it took 4.77 years to reach the final binding decision after the presumed medical injury happened (Liu 2016).

In 672 civil medical malpractice cases in district courts (January 1997–February 2010), three leading medical specialties complained of are internal medicine (26%), surgery (24%) and gynecology/obstetrics (17%). The basis of the complaints was mainly tort or medical contract violation. As regards the damage amount requested by the plaintiffs, in 24% of cases the amount was around 33,000–66,000 U.S. dollars. Only in 12% of cases, the requested damage amount exceeded 333,000 U.S. dollars. In 79.6% of civil cases, the courts made decisions after the referral of the cases for the reviews of the MRC or medical centers. 90% of the courts that referred their cases for a medical malpractice review adopted the conclusions of the reviews. Only 20.6% of the plaintiff won their cases and the majority of the awarded damages were below

100,000 U.S. dollars (Shen and Chuang 2012). In 1,270 district court civil cases, between 2002 and 2013, plaintiffs won 15.0% of cases. Among the court decisions for the plaintiff that were appealed (50.5% of those for the plaintiff), 67.7% were ruled for the plaintiff again. In the court decisions for the defendants that were appealed (34.4% of those for the defendants), 92.7% were maintained by the appellate courts (Wu et al. 2017). On average, the civil medical malpractice litigation last 4.02 years in the district courts, 1.6 years in the appellate courts, and an extra 0.9 years in the supreme court (Shen and Chuang 2012).

In medical malpractice litigation, the courts usually have to address complicated and difficult medical technical issues. It is hard for the courts or the prosecutors to grasp what the duty is of a good administrator or an ordinary healthcare professional with reasonable knowledge, experience, and integrity. The reports of the MRC or medical centers on medical malpractice have played an important role in the courts' free evaluation of evidence and inner conviction (Wu 2019). The names of the members of the MRC or the experts of medical centers are not listed in the reports. They do not need to testify in court or face cross examinations. It takes about 6–9 months to complete the medical malpractice reports through medical chart reviews. Due to their lack of medical knowledge, the courts or the prosecutors (under the requests of complaining or litigating parties) sometimes could not pose the precise, relevant questions when they entrusted the MRC or medical centers to conduct the medical malpractice review. About 27.6% of cases had repeated medical malpractice reviews to clarify disputed issues. This is one of the reasons why medical malpractice litigation consumes longer time than other types of litigation (Liao 2015; Chu 2018).

4 Alternative Medical Disputes Resolution Mechanisms in Taiwan

4.1 The Mediation by Township and County-Administered City

In Taiwan, mediation may be conducted by three different organs: Township and County-administered City (TC), local health authority (LHA) or court (Ct). In the dispute settlement procedure, mediation (TC) and mediation (LHA) belong to the alternative dispute resolution (ADR), while mediation (Ct) is a part of the litigation procedure. Traditionally, people in the gentry level could mediate and reasonably resolve conflicts related to civil or mild criminal affairs between people. This mechanism could reduce the litigation caseload, enhance neighborhood harmony, and promote peace in society. According to the Township and County-Administered City Mediation Act, townships and county-administered cities shall establish the mediation committees to handle the mediation of civil cases or criminal cases in which no trial will begin without complaint. The mediation committee consists of non-partial members who are appointed for their legal knowledge, other expertise, or good reputation (Wu 2016). According to the Act, the mediation (TC) is not mandatory and may not be conducted without the agreement of the disputing parties. Once the mediation (TC) is successful and its agreement is approved by a court before the litigation ruling is final and binding, the litigation is concluded. The court-approved mediation agreement has the power of a final and binding civil court decision and may be used as the ground for civil enforcement.

The mediation (TC) in this Act has the advantage of respecting the autonomy of the disputing parties and adopting a simple and convenient procedure. The court-approved mediation agreement has the effect of res judicata. However, the members of the mediation committee actually do not have medical expertise and are not able to examine the medical malpractice review. The use of mediation (TC) to resolve medical disputes is hindered because it cannot satisfy the need of patients and their family to know the truth of medical malpractice (Chen 2002). Medical disputes were seldom resolved through this mechanism of mediation (Chu 2018).

4.2 The Mediation by Local Health Authority

According to the Medical Care Act that came into force in 1986, local governments have to establish local medical review committees, the missions of which include the mediation of medical disputes. The design of alternative medical dispute resolution is customized and localized based on the need and resource of different local governments.

According to the Act, either parties in the medical disputes may apply, in writing, to local health authority for conducting mediation (LHA). Screening out the unqualified application, the local health authority will inquire whether the other party agrees to the conduction of mediation. As both disputing parties agree to mediation, local health authority will designate one to several mediators to conduct mediation at the mediation meeting. The mediators may be healthcare professionals, legal professionals or impartial community members. When deemed necessary, the mediators may seek expert opinions before conducting the mediation. Expert opinions are not binding. During mediation, there is no review on the attribution of fault and the expert opinions may not be admissible as evidence in medical malpractice litigation. According to the official statistics of the Ministry of Health and Welfare (MOHW) in Taiwan, in 2002–2011 there were 4,540 cases of mediation by the local health authority, in which 1,671 (36.8%) were successfully mediated (Huang et al. 2020).

There are several disadvantages in this mediation's design. It does not provide medical malpractice review and may not restrict the rights of patients or their family to complain to the courts. The mediation agreement does not have the legal power of compulsory enforcement. The disputing parties have not been highly motivated to agree to use the mediation (LHA) procedure (Chu and Lin 2003; Chen 2013a). Due to its lack of medical expertise, local health authorities have to rely on representatives from medical associations in conducting mediation. This may raise the patient party's stereotyped suspicion of doctors shielding one another and indirectly reduce the motivation for negotiation (Chen 2011). Some patient parties might look forward to disciplining healthcare professionals or facilities who were responsible for medical injuries. To the disappointment of these patient parties, discipline is not part of the goal of the mediation (LHA) (Li 2015).

4.3 The Mediation by the Court or Referred by the Prosecutor

In Taiwan, since mediation (TC) and the mediation (LHA) are not mandatory, a patient party, in a medical dispute, may choose to skip mediation (TC) or mediation (LHA) procedures and engage in medical malpractice litigation directly.

In criminal cases, if the patient party complains to a prosecutor or engages in private prosecution, the prosecutor or the court may transfer the case for mediation (Ct) ex officio or with the agreement of the disputing parties (Articles 248–2, 271–4 in the Taiwan Code of Criminal Procedure). In civil cases, unless a patient party has gone through an unsuccessful mediation (Ct), it may not initiate a civil action in a court or append a supplementary civil action to a medical malpractice criminal litigation (Article 403 of the Taiwan Code of Civil Procedure). The mediation (Ct) for civil medical malpractice may be conducted by court-appointed mediation members or the sitting judges (Article 406–1 of the Taiwan Code of Civil Procedure). If the dispute was not successfully mediated, outside of the litigation procedure, it is also difficult for the disputing parties to reach an agreement via the mediation by the court or referred by the prosecutor (Chen 2011). Courts could skip the mediation (Ct) procedure based on the following reasons: mediation is not necessary; there is little hope of successful mediation; or there was a previous unsuccessful mediation (Article 406 of the Taiwan Code of Civil Procedure) (Lin 2014).

The court not having good enough medical knowledge, it is not clear whether the court performs better in mediation than the mediation members in the above-mentioned other mediation mechanisms. As medical disputing parties seek litigation, the appropriateness or liability of medical practices has been the focus of disputes, the court has to count on medical malpractice review to conduct the mediation. As the number of medical malpractice review increases, it may take up to 5–6 years for a medical malpractice litigation to finalize (Chen 2013b). The dream of using court mediation to efficiently address medical disputes is yet to come true in Taiwan.

4.4 Reconciliation

In medical disputes, often patients or their family members argue with medical staff or medical facilities and seek an explanation, apology and/or remedy. One of the best ways to avoid medical malpractice litigation is to clarify the facts, soothe the emotion of the patient party and obtain its understanding at the early stage of the dispute. In the 516 events of medical disputes in a medical center in Taiwan in 2002–2004, 80% did not evolve into litigation through immediate risk management (Chen 2011). In Taiwan, instead of objective truth and legal norm, the prioritized cultural considerations in a negotiation between both parties in a medical dispute are favors, face saving, moral responsibility, and harmony. It was argued that to resolve medical disputes, reconciliation is the best practice that is compatible with Taiwan's culture (Chu and Lin 2003).

4.5 *Arbitration*

According to Articles 3 and 5 in the Arbitration Act in Taiwan, arbitration could be initiated only based on an arbitration agreement between the disputing parties or a contract that has an arbitration clause. The target of arbitration should be limited to those that may be settled in accordance with the law. Basically, cases of civil medical malpractice litigation could be resolved through arbitration according to the agreement of the disputing parties. As regards complaint-mandated criminal medical malpractice litigation, one could withdraw the complaint and initiates an arbitration based on agreement.

Because arbitration is not open to the public, it was rarely heard that a medical malpractice dispute was resolved by arbitration. The number of this kind of arbitration is unknown (Chang 2017). Arbitrators in medical malpractice cases tend to include medical experts. Compared to mediation that is free of charge, arbitration is not favored because the parties have to make an agreement to pay for the arbitration. In the circumstances that arbitration fee is no less than the litigation fee, disputing parties may prefer using the familiar litigation procedure.

In Table 1, we show a comparison of different alternative dispute resolution mechanisms regarding professionalism (the mediator's medical expertise), patient party's

Table 1 Alternative medical dispute resolution mechanisms

Category	Reconciliation	Mediation			Arbitration
		Township/City	Health authority	Court	
Professionalism	Not related	Weak	Strong	Moderate	Strong
Fairness impression	Weak	Strong	Moderate	Strong	Strong
Fee payment	Nil	Nil	Nil	Nil	Yes
Res Judicata	Nil	Yes	Nil	Yes	Yes
Enforcement title	Nil#	Yes	Nil#	Yes	Yes

If the medical party refuses to pay, the patient party has to litigate for obtaining the enforcement title

fairness impression, the party's fee payment for utilizing the procedure, and the res judicata and enforcement title of the results.

5 Public Attitudes Towards Medical Malpractice in Taiwan

In December 2012, one of the authors conducted a telephone questionnaire survey of a representative sample (N = 1,367) of the public in Taiwan about their attitudes towards medical malpractice. 59.8% of the surveyees agreed that the goal of medical malpractice is for recovering damage and 58.1% for blaming or punishing physicians and medical facilities. Much larger proportions of the surveyees recognized the goals as enhancing the quality of care (91.4%) or finding the truth in medical malpractice (89.9%). 50.3% of the surveyees agreed that civil litigation is enough for addressing the fault of healthcare professionals, but 71.6% agreed that criminal punishment is needed only when physicians commit a serious fault in harming patients (Wu et al. 2013).

69.9% of the surveyees accepted the statement that current medical malpractice institution could not award those malpractice victims the damage they are justified to recover. 36.9% of the surveyees still thought that the plaintiffs had a more than 20% chance of winning a malpractice case. Based on the empirical data about medical malpractice litigation, their impressions were incorrect.

In the circumstances of mild medical injury, 94.8% agreed that they would not sue physicians or medical facilities if they received explanations about what happened and were offered a remedy. In the circumstances of severe medical injury and death with explanations and remedy offered, 63.3% and 65.5% of surveyees will still sue the physicians or medical facilities (Wu et al. 2013). It shows that, unless there is legal protection, healthcare professionals' apology and explanation regarding severe medical injury carries a significant risk of medical malpractice.

80.1% of the surveyees agreed that compared to litigation, no-fault remedy institutions could benefit more medical injury victims and their family members. 84.1% agreed that medical experts in the no-fault institution could make an accurate determination about medical injury than the judges. 86.9% agreed that we should set upper limits of damage awarded for different levels of harm in the no-fault institution. 79.0% of the surveyees agreed that in the no-fault institution medical professionals are more willing to disclose the facts and thus patient safety planning could be enhanced. 66.3% of them agreed that this institution could diminish the opposition between the medical professionals and the patients and their family members (Wu et al. 2013).

Although in the survey the public did not favor criminal punishment as a way of addressing all medical injuries, above empirical statistics still showed that criminal complaints of medical malpractice outnumbered the civil action cases. As the proportion of indictment was about 10% of all criminal complaints, the prosecutors actually act as gatekeepers who screen out the litigation unworthy complaints. Public opinions disfavoring criminal punishment for medical malpractice policy are different from the strategic moves of the complaining parties in medical injury events.

6 No-Fault and Quasi-no-Fault Medical Injury Compensation Programs in Taiwan

There has been a call to set up a medical malpractice no-fault liability system in Taiwan. The above failed venture to apply the Consumer Protection Act to medical malpractice, is just one example. Although Taiwan does not have a no-fault medical malpractice liability system, it has incorporated no-fault remedy institutions in different fields of healthcare practices. In the beginning only the use of vaccines and pharmaceuticals were covered. Later endeavor to apply similar institutions to medical procedures succeeded only in the field of obstetrics. The subsections will introduce the vaccination injury, pharmaceutical injury and birth incident emergency compensation programs. Table 2 shows a concise comparison among the three programs.

Table 2 Comparisons among compensation programs of vaccine injury (VICP), drug injury (DIRP) and birth incident emergency (BIERP)

Category	VICP	DIRP	BIERP
Claimant	Patient, legal representative, heir	Patient, legal representative, heir	Patient, heir, mother of the fetus
Period of prescription	Within 2 years after the injury is known or within 5 years after the injury	Within 3 years after the injury is known	Within 2 years after the incidence is known or within 10 years after the incidence
Upper limits of compensation (one U.S. dollar = 30 New Taiwan dollars)	200 thousand U.S. dollars	66.7 thousand U.S. dollars	133.3 thousand U.S. dollars
No-fault compensation	Yes	No	Yes
Duration for review	6 months; no more than 9 months	3 months; no more than 4 months	3 months; no more than 6 months
Permission for concurrent litigation	Yes	Yes	No
Compensation recovery by competent authority	No	Yes, if the patient is awarded damage or other remedy based on the same fact	yes, if the court rules that healthcare professionals are liable
Subrogation by competent authority	No	Yes, towards those who are liable	Yes, towards those who are liable

6.1 Vaccine Injury Compensation Program (VICP)

After an incident of polio infection, caused by an oral polio vaccination in 1986, Taiwan government promulgated a regulation regarding vaccine injury compensation in 1988. The government established a fund to compensate for those who suffered from vaccine regardless of whether healthcare professionals were negligent in vaccination. For each dose of the vaccine, the vaccine manufacturers or the import companies had to donate 1–1.5 NT dollars (about 0.033–0.05 US dollar) to the fund. A Vaccine Injury Compensation Working Group under the MOHW in Taiwan has been in charge of determining whether an injury was caused by a vaccination. Based on the severity of injury, there have been four categories of compensation upper limits: death (maximum amount 200,000 U.S. dollars), disability (maximum amount 167,000 U.S. dollars), serious illness (maximum amount 33,300 U.S. dollars) and other adverse reactions (maximum amount 6,700 U.S. dollars). There are three levels of strength of causal relationship between vaccination and injury: positive, non-excludable, and nil. Those expected mild and usually seen vaccine injuries are not compensated. Compensation will not be awarded to those suffering from conversion or psychogenic symptoms related to vaccination. In cases where the causal relationship between vaccination and the injury was nil, the Working Group may determine to cover the claimant's healthcare fees for clarifying the causal relationship or funeral fees. In general, the determination of the compensation would be issued within 9 months (https://www.cdc.gov.tw/Category/Page/OM4QgMRlmzYg5UDLHlnXRw, in Chinese, accessed on July 17, 2020).

Through 2019, there were about 1,900 applicants for the vaccine injury compensation. In total, 4 million U.S. dollars of compensation were awarded to about 45% of the claimants. As the Working Group's determination is deemed an administrative sanction, any claimant who is not satisfied with the determination may petition the decision and then complains at the administrative court if his or her petition fails (https://www.cdc.gov.tw/Category/Page/OM4QgMRlmzYg5UDLHlnXRw, in Chinese, accessed on July 17, 2020). In general, there were only a few litigated cases regarding vaccine injuries. In 2017, in one case regarding vaccine induced autoimmune disease the court ruled that the Working Group should have awarded compensation to a claimant if it was unable to offer an explanation other than vaccination injury to the death of a vaccinated adolescent (Supreme Administrative Court. 106 Sentence No. 355 (2017)). A mere expert assertion that vaccination did not cause the death may not be construed as excluding vaccination from being the cause of death. After this court decision, Taiwan Centers for Disease Control modified the term of remedy from "non-excludable" to "non-ascertainable", hoping that the Working Group does not need to award a remedy in circumstances where the possibility of vaccine injury is very low (yet, non-excludable). As the courts sometimes tended to expand the domain of compensation, there has been a trend to limit the amount of compensation in the regulation and practice of the Work Group.

6.2 Drug Injury Relief Program (DIRP)

In the 1970s–1980s, many people with hemophilia, including those living in Taiwan, died due to HIV infection after their use of contaminated blood products (Chou 2005). In 1997, there were more than 100 cases of patients who suffered or even died from liver toxicity induced by Lamisil or Sporanox (Lee and Yang 2014). Addressing the important drug safety problem, Taiwan government established a drug adverse reaction report system in 1998 and promulgated the Drug Injury Relief Act that came into effect in 2000. In 2001, Taiwan Drug Injury Relief Foundation was established to take charge of the affairs of drug injury relief. According to the Act, using the levy from pharmaceutical manufacturers and the importing companies as the major source, Taiwan government sets up a Drug Injury Relief Fund to compensate for the drug injury. In 2019, the amount of levy reached about 2.76 million U.S. dollars (Wu and Chen 2020). Through 2019, there have been 3,505 applications for drug injury relief. In total, over 16.6 million U.S. dollars were awarded to 58% of the claimants (https://www.tdrf.org.tw/apply04/, in Chinese, accessed on July 13, 2020).

As the drug injury relief fund only affords "limited liability", it does not cover mild injuries, usual and expectable drug injuries, injuries by experimental drugs, or drug overdose during the emergency care. Designating upper limits of relief amount for each injury level, it only covers severe drug injury (maximum amount 20,000 U.S. dollars per case), disability cause by drug injury (maximal amount 66,700 U.S. dollars per case) or death (maximal amount 66,700 U.S. dollars per case).

The MOHW in Taiwan has established the Drug Injury Relief Review Committee to review the applications. Different from the above no-fault scheme of vaccine injury compensation, the Review Committee will not award the relief if it is ascertained that the drug injury victims, pharmaceutical manufacturers, importing companies, the prescribing physicians or others are at fault in causing the drug injury. In addition, the scheme only covers the justified and reasonable use of drugs licensed by the competent authority. An off-label use that is supported by the known, credible medical literature is also considered justified and reasonable use. This is a quasi-no-fault relief scheme (Lee and Yang 2014). It only covers the cases in which no one should be blamed or in circumstances where no cause, other than drug adverse reaction, could reasonably explain the injury. The Review Committee is required to provide relief less than the upper-limit amount at its discretion.

Similar to the VICP, the decision of the Review Committee is deemed an administrative sanction. The claimant for the drug relief may petition for an administrative remedy and then complains at the administrative court to revoke the petition committee's decision that does not support his or her petition. Irrespective of the decision the Review Committee makes, the claimants still hold the right to the conduction criminal or civil litigation based on the drug injury. Few cases of drug injury litigation were noted. In one unusual case that was appealed to the Constitutional Court, the majority opinion (Interpretation No. 767 on July 27, 2018) ruled for the exclusion of the usual and expectable drug injury (probability > 1%) from relief is constitutional (https://cons.judicial.gov.tw/jcc/zh-tw/jep03/show?expno=767, in Chinese, accessed on Aug. 28, 2020). Accepting the exclusion's policy goal to avoid the fund's financial infirmity and the pharmaceutical companies' reluctance to manufacture or import effective drugs, the opinion held that the regulation does not violate the principle of legal certainty, the principle of proportionality and people's right to life and health. The constitutional court counted on healthcare professionals' informed consent practices to allocate the risk of drug injury among patients, healthcare professionals, the drug relief fund, and other liable entities. Based on respect for the legislative power, the interpretation actually is cautious in enlarging the pool of persons receiving drug relief.

6.3 Childbirth Accident Emergency Relief Program (BIERP)

Gynecology/obstetrics have been one of the leading specialties with high medical malpractice risk in Taiwan. About a decade ago, it was noted that the number of medical students applying for gynecology/obstetrics was decreasing and many qualified gynecologists/obstetricians even refused to practice obstetrics. This trend was attributed to increased risk of medical malpractice in obstetrics (Wang et al. 2017).

To offer pregnant women reasonable protection against the risk of birth incident and reduce the conflicts between obstetricians and patients, the MOHW in Taiwan set up a Compensation Pilot Program on Birth Incidents in 2012. The program is medical facility based. Both the obstetricians and the patients have to sign an agreement on the compensation first, and then medical facilities may apply for compensation from the government (Kao and Kao 2014). If a patient raises a civil suit in the court and the fault is attributed to either party, the liable party has to return the proportion of compensation to the government. The upper limit of compensation amount was categorized according to the severity of the birth incident: death of the pregnant woman (maximal amount 66,700 U.S. dollars), death of the fetus or the newborn (maximal amount 10,000 U.S. dollars), profound disability of the pregnant woman or the newborn (maximal amount 50,000 U.S. dollars), severe disability of the pregnant woman or the newborn (maximal amount 43,300 U.S. dollars), and moderate disability of the pregnant women or the newborn (maximal amount 36,700 U.S. dollars). In general, the decision on the compensation was made within 3–4 months.

After three years of implementing the pilot program, the number of medical malpractice litigation in obstetrics diminished by 70% and the number of medical students applying for gynecology/obstetrics increased gradually (Ministry of Health and Welfare 2019). This scheme of the pilot program was transformed into the provisions of the Childbirth Accident Emergency Relief Act that came into effect in 2016. The chief source of the relief comes from the grants from the government budget and the Health and Welfare Surcharges on Tobacco Products.

In the pilot program, once the medical facility received compensation from the government, the obstetrician would be deemed not liable by a review committee that determined the compensation. There is criticism against the review committee's taking the place of the court in determining liability (Huang 2016). Similar to the VICP, the Act has adopted a no-fault relief scheme covers injuries or death similar to those in the pilot program. The range of coverage has been expanded in the Act to include loss of fertility due to uterine resection (maximal amount 26,700 U.S. dollars) and other injuries to the body and health that are severe and incurable or difficult to cure as recognized by the central competent authority (maximal amount 10,000 U.S. dollars). Upper limits of the relief amounts have been increased for the death of pregnant women (maximal amount 133,000 U.S. dollars), profound disability for pregnant women and newborns (maximal amount 100,000 U.S. dollars), severe disability (maximal amount 66,600 U.S. dollars) and moderate disability (maximal amount 50,000 U.S. dollars).

From 2016 through 2018, there were 576 applications for the birth incident emergency relief, 557 of which (96.7%) were granted relief by the review committee. The total amount of emergency relief added up to 9.2 million U.S. dollars (Ministry of Health and Welfare 2019).

7 Bills on the Medical Dispute Management and Compensation

In the twenty first century Taiwan, there have been two opposing positions (the mediation camp v. the compensation camp) in drafting bills to deal with medical disputes. The mediation camp favors pre-litigation mandated mediation and advocates for strengthening current mediation mechanisms and arbitration agreement. Emphasizing the importance of reducing the amount of litigation and allowing the patient party to be awarded as soon as possible, the compensation camp promotes a quasi-no-fault compensation institution. If later medical malpractice review shows that medical professionals or facilities should be liable, then the liable entities need to make up the loss of the compensation fund for the previous payment to the patient party. The government did not have any convincing actuarial analysis of the potential payment through the quasi no fault payment. The mediation camp worries whether it is fair to distribute the cost of medical care risk to the whole society and whether the quasi-no-fault payment would induce moral hazard and threaten the financial health of the compensation fund. The compensation camp argued that the mediation camps for its conservative emphasis on procedure and overlapping designs of mediation and litigation. The mediation camp was criticized for its failure to adopt complementary compensatory measures of insurance or fund to support compensation. Without an adequate remedy institution, the mediation camp's proposal was deemed not supportive enough to the healthcare professionals when facing patients and their family members. In the stalemate, no bill proposed by both camps could consolidate and prevail to become law (Legislative Yuan nd).

7.1 The 2012 Bill Regarding Management of Medical Disputes and Compensation for Medical Incidents

In 2012, integrating the opinions of both camps, the Executive Yuan proposed the "Bill Regarding Management of Medical Disputes and Compensation for Medical Incidents." The Bill emphasized both the strengthening of mediation procedure and the provision of immediate compensation. To enhance quality of medical care, it incorporated mechanisms of the sentinel event report, root cause analysis and quality improvement plan (https://www.moj.gov.tw/cp-21-115659-9dd1a-001.html, in Chinese, accessed on September 2, 2020). To facilitate the mediation process and soothe the feelings of the patient party, it adopted a simple version of the apology law by which healthcare professionals' expressions of apology could not be used as evidence against the professionals in the court of law. It established a quasi-no-fault compensation program, in which the compensation would be offered only when it is uncertain whether the professionals have faults. Different from the Childbirth Accident Emergency Relief Act, the Bill required the healthcare professionals and facilities to afford a proportion (no more than 30%) of the compensation fund (https://www.moj.gov.tw/cp-21-115659-9dd1a-001.html, in Chinese, accessed on September 2, 2020). However, the Bill did not get full supports from the legislators. In 2012–2014, there were up to 11 related competing bills proposed by different legislators. Medical societies could not agree on the monetary shares they need to dedicate out of pocket to the compensation fund. They issued an official statement opposing the adoption of the Bill (https://www.tma.tw/meeting/meeting_info.asp?meete_id=5736, in Chinese, accessed on September 1, 2020). The Bill never made to pass the second reading in the legislation process.

7.2 The 2018 Bill Regarding Medical Incident Prevention and Dispute Management

The mediation thought dominated the trend of later legislation. In 2018, after having shelved the controversial quasi-no-fault compensation scheme, the Executive Yuan proposed the Bill Regarding Medical Incident Prevention and Dispute Management. The Bill emphasized communication and caring, dispute mediation, and error reporting and prevention (https://www.mohw.gov.tw/cp-16-40687-1.html, in Chinese, accessed on September 2, 2020).

As regards communication and caring, the Bill requires hospitals to set up a communication and caring team to offer immediate care and support to the patient party who has complaints against a hospital or its employees. It incorporates apology law to encourage healthcare professionals to disclose the truth and apologize to the patient party without the fear of their apologies used against themselves. It aims to establish a specific review entity in charge of clarifying disputing issues and providing professional analysis as an impartial third party.

With the inputs from the specific review entity, according to the Bill, mediation is mandatory before the initiation of medical malpractice litigation. The result of the mediation may have binding force after it is approved by the court.

The Bill requires medical facilities to set up a patient safety management system and to investigate the root cause of sentinel event. Based on the results of the investigation, the facilities have to propose patient safety improvement plan and report to the central competent authority. For some severe sentinel events, the central competent authority may set up a task force to engage in investigation and make public the report. The investigation reports could not be used evidence in related medical malpractice litigation.

The Bill also did not go through the legislation process. Whether the Executive Yan would continue to promote the Bill in 2020 is still uncertain. The Bill lays out several important strategies to manage medical disputes that are developed separately at the local level through the efforts of administrative and judicial branches.

8 Later Development in Legislation Related to Medical Malpractice

The bills to systematically manage medical disputes did not prevail. Focusing on specific topics, later legislation has aimed to clarify the conditions of informed consent and duty of care in medical practices.

Patient Right to Autonomy Act was promulgated in 2016 and came into effect in January 2019. Its Article 5 modifies the practices of informed consent in Taiwan by requiring healthcare facilities or professionals to first inform the patient the information (disease condition, treatment policy, management, medication, prognosis, side effects, etc.) relevant to the medical treatment. Before that, when deemed appropriate by healthcare professionals, the patient may be excluded from the process of information provision. The promulgation of Article 5 of the Patient Right to Autonomy Act signified the shift of healthcare policy away from family-centered decision making. It is possible that the traditional practice of family consent might become an issue of civil medical malpractice in the future. It is worthy of exploration whether the individual-based scheme could be consolidated in real life practices by this kind of civil medical malpractice in the future.

In Taiwan, there were several versions of interpretations of the duty of care in court decisions. In 2017, for the first time, the Medical Care Act defined the components for the court to determine the duty of care and professional discretion in healthcare and makes the standard reasonable, tangible and concrete. According to the revised Article 82 of the Medical Care Act, the court should consider the objective conditions of medical custom, medical standards, medical equipment, work conditions, and emergency situation in the locality at the time of practice in the medical field concerned. It is still unknown whether this formulation could lessen the uncertainty in courts' decision of medical negligence. Urging the court to consider professional discretion, the revision might facilitate the courts to determine duty of care in favor of healthcare professionals. This formulation has been supported by a Taiwan Supreme Court ruling that the goal of the revision is to restrict the range of negligent liability of physicians (Taiwan Supreme Court, 107 Tai-Appeal No. 4587 (2019)). It is hard to define medical custom, medical standards and other conditions and to draw the normative line between what is due and not. It may still not be easy for the court to make a determination of negligence.

In May 2019, the provisions of heightened penalty for negligence in business practice was abolished in Articles 276 (negligent homicide) and 284 (negligent harm and severe harm) of the Criminal Code in Taiwan. The listed reasons for the revision are as follow: (a) the harm rendered by the professionals are not necessarily larger than that by the laypersons; (b) it is against the equality principle to expect and require the professionals to bear a higher duty of care to avoid risk; (c) in practice judges tended to expand the domain of business such that these articles were turned into the foundation of over-deterring practices (https://www.moj.gov.tw/cp-21-115659-9dd1a-001.html, in Chinese, accessed on September 2, 2020). Thus, the revision is a good news for healthcare professionals since it lessens their worry of harsh punishment for malpractice.

The later legislation seems to make the legal milieu of medical malpractice more friendly than ever to healthcare professionals in Taiwan.

9 Later Development of Mechanisms of Alternative Medical Dispute Resolution in Taiwan

Mediation has yet to accomplish its goal of diminishing the case numbers of medical malpractice litigation, as the number of medical disputes continued to increase and disputing parties have been reluctant to utilize the mediation procedure to resolve disputes.

To increase the effectiveness of court mediation, since 2012, Taiwan Taichung District Court initiated a pilot program that integrates medical dispute mediation, counseling and review. In each mediation, there are two expert mediation members, one having expertise in medicine and the other in law. In charge of providing medical opinions, mediation members with expertise in medicine are recommended by the Greater Taichung Medical Association. Retired judges, current judges or legal associative officers hold the positions of mediation members with expertise in law. They are in charge of providing legal opinions and making mediation plans based on the statement of the disputing parties (Lin 2014; Chen 2013). In the medical malpractice litigation, medical expert members are employed to provide counseling to the court. They help sort out the disputed issues and thus make clear the questions posed in the medical malpractice review. In Taichung District Court, medical malpractice review groups comprised of local medical centers are in charge of malpractice review. For hastening the completion of the medical malpractice review and avoid procrastination of court procedures, the service of the MRC is not utilized (Chen 2013).

After the pilot program was implemented, the mediation success rate reached above 40%. Medical counseling and local medical malpractice review were used in more than 40% of medical malpractice litigation in Taichung District Court. The time needed for completing medical malpractice reports was shortened by a wide margin (Chen 2016). Seeing this achievement, other district courts have imitated the Taichung District Court and customized the design of the court mediation procedure based on local resources and competency.

In 2017, the MOHW in Taiwan began to promote a plural-discipline pilot medical dispute mediation program. Two expert mediation members (one in medicine and the other in law) will sit in the same mediation procedure. For clarifying an unresolved issue, the third expert may join to express opinions on the issue. If a patient party makes a complaint in criminal procedure, the prosecutor may refer the case to the local health authority for mediation when (s)he deems mediation feasible for resolving the dispute. This scheme may facilitate the success of mediation and further reduce the number of medical malpractice litigation (Cheng and Chen 2018). In 2014–2018, in total 3,200 cases of mediation by the local health authority, 1,141 (35.7%) were accomplished (https://dep.mohw.gov.tw/DOMA/cp-2712-7681-106.html, in Chinese, accessed on August 20, 2020). As compared with the statistics in 2002–2011 (4,540 mediation cases with a success rate of 36.8%) (Huang et al. 2020), the statistics in 2014–2018 revealed a trend of increased use of this mediation mechanism. However, the mediation success rate did not improve much. The long-term effectiveness of this pilot mediation scheme is still unknown.

Although previous Bills failed to set up the legal foundation for communicating and caring programs, administrative efforts on this aspect have continued to grow. Since 2013, the MOHW has entrusted local health authorities to coach medical facilities in their jurisdictions to set up medical disputes communicating and caring groups (Ministry of Health and Welfare 2017). Led by the administrative supervisor of a medical facility, the communicating and caring group comprises legal staff, department chairpersons, head nurses, social workers, psychologists, experts and scholars, and disinterested community members. In some medical facilities supported by Christian organizations, chaplains are also one of the members in the group. Understanding that community clinics and district hospitals are unable to set up a full mediation team, in 2017, the MOHW initiated the program for quality improvement in medical dispute management. Through the program, local medical associations have been coached to set up community and caring groups to facilitate the reconciliation process in medical disputes (Ministry of Health and Welfare 2017).

Other than engaging in post hoc communication and caring to manage medical disputes, some medical facilities actively set up a proactive dispute resolution group to monitor and intervene into events that may potentially develop into medical disputes (Lin 2016). In general, once notified that a medical dispute has happened, the communicating and caring group will designate members to form a task force based on the types of disputes and what medical specialties are involved. One member is designated the role of a liaison person who understand the patient party's needs through establishing and maintaining a trust relationship with the patient party. The task force will collect relevant information, investigate the event and offer help and emotional support to the colleagues complained about by the patient party. Meetings between the disputing medical and patient parties are arranged. The task force will facilitate the dialogue and communication between the disputing parties through explanations, timely disclosure of investigation results, and empathy and emotional support to the patient party. No matter whether reconciliation is achieved, the communicating and caring group will continue to follow the development of the dispute via the contact person (Shih 2015). In recent years, experts have been developing courses of communicating and caring in medical disputes to train medical personnel. Some courses focus on facilitated mediation, some emotional support and others coordination skills (Lee, Chen, Research Team 2019). Lectures and training courses have been conducted (https://www.tdrf.org.tw/2019/06/26/news02-8/, in Chinese, accessed on September 1, 2020). Thus, communicating and caring to facilitate reconciliation has become an important field of alternative medical dispute resolution in Taiwan.

Finally, in 2020, in the 908 listed arbitrators, 19 already have the background in medicine, dental medicine, or hospital management (http://www.arbitration.org.tw/ArbitratorResults.php, in Chinese, accessed on August 17, 2020). It seems they could afford a certain amount of medical dispute arbitration. Scholars in Taiwan have been advocating for the use of arbitration to resolve medical disputes or the incorporation of arbitration in the medical dispute resolution bill. Like a court decision, arbitration decision could have res judicata. In addition, arbitration procedure is more rapid and private than litigation. It may become an alternative procedural choice that could be written into the medical care contract (Lin and Lu 2016; Liu et al. 2020).

10 Conclusion

The number of criminal medical disputes has diminished from 2012 in recent years (Fig. 1). Although it is difficult to tease out all the factors contributing to the diminution trend, active development of alternative dispute resolution mechanisms must be counted as an important one. Administrative branch both at the central and the local levels, local judicial branch and medical facilities have been working separately or together to diminish the burden of medical malpractice litigation. Through the cooperation of the experts in law and medicine, the Taiwan government has been endeavoring to help local health authorities to develop customized local mediation mechanisms and medical facilities to set up reconciliation mechanisms through communicating and caring. In the medical disputes, counseling and emotional support are provided to both the healthcare personnel and patient parties. Incorporating different stages of medical disputes, such as mediation, expert counseling and the local medical malpractice review, the Taichung District Court's mediation program has become a paradigm for the other court medical dispute resolution programs. The development seems to bring a promising future for medical malpractice management in Taiwan. To know the truth and improve quality of healthcare is more important than blaming health professionals and damage award. If the new mechanisms of alternative medical dispute resolution could achieve the prioritized policy goals (truth and quality), blaming healthcare professionals is not that important if the patient party could receive acceptable compensation following the above mechanisms. The prominent tension in the relationship between the healthcare professional party and the patient party could be relieved to a certain extent.

Although previous bills, intending to systematically manage medical disputes, did not succeed, the fierce debate has anchored the policy key points and facilitated the development of some domain-specific efforts to resolve medical disputes. No-fault or quasi-no-fault compensation programs were adopted incrementally only in vaccine injury, drug injury and childbirth incidents. The risk and cost redistribution through the levy of each vaccine or drug sales to establish a compensation fund is well accepted to the public in Taiwan. Not required to pay out of pocket to set up a fund to compensate for the childbirth incidents, gynecologists/obstetricians as the medical specialty carrying a high risk of medical malpractice litigation supported the legislation. In the legislative procedure of the 2012 ambitious Bill that intended to integrate the policy goals of mediation, quality improvement, and quasi-no-fault compensation, the unresolved issues of distributive justice finally failed the Bill. It means that based on current progress we need further discussion about distributive justice regarding risk, responsibility and wellbeing. One of the officers involving in the medical dispute resolution legislation once commented (Legislative Yuan nd): "*In the past, much information regarding medical dispute management was not disclosed because of its conflicting characteristics.*" "*As more empirical information is gathered and more ideas discussed, society will learn to a certain extent to determine whether to adopt a no-fault compensation scheme...*" As mediation is effective in managing the trend of medical disputes, the impetus to promote (quasi-)no-fault compensation has subsided.

Young physicians in residency training programs are deemed laborers in Taiwan. Some media reports and messages have revealed the work burden of healthcare professionals and their sufferings in medical malpractice litigation. Recent legislation efforts aim to lessen the risk of healthcare professionals being attacked, being over-punished, or being liable based on an uncertain standard. The recruitment of residents in the above medical specialties with insufficient supply of physicians began to improve (Huang 2018). There has been collaboration by different disciplines and governmental branches at different levels, the authors sincerely hope that with further inputs from academia and social discussion, Taiwan could reach a consensus on the policy regarding medical disputes and medical malpractice.

References

Chang T (2017) Research on applying arbitration to medical disputes: centered on the ADR experiences in the U.S. (in Chinese). Tunghai Univ Law Rev 51:217–69

Chen TC (2002) Issue discussion in the meeting regarding the current situation and prospect of the problems of medical incident liability in Taiwan, part 2 (in Chinese). Taiwan Law J 40:64–104

Chen TF (2011) Mechanisms for medical disputes resolution in taiwan: facts and criticisms (in Chinese). Cross-Strait Law Rev 34:5–22

Chen TF (2013a) Contentions on the legislation of medical malpractice mediation institution (in Chinese). Taiwan Law Rev 213:60–72

Chen HT (2013b) Ways to resolve medical risk and disputes: a discussion based on the pilot medical program in Taichung District Court (in Chinese). Taiwan Law Rev 174–215

Chen TF (2014) Formation and evolution of medical liability (in Chinese). Taipei: National Taiwan University Press

Chen WY (2015) Practices and legilation of mandated medical liability insurance (in Chinese). In: Chen HT (ed) Leal system and evidence of medical dispute management (in Chinese). Taipei: Angle Publishing, pp 253–89

Chen HT (2016) A humble proposal to improve civil medical malpractice litigation in Taiwan (in Chinese). Cross-Strait Law Rev 53:73–96

Chen HT (2019) Law and Economics analysis of the management of medical disputes (in Chinese). Medical liability insurance and law and economics (in Chinese). Taipei: Angle Publishing, pp 67–102

Cheng JS, Chen YC (2018) The challenges faced by the mediation program in the Medical Incident Prevention and Dispute Management Act (in Chinese). Taiwan Bar J 22(8):4–12

Chou FM (2005) Hemophilia and HIV-infected Hemophilia Patients' Illness Experiences in Taiwan (in Chinese). Taipei: Taipei Medical University

Chu CM (2018) The mediation of medical disputes by local health authority and township (in Chinese). The resource manual for managing medical disputes (in Chinese). Taipei: Joint Commission of Taiwan, p 51–6

Chu JJ, Lin DL (2003) How to obtain fairness in medical practice?: an exploration of the deficits in the mechanisms of medical dispute management (in Chinese). J Law Med 11((3.4)):31–61

Health Promotion Administration of the Ministry of Health and Welfare (2015) National Health Insurance 2015–2016 Annual Report 2015

Huang MC (2016) How to interpret the compensation law of childbirth-related Injury (in Chinese). Hospital 49(2):1–11

Huang TR (2018) The manpower in gynecology/obstetrics stops decline and began to inrease. Why is the vacancy of resident positions in gynecology/obstetrics completely filled after more than 10 years of difficult recruitment? (in Chinese, https://www.storm.mg/article/538631?page=1. Accessed September 1, 2020

Huang HH, Shen MZ, Liu XS, Yang ML (2020) The Control Yuan Investigation Report, 101 Finance Investigation No. 0120 (in Chinese). https://www.cy.gov.tw/CyBsBox.aspx?n=133&CSN=1&page=14&PageSize=200. Accessed August 20, 2020

Hung CL (2017). Resolving medical disputes! The Ministry of Health and Welfare proposed Medical Dispute Act again and dropped the controversial compensation design. https://www.healthettodaynet/news/1014555, in Chinese. Accessed September 2, 2020. 2017

Kao TF, Kao MY (2014) From the 'birth-related dispute incident pilot plan' to explore the 'medical disputes and medical incinent compensation law' legislative trends to view the medical community (in Chinese). J Law Med 21(2):21–34

Lee SY, Chen YC, Research Team (2019) The great reconciliation between physicians and patients: A educational manual to help physicians, nurses, phamacists, social workers, medical technologists, hospital administrative staff, patients and family members to learn empathy, care and self protection together Taipei: Ark

Lee MJ, Yang HI (2014). Is no-fault liability equal to no-blame?: discussion based on Subsection 1 Article 13 of Drug Injury Relief Act (in Chinese). Taiwan Law Rev 228:119–40
Li FA (2015) Addressing the practices of medical dispute mediation by local health authority (in Chinese). J Healthcare Quality 9(5):48–51
Liao JY (2015) The role of medical review in litigation (in Chinese). J Healthcare Quality 9(3):96–100
Lin YL (2014) Legal theory and practice of medical disputes: ADR Taichung experience (in Chinese). J Law Med 21(1):1–14
Lin DL (2015) The experience and implication of the open disclosure mechanism implemented in the U.S. and Australia: Exploring medical injury events in positive and constructive contexts (in Chinese). In: Chen HT, editor. Leal system and evidence of medical dispute management (in Chinese). Taipei: Angle Publishing, p 79–110
Lin HJ (2016) The first shot for preventing medical disputes: Crossing the strait between medical disputes and patient safety -addressing Proactive Dispute Resolution (PDR) (in Chinese). J Healthcare Quality. 10(3):18–23
Lin WC (2018) The current situation of medical dispute litigation and empirical research in Taiwan (in Chinese). China Law J 63(2):101–24
Lin CC, Lu LH (2016) The character of medical arbitration in ADR (Alternative Dispute Resolution) and the future in medical malpractice law (in Chinese). J Healthcare Quality 10(3):58–65
Liu PY (2011) An empirical study of medical malpractice judgments from district criminal courts in Taiwan: 2000–2010 (in Chinese). Technol Law Rev 8(2):257–94
Liu PY (2016) Empirical research on the appeal court decisions on criminal medical disputes (in Chinese). Academia Sinica Law J 18:267–313
Liu MS (2020) The allocation and shift of burden of proof in the causal relationship in establishing physician liability: centered on German law (in Chinese). Taiwan Law Rev 269:106–32
Liu HE, Wu TW (2019) A socio-legal study of aesthetic medicine and consumer protection act (in Chinese). Angle Health Law Rev 32:7–30
Liu PW, Chiu CH, Yang MG (1997) A study on medical disputes handled by the consumers' foundation in Taiwan (in Chinese). Chinese J Public Health 16(1):77–85
Liu CT, Shen RN, Wen CW, Huang YY (2020) A preliminary study on korean act on remedies for injuries from medical malpractice and mediation of medical disputes (in Chinese). Medical Disputes Manag. Taipei: Angle, pp 116–35
Lu YC, Liang HL (2018) Principl of informed consent and the liability of criminal negligence of medical act—development and evaluation of practical judgment in Taiwan (in Chinese). Court Case Times 69:90–107
Ministry of Health and Welfare (2017) Project report of the 10th Plenary Session of the Committee on Social Welfare and Health and environment of the Ninth Fourth Session of the Legislative Yuan
Ministry of Health and Welfare (2019) Annual report of childbirth incident relief (in Chinese). Taipei: Ministry of Health and Welfare
Shen KL, Chuang CH (2012) Evidence law and empirical study in medical malpractice litigation (in Chinese). Chengchi Law Rev 127:167–266
Shih CL (2015) Establishing effective patient safety communication model: the compositon and operation of communicating and caring group (in Chinese). J Healthcare Quality 9(6):4–8
Wang TH, Lin SF, Tsai KY, Liu YF (2017) Lessons from the MOHW compensation pilot program on birth incidents: First step and looking forward. Taiwanese J Obstetrics Gynecol 56(3):320–324
Wei LC (2017) A study on non-therapeutic micro cosmetic surgery and its appropriateness of applying consumer protection act (in Chinese). Nat Univ Kaohsiung Law J 12(2):245–98
Wu KP (2016) The method for civil mediation for medical dispute (in Chinese). Health Law Policy J 4:19–42
Wu ZZ (2019) The criteria of judging medical negligence (in Chinese). Chengchi Law Rev 158:87–159

Wu YS, Chen WW (2020) The execution results of the levy for the drug injury relief fund in 2019 (in Chinese). Drug Safety Newsletter 70:18–9

Wu KCC, Chen WC, Chiang DL (2013) Analysis of no-fault compensation for medical injury and pilot exploration of the public's attitude towards it in Taiwan (in Chinese). http://www.cppl.ntu.edu.tw/research/2012research/10101Final.pdf, Center for Public Policy and Law, National Taiwan University 2013

Wu CY, Yang TW, Chen RC (2017) An empirical study on medical litigation: appeal rate and consistency of civil case (in Chinese). Nat Chung Chen Univ Law J 55:137–78

Published in Gazette (in Chinese), Legislative Yuan. 89(21):406–28

Published in Gazette (in Chinese), Legislative Yuan, 91(48):5–28

Published in Gazette (in Chinese), Legislative Yuan, 92(3):305–8

Published in Gazette (in Chinese), Legislative Yuan. 96(17): 383–93

Yang HI (2005) The development of the informed consent principle in judicial practice: comment on the ruling in 94 Tai-Appeal No. 2676 (in Chinese). Taiwan Law J (73):212–4

Yang HI, Huang YY (2015) When law meets medicine: two proposals for medical dispute legislation (in Chinese). Judicial Aspiration 115:7–31

Printed by Printforce, the Netherlands